Micro-frontends for Modern Web Development

A practical approach to scalable frontend architecture

Muthu Vijayan

www.bpbonline.com

First Edition 2026

ISBN: 978-93-78541-483

LIMITS OF LIABILITY AND DISCLAIMER OF WARRANTY

The information contained in this book is true and correct to the best of author's and publisher's knowledge. The author has made every effort to ensure the accuracy of these publications, but the publisher cannot be held responsible for any loss or damage arising from any information in this book.

All trademarks referred to in the book are acknowledged as properties of their respective owners but BPB Publications cannot guarantee the accuracy of this information.

Distributors:

BPB PUBLICATIONS
20, Ansari Road, Darya Ganj
New Delhi-110002
Ph: 23254990/23254991

DECCAN AGENCIES
4-3-329, Bank Street,
Hyderabad-500195
Ph: 24756967/24756400

MICRO MEDIA
Shop No. 5, Mahendra Chambers,
150 DN Rd. Next to Capital Cinema,
V.T. (C.S.T.) Station, MUMBAI-400 001
Ph: 22078296/22078297

To View Complete BPB Publications Catalogue Scan the QR Code:

Published by Manish Jain for BPB Publications, 20 Ansari Road, Darya Ganj, New Delhi-110002 and Printed by him at Repro India Ltd., Rewari.

www.bpbonline.com

Dedicated to

My parents, my wife, and my daughters —
my foundation, my strength, and my inspiration

About the Author

Muthu Vijayan is a frontend architect with nearly 20 years of experience in web application development and platform engineering. He has worked extensively on large-scale frontend systems, micro-frontend architectures, and modular UI platforms in enterprise environments.

His areas of expertise include distributed frontend design, performance optimization, observability practices, deployment strategies, and governance models for scalable web applications. He has led modernization initiatives and contributed to building independently deployable frontend ecosystems that support organizational scale and engineering autonomy.

Muthu also explores emerging technologies such as artificial intelligence and how they can be embedded into user experiences within modern web architectures.

Through this book, he shares practical insights and architectural lessons gained from building and evolving production-grade frontend systems.

About the Reviewer

Krishna Kandi is a senior software engineer with over two decades of professional experience designing and operating large-scale distributed systems. His work spans high availability platforms, observability, frontend and backend integration, and secure system design in regulated and mission-critical environments, including global financial infrastructure and enterprise SaaS platforms.

Krishna specializes in building resilient systems and enjoys working on problems related to system reliability, performance visibility, and platform scale. He has contributed to systems that support complex workflows, strict compliance requirements, and large user bases, and regularly reviews technical material related to modern frontend architecture, distributed systems, and platform engineering.

He is currently working as a senior software engineer at Convoke, where he contributes to the design and development of enterprise-grade compliance and data platforms.

Acknowledgement

This book would not have been possible without the collective experience of the many engineers and architects I have had the privilege to work alongside. The real-world systems we built, and the challenges we navigated together, form the backbone of this book. Every architectural debate, performance regression, production incident, and hard-earned lesson contributed in some way to the ideas presented in these chapters.

I am especially grateful to the platform engineers and frontend teams who continuously strive to balance autonomy with architectural discipline. Their commitment to performance, security, governance, and long-term maintainability has shaped much of the thinking captured here. Working alongside individuals who challenge assumptions and elevate standards has been both inspiring and humbling.

I would like to extend my sincere thanks to my reviewers, Mr. Dale Gillespie, Mr. Vinothkumar Kalyanasundaram, and Krishna Kandi, for their valuable time, thoughtful feedback, and consistent guidance throughout the writing process. Their insights helped refine the technical depth, clarify complex concepts, and strengthen the overall structure of this book.

My gratitude also goes to the BPB Publication team for their support, patience, and direction. Bringing a technical manuscript to completion requires far more than writing; their steady guidance helped transform ideas into a finished work.

Finally, and most importantly, I thank my family. Writing this book required long evenings and weekends that could have been spent with them. Their understanding, encouragement, and quiet support made this journey possible. I am deeply grateful for their patience and for being my constant source of strength and inspiration.

Preface

Frontend development has undergone a remarkable transformation over the past two decades. What began as static markup layered with minimal interactivity has evolved into highly dynamic, distributed application ecosystems. Today's frontend systems are not merely presentation layers; they are sophisticated platforms responsible for rendering complex user experiences, orchestrating business workflows, integrating with distributed services, and delivering measurable business value.

As organizations scale, frontend architecture becomes a strategic concern. Teams grow, codebases expand, release cycles accelerate, and user expectations increase. The monolithic frontend, once manageable within a single team, begins to strain under the weight of coordination overhead, shared dependencies, and competing priorities. Architectural decisions that once seemed tactical become organizational constraints.

Micro-frontends emerged as a response to this scale problem. They offer a way to decompose large frontend systems into independently developed, tested, and deployed units. When implemented thoughtfully, micro-frontends enable team autonomy, faster delivery, and clearer ownership boundaries. However, they are not a silver bullet. Distributing the frontend introduces its own complexities: performance drift, security boundaries, dependency management, runtime coordination, and governance challenges.

This book approaches micro-frontends not as a trend or a tooling choice, but as an architectural discipline. It examines the technical, operational, and organizational considerations required to build and scale micro-frontend ecosystems responsibly.

This book is intended for senior engineers, architects, platform engineers, and technical leaders responsible for designing or evolving large-scale frontend systems. It assumes familiarity with modern web development and focuses on architectural decision-making, trade-offs, and real-world implementation patterns. Whether you are evaluating micro-frontends for the first time, migrating from a monolith, or scaling an existing implementation, this book provides a structured, engineering-focused guide.

Readers will gain a deep understanding of micro-frontend principles and mental models, practical implementation strategies and composition patterns, and infrastructure and deployment approaches tailored for distributed frontends. Furthermore, they will acquire communication and interoperability techniques across independently deployed modules, observability, performance, and security practices specific to MFE architectures, and organizational insights for sustaining autonomy without sacrificing cohesion.

This book is divided into 10 chapters:

Chapter 1: Journey of Frontend — In this chapter, we trace the evolution of frontend development from static pages to modern applications. This chapter establishes the context for why monolithic architectures struggle at scale and explains the rise of micro-frontends as a structural response to organizational and technical growth.

Chapter 2: Introduction to Micro-frontend — This chapter builds foundational understanding. It defines what micro-frontends are, explores their core principles, and compares them with microservices. By examining modules and components as core paradigms, the chapter clarifies how distributed frontend systems are conceptualized and structured.

Chapter 3: Designing Micro-frontends — In this chapter, we move into architectural thinking. This chapter introduces the mental models required to treat each MFE as both independent and part of a larger system. It explores composition, strangulation, adapter, pub-sub, and facade patterns. It also examines stateful versus stateless architectures and addresses the often-overlooked challenge of maintaining UX consistency across distributed teams.

Chapter 4: Laying Infrastructure — This chapter focuses on foundational decisions. Framework-specific versus framework-agnostic approaches, repository strategies, project setup, testing isolation, and CI/CD customization are explored in depth. Infrastructure choices shape long-term scalability, and this chapter provides guidance for building resilient, flexible foundations.

Chapter 5: Implementation Strategies — This chapter's discussion becomes hands-on. Modularization techniques, integration modes, composition strategies, Web Components, Module Federation, siteless UI, **backend-for-frontend (BFF)** patterns, and GraphQL integrations are examined. Native platform integration and real-world case studies demonstrate practical application, while antipatterns and error-handling strategies highlight common pitfalls.

Chapter 6: Communication and Interoperability — This chapter addresses one of the most critical aspects of MFEs: coordination without tight coupling. It explores shared and local state management, event-driven communication, dependency sharing, and routing strategies. The chapter emphasizes how loosely coupled modules can still deliver a unified experience when guided by clear communication contracts.

Chapter 7: Deployment Strategies — In this chapter, we examine how independence is preserved at scale. Artifacts, bundlers, module formats, runtime integration patterns, federated artifacts, and automated pipelines form the backbone of reliable MFE delivery. This chapter connects architectural intent with operational execution.

Chapter 8: Observability and Monitoring — This chapter shifts focus to visibility, distributed frontends introduce runtime complexity that demands robust monitoring. Logs, metrics, traces, correlation identifiers, analytics governance, and real user monitoring are discussed as essential pillars of reliability. The chapter highlights how to maintain a unified operational view across independently shipped modules.

Chapter 9: Performance and Security — Performance and security take center stage in this chapter. The MFE systems; these concerns are deeply intertwined. Performance budgets, browser APIs, runtime measurement techniques, dependency control, and cross-origin considerations are examined alongside security guardrails such as isolation policies, HTTP headers, and mitigation strategies for XSS and CSRF. Governance models that support both performance and security discipline are also explored.

Chapter 10: Organizational Impact — This chapter broadens the lens. Micro-frontends influence not just codebases but team structures, workflows, leadership alignment, and long-term strategy. This chapter explores industry adoption patterns, common organizational challenges, governance approaches, leadership engagement strategies, and emerging trends such as AI-assisted development and composable platforms. It underscores that technical autonomy must be balanced with product coherence.

Throughout this book, the emphasis remains consistent: micro-frontends succeed not because of a particular framework or bundler, but because of architectural clarity and organizational discipline. The goal is not to advocate for micro-frontends universally, but to equip you with the principles needed to evaluate, design, implement, and scale them responsibly.

The technologies discussed will evolve and new frameworks will emerge. Integration patterns will mature. However, the underlying architectural questions about ownership, isolation, coordination, performance, and governance will remain.

This book is an invitation to approach micro-frontends with rigor, balance autonomy with cohesion, and design frontend systems that scale not only technically, but organizationally.

Code Bundle and Coloured Images

Please follow the link to download the
Code Bundle and the ***Coloured Images*** of the book:

https://rebrand.ly/a27bca

The code bundle for the book is also hosted on GitHub at
https://github.com/bpbpublications/Micro-frontends-for-Modern-Web-Development.
In case there's an update to the code, it will be updated on the existing GitHub repository.

We have code bundles from our rich catalogue of books and videos available at **https://github.com/bpbpublications.** Check them out!

Errata

We take immense pride in our work at BPB Publications and follow best practices to ensure the accuracy of our content to provide an indulging reading experience to our subscribers. Our readers are our mirrors, and we use their inputs to reflect and improve upon human errors, if any, that may have occurred during the publishing processes involved. To let us maintain the quality and help us reach out to any readers who might be having difficulties due to any unforeseen errors, please write to us at: **errata@bpbonline.com**

Your support, suggestions and feedback are highly appreciated by the BPB Publications' Family.

Piracy

If you come across any illegal copies of our works in any form on the internet, we would be grateful if you would provide us with the location address or website name. Please contact us at **business@bpbonline.com** with a link to the material.

If you are interested in becoming an author

If there is a topic that you have expertise in, and you are interested in either writing or contributing to a book, please visit **www.bpbonline.com**. We have worked with thousands of developers and tech professionals, just like you, to help them share their insights with the global tech community. You can make a general application, apply for a specific hot topic that we are recruiting an author for, or submit your own idea.

Reviews

Please leave a review. Once you have read and used this book, why not leave a review on the site that you purchased it from? Potential readers can then see and use your unbiased opinion to make purchase decisions. We at BPB can understand what you think about our products, and our authors can see your feedback on their book. Thank you!

For more information about BPB, please visit **www.bpbonline.com**.

Join our Discord space

Join our Discord workspace for latest updates, offers, tech happenings around the world, new releases, and sessions with the authors:

https://discord.bpbonline.com

Table of Contents

CHAPTER 1
Journey of Frontend

Introduction

This chapter will explain the basics of frontend development, its key components, and its importance in today's web. We will explore how the web has evolved from static pages to modern frontend applications. Additionally, we will discuss the limitations of monolithic architectures and the need for a more flexible, modular approach to meet changing user and business needs. Lastly, we will look into the rise of micro-frontends, their impact on organizations, and the challenges and solutions they bring, showing how they have transformed web development.

Structure

The chapter covers the following topics:

- Visible side of software
- Evolution over the decades
- Challenges that impact large-scale web apps
- Rise of micro-frontends

Objectives

By the end of the chapter, you should be able to understand the basics of frontend development and its evolution over time. You will also have a clear understanding of why modular architecture is preferred over monolithic design, after evaluating its limitations and impact on modern, scalable frontends. Finally, you will gain insight into the benefits of using micro-frontends, along with the challenges and the solutions currently in use.

Visible side of software

Think of humans: each one is unique, yet they share fundamental capabilities such as walking, talking, and seeing. These functions are powered by internal organs like the brain, heart, and lungs. However, when we encounter a person, we do not focus on their internal workings. We see their outward appearance, their **frontend**, and it is this that helps us identify and connect with them. Similarly, in software applications, the core functionality resides beneath the surface, driven by underlying systems and algorithms. However, to make that functionality accessible and useful, it needs an interface, a frontend.

Each frontend may take a different shape or style, but it offers one essential feature: interactivity. Just as a person's talents are only valuable if they can be communicated with, the true power of a software application is only unlocked through its frontend. It is the visible side, the interface that enables users to interact with the core functionality of the system, whether through a website, app, or platform. Without a well-designed frontend, even the most sophisticated software remains out of reach.

In the modern digital age, we interact with many frontend interfaces in our daily lives, be it a digital clock that wakes you up in the morning, a digital calendar that tells your schedule, or even a kiosk at the train or bus station that you cross every day. Although each of those serves different purposes, all of them have one thing in common, which is the **frontend** of that product that you can interact with. However, what exactly is a frontend, and how has it evolved over time? To answer this, we must delve into the world of user interfaces, explore the technologies that shaped their development, and understand the impact frontend development has on those products' interfaces.

Frontend development

Well, for starters, frontend development is a part of software development that deals with everything the user interacts with. It is the **face** of an application, which includes the design, the layout, the buttons, the navigation, and even the animations. When you see a web, mobile, or even a smart TV application, the first thing you notice or interact with is the frontend of those applications. The goal of the frontend is to ensure the users can interact with the application smoothly, intuitively, and efficiently.

Frontend is not only about making things look pretty. It is about functionality, accessibility, and user experience. To understand what it takes to create an effective frontend of an application, we must know the key concepts of frontend development, and they are as follows:

- **User experience** (**UX**) design
- **User interface** (**UI**) design
- Interactivity
- Accessibility
- Responsiveness

User experience design

UX design plays a pivotal role in shaping the user journey within an application or product. Unlike UI design, which focuses on the visual structure and interactive elements, UX design is centered around creating an experience that is intuitive, engaging, and meaningful to the user. The canvas of UX design is expansive. It can evolve and adapt to meet changing user needs, technological advancements, and business goals.

The process starts with extensive user research, which is both qualitative (feedback-driven) and quantitative (data-driven). Through the means of surveys, interviews, usability testing, and analytics, the UX can collect valuable insights into the user behavior and their pain points. This research provides the essential knowledge to understand what the user wants and expects, allowing UX to make informed decisions. The main goal is not just to know the user needs, but to create an engaging experience for the users.

Once the research is complete, the insights will be translated into an interactive design, often as a wireframe. Wireframes are like a blueprint that contains the user's entire journey through the application. It acts as the skeleton of the design, which helps to organize the content, decide the user workflows, and interactions. These early-stage designs help to visualize the structure of the application, test interactions, and identify any potential issues before it is developed.

Figure 1.1 shows a wireframe that acts as a blueprint that will be discussed and finetuned before starting development:

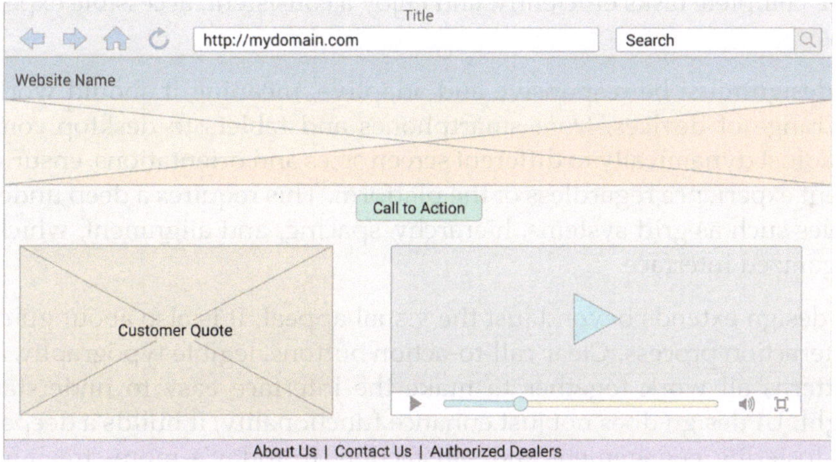

***Figure 1.1:** Example of a wireframe*

A core principle of UX design is **information architecture** (**IA**), the process of organizing and structuring content in a way that makes it easy for users to find and consume. Effective IA ensures that the information can be quickly located by the users without feeling overwhelmed or lost. A well-organized IA not only improves usability but also supports accessibility by providing clear structure, consistent navigation, and meaningful labels, while simultaneously optimizing search functionality to create a smooth and intuitive experience.

In a nutshell, user experience is about understanding users' needs and optimizing the way they interact with the product. More importantly, it is an iterative process that takes into account both user expectations and business objectives to deliver an intuitive and engaging user experience throughout.

User interface design

UI design is a critical aspect of application development that focuses on implementing the visual and interactive elements of an interface, translating UX decisions into concrete user-facing components. It encompasses the selection of visual elements, such as colors, typography, icons, buttons, and layouts, ensuring that each element is purposefully designed to enhance usability and engagement. A well-executed UI design not only draws users into the application but also creates a seamless, intuitive experience that makes navigation effortless. The goal is to make the application feel intuitive and aesthetically pleasing, aligning the interface design with the overall branding and user expectations.

UI design works in tandem with UX design, ensuring that both visual and interactive aspects of the application are thoughtfully crafted to meet the needs and behaviors of the end user. While UX focuses on the overall experience and user journey, UI design addresses the finer details of how users interact with the application at a visual level. It ensures that users can easily find what they need, complete tasks efficiently, and enjoy a consistent, accessible experience across various devices.

Moreover, UI design must be responsive and adaptive, meaning it should work seamlessly across a wide range of devices, from smartphones and tablets to desktop computers. The layout should adjust dynamically to different screen sizes and orientations, ensuring that users have a consistent experience regardless of the platform. This requires a deep understanding of design principles such as grid systems, hierarchy, spacing, and alignment, which help create a clean and organized interface.

The role of UI design extends beyond just the visual appeal. It is also about guiding the user through the interaction process. Clear call-to-action buttons, legible typography, and intuitive navigation patterns all work together to make the interface easy to understand and use. When done right, UI design does not just enhance functionality; it builds a deeper connection with the user, fostering engagement and satisfaction. In today's more streamlined product teams, these responsibilities often converge, with UX, information architecture, and UI design frequently handled by a single UX designer who wears multiple hats and shapes the experience holistically.

Interactivity

Interactivity in frontend development refers to how users engage with a website or application through responsive elements like buttons, forms, sliders, and navigation menus. These dynamic components allow users to take actions, such as submitting forms or clicking buttons, and receive immediate feedback. This creates a more engaging and intuitive experience, making the interface feel responsive and interactive rather than static.

JavaScript plays a vital role in enabling interactivity by allowing developers to dynamically update content without page reloads. Event listeners detect user actions and trigger changes in the UI, while technologies like **AJAX** and the **Fetch API** enable asynchronous data loading, improving responsiveness and overall user experience. This creates seamless real-time interactions, especially in **single page applications** (**SPAs**).

On mobile devices, interactivity must be optimized for touch-based navigation with buttons and links large enough to tap easily, and animations that run smoothly. Balancing dynamic interactions with performance is crucial to ensure fast load times and a consistent experience across different devices, enhancing both usability and engagement.

Do you know: **In the year 1997, Microsoft extended HTML to make it interactive and called Dynamic HTML (DHTML), which forms the foundation of what we use as a SPA today.**

Accessibility

Accessibility is about making sure that websites and applications can be used by everyone, regardless of ability. The **Web Content Accessibility Guidelines** (**WCAG**) describe this through four core principles. **Perceivable** means users must be able to see or hear the information being presented, whether through text, images, audio, or alternatives like captions and screen readers. **Operable** means users must be able to interact with the interface using different input methods, such as a keyboard, mouse, touch, or assistive devices, without getting stuck or blocked. **Understandable** means content and interactions should be clear, predictable, and easy to follow, so users know what will happen when they take an action. **Robust** means the application should work reliably across different browsers, devices, and assistive technologies, both today and as technology evolves. Keeping these principles in mind helps teams build experiences that are inclusive, practical, and resilient over time.

Importance of accessibility

Web is for all; therefore, the web is an essential part of modern life, encompassing daily activities like shopping, education, work, and entertainment. Accessibility ensures that everyone, regardless of their abilities or disabilities, can access and use the web effectively. Whether it is a person with color blindness, hearing loss, or visual impairment, they deserve equal access to information and services. As frontend developers, we hold the responsibility to design and build web applications that are inclusive and accessible to all users, promoting equity and usability for everyone.

Accessibility is a web standard

Web accessibility is not just a best practice; it is a standard. Organizations like W3C have established guidelines such as WCAG, **Authoring Tool Accessibility Guidelines** (**ATAG**), and **Accessible Rich Internet Applications** (**ARIA**) to help developers create accessible web applications. Governments worldwide are enforcing accessibility regulations, making compliance with AAA standards a legal and ethical obligation. Despite this, many developers still view accessibility as optional. By embracing these standards, we contribute to creating a web that is truly for everyone.

Consider accessibility at the design stage

Incorporating accessibility early in the design process is both cost-effective and efficient. Many accessibility features, such as appropriate color contrast, semantic HTML, and keyboard navigability, are simple to implement when planned upfront. Delaying accessibility considerations often results in costly redesigns and retrofitting. The WCAG guidelines categorize accessibility into three levels:

- A (minimum requirements)
- AA (addresses the most common barriers)
- AAA (highest level of accessibility)

By striving for at least AA compliance and aiming for AAA wherever possible, we can ensure that our web applications are as inclusive as they can be. Accessibility is not an afterthought; it is an integral part of good design and development practices. Let us build a web that welcomes everyone!

Do you know: **In 2006, the National Federation of the Blind (NFB) filed a lawsuit against Target Corporation, alleging that its website was inaccessible to visually impaired users. The case resulted in a $6 million settlement and mandated Target to enhance its website's accessibility (Source: www.w3.org).**

Responsiveness

Responsiveness ensures that web applications look and function well across a variety of devices, from desktops, smartphones, and even smart TVs. Responsive design uses flexible layouts, media queries, and fluid grids to adapt the content to different screen sizes and orientations. This allows users to have a smooth experience, whether they are viewing the site on a large monitor or a small mobile screen. A responsive design not only improves usability but also contributes to better SEO and user engagement by providing an optimal experience on any device.

Enhancing user satisfaction

Imagine opening a website on your phone and struggling to read tiny text or tap on links because the layout does not fit the screen. Responsive design eliminates such pain points by automatically adjusting the interface to match the user's device. This creates a positive impression and makes visitors more likely to stay longer, explore your content, and return in the future. Prioritizing responsiveness shows that you value your users' time and experience.

Future-proofing your web applications

As technology evolves, new devices and screen sizes continue to emerge. A responsive design ensures your application is prepared for these changes without needing constant updates. By designing with flexibility and adaptability in mind, you create a website that stands the test of time, saving effort and resources in the long run. Responsive design is not just about solving today's problems, but it is also about anticipating tomorrow's needs.

Evolution over the decades

Over the decades, frontend development has transformed from static, text-based websites to dynamic, interactive, and responsive applications that provide rich user experiences. This evolution has been nothing short of impressive, marked by various phases of progress and occasional setbacks. Throughout this journey, countless enthusiasts have contributed to the growth of the web ecosystem, particularly in the frontend space. In this section, we will explore each phase and highlight the key improvements made along the way.

1990s: The static web

In the early days of the web, frontend development was limited to basic HTML, which was used to structure simple, static pages. Websites were mostly text-based, with minimal graphics or interactivity. These text-based pages were connected through links, which is where the term **HyperText** comes from; it refers to the ability to link one document to another, allowing users to navigate information non-linearly. The term **Markup Language** refers to the use of tags or elements within a document to define its structure, such as headings, paragraphs, and links. *Figure 1.2* showcases the first website launched on the World Wide Web, which consisted of simple text and hyperlinks connecting static pages. Its primary goal was to share and organize information across the web.

Designers used tables for layout, and **Cascading Style Sheets (CSS)** were not widely adopted until the late '90s. JavaScript also emerged during this period, but it was used sparingly, primarily for basic client-side interactivity like form validation.

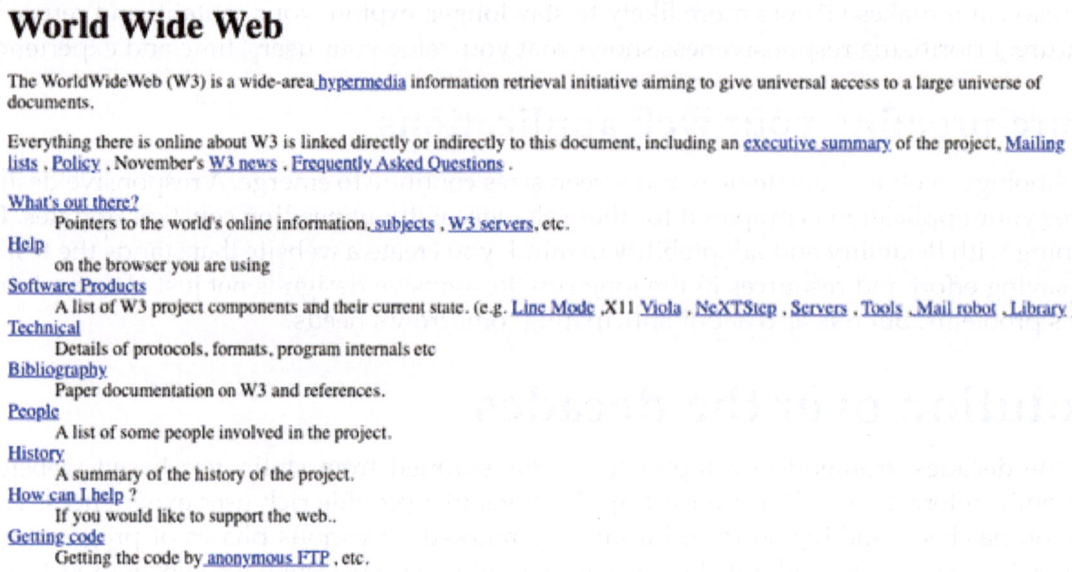

World Wide Web

The WorldWideWeb (W3) is a wide-area hypermedia information retrieval initiative aiming to give universal access to a large universe of documents.

Everything there is online about W3 is linked directly or indirectly to this document, including an executive summary of the project, Mailing lists , Policy , November's W3 news , Frequently Asked Questions .

What's out there?
Pointers to the world's online information, subjects , W3 servers, etc.
Help
on the browser you are using
Software Products
A list of W3 project components and their current state. (e.g. Line Mode ,X11 Viola , NeXTStep , Servers , Tools , Mail robot , Library)
Technical
Details of protocols, formats, program internals etc
Bibliography
Paper documentation on W3 and references.
People
A list of some people involved in the project.
History
A summary of the history of the project.
How can I help ?
If you would like to support the web..
Getting code
Getting the code by anonymous FTP , etc.

Figure 1.2*: First website, World Wide Web launched on August 6th, 1991*

*(****Source****: http://info.cern.ch)*

2000s: The rise of CSS and JavaScript

The 2000s saw significant growth in frontend development with the adoption of more advanced CSS for layout and design. CSS allowed developers to separate the structure of content from its presentation, making web development more efficient and scalable. It also marks the era where server scripting languages such as **Active Server Pages** (**ASP**), **Hypertext Preprocessor** (**PHP**), and **Java Server Pages** (**JSP**) thrived.

Also, JavaScript usage expanded with libraries such as Prototype.js, Scriptaculous, and jQuery, simplifying **Document Object Model** (**DOM**) manipulation and enabling more interactive features, such as dynamic content loading and animations. During this time, websites became more visually appealing, with improved navigation and basic forms of interactivity.

Figure 1.3 displays a screenshot of Amazon.com from the early 2000s, featuring all the basic elements necessary for online shopping at the time:

***Figure 1.3**: Amazon.com in the early 2000s*

*(**Source**: https://www.webdesignmuseum.org)*

2010s: The age of responsive design

The 2010s introduced a major shift in frontend development with the rise of responsive design. The growing use of mobile devices prompted developers to design websites that could adapt to different screen sizes and resolutions. Media queries in CSS became essential for creating flexible layouts that adjusted based on device characteristics. The introduction of HTML5 and CSS3 brought new features like multimedia support, animations, and advanced styling, enabling developers to build more interactive and visually rich experiences without relying heavily on software like Adobe Flash, which had previously been widely used to create animations, games, and interactive websites when HTML and CSS were more limited.

Figure 1.4 shows the Twitter mobile website in 2010. This decade also saw the widespread adoption of JavaScript frameworks like Angular, React, and Vue.js. These frameworks allowed developers to build SPAs, where content is loaded dynamically without page refreshes, leading to faster and smoother user experiences. Frontend development became more modular and component-based, emphasizing reusability and maintainability.

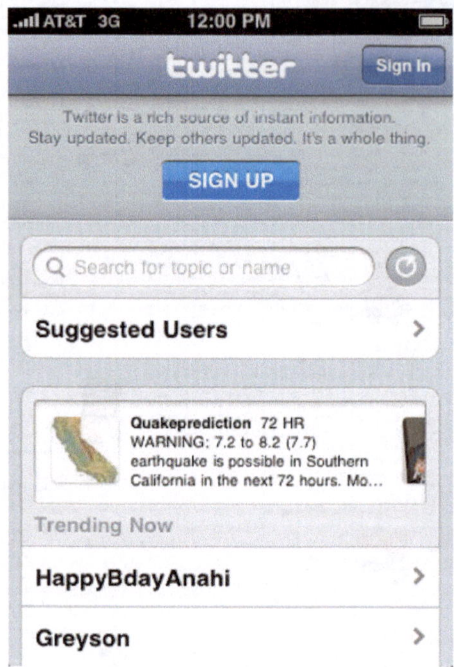

***Figure 1.4**: Twitter mobile responsive website from 2010*

*(**Source**: https://www.webdesignmuseum.com)*

2020s: Modern web and the rise of JAMStack

In the current decade, frontend development has evolved towards faster, more efficient applications powered by modern tools and workflows. The rise of **JavaScript, APIs, and Markup Stack (JAMStack)** represents a shift toward static site generation and serverless architectures, where frontend code is decoupled from backend systems, enabling faster performance and scalability.

During this period, **server-side rendering (SSR)** also re-emerged as a complementary technique, used selectively to optimize initial load performance and search engine visibility while retaining rich client-side interactivity. Tools like Gatsby, Next.js, and Hugo have become popular for building optimized web experiences that load quickly and deliver strong user experiences. *Figure 1.5* shows the popular ride-share web application Uber built with JAMStack around 2020:

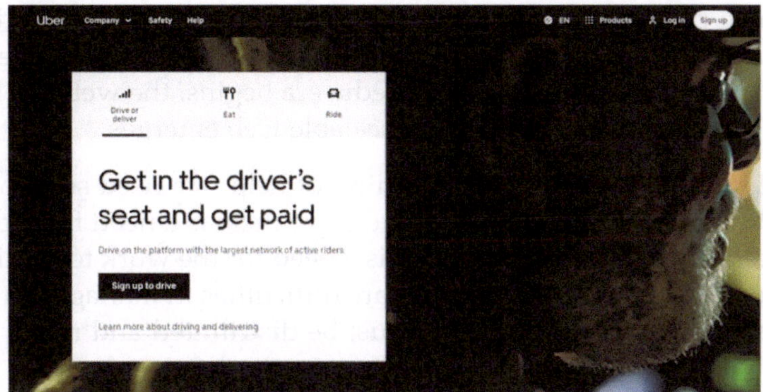

***Figure 1.5**: Uber built with JAMStack, 2020*
*(**Source**: https://www.staticmania.com)*

Moreover, WebAssembly is gaining traction, allowing frontend developers to run compiled code (like C or Rust) in the browser for high-performance applications. **Progressive Web Apps (PWAs**) have become more prevalent, offering app-like experiences directly in the browser with offline capabilities and push notifications.

The focus on accessibility, performance, and user experience is stronger than ever, with tools like lighthouse and automated testing helping developers ensure that websites meet modern standards. CSS Grid and Flexbox have become essential layout techniques, making complex designs more achievable without relying on outdated methods like floats or tables.

Future

From static HTML pages to dynamic, interactive applications, frontend development has evolved to meet the growing demands for rich, accessible, and performant user experiences. The combination of powerful JavaScript frameworks, responsive design principles, and modern development tools has revolutionized how web applications are built and used. The future promises even more innovation, with continued advancements in performance, AI-driven user interfaces, and immersive web technologies like AR and VR.

Challenges that impact large-scale web apps

Web, what we have today, is not the same as a few decades ago. It has moved away from being a static webpage to a dynamic, data-intensive web application. At one point, there were designers who designed the idea in photoshop and converted it into HTML, and on the other hand, there were developers who made the web application interactive by using a scripting language. There could be multiple pages on the website, and those will be handled by the same set of designers and developers. It is more than enough, as the scope is minimal. Now, every job that requires an in-person visit has been made online; be it visiting a bank for a deposit, withdrawing an amount, visiting a doctor's office for an appointment, or buying groceries from a store, it can all be done by sitting comfortably at home. That evolution increases the day-to-day traffic to those web pages, and the usage of the web has grown enormously from a few thousand to billions now. As the social media era begins, the web has become a part of human life. As the usage grows, the need for a scalable web emerges.

The strategies once used became obsolete and did not help. We need solutions that can scale automatically. As the scope of web applications creeps, there is a need for more hands to help in delivering a successful product, and so there is a need for the work to be distributed. When more people are working towards a goal, there are difficulties in managing a single codebase. So, it is not just the work, but even the code must be distributed and needs to be developed independently.

Monolithic

The word **Monolithic** refers to something massive, crafted from a single stone (Refer to *Figure 1.6*). In software systems, monolithic is an architectural way of organizing the code to build a product.

It stresses the cohesive nature as each component is interdependent and should be tightly coupled. No matter how big the product or codebase is, it should all exist in a single codebase and work cohesively. Though it comes with some advantages, such as rapid application development, easy testing, and debugging, the main concern of this model is scalability.

Figure 1.6: *Monolithic stone pillar*

*(**Source:** OpenAI DALL-E)*

Meeting the demand

As mentioned above, the need for a scalable solution is not an afterthought. It is a must-have for any web application that is consumer-facing. The reason is the userbase. *Figure 1.7* displays the total number of internet users from the year 2005 to 2025:

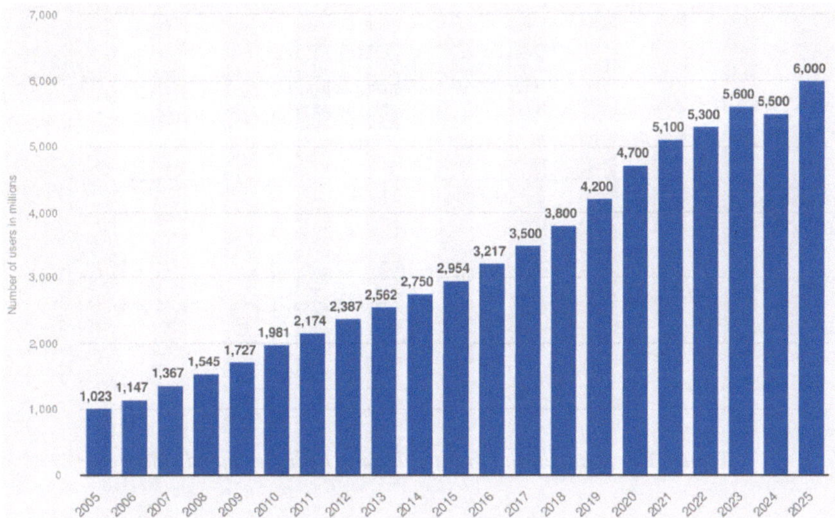

***Figure 1.7**: Number of internet users worldwide from 2005 to 2025*

*(**Source**: www.statista.com)*

As the user base increases, so does the application, and it needs an infrastructure that can accommodate that growing demand. Around 2010, the need for scalability pushed top companies to migrate from Monolithic. A few companies that transformed their architecture include Netflix, Amazon, and eBay. In 2009, popular video platforms like Netflix took that decision to migrate from monolithic, and it took 2 years for them to fully migrate. It was not an easy journey as they had to keep the lights on while they gradually decomposed their code and infrastructure. Not to forget the sentiment and push back even from their stakeholders. Another company that not only migrated to scalable architecture successfully but also foresees the future in modular services is Amazon. Thanks to its compelling, ever-growing userbase, it sensed the need for scale around 2001 and started prepping for that. Though they have not invented it, Amazon's most successful product, **Amazon Web Services** (**AWS**), has been a stepping stone for many companies to onboard to the modular services journey.

Development concerns

As frontend applications grow, a monolithic architecture typically consolidates user interface components, application logic, state management, and styling into a single shared stack. While this approach can simplify early development, it becomes increasingly difficult to manage as both the codebase and the number of contributing teams expand.

Figure 1.8 illustrates a monolithic frontend organized around a single, shared application stack. All core layers, including UI, business logic, global state, and styles, are tightly coupled and evolve together as part of one deployment unit. Multiple features and teams depend on the same shared layers, which means that even small changes can have unintended ripple effects across the application:

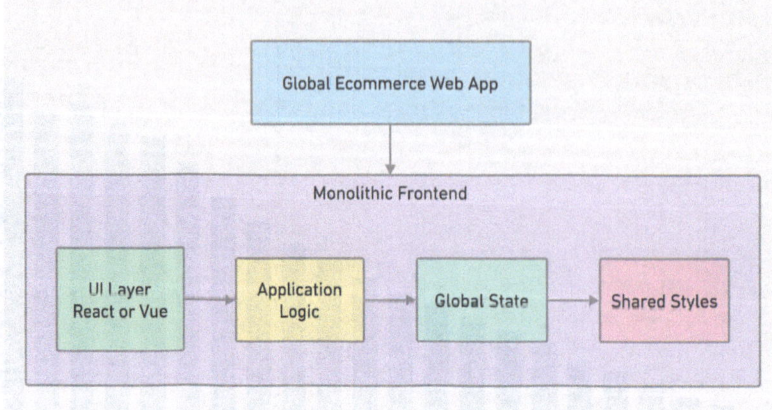

Figure 1.8: *A monolithic frontend using a single shared stack*

In this model, teams are required to coordinate closely when making changes, as modifications in one area may impact other features that rely on the same shared state or logic. This tight coupling slows development, complicates testing, and makes parallel work harder to sustain. Over time, frequent merge conflicts, fear of regressions, and release dependencies can reduce team autonomy and negatively affect developer morale.

As applications continue to scale, these development concerns become a significant bottleneck, often prompting teams to explore architectural alternatives that better support independent development and evolution.

Deployment

Once the application feature is developed, it must be deployed to the infrastructure, probably on a server, so that it can be accessed by the end user. In monolithic, we had to deploy the entire application even though only a small change had been made to the code, and the same is true if we had to roll back the changes as well. If there are more teams involved, it makes the situation worse as their releases are dependent, and a scenario such as a rollback could create chaos. Moreover, each team must rebuild and redeploy its features, which could slow down the deployment pipelines and lead to delays in updates and increased risks for bugs and potential downtime.

Another issue is with managing the version compatibility. Managing versions and ensuring backward compatibility is tricky, as multiple teams could be working on different components. Any updates could potentially break other parts of the components, causing instability during deployment. In a modular environment, application components can be developed and deployed independently without affecting any other components, and a failure in one component's deployment cycle should not affect the others.

Error handling

In a monolithic architecture, errors in one part of the system often propagate throughout the application, affecting multiple components. This can make it harder to isolate and fix issues quickly, leading to system-wide failures.

As the application grows, error tracking and monitoring become increasingly complex. In monolithic systems, logs from various components are often mixed, making it difficult to identify and resolve specific errors. Centralized logging and monitoring solutions can help, but they require careful setup and management.

Since everything is tightly coupled in a monolithic architecture, fault isolation is harder to achieve. A bug in one module can bring down the entire application, whereas in a modular architecture, failures are often isolated to specific components or modules, minimizing the impact on the overall system.

Locked into a technology stack

When the application is in the design or prototype stage, the architects tend to finalize the tech stack they plan to build the application. Most of the time, the technologies or tools that have been trending at that time would be picked unless there are any other concrete reasons. However, as the day goes on, technologies and tools evolve, and it gets better day by day. In a monolithic environment, once a tech stack or tools are decided, we are stuck with that until the lifetime of that application. It gives little or no opportunity to upgrade the tools as they evolve, and we will not be able to choose a different set of tools that have been trending at that time.

This challenge becomes even more pronounced when organizations acquire other companies or integrate with partner products that are built using different frontend technologies. In such scenarios, monolithic architectures often force costly rewrites or long-term compromises to align on a single stack.

By embracing modularity, teams gain the ability to evolve parts of the application independently. Development teams may have expertise in different technologies, and modular architectures allow those skills to be applied more effectively without forcing uniform adoption of a single framework across the entire codebase. While this approach introduces additional integration considerations, these challenges can be managed through clear boundaries, contracts, and governance.

Rise of micro-frontends

The challenges of developing, deploying, and maintaining monolithic applications have led to groundbreaking solutions. Companies like Netflix, Amazon, and eBay pioneered the adoption of microservices, an approach that revolutionized how we think about backend architecture. These companies faced a growing need for scalability, faster feature delivery, and operational resilience, which monolithic architectures could not provide.

Microservices follow a service-oriented architecture where each service is developed and deployed independently. This independence allows teams to make changes to one service without affecting the entire application. Moreover, teams working on these services can choose their preferred tech stacks, workflows, and locations, making cross-functional collaboration more dynamic and efficient.

Microservices quickly proved to be a game-changer. Teams delivered faster, scaled effortlessly, and saw tangible returns on investment. This architectural shift empowered organizations to innovate at an unprecedented pace. Yet, this innovation solved only one side of the equation, the backend.

Frontend lag

While the backend embraced modularity and scalability, the frontend continued to rely heavily on monolithic architectures. Despite advancements in frontend technologies, such as the advent of SPAs and frameworks like Backbone, Ember, and Angular, developers struggled to create modular and scalable frontend applications.

In monolithic frontend applications, even small changes to a single feature often require testing and redeploying the entire application. This lack of modularity created bottlenecks, especially in large teams or organizations managing complex applications with numerous features.

Imagine a global e-commerce platform where teams in different regions work on region-specific features. A monolithic architecture would force these teams to coordinate their changes meticulously, resulting in delays, inefficiencies, and higher risks of introducing bugs. The lack of independence in frontend development became an obstacle to scaling engineering teams and accelerating delivery.

Birth of micro-frontends

In 2016, ThoughtWorks coined the term micro-frontends to address this challenge. Inspired by the principles of microservices, micro-frontends brought the same modularity and independence to the frontend. The idea was simple yet transformative, and it broke the frontend into smaller, independently deployable pieces, where each piece corresponds to a specific feature or functionality.

Micro-frontends enable teams to own individual features end-to-end, from development to deployment. Each feature can have its own technology stack, independent lifecycle, and isolated testing, reducing dependencies across teams. For instance, one team might use React for a user authentication module, while another uses Vue.js for a product catalog. These micro-frontends integrate seamlessly into a cohesive user experience. This has been illustrated in the following figure:

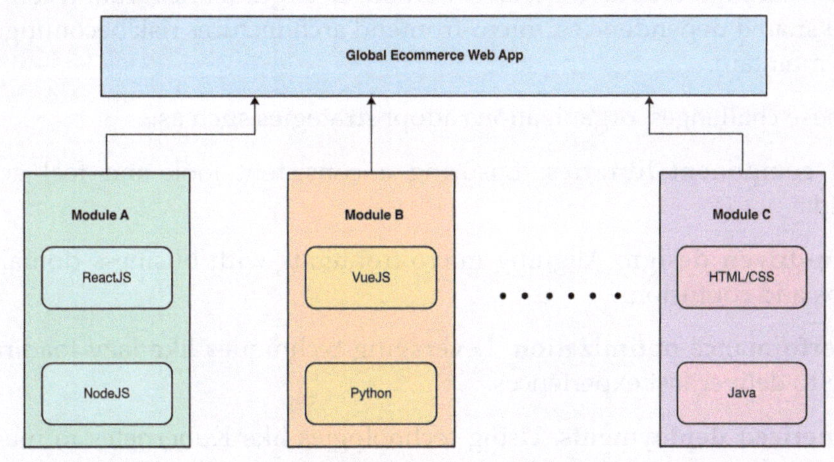

Figure 1.9: *Modules with different tech stacks developed and deployed independently*

Organizational impact

The benefits of micro-frontends extend far beyond the technical realm. By decentralizing ownership, they empower smaller teams to focus on their specific domain. This not only reduces the pressure on engineering teams but also fosters a culture of accountability and innovation.

From a business perspective, micro-frontends enable faster time to market for new features. Teams can iterate on their respective features without waiting for other parts of the application to be ready. This agility translates to competitive advantages, especially in industries where speed and user experience are critical.

For example, consider an online streaming platform introducing region-specific recommendations. A micro-frontend approach would allow the recommendations team to deploy updates independently, ensuring the rest of the application remains unaffected. This modularity also makes the platform more resilient, as failures in one feature do not cascade to others.

Challenges and solutions

While micro-frontends offer numerous benefits, they also introduce challenges. For example, ensuring seamless integration between multiple micro-frontends requires careful planning. Performance can also be a concern if micro-frontends are not optimized for efficient loading and rendering. In addition, effective governance is essential to define interaction patterns, shared contracts, and standards across teams. Without clear guidelines around communication, versioning, and shared dependencies, micro-frontend architectures risk becoming fragmented and difficult to maintain.

To overcome these challenges, organizations adopt strategies such as:

- **Shared component libraries**: Ensuring a consistent look and feel across micro-frontends.
- **Domain-driven design**: Aligning micro-frontends with business domains to avoid overlaps and confusion.
- **Web performance optimization**: Leveraging techniques like lazy loading and edge caching to deliver fast experiences.
- **Containerized deployments**: Using technologies like Kubernetes to manage micro-frontend deployments efficiently.
- **Platform governance and ownership**: Establishing shared standards, versioning policies, and architectural guidelines across teams.

Paradigm shift in frontend development

The rise of micro-frontends represents more than just a technical solution, and it is a paradigm shift in how we think about building and scaling web applications. By aligning technology with business goals, micro-frontends enable organizations to deliver faster, innovate continuously, and meet the demands of modern users.

Looking ahead, micro-frontends are poised to play a crucial role in the evolution of web development. As edge computing, serverless architectures, and AI-driven personalization become mainstream, the principles of modularity and independence will remain foundational. The adoption of micro-frontends is not just about solving today's problems; it is about future-proofing the frontend for the challenges of tomorrow.

As with any transformative approach, the journey to adopting micro-frontends comes with its own learning curve. However, for organizations willing to embrace change, the rewards are immense. It could result in happier teams, faster delivery, and a competitive edge in the digital economy. The rise of micro-frontends is a testament to how innovation in architecture can unlock new possibilities in web development.

Conclusion

The journey of the frontend has been nothing short of transformative, evolving from simple static web pages to dynamic, interactive, and highly scalable applications that power modern businesses. This chapter outlined how the visible side of software has grown to meet the demands of an ever-changing digital landscape, shaped by user expectations and technological advancements.

We discussed the foundational elements of frontend development, such as HTML, CSS, and JavaScript, and delved into the rise of scripting languages like PHP, ASP, and JSP that helped build dynamic experiences. Along the way, we uncovered the limitations of traditional monolithic architectures and the challenges faced by large-scale web applications. These challenges, combined with the need for flexibility and modularity, have given rise to Micro-frontends as a game-changing paradigm.

Understanding this journey sets the stage for the next chapter, where we will discuss the world of micro-frontends by exploring the key principles and benefits along the way. Also, we will discuss the benefits of modularity, team autonomy, and scalability, as well as a few real-world examples where micro-frontends solve critical issues. We will also see the overview of microservices and how they converge and differ from micro-frontends. Finally, we will discuss the two key pillars, modularity and components.

Join our Discord space

Join our Discord workspace for latest updates, offers, tech happenings around the world, new releases, and sessions with the authors:

https://discord.bpbonline.com

CHAPTER 2
Introduction to Micro-frontends

Introduction

This chapter will introduce micro-frontends in detail to the readers, explaining what they are, the principles behind them, and the numerous advantages they add to frontend development in the modern web arena. Furthermore, it discusses a few real-world examples where micro-frontends shine. Also, readers would learn about the popular backend API pattern, **microservices**, and how it converges and diverges with micro-frontend. Finally, we would discuss the two core paradigms, *modules* and *components,* to understand the idea behind the distributed frontends.

Structure

The chapter covers the following topics:

- Understanding micro-frontends
- Core principles
- Benefits of micro-frontends
- Microservices
- Modules and components

Objectives

By the end of the chapter, you should be able to understand what micro-frontends are and where they can be used in real-world scenarios. You will also learn the core principles that frame the micro-frontends and their benefits of using them in a large, distributed system. You will understand how it emerges from the concept of microservices and how micro-frontends differ. Furthermore, you will have an introduction to the modules and components and how they paved the way for a distributed frontend architecture.

Understanding micro-frontends

Micro-frontends (**MFE**) is an architectural pattern that allows teams to build features independently in a composable fashion that can be distributed and reused across several applications. Let us think of a real-world use case with an e-commerce application like Amazon, though it needs the user to be logged in to complete a purchase, those websites do not enforce it upfront; they prompt the user to login before attempting to do certain tasks, such as checkout or modifying user account information, and so on. A more common way of handling this is to have a login page and redirect the user to that page to perform the respective action, such as logging in. However, doing so would not only create a bad user experience but also have the drawback of the user losing focus on the context. Displaying the login in a pop-up on the same page enhances user experience and maintains context. The following figure illustrates how a login pop-up can appear over the existing page content, allowing users to sign in without being redirected:

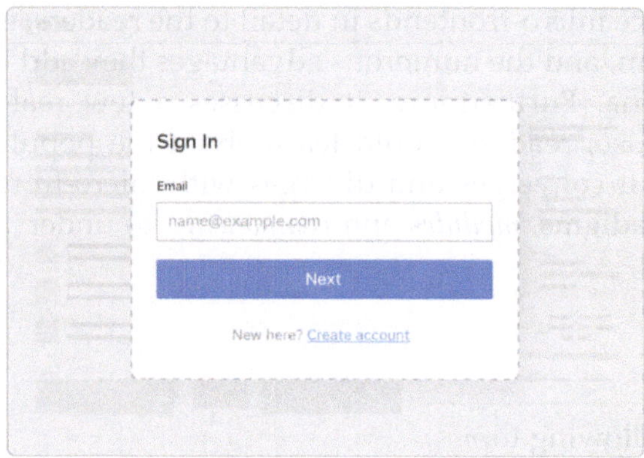

Figure 2.1*: The login pop-up appears within the same page*

Figure 2.1 shows a login screen that is embedded as part of the existing page. It could have been a separate page, but displaying this as a pop-up would leave the user in the same context. While it is certainly possible to display the login as a pop-up for a better experience, it would raise several questions on how it can be built and reused across the application, especially in a large organization, as each of those functionalities would be handled by different teams. That is where MFEs shine, as each team can build these features autonomously without worrying about the actual context of where this will be displayed. Let us explore the various approaches to designing MFEs in the following sections.

Horizontal split modal

An application can be split horizontally, where there can be multiple MFEs on the same page. A simple example would be to have a **Header**, **Navigation**, **Article**, and **Footer** as MFE on a single page (see *Figure 2.2*). These MFEs not only co-exist on the same page but can also share data with each other. The look and feel can be dictated by a common design system to ensure the **user experience** (**UX**) is consistent across. This kind of setup requires strong coordination with peer teams, and cross-cutting concerns such as authentication and analytics could be tricky to implement.

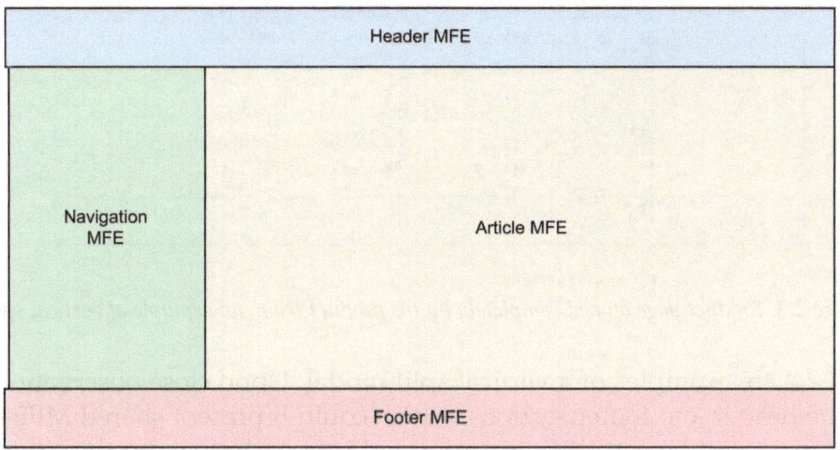

Figure 2.2*: Typical horizontal split of MFEs*

Vertical split modal

Vertical split divides the application based on **business domains or features**, where each MFE owns its full stack of functionality within its scope. For example, there may be separate MFEs, one for each domain, such as Profile MFE, Search MFE, each designed as if it were a separate **single page application** (**SPA**) and can be accessed by its own route */profile* and */search*, respectively. This technique allows teams to be truly autonomous with their own deployment pipelines and scales well across domains. However, it might be difficult to share any existing designs unless it is centralized and might need coordination to orchestrate application-level routing.

In vertically split MFE architectures, individual domain modules may internally adopt different rendering strategies. For example, a domain-specific MFE may use React Server Components to render data-heavy views on the server while preserving client-side interactivity where needed. The following figure is an example of a product page managed by a dedicated product team within the company. Since the team owns the entire page, there is a limited opportunity to share components or modules unless they are maintained in a centralized system.

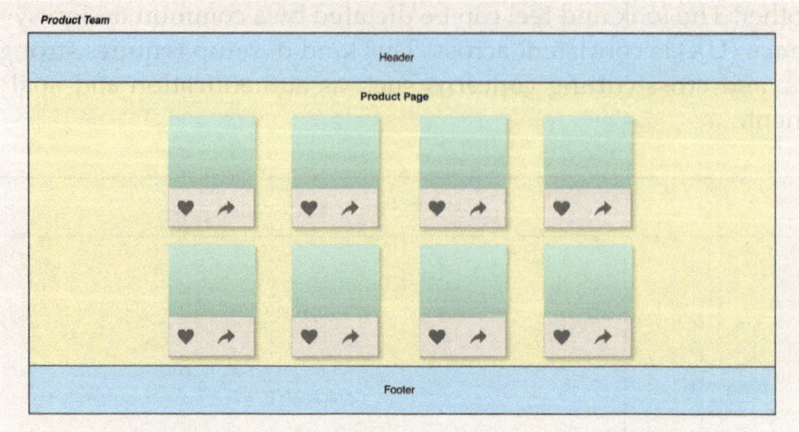

***Figure 2.3**: Product page owned completely by the product team, an example of vertical split*

Figures 2.3 and 2.4 are examples of a vertical split modal. Upon close observation, you might have noticed the header and footer sections, which could represent shared MFEs in this case. However, they must still be explicitly incorporated into each page by the respective teams. This approach allows for visual and functional consistency across the application, while still giving individual teams the autonomy to manage their own domains. It also highlights the importance of having a well-defined contract or interface for shared components to ensure seamless integration and reduce redundancy.

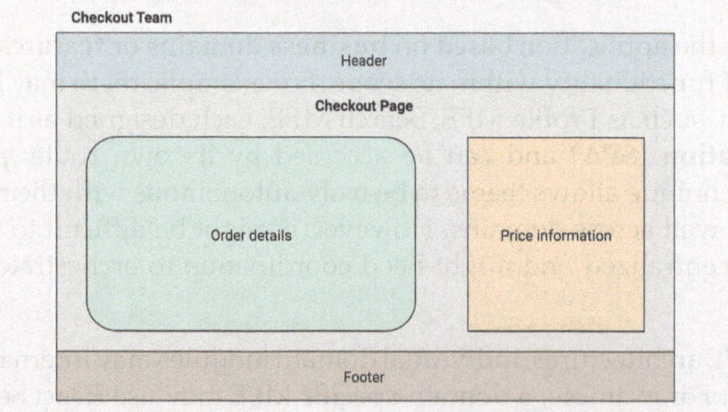

***Figure 2.4**: Example of vertical split, where the checkout page of the same application is owned by another team*

Hybrid model

The **hybrid model** MFE architecture combines both **horizontal and vertical splits**, aiming to leverage the strengths of each approach. It allows shared layout and common components through a horizontal split, while enabling independently developed and deployed business features through a vertical split. In this model, a shell application owns the container and common frame, such as the header, navigation, footer, and shared layout, while feature MFEs are dynamically loaded into the content area based on routing. This structure enables reuse of common user interface elements while preserving domain-based ownership and team autonomy.

Figure 2.5 illustrates how a typical hybrid approach could be; here, there has to be an application team that owns the container or the shell for other teams to incorporate their MFEs. The shell is responsible for cross-cutting concerns such as routing, authentication, analytics, and shared layout elements, including the header, navigation, and footer.

Feature MFEs are composed within this shared frame and may require contextual actions, such as a call to action specific to a business flow. Rather than directly modifying shared layout components, feature teams interact with the shell through well-defined extension points, allowing them to contribute domain-specific behavior while the shell team retains control over placement, styling, and accessibility. This approach suits MFEs built as an SPA and is a widely adopted approach in a client-driven application.

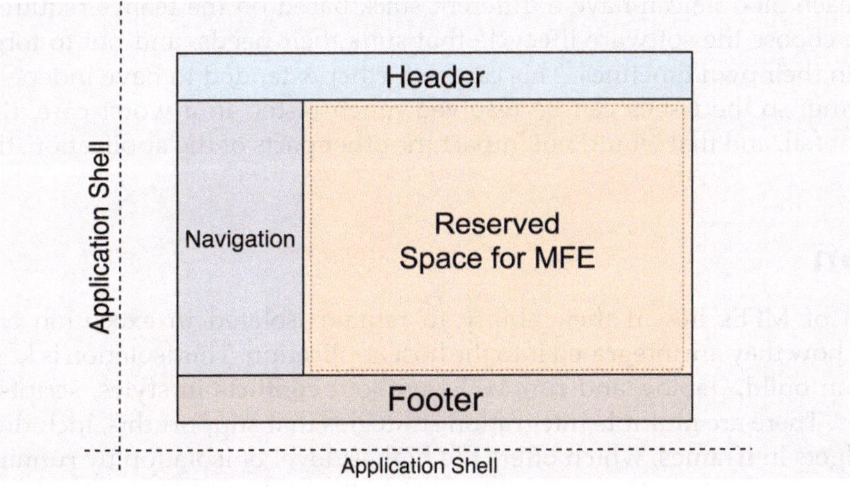

***Figure 2.5**: Hybrid approach with application shell*

As we have navigated around various approaches, let us quickly look into the core concepts behind MFEs that make it an obvious choice to build distributed and scalable frontend applications.

Core principles

At the heart of MFEs are three foundational principles: **autonomy**, **isolation**, and **composability**, which ensure that each MFE can be developed, deployed, and maintained independently, while still integrated to create a unified user experience. These principles enable organizations to scale teams, reduce cross-team dependencies, and deliver features more efficiently. Let us explore these to understand the need for each principle.

Autonomy

The power of autonomy relies on the self-belief that one can produce a better outcome. The most important principle is being **autonomous,** as it allows the team to operate independently without depending on the rest of the organization. They can fully own the domain and take decisions themselves with respect to the technology stack, development methodology, and, in fact, the release cycles. In a large organization, this could create wonders as each team can iterate faster, producing results.

In a siloed environment, where each team must contribute to the higher goal, it is important to reduce the interdependencies so teams can focus only on their target and deliver it with excellence. Being nimble allows us to set up a team focused on the mission, and it can include product and UX to assist the development team as well.

With the ever-changing software landscape, it is important to keep the technology stack updated. With the monolithic setup, this is hard as it impacts the entire codebase. However, with MFEs, each module can have a different stack based on the team's requirements. Also, the team can choose the software lifecycle that suits their needs, and not to forget, they can also deliver in their own timelines. This can be further extended to have independent testing and monitoring, so the issues can be resolved much faster. In a worst case, the respective module might fail, and that would not impact the other parts of the application, thus ensuring resiliency.

Isolation

The strength of MFEs lies in their ability to remain isolated in execution and behavior, regardless of how they are integrated into the host application. This isolation is key to ensuring that teams can build, deploy, and run MFEs without conflicts in styles, scripts, or runtime dependencies. There are multiple integration strategies that support this, including rendering MFEs as widgets in **iframes**, which offers the highest level of isolation by running each MFE in its own browsing context. This approach requires the MFE to be hosted by the owning team and communicates with the host via postMessage or shared interfaces.

Other integration patterns include packaging MFEs as **npm modules**, loading them as **external JavaScript bundles**, or using **Module Federation** to dynamically import and mount them at runtime. These methods provide varying degrees of runtime and style isolation, often relying on **Shadow DOM**, **scoped CSS**, or **sandboxed execution contexts** to prevent cross-contamination between MFEs and the container or between MFEs themselves. Ultimately, the goal of isolation is to allow MFEs to operate independently, reducing the risk of regressions, improving fault tolerance, and enabling multiple teams to collaborate at scale without stepping on each other's toes.

Composability

Composability in MFEs refers to the ability to assemble independently developed UI components or applications into a cohesive whole without sacrificing modularity. This principle enables teams to design MFEs like building blocks, each focused on a specific domain that can be dynamically combined within a layout or page. Composability ensures that these blocks can work together seamlessly through well-defined interfaces such as shared events, APIs, or Host-to-MFE contracts. Whether rendered client-side, server-side, or at the edge, each MFE must be able to integrate smoothly without introducing tight coupling or interdependencies that break autonomy.

A composable architecture encourages flexibility, scalability, and maintainability. It allows product experiences to evolve rapidly. MFEs can be rearranged, replaced, or extended with minimal impact on the overall system. For example, a homepage could be composed of separate MFEs for recommendations, header, navigation, and notifications, all deployed and updated independently. The host app or shell acts as a layout orchestrator, managing composition logic while delegating responsibility for UI behavior to the individual MFEs. This level of composability is essential for delivering consistent user experiences while empowering teams to move fast and innovate within their own domain boundaries.

Benefits of micro-frontends

While MFEs offer numerous benefits across an organization, the true value lies in their **return on investment** (**ROI**). The following sections highlight some of the most impactful advantages that make this architectural approach stand out. MFEs reduce the coordination overhead between teams, streamline deployment pipelines, and make it easier to roll out or roll back features with minimal risk. Let us discuss these benefits to understand how MFEs can transform development processes, enhance team productivity, and deliver better business outcomes.

Decentralized

In today's fast-paced digital landscape, the concept of decentralization has become increasingly important. In the context of MFEs, decentralization refers to the freedom that teams have to build, test, and deploy individual applications or modules at their own pace. This decentralized approach allows teams to work independently, making decisions that best serve their specific goals and objectives. When working with MFEs, teams are often siloed, focusing on a specific goal or objective. This siloed nature of the team allows them to be highly focused and dedicated to achieving their goal. With MFEs, each team is responsible for building and maintaining its own application or module, which reduces dependencies and makes it easier to manage.

MFEs, while carefully designed, could reduce the number of dependencies that need to be managed. When working with monolithic applications, teams often struggle with a multitude of interconnected components, each with its own set of dependencies. In contrast, MFEs allow teams to focus on their specific application or module, minimizing the complexity and reducing the risk of dependencies causing issues. It also provides the freedom to choose the tech stack that is most comfortable for them. This means that each team can select the technologies they know best and are most familiar with, allowing them to work more efficiently and effectively. Without the constraints of a monolithic application, teams have the flexibility to use different programming languages, frameworks, and tools to achieve their goals. In addition, MFEs also offer the opportunity to become a platform team addressing common use cases. This means that multiple teams can work together, sharing knowledge and expertise, to build solutions that benefit everyone. By working together as a platform team, you can create reusable components, share best practices, and accelerate development.

Faster time to market

In today's fast-paced digital landscape, speed is crucial. When it comes to MFEs, faster time to market can be a game-changer. By adopting a modularized approach, teams can work independently, making decisions quickly and iteratively, resulting in a significant reduction in the time it takes to bring new features or applications to market. In traditional monolithic application development, requirements are often complex and interconnected. With MFEs, you can sort your requirements and prioritize what matters most. By focusing on specific goals and objectives, teams can quickly identify the most critical tasks and start building. This prioritization enables teams to deliver value faster, reducing the time it takes to bring new features or applications to market.

In the context of MFEs, the **Minimum Viable Product** (**MVP**) approach is incredibly effective. By focusing on delivering a minimal yet functional product, teams can quickly validate assumptions and gather feedback from stakeholders. This rapid iteration enables teams to refine their product, adjust, and deliver value faster. In traditional monolithic application development, iterations are often slow and cumbersome. With MFEs, teams can iterate faster, thanks to the agility and flexibility offered by being autonomous. By embracing agile development methodologies, teams can quickly respond to changes in market conditions, user needs, or stakeholder feedback.

When working with MFEs, teams are no longer constrained by a single, tightly coupled frontend codebase. By enabling domain-level ownership and independent development, teams can make localized decisions more efficiently, without being blocked by unrelated changes in other parts of the application. This autonomy allows teams to iterate faster, experiment safely, and address issues earlier in the development cycle, while still operating within shared architectural and governance boundaries.

Fault tolerance

In large-scale frontend applications, failures are inevitable, whether they arise from code defects, network instability, or dependencies on external services. One of the key benefits of adopting MFE is improved fault tolerance through architectural isolation. Because MFEs are designed as independent and self-contained units, failures can often be confined to a specific feature or domain rather than impacting the entire application. This isolation reduces the blast radius of errors and helps ensure that critical user journeys remain functional even when individual modules encounter problems.

MFE architectures also encourage deliberate error-handling strategies at the module level. Instead of relying on a single global error handling mechanism, each MFE can detect, handle, and recover from failures within its own scope. This enables applications to degrade gracefully, for example, by displaying partial content or fallback experiences, rather than failing entirely. By localizing error handling, teams can address issues more quickly and with greater confidence, without introducing unintended side effects across unrelated features.

Observability further strengthens fault tolerance by providing visibility into how individual MFEs behave at runtime. By instrumenting modules independently, teams can monitor health indicators such as error rates, latency, and availability within their own domains. This localized observability makes it easier to identify emerging issues, understand their impact, and take corrective action before they escalate into broader system failures.

Distributed tracing complements observability by helping teams understand how failures propagate across frontend modules and backend services. High-level tracing of requests, events, and interactions allows teams to follow execution paths across MFEs, making it easier to diagnose complex issues in distributed systems. Together, structured error handling, observability, and tracing form the foundation of resilient MFE architectures. These topics are explored in greater depth in *Chapter 8, Observability and Monitoring*.

Parallel execution

One of the key benefits of MFE is the ability for teams to work in parallel on different parts of the application. By decomposing the frontend into independent modules, multiple teams can develop, test, and evolve their features simultaneously without being blocked by changes in unrelated areas. This parallel execution increases overall development throughput and enables organizations to scale frontend delivery as teams and applications grow.

In hybrid MFE architectures, as illustrated in *Figure 2.5*, parallel execution is supported by a shared container or shell that defines clear integration boundaries. While individual feature MFEs are developed independently, they are composed within a common framework that handles routing, layout, and cross-cutting concerns. Establishing clear integration contracts and composition mechanisms allows teams to converge their work without tightly coupling their development cycles.

Effective parallel execution also depends on minimizing dependencies between teams. MFEs encourage loose coupling by limiting shared state and avoiding direct dependencies between feature modules. This allows teams to make progress independently, leverage their specific expertise, and deliver changes without waiting for other teams. While some level of coordination is still required, the architectural separation provided by micro-frontends significantly reduces friction and enables sustained parallel development at scale.

Scalable at ease

One of the most significant advantages of MFEs is their ability to scale and manage easily. Scalability ensures that we scale not only our infrastructure based on the needs, but also the features, teams, and the application architecture. Composability allows organizations to scale development across multiple teams, with each team owning a specific feature or a domain. For instance, in a **software as a service** (**SaaS**) application, the billing team can independently build and iterate on the payment component while the analytics team works on user metrics, both of which integrate seamlessly into the user portal.

MFE encourages the reuse of components or modules. It has been made possible by its composable nature. Instead of rewriting similar components for different parts of an application or across multiple apps, teams can build **shared components** such as login boxes, search bars, modals, or data visualizations that can be used wherever needed. This reduces duplication, improves consistency, and saves engineering effort.

From a delivery perspective, MFEs support independent releases and incremental upgrades. Teams can introduce new features, roll out changes gradually, or deploy updates without requiring a full application redeploy or downtime. This flexibility allows organizations to respond more effectively to changes in business priorities or market conditions. As organizational needs evolve, individual MFEs can be scaled up, evolved, or retired without forcing large-scale architectural changes, enabling teams to focus on delivering new capabilities that drive growth and innovation.

Microservices

Microservices is an architectural style that structures an application as a collection of small, independent services that communicate with each other using lightweight protocols and APIs. Each service runs in its own process and communicates with other services using its own APIs. The term *microservice* was coined by *Martin Fowler* in 2012, who described it as a way to build scalable, maintainable systems by dividing the application into small, independent components that can be developed, tested, and deployed independently.

As depicted in *Figure 2.6*, in a modular e-commerce architecture, the application is decomposed into domain-specific services that reflect core business capabilities such as **Product Discovery**, **Order Management**, and **User and Access Management**:

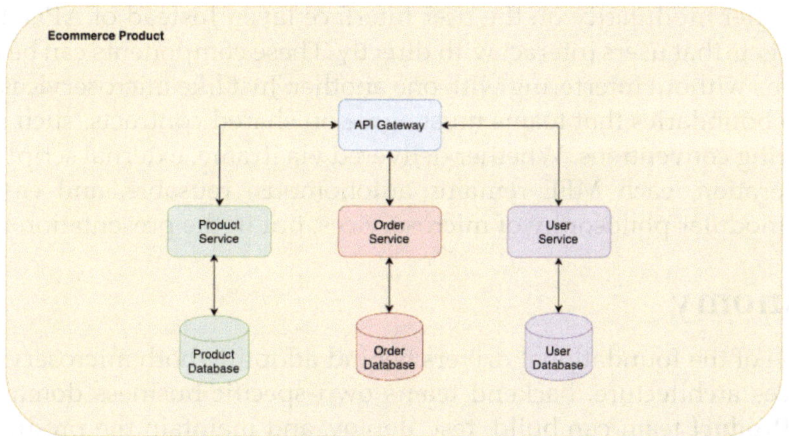

Figure 2.6: *Example of microservices in a typical e-commerce application*

Each of these domains is owned by an autonomous team, responsible for the full lifecycle of their service, including its data storage, business logic, and API surface. For example, the **Order** service manages and stores all order-related data, while user identity and profile information are exclusively managed by the **User** service. This separation of concerns ensures that services remain decoupled, enabling independent development, deployment, and scaling, while still collaborating to deliver a cohesive customer experience.

Similarities between microservices and MFEs

Though microservices and MFEs operate at different tiers, both aim to break down large, monolithic systems into smaller, independently manageable units. This shared philosophy brings several important similarities that help organizations scale both their technology and teams effectively. In this overview, we will explore how microservices and MFEs support **team autonomy**, enable **independent deployments**, encourage **technology of choice**, align with **domain-driven design** (**DDD**), promote **continuous delivery**, and contribute to overall **scalability**. These characteristics not only streamline development workflows but also foster a more resilient and adaptable system architecture.

Modular architecture

Both microservices and MFEs embrace modularity by decomposing complex systems into smaller, manageable, and independently deployable units. In microservices, this is achieved by designing services around business capabilities. For example, an *Order Service* that encapsulates all logic related to order processing. Such a service can be reused across multiple applications or domains, with access controls and feature toggles implemented at the application or user level. Importantly, the team owning the service maintains full control over its behavior and evolution. The service communicates through a well-defined contract that consumers agree to, typically a REST or GraphQL API.

Similarly, MFEs offer modularity on the user interface layer. Instead of APIs, they expose UI interfaces or widgets that users interact with directly. These components can be composed into larger applications without interfering with one another. Just like microservices, MFEs require clear integration boundaries that teams must agree on shared contracts, such as input props, events, or rendering conventions. Whether delivered via iframe, external script, npm package, or Module Federation, each MFE remains autonomous, reusable, and easily integrated, focusing on the modular philosophy of microservices, but in the presentation layer.

Team autonomy

Autonomy is one of the foundational drivers behind adopting both microservices and MFEs. In a microservices architecture, backend teams own specific business domains end-to-end. For instance, a **Product** team can build, test, deploy, and maintain the product microservice independently. This enables faster decision-making, internal problem-solving, and minimizes dependencies across teams. The same principle applies to MFEs. A team responsible for the **Checkout** experience on the frontend can design, develop, and deploy its own user interface module without waiting on or coordinating with other frontend teams. Autonomy also allows these teams to define their own testing practices, release cadence, and roadmap. In both models, team autonomy leads to increased velocity and a higher sense of ownership, where the success or failure of a component directly maps to the team responsible.

Independent deployments

Independent deployment is an important feature that gives both architectures their agility. In traditional monolithic systems, even a minor change to a small feature could trigger a full-system deployment, risking regression or downtime. With microservices, teams can deploy individual services without touching the rest of the system. Similarly, MFEs can be deployed independently, either by publishing to a **content delivery network** (**CDN**) or through dynamic Module Federation techniques. For example, a change to the product listing component in an e-commerce site does not require rebuilding or redeploying the entire frontend. This leads to faster time-to-market, safer rollbacks, and more resilient systems. Both architectures support various deployment strategies such as blue-green deployments, canary releases, and progressive delivery, empowering teams to ship often and with confidence.

Technology of choice

Freedom of technology choice is a strong enabler for both backend and frontend teams in modular architectures. In microservices, a team can choose Node.js, Go, or Python based on the specific needs of their domain. For instance, a machine learning service may be written in Python, while a high-performance API might use Go. This polyglot approach allows teams to optimize for their domain-specific problems. MFEs bring the same flexibility to the UI layer. One team might use React to build a dashboard widget, while another may prefer Angular for a form-heavy admin interface. Though this introduces complexity in integration and consistency, the ability to choose the right tool for the job drives innovation and team satisfaction. Both systems succeed by enforcing boundaries, APIs in microservices, and interfaces or **Document Object Model** (**DOM**) contracts in MFEs, thus ensuring teams stay loosely coupled even with diverse technology stacks.

Domain-driven design

Both microservices and MFEs are naturally aligned with DDD principles. In microservices, the concept of bounded contexts ensures that each service models a specific domain and handles all logic, data, and interactions relevant to that domain. This clarity helps avoid shared states or tightly coupled logic. Similarly, in MFEs, each UI module often maps to a distinct user-facing domain such as a user profile, shopping cart, or analytics dashboard. These modules do not just reflect backend data but encapsulate the workflows, user interactions, and even routing logic specific to their domain. This kind of mirroring between the frontend and backend domains leads to vertical alignment, where one cross-functional team can own a slice of the system end-to-end. It improves maintainability, reinforces business logic boundaries, and promotes a product-focused architecture.

Continuous delivery enablement

One of the key enablers of rapid product development is the ability to continuously deliver changes into production. Microservices, by being independently deployable and decoupled from each other, lend themselves naturally to CI/CD pipelines. Teams can build, test, and push their services with minimal friction. MFEs extend this paradigm to the frontend world. With proper tooling, teams can integrate CI/CD practices like automated testing, static analysis, and deployment previews per UI module. For example, a documentation portal may continuously deploy its UI changes after each pull request is merged. This granular delivery capability reduces the risk of large releases and promotes iterative improvement. Combined, microservices and micro-frontends empower organizations to practice true continuous delivery, not just in the backend but across the full product experience.

Scalability

There is a popular myth that scalability is a backend concern, though it is not true. In microservices, each service can scale independently based on load. A high demand service like **Search** or **Payments** can be replicated horizontally without scaling the entire application. This fine-grained scalability ensures resource efficiency and optimal performance. Micro-frontends offer similar benefits on the UI side. Individual components or routes can be lazy loaded, offloaded to CDNs, or rendered at the edge to optimize for performance and resource usage. For example, a product catalog MFE can be served statically, while a real-time analytics MFE uses dynamic rendering. This separation allows frontend systems to respond to usage patterns just as granularly as the backend. Together, the architectures offer true end-to-end scalability, tuned to the demands of each part of the application.

Differences between microservices and MFEs

While microservices and MFEs share many architectural principles, they diverge in critical ways due to their roles in the technology stack. Microservices are inherently backend-focused. They operate server-side, managing business logic operating on data and access management. Also, they expose APIs and protocols like REST, gRPC, or event streams for communication, and their complexity often lies in consistency models, distributed transactions, and observability across service boundaries. In contrast, MFEs deal with client-side delivery, rendering UI elements, handling browser events, managing client state, and ensuring a cohesive user experience. Their complexity is more visual and interaction-focused, including challenges like styling, shared dependencies, cross-framework interoperability, and runtime integration.

Another key difference is in runtime execution environments. Microservices typically run in containers, VMs, or serverless functions on infrastructure like Kubernetes or AWS Lambda. Their lifecycle and scaling strategies are bound to server-side orchestration. MFEs, however, run inside the user's browser. They are shipped as static assets, dynamically loaded via techniques like Module Federation or iframes, and executed in a constrained, sandboxed environment. This introduces unique considerations like bundle size optimization, initial page load performance, and compatibility across browsers and devices.

Lastly, testing differs significantly. Microservices emphasize unit tests, contract tests, and integration tests across APIs and services. MFEs need those too, but add visual regression testing, accessibility checks, and interaction flow validation to ensure the user interface remains consistent and intuitive. While microservices evolve with a backend-centric lens on performance and logic correctness, MFEs must account for human-facing usability, brand consistency, and client-side performance at every iteration.

Did you know: There is a common misconception that micro-frontends have to be used along with microservices, which is not true. MFEs can be used with a Monolithic backend as well. Moreover, it can also be composed on the server-side, edge (e.g., Lambda@Edge), or during build time if consumed as node modules.

Vertical slicing

A common and inevitable question arises: *Can micro-frontends and microservices work together?* The answer is *yes*. In a well-architected, decoupled system, a single product team might own both a microservice and its corresponding micro-frontend. For example, a user profile module. The micro-frontend could provide a consistent, user-facing interface to collect and display user information, while the associated microservice handles backend responsibilities like storing, retrieving, and sharing that data across other systems within the organization to support various operational needs.

Often, the micro-frontend directly consumes the microservice built by its own team, being a *First Party Consumer* promotes reusability and ensures tight alignment between the frontend and backend. Alternatively, the team may introduce a middleware layer, adopting a **backend for frontend** (**BFF**) approach to tailor backend interactions specifically for the frontend's needs. Architectures like these reinforce the principle of **vertical slicing**, empowering teams to independently deliver complete end-to-end features.

Modules and components

In modern web development, especially within large-scale applications and micro-frontend architectures, two foundational building blocks emerge repeatedly: modules and components. While they may sound interchangeable, understanding the clear distinction between the two is vital for architecting scalable and maintainable systems. Recognizing the roles of modules and components allows developers to design systems that promote reusability, separation of concerns, and easier collaboration among teams. This distinction also impacts deployment strategies, testing approaches, and how teams coordinate development efforts, especially when working in distributed environments.

Components

A component is a self-contained UI element such as a button, an input field, a modal dialog, or even a whole form. It encapsulates structure (HTML), style (CSS), and behavior (JavaScript), often with reusability in mind. Components are analogous to Lego blocks, each of different shapes and sizes, where they can be integrated to form another shape.

Components are UI focused; they mainly reside in the presentational layer of the application to set the brand of the product, ensuring a consistent user experience. It is tailored to be designed in a way that it is composable. That is, a new component can be formed by composing several other components, thus ensuring each of those is reusable. A component can be a stateful (functional components) or stateless, as per the needs.

The following is an example of a component in ReactJS:

```
// Button.tsx
type ButtonProps = {
  label: string;
  onClick: () => void;
};
export const Button = ({ label, onClick }: ButtonProps) => (
  <button onClick={onClick} className="p-2 rounded bg-blue-600 text-white">
    {label}
  </button>
);
```

The above code is for a simple button component. If you closely observe, it follows the **single responsibility principle** (**SRP**) and does one thing with reusable parameters, such as label or onclick function callbacks, and is agnostic of where or how it is used.

Note: In real-world applications, components often need to handle additional concerns beyond basic rendering and interaction. These may include supporting multiple visual variants, managing disabled or loading states, adhering to accessibility standards, and aligning with shared design systems or style guidelines. While such considerations add complexity, they are essential for building reusable, consistent, and production-ready components. The example above intentionally remains simple to illustrate core component principles without introducing these additional concerns.

Modules

Modules are self-contained applications, a widget, or a simple, organized unit that can be distributed and reused across several other parts of the organization. It is like a mini-program within your main program. Modules can be used to group related functions together, encapsulate complex logic, or reuse code across multiple parts of your application.

Modules are often considered a higher-level unit of composition. It is often a **feature-level** or **domain-specific** grouping of components, logic, styles, and sometimes even state management. In a micro-frontend context, a module might represent an independently deployable unit.

Modules are feature-focused compared to components, which are UI centric. It could include multiple components with backend logic that can be reused as a cohesive unit. The following is an example of a module layer within an application:

```
🗀 user-profile-module/
├── components/
│   └── UserCard.tsx
├── services/
│   └── userService.ts
├── index.ts
```

Here, the user-profile-module is a cohesive unit composed of the `UserCard` component and an associated `userService`, which is used to fetch the user details from another microservice. Ideally, it is exported to the consumer as one single module that displays the user information:

```
// user-profile-module/index.ts
export { UserCard } from './components/UserCard';
```

Module consumed as follows:

```
// App.tsx
import { UserCard } from 'user-profile-module';
```

```
const App = () => {
  return <UserCard />;
};
```

Note: Modules can be composed of components. Applications can be composed of modules.

In MFEs, modules define the boundary of ownership. A team might own a **`PaymentModule`** or **`UserSettingsModule`** and expose those as standalone deployable units. Each module could be composed of several components, such as buttons, fields, and forms that stay private to that module.

As a matter of good practice, components can be reused across modules via a well-designed component library such as MUI (formerly **Material-UI**). Also, it is imperative that modules should abstract and encapsulate the behavior and should not leak the internals.

While designing MFEs, we should think of components as *Atoms* and modules as *Molecules*. We need both, but understanding their hierarchy, scope, and purpose will dramatically improve how we scale our frontend, especially in a distributed environment.

Conclusion

As modern web applications grow in complexity and scale, the need for modular, maintainable, and scalable architectures becomes paramount. We began by building a clear understanding of MFEs and why they matter in today's fast-paced development landscape. We then explored the core principles: Autonomy, isolation, and composability, which provide the foundation for building robust and flexible frontend ecosystems. By highlighting the benefits, such as faster delivery, improved fault tolerance, and enhanced scalability, the chapter outlined how MFEs can address common challenges faced in traditional frontend development.

We also drew a clear comparison with microservices, demonstrating how MFEs align with backend practices while addressing the unique demands of the user interface. Finally, by delving into the structure of modules and components, we emphasized the importance of designing MFEs in a way that supports maintainability, reusability, and consistent user experiences.

In the next chapter, we explore designing MFEs, moving beyond architecture to practical considerations that drive successful implementations. We will examine the mental models and design patterns essential for component and module design, discuss the importance of future-proofing, and weigh the trade-offs between stateful and stateless components. Finally, we will cover how to ensure UX consistency across MFEs. This chapter will equip you with strategic insights and best practices to design MFEs that are scalable, cohesive, and ready for the future.

Chapter 3
Designing Micro-frontends

Introduction

This chapter will discuss the essential approaches and practices for crafting effective and cohesive **micro-frontend** (**MFE**) architectures. We will discuss the appropriate mental model that allows developers to think of each MFE as an independent unit, but part of a larger system. The chapter further explores the necessary design patterns that would add consistency and structure to MFE projects, covering approaches like composition, strangulation, adapter, pub-sub, and facade patterns.

In addition, we will discuss approaches and forward-thinking practices that support scalability and adaptability, allowing applications to evolve alongside business and technology demands. Also, this chapter focuses on the trade-offs between stateful and stateless MFE architectures. Each approach offers distinct advantages, and we will discuss the comparison. By understanding these trade-offs, we can choose the approach that best fits our application's goals and constraints.

We also explore the importance of UX consistency across an organization. As systems grow and teams become more distributed, maintaining a unified user experience becomes critical. This section outlines practical strategies for building and scaling design systems, and demonstrates how MFEs can be designed to deliver a seamless, cohesive interface. Together, these topics lay the groundwork for making informed, future-ready architectural decisions.

Structure

The chapter covers the following topics:

- Mental model
- Design patterns
- Architecting for the future
- Stateful vs. stateless
- UX consistency

Objectives

By the end of this chapter, you should know the right approach to the application design. You will understand the mental model behind crafting the application and why it is important to have it as part of the design stage itself. Moreover, you will also learn the design patterns that preach the qualities of composition, isolation, and encapsulation that resonate with the idea of MFEs. Also, we will learn the need to design the architecture considering a futuristic mindset. Along the way, we will discuss the importance of understanding stateful and stateless applications when it comes to modularity. By the end, you will understand the necessity of MFEs in the world of user experience.

Mental model

One of the most important considerations when thinking of a product is understanding where it all begins. Often, it starts as a simple idea that gradually evolves into a billion-dollar product. The architecture, while not always fully defined at the outset, plays a crucial role from the beginning. Although it is impossible for a developer or architect to predict the exact scale the system will need to reach, thoughtful planning and flexible design are essential parts of any successful software journey. These are common realities faced throughout the development process.

Some argue that scalability should be built into the foundation from day one. Others say it can be addressed later, as the product matures. However, in today's world, scalability is no longer an afterthought. That does not mean early-stage teams must stress over scale from day one. This is because of modern cloud infrastructure, and we have abstracted away much of that burden on the backend. However, the frontend still presents its own set of challenges that have to be addressed.

Unlike backend microservices, frontend applications do not scale horizontally in the same way. They demand careful thought at the design phase, especially if you want to isolate features, enable parallel development, and avoid shared ownership bottlenecks later. This forces the developer to have the right mental model from the start.

A mental model is an architect's thought experiment, a process of building the system in an imaginary world, using only the resources, constraints, and goals available. It allows teams to stress test decisions before writing code. It helps visualize complexity, team boundaries, and long-term evolvability, way before they become painful realities.

It would start at the design stage, where the discussion of what part of it is discussed, and once we are clear on what, we can think about *how*. As we have seen in the previous chapters, there are multiple ways we could design the application, and each has its own advantages and disadvantages. Keeping those in mind, we know it is tricky to decide on the architecture at the design stage. Let us discuss a few parameters that could help draft the right mental model.

Fractal design

Rather than trying to land on a single architectural blueprint at the beginning, we can evolve our approach the way nature does. In biology and in complex systems, growth often follows a fractal pattern, where the smallest units reflect the structure of the whole. Each part is independently shaped but still fits into a greater system. This same concept can be applied to design the mental model around an application. It could be small, self-similar units that compose a complete, cohesive product.

Instead of thinking linearly, either top-down or bottom-up, we adopt a *recursive*, self-similar model. Fractal design does not just mean *small pieces;* it means every piece, regardless of its position or size in the hierarchy, adheres to a common contract that is independent, reusable, replaceable, and interoperable. From the tiniest UI component to an entire domain-level frontend module, the same principles should apply. As shown in the following figure, the system evolves in phases, similar to natural ecosystems:

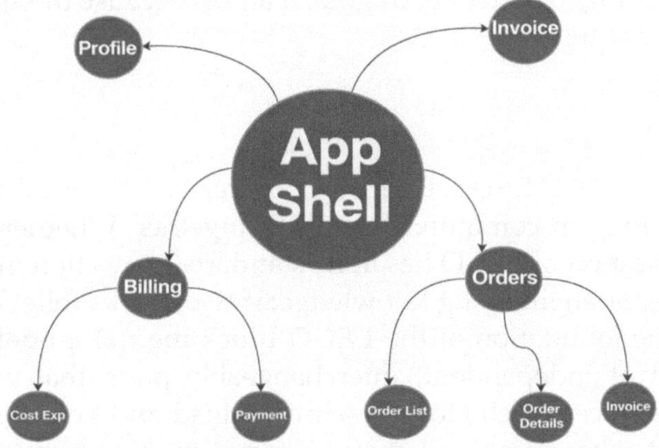

Figure 3.1*: Fractal design in a typical e-commerce application*

Figure 3.1 illustrates the concept of fractal design using an e-commerce application. In this model, smaller, self-contained units such as orders, billing, and invoice fragments function independently yet contribute to the larger system as a cohesive whole. Notably, the invoice module is reused both within the **App Shell** and as a sub-fragment of the **Orders** section, demonstrating its modularity and reusability across different parts of the application.

A real-world analogy to fractal design can be explained via a car; it is not just one big machine, but a collection of smaller parts, each working together to make the whole function. Imagine you need to change a flat tire. You do not need to take the entire car apart to do that; you only work with the tire. That is possible because the tire is designed as an independent part with clear boundaries. It connects to the car in a specific way, using bolts and a rim that match the car's design. You can replace just the tire, and the rest of the car keeps working. The same idea applies to the seats; they are attached securely, but if needed, they can be removed or replaced without affecting the rest of the vehicle. This replaceability is a feature of fractal design. Every part is complete, and it connects to others through standard ways, like a puzzle piece fitting into a larger picture.

However, even though the parts can work independently, they also work together smoothly to make the whole system function. When you drive the car, pressing the brake pedal slows down the wheels, switching on the wipers clears the windshield, and turning the steering wheel changes direction. Each of these actions feels simple, but behind the scenes, many small parts are working together. The amazing thing is that you do not have to think about all of them; the car just works. That is the elegance of a system built using fractal design: the broader system emerges from many small actions happening simultaneously, each within its own distinct context. The overall driving experience will be smooth, safe, and controlled, and it is not coming from one big machine doing the big job. It comes from many smaller parts, each designed carefully, doing its small job well, and all following a pattern of repeatable structure and interaction. That kind of design not only makes the car easier to build and fix but also helps it last longer and adapt to new features, whether it is adding a new speaker, changing the upholstery, or upgrading to better headlights. It all fits because the structure is predictable, modular, and fractal in nature.

LEGO blocks

Imagine opening a box of LEGO bricks. Each block comes in different shapes, colors, and sizes, but they all have one thing in common: they all fit together. Whether it is a tiny stud or a long flat plate, the application of LEGO lies in its standard connection mechanism. You do not need custom tools, glue, or engineering knowledge; if two blocks follow the basic shape, they just click. This forms the foundation of the **LEGO block mental model**, in which the design systems are composed of independent, interchangeable parts that connect through well-defined, predictable interfaces. Each block is self-contained and knows nothing about what it will be connected to. Yet, when combined, they can form anything from a small house to a giant spaceship. This exemplifies the principle that simplicity fosters flexibility. The following figure illustrates how a module or component can be conceptualized according to the LEGO model:

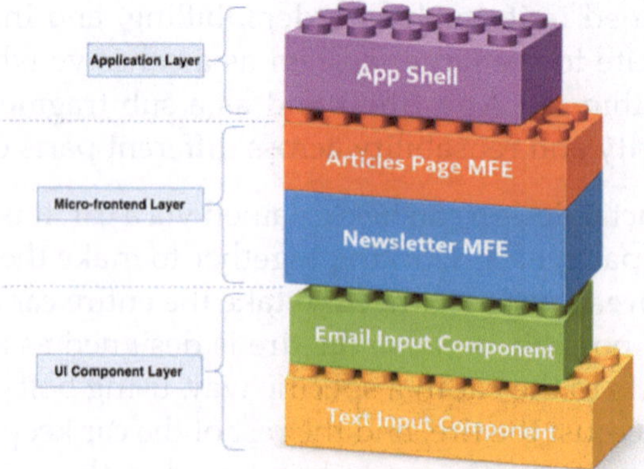

Figure 3.2: *Lego block representation of UI components and modules*

Embracing a mindset focused on granularity leads to greater long-term benefits. As illustrated in *Figure 3.2*, each block is designed to function independently, while still being flexible enough to integrate into larger systems. For example, a simple **Text Input Component** evolves into an **Email Input Component**, which is then incorporated into a **Newsletter MFE**. That **Newsletter MFE** is further embedded within an **Articles Page MFE**, ultimately contributing to the full application. You can now observe the pattern at play. While designing such granular components requires thoughtful planning and effort upfront, it significantly accelerates development in the long run. This exemplifies strategic thinking, a topic we will explore in more detail later in this chapter under the *Architecting for the future* section.

At first glance, LEGO might seem limited! After all, you are restricted to plastic blocks with fixed sizes and connection patterns, but this limitation is what unlocks creativity. The boundaries are very clear. You cannot bend a LEGO block, but you can stack it, rotate it, or combine it with others to create shapes. Within these constraints, people have built entire cities, functioning robots, and replicas of famous landmarks. The key insight is that having a standard does not reduce creativity; it enables it. When all parts share a common language, you can combine them in countless ways without starting from scratch. The same applies in technology, design, and even business. When every team builds components using the same interface contract, the entire organization can innovate faster. One team can build a user profile widget, and another team can use it without needing to understand its internals. This decoupling means teams move independently but stay connected through shared rules, which is just like LEGO builders working on different sections of the same castle.

Another strength of this model is replaceability and evolution. Imagine building a LEGO car and later deciding to upgrade the wheels. You do not need to rebuild the entire car. You simply remove the old wheels and attach new ones. In system design, this translates to improving a single module, such as a login form or analytics component, without rewriting the entire application. As long as the module continues to honor the same interface and behavior contract, the rest of the system remains unaffected.

This is what makes software, products, and even organizational systems scalable and maintainable. You are assembling from a library of parts, each with a clear role and a well-defined plug point. As systems grow, the ability to reuse, reconfigure, and remix parts becomes more valuable than building everything from scratch. The LEGO block model demonstrates how systems can evolve safely and creatively without chaos when modularity and standardization are trusted.

Note: **Components are reusable UI building blocks that remain largely context-agnostic. Micro-frontends, by contrast, encapsulate business capabilities and combine multiple components with domain-specific logic to deliver a functional feature.**

Bounded context

We have explored two models so far, *fractal design*, which favors nested, self-similar structures, and the *LEGO model*, which promotes plug-and-play modularity through standardized interfaces. However, in real-world systems, we also need a way to manage meaning and language. Otherwise, modular pieces might connect physically but conflict conceptually. That is where the third mental model, *Bounded Context,* becomes essential.

Imagine you are traveling across India. You begin in Punjab, where people speak Punjabi, enjoy rotis, and wear salwar suits and turbans. A few hours later, you are in Rajasthan, where the language shifts to Rajasthani dialects, the food emphasizes spices and dry textures, and the clothing becomes more colorful and desert-adapted. Travel further south to Tamil Nadu, and the world changes again; now people speak Tamil, eat off banana leaves, and wear veshti and sarees. Though all these states are part of the same country, each has its own distinct culture, language, cuisine, and customs. This similar concept is found in the *Bounded Context*. Each state is like a context with its own internal rules, vocabulary, and expectations. While they may share a national identity, currency, and constitution, the way of life inside each state is self-consistent and unique.

Similarly, in software systems, a Bounded Context represents a *clear conceptual boundary* within which words, models, and behaviors are aligned and meaningful. What something means in one context may mean something in another. That is not a conflict; it is a design choice. Just as no one expects Tamil to be understood in Punjab, we do not expect a data model from the payment system to be used unchanged in the customer support module. Instead, we design each context to be internally coherent, and use well-defined interfaces like translation, protocols, or **application programming interfaces** (**APIs**) when information needs to cross these boundaries. This mental model ensures that each domain can evolve independently while still participating in a shared ecosystem, just like India's diverse states form one nation. The following figure illustrates different independent modules within their own bounded context that establish communication with each other via a shared communication layer:

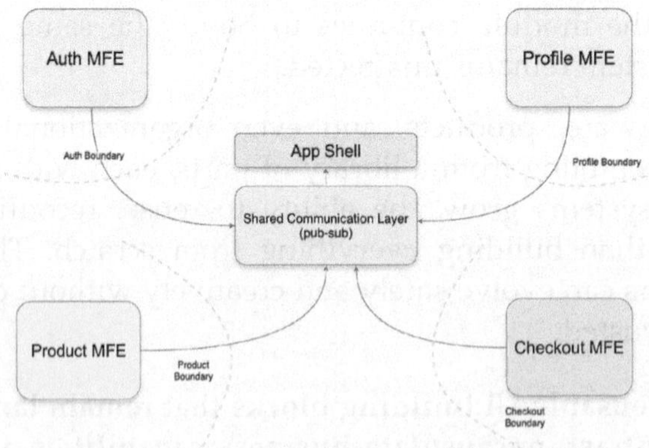

Figure 3.3: *Modules with their own boundaries, communicating via a shared layer*

As shown in *Figure 3.3,* each MFE operates within a clearly defined bounded context. These boundaries, such as the **Auth Boundary** controlling the **Auth MFE**, the **Profile Boundary** managing the **Profile MFE**, and similarly for **Product** and **Checkout,** ensure that each module encapsulates its own domain logic, data, and behavior. This separation allows MFEs to evolve, deploy, and scale independently without tightly coupling to others. Bounded contexts, a concept from **domain-driven design** (**DDD**), help in drawing clear lines around functionality and ownership. Each MFE is aligned with a specific business capability, reinforcing modular thinking and reducing cross-cutting dependencies. However, collaboration is still essential in a full-fledged application. To facilitate inter-module interaction, a shared communication layer is introduced. This layer enables MFEs to exchange information when needed using event-driven mechanisms or a publish-subscribe model without violating their autonomy. This approach fosters loose coupling while supporting a coordinated user experience across domains.

Design patterns

MFE embraces modularity at the UI level by breaking a large frontend monolith into independently developed, tested, and deployed components. This approach enables teams to work in parallel, scale development efficiently, and adopt technology stacks best suited to each feature or domain. However, distributing the frontend in this way introduces new complexities, such as ensuring consistency in user experience, managing cross-team dependencies, and handling communication between isolated modules.

To effectively orchestrate these distributed pieces into a seamless experience, proven design patterns come into play. Patterns like Composition, Strangulation, Adapter, Facade, and **Publish-Subscribe** (**Pub-Sub**) help manage concerns such as interoperability, abstraction, communication, and scalability. Understanding and applying these patterns ensures that MFEs remain maintainable, resilient, and cohesive even when built by multiple teams using different technologies.

In the following sections, we will explore these design patterns in greater depth, examining how each one supports the development of scalable, maintainable, and resilient micro frontend architectures.

Composition pattern

The composition pattern in MFE refers to how independently developed frontend pieces are assembled to form a cohesive application. Unlike monolithic frontends, where all components are tightly coupled and bundled at build time, MFEs thrive on loose coupling and runtime integration. This pattern is essential in enabling autonomy and scalability across frontend teams, allowing them to own and ship features independently. The composition can occur at different stages, build time, server-side, or client-side, each with its trade-offs in flexibility, performance, and complexity.

Imagine an airport terminal where multiple airlines operate side by side. Each airline manages its own check-in counters, staff, booking systems, and boarding processes. Yet they all rely on shared airport infrastructure such as security checkpoints, baggage handling systems, gates, and passenger information displays. To travelers, the airport appears as a single coordinated experience even though many independent organizations operate within it.

MFE composition works in a similar way. Each airline represents an independent MFE that owns its functionality and release cycle. The airport infrastructure represents the host application and shared platform services, such as routing, authentication, and design systems, that enable these independent modules to function together as a unified product.

While composition enables flexibility, it introduces new responsibilities for frontend architects. A major challenge is style and dependency isolation. If MFEs ship their own CSS globally, styles can leak and override each other. This is often solved using CSS Modules, Shadow **Document Object Model** (**DOM**) (via Web components), **Block, Element, Modifier** (**BEM**) naming conventions, or CSS-in-JS solutions such as styled-components and Emotion. CSS-in-JS libraries scope styles at the component level and often generate unique class names at runtime, reducing the risk of style collisions across independently developed MFEs. Another challenge is dependency sharing. For example, if multiple MFEs load different versions of React, bundle size and runtime conflicts can grow. This is mitigated using Webpack Module Federation, which allows shared libraries to be dynamically linked and reused at runtime. The following code block explains how a simple component, such as a card, can be generated in a composable way:

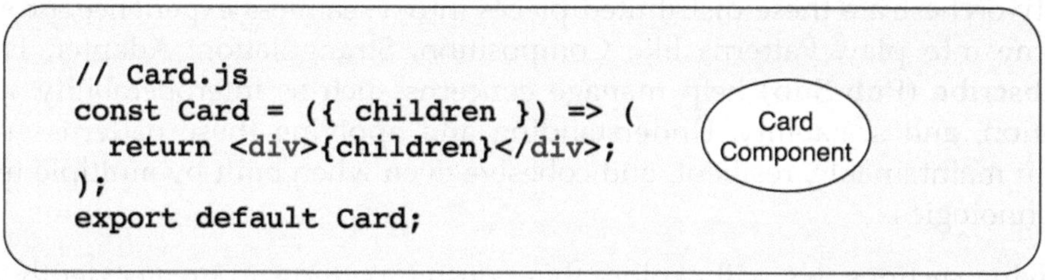

```
// Card.js
const Card = ({ children }) => (
  return <div>{children}</div>;
);
export default Card;
```


Figure 3.4 (a): Simple card component that displays the content passed to it

In *Figure 3.4 (a)*, we have a simple card component built using ReactJS, which is pure and displays whatever is passed to it. As this is a component, by default, it is reusable and composable. Such composability is explained in the following figure:

```
// Section.js
import Card from './Card';
const Section = ({ title, children }) => {
  return (
    <section>
      <h2>{title}</h2>
      <Card>{children}</Card>
    </section>
  ));
};
export default Section;
```


Figure 3.4 (b): *Section component is created by composing card component*

Figure 3.4 (b), you might notice that the card component has been used to form another component, which is the section component. Now, the card component is not only reused, but it is also composed into another component. These components can further be included into either a page component as *Figure 3.4 (c)* or only the **Card** can be used as needed.

```
// Page.js
import Section from './Section';
const Page = () => {
  return (
    <>
      <Section title="User Profile">
        <p>User Profile Section </p>
      </Section>
      <Section title="Recent Activities">
        <p>Recent Activities Section </p>
      </Section>
    </>
  );
};
export default Page;
```


Figure 3.4 (c): *The page that consumes the section indirectly uses the card component*

Composition also requires error boundaries and fallback logic. If one MFE fails to load due to a network issue or deployment error, the container should catch the failure and provide a fallback or remove that section gracefully. This is particularly important in client-side composition where MFEs are loaded dynamically and asynchronously. Moreover, shared routing and context management become critical. Whether it's an authenticated user or an A/B test group, some level of shared state or identity must flow across MFEs without tightly coupling them.

Strangulation pattern

One of the most common challenges in large frontend applications, especially in legacy monoliths, is their incremental modernization. Rewriting the entire UI from scratch is risky, time-consuming, and often infeasible for enterprise systems that must remain operational. Businesses still need to ship features, fix bugs, and serve users while transitioning to modern architectures like MFE. This is where the strangulation pattern offers a pragmatic solution. Instead of a *big bang* rewrite, the strangulation pattern enables teams to gradually replace parts of a monolithic frontend with MFEs, one feature or route at a time, until the legacy is fully retired.

Inspired by *Martin Fowler's strangler fig* analogy from nature, where a new vine wraps around a host tree and eventually replaces it, the strangulation pattern works by routing parts of the application to newer implementations while preserving the old where necessary. Imagine a legacy e-commerce portal built in AngularJS, but your team wants to modernize it using React-based MFEs. Rather than replacing the entire app, you might start by extracting the product listing page as a standalone MFE. Users navigating to the products page will see the new implementation, while the rest of the app continues to rely on the legacy codebase. Over time, you strangle more of the old UI as new MFEs take over.

A real-world analogy would be renovating a restaurant without closing it. Rather than shutting the whole place down for months, you renovate one section at a time, the kitchen, then the dining hall, then the restrooms, while keeping the rest functional. Diners still get served, and the business does not lose revenue. Similarly, with strangulation in MFEs, you avoid downtime and risk by slowly migrating user-facing routes, services, and shared components while keeping the application available and maintainable.

Technically, the strangulation pattern often uses routing logic at the edge (e.g., Lambda@ Edge, **content delivery network** (**CDN**) redirect rules) or within the container app shell to decide whether to render the legacy view or load a micro frontend. In some cases, wrapper components or iframe bridges can be used to mount MFEs inside legacy pages. When routing users between two architectures, care must be taken with shared state (like auth tokens or user sessions), consistent styling, and navigation continuity. Feature flags are often used to enable A/B testing and roll out new MFEs incrementally to users. The following figure shows an example of the strangulation pattern:

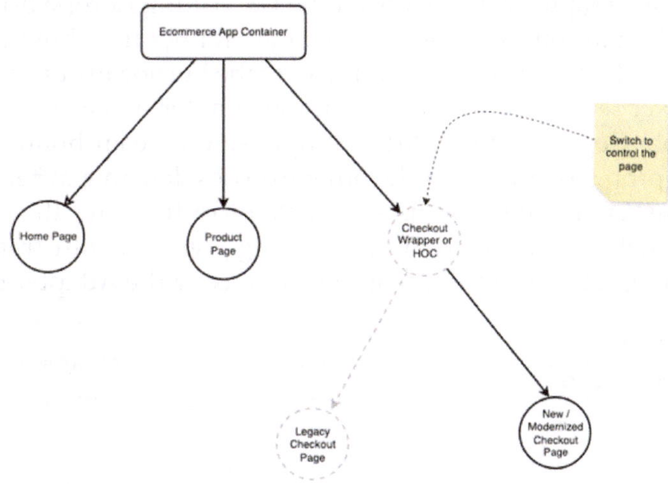

Figure 3.5: *Checkout page replaced using the strangulation pattern*

As depicted in *Figure 3.5*, an e-commerce company can decide to replace the checkout page incrementally using a wrapper or a **higher-order component** (**HOC**) that can decide the new or the old checkout page based on some condition, usually a feature flag or toggle controlled at run time. Though we have showcased the split at one level, in an ideal scenario, it can happen at any level or even at the routing, edge, or on the server. The important point to understand is how this helps to incrementally deliver the modernized page without impacting the business. Also, the greyed area in the image (HOC and the legacy page) can be removed easily once the migration is over.

The real strength of the strangulation pattern is risk reduction. It allows the frontend architecture to evolve while delivering continuous value to users and business stakeholders. It aligns well with agile delivery, promotes parallel development, and avoids rewriting known working systems from scratch. Eventually, once all routes and features have been offloaded to modern MFEs, the legacy application can be safely decommissioned, and by that time, users will not have even noticed the transition. In essence, strangulation provides a flexible pathway to modernization with less hassle.

Adapter pattern

The *Adapter pattern* in MFEs is a structural design solution that enables independently built components or modules to work together despite differences in their interfaces, formats, or expectations. In large organizations, different teams may use varied frameworks, data contracts, or communication models. Instead of forcing all teams to conform to a shared spec or refactor legacy modules, an adapter acts as a translator layer. It allows an MFE to consume or expose interfaces that do not natively match the surrounding system, ensuring seamless integration without compromising modularity or autonomy.

Imagine a world travel adapter. A tourist from the US visiting Europe brings a phone charger with flat pins, only to find round sockets in the hotel. Rather than buying a new charger, the tourist uses a plug adapter that bridges their device to the European outlet. The charger remains unchanged, the socket remains unchanged, but the adapter makes them compatible. This is precisely how adapter logic works in MFEs. Suppose one team builds a React component expecting a specific prop structure, and the other exposes data in a different shape. Instead of altering both systems, an adapter reshapes the data or restructures the component interface, letting both work together effortlessly. The following *Figure 3.6* illustrates how a non-React component can be integrated into a React application using the Adapter pattern:

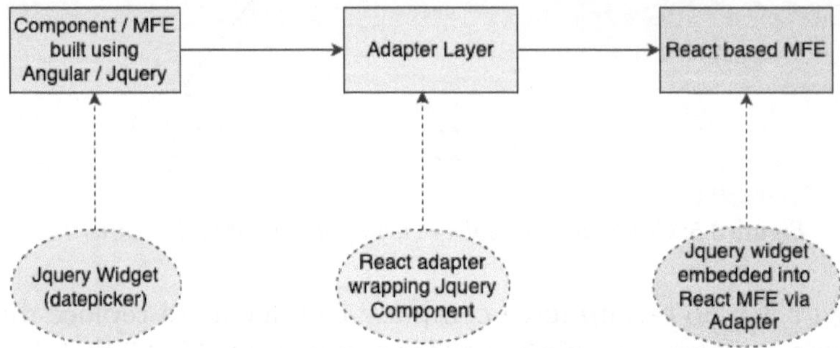

Figure 3.6: *A non-react component can be used in React using the Adapter layer*

Adapters become especially useful in scenarios where systems evolve at different speeds. A common use case is integrating legacy applications with modern MFE modules. If a legacy AngularJS component emits custom DOM events and the surrounding system expects Redux actions, an adapter captures those events and dispatches the necessary actions. Similarly, APIs with different field names or date formats can be normalized by lightweight adapter utilities before being passed into components. These adapters help avoid tight coupling and allow migration or experimentation without risking production stability.

However, adapters must be used thoughtfully. Too many adapters can hide complexity and introduce maintenance overhead. When used correctly, the adapter pattern allows MFEs to communicate across technical boundaries and evolution cycles, serving as the quiet enabler of interoperability in modern frontend architectures.

Facade pattern

The *Facade pattern* in MFEs is a structural design approach that introduces a simplified and unified interface to a set of complex, underlying subsystems or MFE modules. It acts as an abstraction layer that hides the inner complexities of multiple MFEs, allowing consumers to interact with them through a single, clean API. In MFE systems where multiple pieces may involve interdependent behavior (like fetching user details, feature flags, and permissions), the facade ensures consumers are not overwhelmed by low-level orchestration or inconsistent APIs. Instead, it offers a cohesive contract that remains stable even as the internals evolve.

Think of a hotel concierge desk as a real-world analogy. Behind the scenes, a hotel operates numerous departments, including housekeeping, maintenance, room service, transportation, guest services, and more. As a guest, you do not need to call each department individually. Instead, you speak with the concierge, who then coordinates the necessary departments on your behalf. The concierge simplifies your interaction with a complex system. Similarly, an MFE facade could provide a single component, such as Product List, in which it can talk to multiple teams to aggregate the product from various sources that are available in that company and display those in a simple dropdown for the user to interact with. The consumers of that component or MFE do not need to know the internal logic or the teams that it interacts with on the fly. The following figure illustrates an example of the facade pattern.

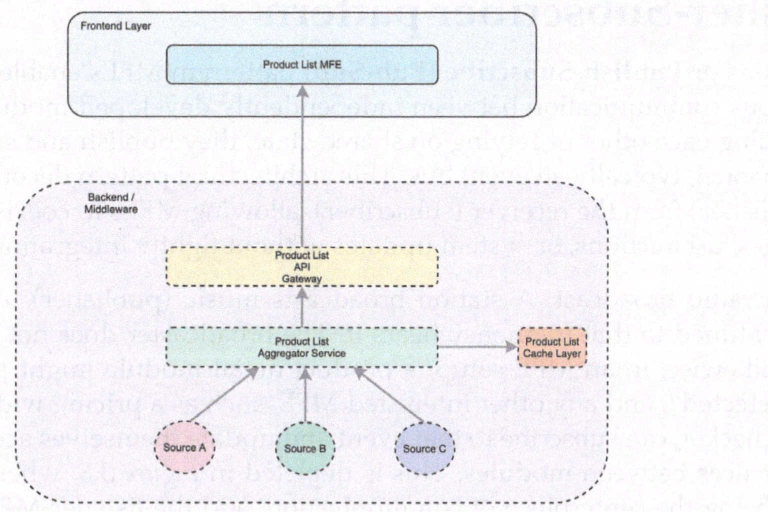

***Figure 3.7**: Product list MFE facades the business logic from consumers*

Figure 3.7 shows the **Product List MFE** sitting in the frontend layer. To the user (or even to another developer consuming the component), it appears as a simple dropdown, or maybe a table of product information. However, behind this clean UI lies a complex network of systems, API gateways, aggregation layers, cache strategies, and external data sources. This is where the Facade Pattern plays its role. The MFE acts as a facade, which is an interface that masks the internal complexity of the product retrieval logic. Consumers of this MFE do not need to know how the data is fetched, merged, cached, or formatted. They simply use the component and get consistent product data.

In practice, the Facade Pattern helps MFEs remain modular yet consumable. For example, in an enterprise dashboard with widgets built by different teams, each MFE might have its own logic to fetch configuration, user permissions, and localization data. Instead of making every module handle this logic independently, a shared facade can encapsulate this orchestration. This also centralizes caching, fallback handling, and loading state management, allowing consistent behavior across the experience.

The facade becomes especially powerful when paired with lazy loading or dynamic imports. Rather than initializing multiple MFEs and hoping they play well together, a facade can sequence them, provide fallback UIs, and expose consolidated state or callbacks. This reduces the coupling between the container app and its child MFEs. Moreover, facades serve as an effective integration boundary, especially during migrations. You can change or swap the internals of several MFEs without breaking downstream consumers, as long as the facade contract remains unchanged. Ultimately, the Facade Pattern enhances developer experience, system reliability, and forward compatibility, all crucial attributes for scaling micro frontend architectures.

Publisher-Subscriber pattern

The event bus or **Publish-Subscribe** (**Pub-Sub**) pattern in MFEs enables loose coupling and asynchronous communication between independently developed modules. Instead of MFEs directly calling each other or relying on shared state, they publish and subscribe to events on a shared channel, typically an event bus. This architectural pattern decouples the sender of an event (publisher) from the receiver (subscriber), allowing MFEs to coexist and react to shared state changes, user actions, or system updates without tightly integrating their internal logic.

Think of a radio broadcast. A station broadcasts music (publisher). Anyone with a radio (subscriber) tuned to that frequency hears it. The broadcaster does not know or care who is listening. Likewise, in an MFE setup, a product detail module might publish an event like **"productSelected"**, and any other interested MFE, such as a pricing widget, review panel, or inventory checker, can subscribe to that event and update themselves accordingly, all without direct references between modules. This is depicted in *Figure 3.8*, where you can notice the event bus being the centerpiece of communication, and the listener MFE updates their state according to the event subscribed:

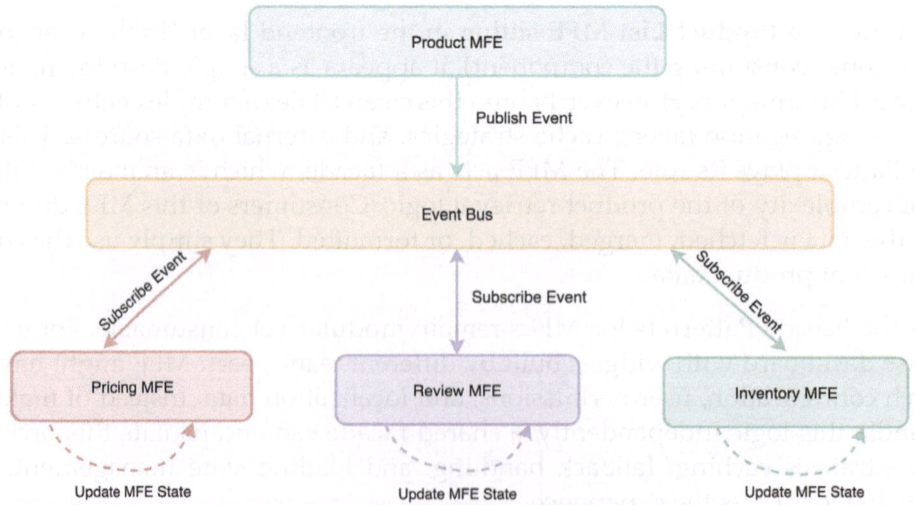

***Figure 3.8:** Pub-Sub event flow example with product MFE*

This pattern becomes especially useful in client-side compositions where MFEs are loaded dynamically. This is because these MFEs may not be aware of each other ahead of time; an event bus allows them to coordinate actions, propagate state, or trigger side effects reactively. Libraries like tiny-emitter or custom event dispatchers using the native EventTarget API are often used to implement lightweight and performant event buses.

However, while Pub-Sub adds flexibility, it can also introduce hidden dependencies and debugging complexity. Since modules are decoupled, it is not always obvious who responds to which events, making it harder to trace flows and reproduce bugs. To manage this, teams often define an event contract, a shared registry of supported event types, payload structures, and publishing conventions. Tools like TypeScript enums or schemas help formalize these contracts. Additionally, monitoring tools or developer consoles can be enhanced to show real-time event traffic, improving observability.

In MFE architecture, the Pub-Sub Pattern plays a vital role in enabling reactive and scalable designs. It encourages autonomy while still supporting cross-cutting features, and it avoids the pitfalls of tightly coupled component hierarchies or global shared states. Used wisely, this pattern becomes the invisible thread that weaves independently crafted modules into a seamless and responsive user experience.

Architecting for the future

Designing an architecture that can scale is mandatory for any application, be it small or big. As the user base changes, the need for scale will increase automatically. The future-proof application tends to satisfy the ever-changing business goals as it has the power of adaptability. As we looked into the mental model that comprises *what* and *how* part of choosing architecture. Now, we will continue to look beyond technical capabilities and see the remaining factors the adds to it.

Strategic mindset

Architectural decisions must be grounded in a strategic mindset that prioritizes long-term vision over short-term gains. It can be tempting to explore the implementation details and deliver tactical solutions quickly, especially when facing deadlines or product pressure. However, strategic thinking enables teams to design systems that are adaptable, scalable, and resilient to change. When we approach requirements strategically, we go beyond immediate features and think about how the system can evolve to support future use cases. This is not about over-engineering. It is about anticipating change and building flexibility into the foundation of the application. For example, creating modular and reusable components may require more time up front, but once in place, these components enable faster development, easier onboarding, and more consistent quality across teams. The investment pays off over time.

A clear mental model of the system's structure, responsibilities, and flows helps us design before a single line of code is written. It provides clarity, reduces ambiguity, and creates alignment across teams. In software, unknowns are inevitable. Early requirements are often defined by internal stakeholders, but the direction and success of a product are ultimately shaped by external users as feedback rolls in; the real iteration begins. Systems that are built with strategic intent are better equipped to accommodate change without becoming brittle or chaotic. In summary, **choose strategy over tactics**. A tactical win might help you ship today, but strategic thinking ensures your architecture remains stable and valuable in the long term.

Architecture driven

Choosing the right framework can contribute to a solid architecture; however, it should not be the primary focus when designing an application. Frameworks are tools, not foundations. A framework should support the architecture you define, not dictate it. Architecture defines the structure, boundaries, and responsibilities within your system. It shapes how components interact, how data flows, and how the application can grow and adapt over time. These decisions should be made at a higher level, independent of whether the implementation will use Angular, React, or any other frontend library.

Choosing a framework too early can influence decisions in subtle ways. You may end up building around what the framework makes convenient, rather than what your product actually needs. This can lead to early wins but create constraints in the long term.

Think of architecture as the blueprint of a house. When designing a house, the focus is on layout, flow, and structure. The choice between materials like steel or cement comes later. It is the plan that drives material choices, not the materials that shape the plan. Similarly, your application's architecture should come first. The framework is simply a tool to implement that vision. This mindset becomes even more critical in an MFE architecture. Each team may prefer different tools or frameworks based on their expertise and product context. If the system is designed with a framework-first mindset, it becomes rigid and tightly coupled. But with architecture-first thinking, you enable interoperability, scalability, and team autonomy regardless of the underlying technologies.

By separating architectural thinking from framework decisions, you preserve flexibility, reduce coupling, and ensure that the system remains adaptable as technologies evolve. Over time, frameworks change, but good architecture endures.

Platform first

A platform-first mindset means designing your systems to enable scale, reuse, and autonomy from the beginning. Instead of focusing only on delivering individual features or modules, the priority shifts to building a strong foundation that can support teams, accelerate development, and enforce consistency across the application landscape. In the context of MFEs, this mindset is especially important. Without a platform approach, teams may struggle with how they build, deploy, and operate their parts of the frontend. Over time, this can lead to fragmentation, duplication, and inconsistent user experiences. A strong platform addresses this by offering shared capabilities that act as a common layer for all teams. This includes not just technical utilities, but also design systems, authentication flows, routing strategies, and deployment standards.

The goal is not to create a heavily centralized system. It is to empower teams by removing repetitive problems and enabling them to focus on their domain. A thoughtfully built platform reduces cognitive load, avoids reinventing the wheel, and increases overall development speed. For example, instead of each MFE handling its own session management or API integration standards, the platform can provide reliable, tested modules for these concerns. Instead of creating build and deploy pipelines from scratch, the platform can offer an extensible build and deployment system that works out of the box and follows best practices.

Adopting a platform-first mindset requires early investment. It means dedicating effort to shared tooling and infrastructure before it becomes a bottleneck, but that effort pays off quickly. New teams onboard faster, shared patterns improve quality, and features ship with greater confidence. Over time, this creates a compounding effect in which every improvement in the platform lifts the entire organization. With a platform-first mindset, your frontend architecture is no longer a loose collection of apps. It becomes a composable ecosystem defined by clear boundaries, enabled by shared infrastructure, and built to grow with confidence.

From mindset to reality

While a strategic mindset, architecture before framework, and platform-first thinking provide a strong foundation, architecture does not exist in a vacuum. In the real world, our decisions are often shaped by practical forces that operate beyond pure design principles. Every architectural choice is influenced by real-world dynamics such as business priorities, team structure, and existing technology investments. These forces do not weaken architecture. In fact, they provide the context that makes architectural decisions meaningful and effective.

To design a resilient and future-ready system, it is essential to understand and align with these driving forces. Let us explore the key realities that shape modern micro frontend architectures.

Business requirements

Business requirements are the cornerstone of any architectural decision. They shape not just what the application does but how it must behave, scale, and evolve. Understanding the business landscape enables architects to make informed decisions about modularity, ownership, deployment strategies, and long-term maintainability.

The following are a few key questions to ask:

1. Are we building a single product or a suite of offerings?
2. Will the product scale across regions or verticals?
3. How fast is the business evolving?
4. Are there multiple brands or customer personas involved?

One of the earliest decisions in a software project is determining the scope of the product. A standalone, tightly focused product used by a small group of users might benefit from a simple monolith. But if the application is a platform used by multiple personas with varied workflows, such as buyers, sellers, admins, or vendors, it becomes essential to explore architectures that can serve each segment with tailored, evolvable experiences.

Scalability is not just technical. It is business-driven. For example, an e-commerce company aiming to expand from a local market to global operations will need its frontend to be adaptable for different languages, currencies, and product offerings. Without careful thought early on, retrofitting these changes into a rigid, monolithic UI can become an expensive, time-consuming challenge.

Most of the time, business velocity also affects architecture. If the company is in a hyper-growth phase, releasing multiple features per week or running many experiments, then the architecture must support continuous delivery. We cannot afford bottlenecks caused by long test cycles or coupled releases. In short, *architecture* should serve the business, not the other way around. The clear thought on the business needs should drive modularity to support global expansion.

Team and organizational structure

Team and organizational structure within the company heavily impact the decision in choosing the right architecture. *Conway's Law states that software systems tend to reflect the communication structures of the organizations that produce them*. This has huge implications for frontend architecture.

The following are a few key questions to ask:

1. Are there multiple teams owning different domains?
2. Do they have separate release schedules?
3. Are teams autonomous or dependent on each other for delivery?
4. Is the organization structured around features, platforms, or capabilities?

A common pattern in modern product teams is the formation of cross-functional squads that own a slice of the product end-to-end. For example, a *search team* might include backend engineers, frontend engineers, designers, and testers, all focused on delivering the search experience. Now, imagine all these teams working in a monolithic frontend. Even with good coding practices, teams will often step on each other's toes. A simple change in one module may trigger regression in unrelated parts. Merging pull requests becomes a coordination game. Release cycles are slowed by dependency hell.

A better model is to give each team their own deployable unit, often as an MFE. This aligns perfectly with the team structure, allowing squads to develop, test, and deploy independently.

Technology and dependency landscape

The technical stack and existing dependencies in your organization are often inherited and not chosen. Legacy codebases, third-party tools, and past architectural decisions shape what is feasible today.

The following are a few key questions to ask:

1. Are teams blocked by shared dependencies?
2. Is there a legacy system that still serves core functionality?
3. Are there mixed technology stacks involved?
4. Is code duplication necessary to move fast?

Every engineering team eventually deals with technology transitions. Maybe you started with AngularJS in 2014, but now you are moving to React or Vue. Migrating a monolithic frontend is like changing the engine of a moving car. You cannot freeze development and break the app. MFEs offer an elegant solution by enabling coexistence. You can gradually rewrite portions of your frontend without breaking the whole experience (Refer to the strangulation pattern in *Figure* 3.5). Each new MFE can use its own tech stack, and legacy systems can be wrapped and embedded as needed.

This is especially helpful when different teams have different levels of expertise or preferences. One team might prefer TypeScript with React, while another experiments with Svelte. As long as communication between modules is well-defined, technology heterogeneity becomes an advantage. Dependency management is another critical issue. Shared libraries, such as design systems, utility functions, or API clients, can create tight coupling. Changes in one place ripple through the entire system. MFEs reduce this blast radius. Teams can pin versions, test in isolation, and upgrade on their own timeline.

Stateful vs. stateless

In micro frontend architecture, one of the most important decisions is how to manage state both within individual modules and across the system. Whether an MFE is stateful or stateless impacts not just its technical design, but also how independently it can evolve, scale, and interact with the rest of the application. This is not a binary choice. It is a spectrum, and every application must choose its place on it based on context, complexity, and collaboration needs.

Stateful design

A stateful MFE is a self-contained unit within a larger frontend architecture that manages its own internal state. It holds the logic and data necessary to render its interface and react to user interactions independently. Unlike stateless MFEs, which rely on a parent container or orchestrator to pass down state, a stateful MFE encapsulates both behavior and data, much like a standalone app.

Stateful MFEs are particularly valuable when:

- The feature needs to work in isolation, including in embedded environments.
- The team building it requires deployment autonomy.
- The MFE has complex logic that should not leak into global orchestration.

This autonomy allows for better encapsulation and testability but comes with trade-offs around shared coordination. In the real-world, we can correlate this with a food truck. It brings everything it needs: ingredients, a cooking station, and even a local brand identity. It can operate independently, serve food without any reliance on the infrastructure of a restaurant, and move between locations. Similarly, a stateful MFE contains its own logic, manages its state (like handling orders and stock), and delivers a full experience to the user regardless of the host application.

The following simplified example illustrates a component that manages its own state locally. In a real micro-frontend architecture, this component would typically be packaged and exposed as a deployable MFE module:

```
// TodoApp.js (Stateful MFE)
import React, { useState } from 'react';
const TodoApp = () => {
  const [tasks, setTasks] = useState([]);
  const [input, setInput] = useState('');
  const addTask = () => {
    if (input.trim()) {
      setTasks([...tasks, input]);
      setInput('');
    }
  };
  return (
    <div>
      <h3>My Todo List (Stateful)</h3>
      <input
        value={input}
        onChange={(e) => setInput(e.target.value)}
        placeholder=»Enter a task»
      />
      <button onClick={addTask}>Add</button>
```

```
      <ul>
        {tasks.map((t, idx) => (
          <li key={idx}>{t}</li>
        ))}
      </ul>
    </div>
  );
};
export default TodoApp;
```

This example manages its own tasks and input state internally and handles user interactions without relying on external state management.

Stateless design

A stateless MFE is a UI module that does not manage its own state internally but instead receives all the necessary data and behavior through props, context, or external orchestrators. In this model, the state is typically lifted up to a container or parent application, which acts as the source of truth. The stateless MFE focuses solely on rendering the UI and reacting to changes, making it highly composable and predictable.

This pattern is ideal when:

- You want centralized control over the application's state.
- You need to orchestrate multiple MFEs around a shared context (e.g., filters, user data).
- You are aiming for consistency and easier testing.

A stateless MFE is like a restaurant waiter. The waiter does not cook food, decide the menu, or store ingredients. They simply take orders from customers and deliver food prepared by the kitchen. The waiter acts based on instructions and inputs; they do not make decisions independently. Just like the waiter depends on others to function and only facilitates interaction, a stateless MFE depends on its parent or host to supply all data and behavior; it focuses purely on rendering and handling basic UI interaction.

The following example illustrates a stateless UI module that renders a list of tasks provided by a parent container:

```
// TaskList.js (Stateless MFE)
import React from 'react';
const TaskList = ({ tasks, onRemove }) => {
  return (
    <div>
```

```
      <h3>Task List (Stateless)</h3>
      <ul>
        {tasks.map((task, idx) => (
          <li key={idx}>
            {task} <button onClick={() => onRemove(idx)}>Remove</button>
          </li>
        ))}
      </ul>
    </div>
  );
};
export default TaskList;
```

Here is how it may be used by a host container that owns the state:

```
// Container.js (Stateful host)
import React, { useState } from 'react';
import TaskList from './TaskList';
const TaskContainer = () => {
  const [tasks, setTasks] = useState(['Buy milk', 'Call John']);
  const handleRemove = (index) => {
    const updated = tasks.filter((_, i) => i !== index);
    setTasks(updated);
  };
  return <TaskList tasks={tasks} onRemove={handleRemove} />;
};
```

In this example, the **TaskList** MFE has no internal state, making it pure, testable, and reusable across projects.

Note: The code snippets above illustrate state ownership patterns using simple UI components. In a real micro-frontend architecture, an MFE also owns a deployment boundary, lifecycle, and integration contract with the host application. These examples intentionally focus only on state management concepts for clarity.

Table 3.1 displays the comparison between stateful and stateless:

Category	Stateful MFE	Stateless MFE
Definition	Manages and owns its own state locally	Receives all state and behavior via props or external sources
Autonomy	High autonomy It is self-contained and works independently	Low autonomy It depends on the host or container for data and coordination
Reusability	Limited reusability, as it is tightly coupled with the internal state	Highly reusable as it is easily reused across different apps or hosts
Communication	Needs explicit inter-MFE communication (events, pub-sub, etc.)	Minimal, as it just renders data passed from the host
Code complexity	Can grow quickly due to state handling logic	Simpler and easier to test
Scalability	Harder to scale as duplication and divergence can occur	Easier to scale with a consistent input/output contract
Example use case	User profile editor, dashboard with local preferences	UI Card, Button, List Renderer

Table 3.1*: Comparison between stateful and stateless MFEs*

There is no one-size-fits-all answer. The decision between stateful and stateless MFEs is not about right or wrong; it is about finding the right fit for the situation. Think of stateful MFEs as independent thinkers. It is capable, complex, and often powerful in the right context. Stateless MFEs, on the other hand, are focused collaborators; it is lean, composable, and highly portable. Great architecture often blends both. Use stateful MFEs where autonomy is essential, and stateless ones where flexibility and reuse are most important. In fact, stateful MFEs can be composed of stateless MFEs that rely on their parent, which is stateful. The key is to design with clarity and purpose. Let the needs of your users, teams, and product guide whether your micro frontend should hold its own logic or follow the lead of its host.

UX consistency

In any application, user experience is one of the most important parts. No matter how well the backend works or how scalable the system is, if the user interface feels disconnected or inconsistent, users will notice. With MFEs, where different teams build different parts of the application, maintaining a smooth and consistent user experience becomes more challenging and more important. A consistent user experience means that things look and feel the same across the entire product. Buttons behave the same way, text sizes are predictable, error messages follow the same style, and navigation feels familiar, no matter which part of the app the user is in. This gives users confidence and reduces confusion. When things change from screen to screen, it makes the product feel unpolished and can break the user's trust.

To make this work in an MFE world, teams need to share the same design language. This is where a strong design system comes in. A design system is more than just a set of UI components. It includes rules, guidelines, and reusable elements that all teams can follow. It covers things like spacing, color palette, typography, icon sets, component behavior, and accessibility standards. It helps teams build faster while staying in sync with others. Several well-known companies have shared their design systems with the world. For example, Google uses material design, which gives a clean and modern look with well-defined rules for motion, layout, and interaction. IBM has the *Carbon Design System*, which focuses on flexibility for enterprise products. Microsoft uses Fluent, which blends well with both web and native apps. Shopify has Polaris, which supports merchants and e-commerce interfaces. Each of these systems provides both design and code resources to help teams build consistent interfaces.

In your own organization, building or choosing a design system should be a key part of your MFE strategy. It reduces the chance of duplicated efforts and makes it easier for new teams to get started. For example, you might have a shared component library that every team uses, like a dropdown, date picker, or a modal dialog. By using the same components, teams do not need to reinvent the wheel, and users enjoy a seamless experience across pages and features.

To apply this effectively, make sure your design system is versioned and published in a way that teams can use it easily. You can host it on a private npm registry or use tools like Storybook to document it visually. You might also want a design token system that allows values like colors and spacing to be changed globally without touching each MFE individually. This kind of setup helps create a clear boundary between design ownership and application logic.

MFEs do not need to mean micro experiences. Even if teams are working independently, a strong shared foundation ensures the output still feels like one product. Make time for regular sync-ups between design and engineering teams. Run audits every few months to see how well the product is following the guidelines. Build tools that highlight visual inconsistencies. Even small things like font mismatches or unexpected button behavior can break the experience. Lastly, remember that consistency is not about making everything look the same. It is about creating a familiar rhythm across your app, where users feel comfortable and confident. The goal is to make the entire system feel thoughtful and well-connected, no matter how many teams are behind it. By treating design systems as a core part of your architecture and culture, you can scale your application confidently without sacrificing the quality of the user experience.

Conclusion

Crafting a successful MFE architecture requires more than just splitting a monolith into smaller parts; it demands a mindset shift, a well-defined design strategy, and a commitment to long-term cohesion. By adopting the right mental model, developers can treat each MFE as an autonomous unit while still aligning with the broader application goals. Leveraging established design patterns like composition, strangulation, adapter, and facade helps bring structure and reusability to otherwise fragmented systems.

At the same time, these benefits do not come without challenges. Decisions around orchestration, shared dependencies, and cross-team coordination become more visible as systems scale. Choices made today, whether to design MFEs as stateful or stateless, or how to enforce UX consistency across teams, directly influence not only scalability and maintainability, but also operational complexity and developer experience. An MFE system is only as strong as its weakest link, and ignoring foundational principles can amplify friction rather than reduce it.

With a solid architectural mindset in place, the next step is laying down the infrastructure to support it. In the following chapter, we will explore the essential groundwork needed to launch and sustain an MFE project, from choosing between framework-specific and framework-agnostic approaches to managing repositories, setting up robust testing strategies, and designing a CI/CD pipeline tailored for independent deployments. This infrastructure is the backbone that transforms architectural vision into a scalable reality.

Chapter 4
Laying Infrastructure

Introduction

This chapter lays the groundwork for building a successful micro-frontend architecture by walking readers through essential setup decisions and best practices. It opens with a comparison between *Framework-specific* and *Framework-agnostic* approaches, offering clear guidance on when to embrace a particular technology stack versus opting for cross-framework flexibility. Following that, it explores various repository strategies tailored to application needs, highlighting how each approach influences team collaboration, dependency management, and version control in a **micro-frontend** (**MFE**) environment.

The chapter then moves into *project setup* and *testing strategies*, providing actionable tips on structuring codebases, writing modular and reusable tests, and ensuring effective isolation between MFEs during testing. Finally, it concludes with a discussion regarding *CI/CD customization*, offering practical advice on designing continuous integration and deployment pipelines that align with the unique characteristics of MFEs, such as independent releases, versioning, and environment configurations. Altogether, this chapter empowers teams to establish a robust, scalable foundation for the efficient development and maintenance of MFE-based applications.

Structure

The chapter covers the following topics:

- Framework vs. framework-agnostic
- Mono-repo vs. multi-repo
- Project setup and testing strategies
- Tailoring CI/CD for MFE architectures

Objectives

This chapter aims to equip readers with a clear understanding of the fundamental choices involved in MFE architecture, including when to adopt a framework-specific versus a framework-agnostic approach. It guides teams in selecting the appropriate repository setup based on their collaboration and project needs, while emphasizing best practices for organizing code and implementing effective, isolated testing strategies. Additionally, the chapter provides practical insights into tailoring CI/CD pipelines to support the independent deployment and versioning demands unique to MFEs. Ultimately, readers will gain the knowledge needed to build a robust, scalable foundation that enhances development efficiency and simplifies the ongoing maintenance and deployment of MFE applications.

Framework vs. framework-agnostic

This section explores the foundational decisions for adopting a framework-specific or framework-agnostic approach in MFE projects. It covers the role of frameworks, their benefits and trade-offs, the considerations for a framework-agnostic mindset, the feasibility of custom MFE frameworks, and the concept of Island Architecture.

Framework

A framework is a pre-built set of tools, libraries, and conventions that helps developers build applications faster and more consistently. Think of it as a blueprint or scaffolding for a house; it provides the structure, so you do not have to build everything from scratch. In web development, frameworks or libraries such as React, Angular, and Vue.js offer reusable components, predefined ways to manage data, and tools to handle common tasks like rendering UI or managing user interactions.

For example:

- React (developed by *Facebook*) is a lightweight library for building dynamic user interfaces using components.
- Angular (developed by *Google*) is an opinionated, full-fledged framework with built-in tools for routing, forms, and state management.
- Vue.js (created by *Evan You*) is a flexible framework known for its simplicity and ease of integration.

Frameworks simplify coding by providing ready-made solutions, ensuring consistency, and reducing repetitive work. In micro-frontends, frameworks play a critical role in structuring individual frontend modules.

Frameworks and micro-frontend

As mentioned in the previous chapters, MFEs extend the microservices concept to the frontend, where an application is split into smaller, independent frontend modules, each developed and deployed by separate teams. Frameworks help streamline this process by providing structure and tools for building and integrating these modules. The concept of modularity has been made simple with the arrival of these frameworks and libraries. As these frameworks adopt many design patterns that we saw in the previous chapters, such as composable and facade patterns, they became the natural fit for building MFEs. Let us look at a few of the key benefits that frameworks offer out of the box.

Component-based development

One of the key pillars of MFEs is their composable nature. MFEs can be architected as a collection of independent, functional units that come together to form a cohesive application. Frameworks like React, Angular, and Vue.js empower this approach by enabling teams to build reusable UI components. For instance, a React-based product card component can be created once and reused across multiple MFEs, ensuring consistency and reducing duplication. These frameworks provide structured ways to build, test, and maintain UI blocks, making it easier to achieve modularity.

In MFE architecture, components are designed to be isolated and self-contained, which minimizes interdependencies between MFEs. This isolation is crucial to maintaining autonomy, a core MFE principle that allows teams to work independently without stepping on each other's toes. It also supports scalability, where different teams can be assigned to specific components or entire MFEs. As a result, teams can focus on building and evolving specific UI elements without being tightly coupled to the rest of the system, fostering parallel development and faster iteration cycles. *Figure 4.1* illustrates how independent functional modules or MFE come together through the app shell or container to create a cohesive application:

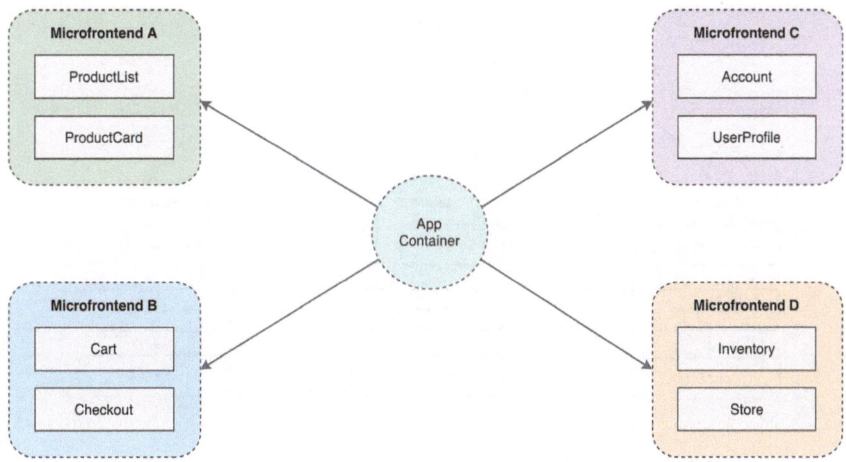

***Figure 4.1**: Component-based development with MFEs*

State management

Another key benefit of using established frameworks in MFEs is their built-in or ecosystem-driven support for state management. In an MFE setup, each MFE is ideally self-contained, including how it manages UI and application state. Frameworks like React provide mature tools such as Redux, Zustand, or React Context that help encapsulate state at the component or feature level. Similarly, Vue.js offers solutions like Vuex and Pinia, which make it easy to maintain local state within an MFE while preserving reactivity. These tools encourage modular design, reducing the likelihood of unintended state sharing or tight coupling between MFEs.

Framework-based meta-frameworks like Next.js and Nuxt enhance this further by offering state management that integrates with **server-side rendering** (**SSR**), API fetching, and static generation. For instance, Next.js developers might use Server Actions or React Query to fetch and hydrate state specific to each MFE, while Nuxt's composable and store modules allow state to be scoped cleanly within individual applications. These capabilities simplify the challenges of state synchronization across different environments (server/client) and allow each MFE to manage its own lifecycle independently. By using these frameworks, teams gain structure, consistency, and built-in best practices for managing state across distributed, autonomous frontends.

Figure 4.2 shows how different MFEs, such as Product, Cart, and Account, manage their own local state but also connect to a shared global state. When a user interacts with a component, like clicking *Add to Cart*, the local event handler updates its own state and may also send an update to the global state, such as updating the cart count. The global state then broadcasts changes to other MFEs so they can react, like updating the cart icon in the header. This way, each MFE stays independent but still stays in sync with the rest of the app.

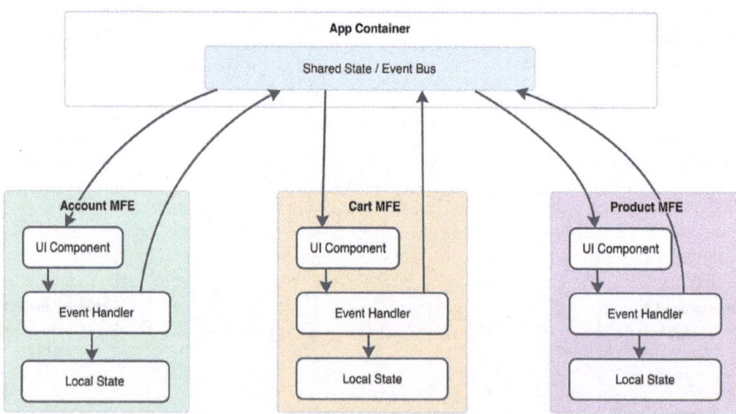

Figure 4.2*: Typical state management flow in an e-commerce application*

Tooling and integration support

A major advantage of using established frameworks in MFEs is the rich ecosystem and mature tooling they bring, which significantly streamlines both development and integration. Frameworks like React, Angular, Vue, and their meta-frameworks such as Next.js and Nuxt offer battle-tested solutions for routing, code splitting, testing, accessibility, and internationalization. These tools help developers build and ship MFEs faster with fewer errors. For instance, Next.js provides built-in support for SSR, dynamic routing, and API handling, all of which are valuable when building MFEs that need to function independently yet harmoniously within a larger app.

On the integration side, these frameworks are often well-supported by orchestration tools like Webpack Module Federation, **Single Page Application** (**SPA**), and Qiankun. The following example illustrates a simple runtime integration where a host MFE dynamically loads a remote component:

```
// Host MFE importing a remote component at runtime
const CartSummary = React.lazy(() => import("checkout/CartSummary"));
```

At runtime, the host application dynamically loads the **`CartSummary`** component from the checkout MFE, without bundling it at build time.

Frameworks like React and Vue are commonly used in conjunction with Module Federation, which enables runtime sharing of components and libraries between MFEs without bundling them together. This support extends to performance tools, testing frameworks (e.g., Jest, Vitest), CI/CD pipelines, and browser DevTools integrations, making the entire development lifecycle more efficient. Using a popular framework means you benefit from a large community, continuous updates, plugin ecosystems, and compatibility with other tools, all of which lower the complexity of adopting and scaling MFE architectures.

Framework-specific MFEs

A framework-specific MFE architecture standardizes the choice of frontend framework (such as React, Angular, or Vue) across all MFEs in the system. Each team still owns and deploys its own MFE independently, but they share the same underlying framework and associated ecosystem.

This approach is common in organizations that prioritize uniformity, maintainability, and shared tooling. By using the same framework across all MFEs, teams can benefit from a shared component library, consistent coding conventions, reusable hooks or utilities, and a unified developer experience. It also simplifies cross-team onboarding and documentation since all teams speak the same *framework language*.

However, this uniformity comes at a cost. Tightly coupling your MFE strategy to a single framework can create vendor lock-in and reduce long-term flexibility. For instance, migrating from React to another framework across multiple MFEs becomes an all-or-nothing effort, defeating one of the core promises of MFEs, incremental evolution. It also introduces friction in scenarios where different teams have different preferences or legacy stacks to maintain.

The following are the advantages of a framework-specific approach:

- **Consistency**: Using a single framework (e.g., React) ensures uniform coding patterns, component libraries, and state management across all MFEs. For example, all teams can use Material-UI with React for consistent styling.
- **Performance optimization**: A single framework reduces the need to load multiple runtime libraries. For example, a React-based MFE setup can share a single React instance, minimizing bundle size.
- **Simplified tooling**: A unified framework allows teams to use the same build tools, testing frameworks (e.g., Jest for React), and CI/CD pipelines, reducing setup complexity.
- **Team alignment**: Ideal for teams with expertise in one framework, reducing training time. For example, a team skilled in Angular can leverage its **command line interface** (**CLI**) and **Reactive Extensions for JavaScript** (**RxJS**) for rapid development.
- **Easier integration**: Frameworks provide built-in mechanisms (e.g., React's Context API, Angular's dependency injection) for communication between MFEs.

The following are the disadvantages of a framework-specific approach:

- **Vendor lock-in**: Committing to one framework (e.g., Vue.js) makes it hard to adopt new technologies without significant refactoring.
- **Limited flexibility**: Teams cannot choose frameworks that better suit specific MFEs. For example, Angular's heavier footprint may not be ideal for lightweight static pages.
- **Framework limitations**: Not all frameworks are suited for every use case. For instance, React's lack of built-in routing may require additional libraries for complex MFEs.
- **Stifled innovation**: Teams may be restricted from experimenting with newer frameworks like Svelte, limiting innovation.

An e-commerce platform using only React for its MFEs (product listing, cart, user profile) benefits from shared components and optimized performance but struggles to integrate a legacy Angular module without a rewrite.

Framework-agnostic approach

A framework-agnostic approach allows each MFE to use different frameworks or technologies (e.g., React, Vue.js, or vanilla JavaScript) and integrates them using framework-neutral tools like Web Components or Module Federation. Adopting this approach requires careful planning and infrastructure.

Key considerations

Adopting a framework-agnostic MFE architecture offers remarkable flexibility and independence for teams, but it introduces a unique set of challenges. Unlike a unified stack where all MFEs follow the same conventions, framework-agnostic setups require greater attention to how components interact, share resources, and maintain consistency. The following are a few key points to consider while choosing a framework-agnostic approach:

- **Integration mechanism**: The core challenge in a framework-agnostic system lies in how to integrate multiple MFEs that might each use different technologies. This integration must allow each MFE to run independently while also coexisting within a shared shell or host application. Module Federation, a feature of Webpack 5, addresses this by enabling MFEs to expose and consume code from each other dynamically at runtime. It helps prevent duplication of shared libraries like React or Vue, which might otherwise be bundled multiple times. Alternatively, Web Components provide a natively supported way to build encapsulated, reusable UI elements without relying on any specific framework. They are especially useful when complete technology neutrality is required. For orchestrating different MFEs within the browser, Single-SPA offers a runtime approach to mounting, updating, and unmounting MFEs, providing a reliable way to bind heterogeneous frontends into a single cohesive application.

- **Design system**: In the absence of a shared framework, maintaining a consistent design and user experience across MFEs becomes more challenging. A centralized design system plays a crucial role in addressing this. Teams can adopt utility-first CSS frameworks like Tailwind CSS, which are inherently framework-agnostic and can be shared across MFEs without conflict. Alternatively, a custom component library built using Web Components ensures that visual elements are consistent regardless of whether they are rendered in React, Vue, or vanilla JavaScript. Tools like Storybook help document and showcase these components in isolation, enabling teams to preview, test, and adopt shared design standards even when building in entirely different frameworks.

- **Team autonomy**: One of the biggest advantages of a framework-agnostic MFE architecture is the autonomy it provides to individual teams. Each team can choose the technology stack that best fits its expertise or project constraints. However, autonomy must come with the responsibility of understanding the integration layer that glues MFEs together. Teams need to be familiar with how their MFE will be mounted into the larger application, what lifecycle events are available, and how communication or routing is handled at runtime. Whether using Single-SPA or a custom loader, the integration model must be documented and easily understandable to avoid inconsistencies or hidden dependencies between MFEs.

- **Performance management**: Loading multiple frameworks on the same page introduces real performance considerations. Without careful planning, this approach can lead to large bundle sizes, duplicated dependencies, and long load times. To manage performance, teams should ensure that MFEs are lazy-loaded when possible, meaning they are only fetched and executed when the user navigates to the part of the app where they are needed. Module Federation can help optimize load times by allowing shared libraries to be loaded once and reused across MFEs. Ongoing monitoring of JavaScript payload sizes, runtime metrics, and real user performance is essential to avoid user experience degradation as the system grows.

- **Tooling diversity**: Each framework brings its own ecosystem of build tools, testing libraries, and developer workflows. In a framework-agnostic setup, this naturally leads to a diverse set of tools and configurations across teams. One MFE may use Webpack and Jest, while another uses Vite and Vitest. This diversity is not inherently problematic, but it must be managed thoughtfully. Building template repositories, internal scaffolding tools, or shared CI/CD modules can help streamline setup while preserving flexibility. However, some aspects, like logging, monitoring, error tracking, and deployment standards, should be unified to ensure observability and operational control across the entire platform.

Figure 4.3 illustrates that a company might decide to use React for an interactive video player, Vue.js for a content management dashboard, and vanilla JavaScript for static pages, integrating them with Single-SPA and a shared Tailwind CSS design system:

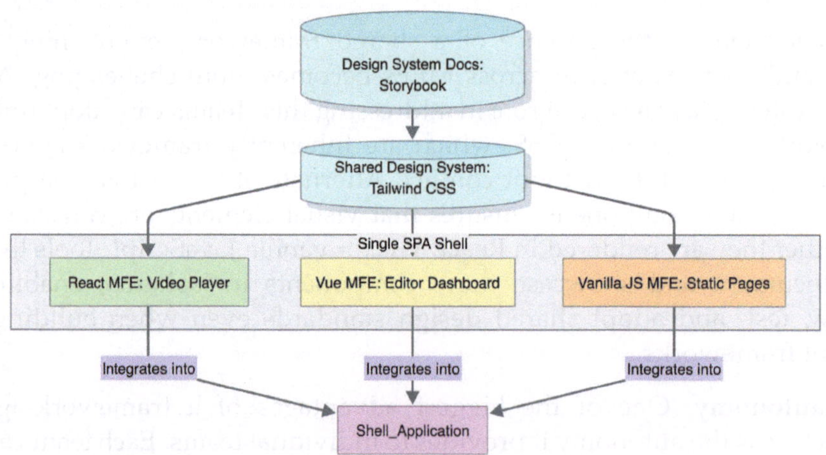

***Figure 4.3**: Example of a framework-agnostic polygot MFE*

The following are the advantages of a framework-agnostic approach:

- **Team autonomy**: Teams can choose frameworks that match their expertise or MFE requirements. For example, a team proficient in Vue.js can use it without learning Angular.
- **Flexibility**: Allows integration of legacy systems or new technologies without rewriting existing MFEs. For example, a legacy Angular app can coexist with a new Svelte-based module.

- **Specialized solutions**: Teams can select lightweight frameworks (e.g., Svelte for performance-critical UIs) or robust ones (e.g., Angular for enterprise apps) based on needs.
- **Future-proofing**: Reduces dependency on a single framework, making it easier to adopt emerging technologies like Lit or Qwik.
- **Innovation**: Encourages teams to experiment with new tools, fostering creativity. For example, a team might use Web Components with Stencil for a lightweight MFE.

The following are the disadvantages of a framework-agnostic approach:

- **Performance overhead**: Loading multiple frameworks (e.g., React and Angular) increases bundle sizes and can cause runtime conflicts. For example, both frameworks may try to manipulate the **Document Object Model** (**DOM**) simultaneously.
- **Integration complexity**: Combining MFEs requires sophisticated tools like Module Federation or Single-SPA, which add setup and maintenance overhead.
- **Inconsistent UI/UX**: Different frameworks may lead to visual or behavioral discrepancies unless a strict design system is enforced.
- **Tooling fragmentation**: Teams may use different build tools (e.g., Vite, Webpack) and testing frameworks, complicating CI/CD pipelines.
- **Higher learning curve**: Developers need to understand multiple frameworks or the integration layer to debug or maintain the system.

Custom MFE framework

A custom or no-framework approach to building MFEs typically involves using plain JavaScript, HTML, and CSS without relying on any mainstream frontend frameworks like React, Vue, or Angular. This method often leans on Web Components or entirely handcrafted modules to structure and render the UI. While this can offer maximum portability, minimal dependencies, and true framework neutrality, it also reintroduces many complexities that modern frameworks have already solved, such as efficient state updates, declarative rendering, routing, and testing conventions. In theory, it grants complete control, but in practice, it shifts the burden of solving low-level problems back to the development team. As a result, adopting a no-framework or custom-framework path often leads to duplicated effort, inconsistent patterns, and slower development velocity. In today's web ecosystem, where mature frameworks come with rich tooling, large communities, and proven scalability, avoiding them altogether is generally not recommended unless there is a very specific use case, such as embedding MFEs in environments where no framework can be assumed or where a minimal footprint is a hard constraint.

Island Architecture

Island Architecture is a modern rendering strategy that combines the performance advantages of static HTML with the flexibility of interactive JavaScript components. Originating from static site generators and evolving alongside performance-conscious web development trends, this approach is now increasingly relevant for complex applications, including MFEs. In Island Architecture, the majority of a web page is rendered as static HTML, either during server-side rendering or at build time, while individual *islands* represent isolated, interactive components that are hydrated independently on the client. These islands load their JavaScript only when necessary, typically in response to user interaction or visibility within the viewport.

The model solves a critical problem that traditional single-page applications often struggle with: excessive JavaScript on initial load. By deferring JavaScript execution to only those parts of the page that need it, Island Architecture significantly reduces time-to-interactive and improves both performance and SEO. For example, a carousel, product review widget, or live chat box could be shipped as individual interactive islands while the rest of the page remains statically rendered. The result is a fast-loading user experience that still allows for rich interactivity where it matters.

This pattern aligns naturally with the principles of MFE architecture. Each island can be developed and deployed independently by a different team, using its own framework, tooling, and deployment pipeline. This is because islands are self-contained and loosely coupled; they reinforce modularity and isolation, two core tenets of MFEs. Additionally, since each island can be rendered using a different frontend technology, the architecture becomes inherently framework-agnostic. A React-based form, a Vue-powered review widget, and a Svelte-based animation component can all coexist on the same page without conflicts, each loading only the JavaScript they require.

Modern frameworks are increasingly embracing Island Architecture as a first-class concept. Astro, for instance, compiles most components to static HTML by default and supports partial hydration for interactivity using frameworks like React, Vue, Svelte, and others. Fresh, built on Deno, promotes server-side routing and renders islands using lightweight JavaScript that hydrates only when needed. Qwik takes this concept further by introducing resumability, a model where the application is streamed to the browser in a serialized form and resumes only specific components when necessary. Enhance is another framework that promotes web standards and builds on the island concept by keeping JavaScript minimal and only where essential. These frameworks offer purpose-built tooling for developers to implement Island Architecture without resorting to custom hydration logic or complex build pipelines.

Figure 4.4 illustrates how Island Architecture is applied within an MFE application using a framework-agnostic approach. The foundation of the page is a statically rendered HTML shell generated on the server, containing essential non-interactive components such as the header, footer, and product grid. Interactive *islands* are layered into this shell as isolated units: a React-based product search that hydrates when the user clicks into it, a Vue.js-powered review widget that initializes on scroll, and a vanilla JavaScript cart badge that activates on hover.

Each island loads its own JavaScript runtime and logic independently, only when needed, which significantly reduces the initial JavaScript payload and enhances performance. This architecture supports modular team ownership, cross-framework development, and a lazy-loading strategy tailored to user behavior, all key principles in scalable MFE systems.

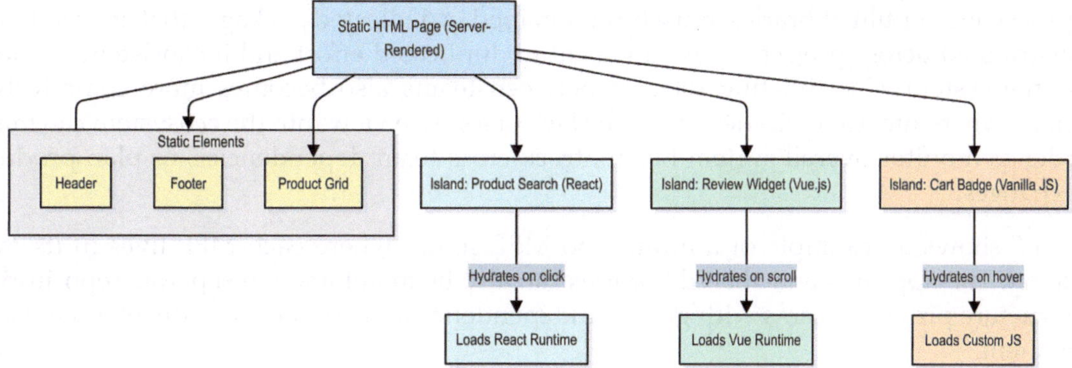

Figure 4.4*: Island Architecture in a framework-agnostic MFE application*

Mono-repo vs. multi-repo

The way we organize code at scale has seen a significant evolution. In the past, version control systems like **Concurrent Version System** (**CVS**) and **SubVersion** (**SVN**) enforced centralized versioning workflows that made branching and collaboration challenging. The rise of Git transformed that landscape by enabling distributed versioning, making it the de facto standard for repository management over the last decade.

When designing an MFE architecture where modularity, independence, and team autonomy are core values, the repository strategy becomes a foundational decision. Each MFE is ideally an independent unit, with its own lifecycle, development team, and technology choices. This independence naturally leads to the question: Should each MFE live in its own repository (multi-repo), or should all MFEs coexist in a single repository (mono-repo)?

This section explores both approaches, weighing their advantages, disadvantages, and the tradeoffs you need to consider when choosing the right model for your team and architecture.

Multi-repo approach

In a multi-repo setup, each MFE lives in its own separate repository. This structure supports the core ideas behind MFE architecture, such as team independence, code isolation, and the ability to deploy features without coordination across teams. Each team manages its own codebase, selects its preferred technology stack, and owns its release lifecycle. This creates a clear boundary of responsibility and enables parallel development without conflict. It also allows teams to control repository permissions more precisely, improving security. An additional benefit is that problems in one part of the system, such as a broken build or runtime error, do not automatically affect other MFEs.

That said, the independence of multi-repos introduces certain challenges. Shared code, such as design systems or utility libraries, must be maintained in dedicated packages that are versioned and distributed across projects. This can result in duplicated effort and inconsistent versions across the system. Coordinating releases between teams also becomes more complicated, especially when integration issues arise. The lack of a single view into the ecosystem can make it harder to monitor overall system health, track cross-team dependencies, or plan product-wide changes.

Figure 4.5 shows an example of a multi-repo MFE setup, where each MFE lives in its own repository. The app shell and shared libraries can also be maintained in separate repositories. This structure provides teams with greater independence and autonomy in development and deployment.

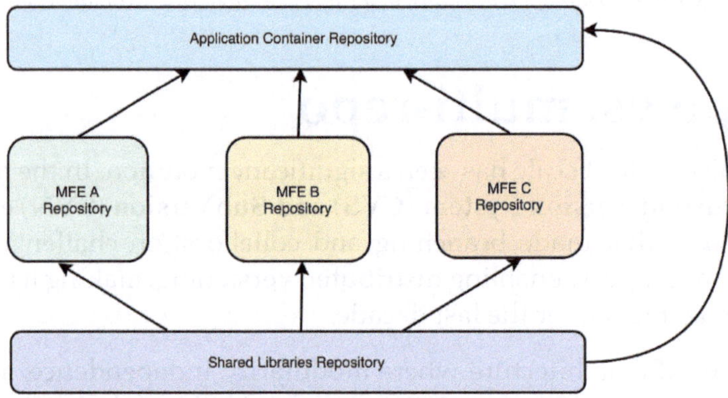

***Figure 4.5**: An example multi-repo setup with each MFE codebase existing separately*

A multi-repo structure is a good choice when teams need full autonomy and are comfortable owning their own delivery pipelines. It suits organizations with strong DevOps practices and clear ownership boundaries. It also works well when micro-frontends are expected to evolve at different speeds or use different frameworks. In these cases, the flexibility of multi-repo outweighs the complexity of integration.

Mono-repo approach

In a mono-repo setup, all MFEs are developed and maintained within a single repository. This structure promotes shared visibility, streamlined tooling, and consistent development practices across teams. Teams benefit from a unified dependency graph, shared configuration files, and centralized linting, testing, and build pipelines. Changes that affect multiple MFEs, such as design system updates or shared utility improvements, can be made in a coordinated way and tested together before deployment. This reduces integration friction and allows for faster iteration across the product.

One of the main benefits of a mono-repo is visibility. Developers can easily trace how different parts of the application interact, which helps improve code quality and onboarding. Shared tooling also means less time spent on DevOps overhead or resolving version mismatches. Mono-repo systems often integrate with tools like Nx, Turborepo, or Bazel to manage builds and enforce boundaries between micro-frontends.

However, a mono-repo also introduces tradeoffs. As the number of MFEs and teams grows, the repository can become harder to manage. Build times may increase unless carefully optimized with caching and affected-only builds. Merge conflicts and branching strategies require clear discipline, especially when multiple teams work on overlapping areas. Repository access must also be carefully controlled to avoid unintended changes across domains.

Figure 4.6 illustrates one way to structure a mono-repo. While there are certainly other valid approaches, a recommended pattern is to separate the codebase into a container and a set of modules. The container hosts the main applications, while the modules contain shared, reusable functionality that can be plugged into any application as needed. This structure provides a scalable foundation and allows teams to grow and extend the system more effectively over time.

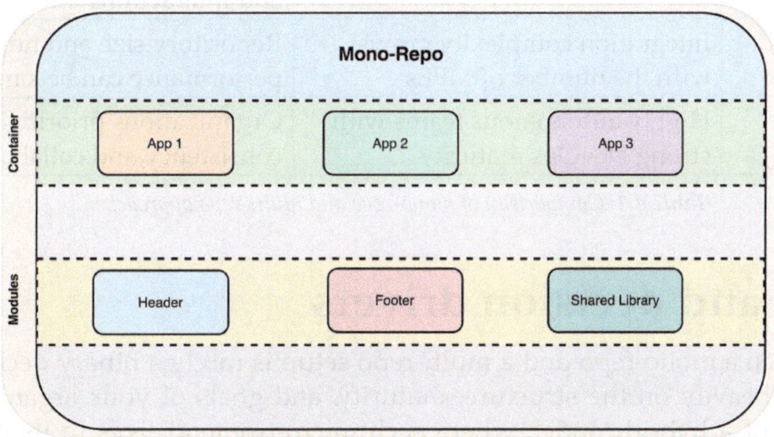

***Figure 4.6:** Mono-repo setup that has all MFEs in a single repository*

Mono-repos work well in environments where cross-team collaboration is frequent and where consistency is a higher priority than total independence. They are particularly useful for organizations that want to encourage shared ownership, enforce design system consistency, and avoid overhead from managing versioned shared packages.

The following table lists the comparison of multi-repo and mono-repo:

Aspect	Multi-repo	Mono-repo
Team autonomy	High, each team fully owns its repository, tooling, and release cycle	Moderate, teams share a repository and must follow common conventions
Code isolation	Strong isolation by default	Logical isolation enforced through tooling and conventions
Technology freedom	Easier to adopt different frameworks and stacks per MFE	Possible, but requires discipline and tooling support
Shared code management	Shared libraries must be versioned and distributed across repos	Shared code is centralized and easier to evolve
Release coordination	Independent releases, but harder cross-team coordination	Easier coordinated changes across MFEs
Build and CI/CD complexity	Simpler per repo, but duplicated pipelines	Centralized pipelines require optimization as the repo grows
Visibility and discoverability	Limited visibility across MFEs	High visibility into dependencies and interactions
Scalability challenges	Integration complexity grows with the number of MFEs	Repository size and build performance can become bottlenecks
Best suited for	Highly autonomous teams with strong DevOps maturity	Organizations prioritizing consistency and collaboration

***Table 4.1**: Comparison of mono-repo and multi-repo approaches*

Tradeoffs and decision drivers

Choosing between a mono-repo and a multi-repo setup is rarely a binary decision. The right choice depends heavily on the structure, maturity, and goals of your organization. In fact, some teams adopt a hybrid model, where each micro-frontend lives in its own repository while shared libraries, design systems, and integration layers are centralized in a mono-repo. This offers a balance between team independence and consistency across the system.

Organizational structure plays a major role in shaping your repository strategy. According to *Conway's Law*, the structure of your codebase will mirror the way your teams communicate. Independent teams with minimal cross-collaboration often benefit from multi-repo setups, where each group can operate in isolation with full control over their own code and workflows.

The release process is another key factor. If MFEs need to be released independently and frequently, a multi-repo approach may offer the flexibility required to deploy without coordination. On the other hand, if your organization follows synchronized release cycles or maintains tight coupling across features, a mono-repo can simplify versioning, testing, and deployment by treating the system as a single unit.

Tooling maturity also affects the decision. Mono-repos demand a more disciplined setup with advanced tooling for build orchestration, caching, and affected-only testing. Without this infrastructure in place, managing a growing mono-repo can become a bottleneck. In contrast, a multi-repo may allow teams to move faster early on, especially when centralized governance and shared tooling are not yet established.

Finally, consider onboarding and developer experience. A mono-repo typically offers a single entry point for local development, making it easier for new developers to explore the system and contribute. In contrast, a multi-repo setup can increase the initial overhead for onboarding but tends to scale better in globally distributed teams with well-defined ownership boundaries.

Real-world architecture models

Understanding how successful organizations structure their micro-frontend repositories provides valuable insight. The following are real-world patterns adopted by engineering teams, each shaped by their scale, product needs, and DevOps maturity:

- **Case study 1**: Spotify, multi-repo model for full autonomy:

  Spotify follows a multi-repo approach in its micro-frontend architecture. Each core feature, such as search, playlists, or the player, is developed and maintained independently by separate teams. These features are integrated at runtime using iframes and coordinated through a shared event system, allowing each team to work without depending on others.

  This approach gives teams full control over their technology choices, deployment schedules, and release cycles. It also limits the impact of failures or bugs to a specific area of the application. While managing shared components and ensuring consistent communication requires coordination, the overall architecture supports scalability and fast-paced development across large organizations.

- **Case study 2**: Google, mono-repo at massive scale:

  Google operates one of the largest mono-repos in the world, containing billions of lines of code across frontend, backend, and infrastructure layers. In this unified codebase, micro-frontend-like modules coexist with other services, following strict organizational and architectural guidelines.

  To make this scale manageable, Google relies on custom tooling such as Bazel, which supports fast, incremental builds and enforces clear module boundaries. Internal APIs and shared libraries are carefully governed through code ownership and mandatory review workflows. These practices ensure consistency, safety, and high development velocity.

This mono-repo model allows for extensive code reuse and organization-wide improvements through atomic changes. Teams can apply updates across multiple modules with confidence, benefiting from a well-integrated ecosystem. While the upfront investment in tooling and governance is significant, it pays off by enabling seamless collaboration at an extraordinary scale.

- **Case study 3**: Shopify, hybrid mono-repo:

  Shopify began with a monolithic architecture and gradually evolved into a modular system that blends traditional server-rendered Rails views with React components and micro-frontends. This transition led to the adoption of a hybrid mono-repo model, where core frontend modules and shared libraries are maintained within a unified repository.

  The majority of MFEs live inside the mono-repo to support shared tooling, consistent development practices, and smooth collaboration across teams. However, Shopify also allows certain teams, especially those experimenting with new features or requiring rapid iteration, to work in separate repositories. This setup preserves the autonomy needed for innovation without losing the cohesion of centralized development.

  Shopify uses tools like Yarn Workspaces and strict linting rules to enforce boundaries within the mono-repo. These practices help teams maintain code ownership and prevent unintended coupling between modules. The hybrid model balances strong governance with the flexibility to support diverse workflows and evolving team structures.

Project setup and testing strategies

Setting up an MFE architecture is both an art and a science. Unlike traditional monolithic frontend applications, where structure and tooling often follow a well-defined path, MFEs offer a broad landscape of options influenced by business goals, team autonomy, and technical maturity. There is no singularly correct way to structure an MFE-based system. The approach taken often reflects the scale of the application, the strength and specialization of the team, the complexity of features, and how independently teams need to work. It is because of this that project setup and testing strategies tend to be highly subjective and evolve alongside the application itself.

Framework vs. framework-agnostic setup

One of the first decisions to make when setting up an MFE project is the choice of framework or the conscious decision to remain framework-agnostic. Using an opinionated framework such as Angular or Next.js can provide a faster, more structured entry point. These frameworks come with a set of best practices, conventions, and pre-configured tooling that simplifies routing, server-side rendering, and testing. Angular, for instance, offers built-in dependency injection, module encapsulation, and standardized testing through tools like Karma or Jest. Similarly, Next.js supports server-side rendering out of the box, file-based routing, and a comprehensive plugin ecosystem. These features can be advantageous when working within a tight timeline or onboarding less experienced developers.

In contrast, using more flexible libraries like React or Vue opens up a different set of trade-offs. While they allow greater freedom in defining the architecture, they also demand more discipline and architectural planning from developers. These libraries do not enforce a specific project structure, so teams must decide on folder hierarchy, module division, state management techniques, and communication protocols between MFEs. While this may appear to be a burden at first, it actually allows teams to tailor the project to fit their specific needs, especially in scenarios where flexibility and customization are more valuable than convention.

An even more agnostic approach involves the use of Web Components or Module Federation. These techniques prioritize interoperability and allow MFEs to be built with different frameworks or no framework at all. This approach grants architects and developers the highest degree of freedom in defining structure, runtime behavior, and orchestration strategies. With Module Federation in particular, it becomes possible to dynamically load remote modules at runtime, creating an environment where each MFE can be developed, deployed, and updated independently. However, this level of control comes with additional responsibilities. Developers must handle shared dependencies, global styling conflicts, routing coordination, and versioning carefully to avoid regressions and unpredictable behavior.

The subjectivity in setting up an MFE system is not a disadvantage; rather, it is a reflection of the architecture's adaptability. Whether the team leans on a highly opinionated framework for consistency or chooses a framework-agnostic path for control and modularity, the key is to design the setup in a way that aligns with organizational goals. These choices influence everything downstream, including developer experience, CI/CD pipelines, deployment independence, and, importantly, testing strategy.

Testing in a modular world

Testing in MFEs is a natural extension of the modularity that defines the architecture itself. Since each MFE is encapsulated and often managed by a separate team, it becomes crucial to ensure each module functions correctly in isolation before it integrates into the broader application. This decoupled nature promotes more maintainable and scalable testing strategies, especially when coupled with component-based development.

Component-based testing practices

Component-based architecture simplifies testing by reducing interdependencies and isolating behavior within well-defined boundaries. In such an environment, unit tests focus on individual functions or small components, ensuring that the logic behaves as expected. Integration tests validate interactions between components or between the component and mocked services. **End-to-end** (E2E) tests evaluate user flows across multiple MFEs, replicating real-world usage scenarios.

Testing models

The testing pyramid remains a foundational model in software testing. It advocates for a large number of fast and reliable unit tests at the base, a moderate number of integration tests in the middle, and a small number of E2E tests at the top. This structure ensures that bugs are caught early and cheaply, with minimal reliance on slow, brittle E2E tests. However, in the context of MFEs, the boundaries between these layers often blur. The triangle model shifts more emphasis to integration tests, which can be more relevant when multiple MFEs must interact in production. This model acknowledges that while unit tests are necessary, the real complexity in MFE systems lies in inter-module communication, shared state, and runtime composition. Refer to *Figure 4.7* for an illustration of typical testing strategies as defined in the pyramid model:

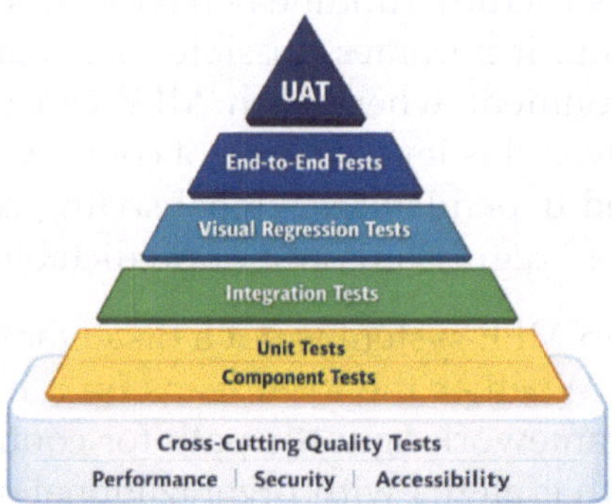

Figure 4.7*: Traditional pyramid testing*

The following are the types of testing:

- **Unit testing**: Unit testing focuses on verifying the smallest pieces of an MFE, such as individual components or utility functions. These tests are fast and isolated, designed to catch bugs early by validating the internal logic and UI rendering of each component without depending on other parts of the system. Common tools include Jest and React Testing Library. Unit tests are typically run frequently during development and form the foundation of a reliable codebase.

- **Component testing**: Component testing focuses on validating individual UI components in isolation, but from a user's perspective rather than purely internal logic. These tests verify that a component renders correctly, responds to user interactions, handles props and local state changes, and integrates properly with mocked dependencies such as APIs or context providers. Unlike low-level unit tests, component tests treat the component as a black box and assert behavior through the rendered output, making them more resilient to implementation changes. In MFE architectures, component testing is especially valuable because components often serve as shared or contract-based building blocks across teams. Tools like React Testing Library and Storybook test runners are commonly used to implement component tests efficiently.

- **Functional or integration testing**: Integration testing checks how multiple components or modules within the same MFE work together. Unlike unit tests, which isolate single pieces, integration tests simulate real interactions among related parts of an MFE, such as a form component interacting with validation logic or data fetching. These tests help ensure internal cohesion and usually run alongside or after unit tests using similar frameworks, but with less mocking of internal dependencies.

- **E2E testing**: E2E testing simulates full user journeys that span multiple MFEs working together in a production-like environment. These tests verify that integrated MFEs deliver a seamless and functional experience, covering scenarios like user authentication, navigation, and critical workflows. Popular E2E frameworks include Cypress and Playwright. This is because E2E tests can be slow and fragile; it is best to focus them on key user paths and run them in staging environments that closely resemble production.

- **Visual regression testing**: Visual regression testing automatically detects unintended UI changes by comparing screenshots taken from different builds of an application. This is particularly valuable in a micro-frontend architecture where multiple teams contribute separate UI modules, helping maintain consistent styling and prevent layout breakages. Tools such as Percy and Applitools are commonly used to automate visual snapshot comparisons within CI pipelines.

- **Performance testing**: Performance testing measures the load time, responsiveness, and resource usage of each MFE individually and as part of the composed application. Since MFEs load independently, it is important to ensure no single module negatively impacts the overall user experience. Tools like Lighthouse and WebPageTest provide metrics to identify bottlenecks, large assets, or inefficient code that could degrade performance, allowing teams to optimize their bundles and runtime behavior.

- **Security testing**: Security testing addresses the increased attack surface introduced by independently developed MFEs running in a shared runtime environment. It focuses on preventing common vulnerabilities such as **cross-site scripting** (**XSS**), **cross-site request forgery** (**CSRF**), and injection attacks. This testing is accomplished using static code analysis, dynamic vulnerability scanners like OWASP ZAP, and enforcing runtime protections like **Content Security Policy** (**CSP**) headers and sandboxing. Security testing is vital to ensure that multiple teams or vendors do not introduce risks into the overall application.

- **Accessibility testing:** Accessibility testing ensures that each MFE is usable by people with diverse abilities and complies with accessibility standards such as WCAG. This is because MFEs are developed independently and later composed into a single application, it is important to verify that accessibility is preserved both within individual modules and across the integrated user interface. This includes validating semantic HTML structure, keyboard navigation, focus management, color contrast, and screen reader compatibility. Automated tools such as axe, Lighthouse, and Pa11y help detect common accessibility issues, while manual testing with assistive technologies ensures real-world usability. Accessibility testing is essential to guarantee that the composed application remains inclusive and usable for all users, regardless of how many MFEs contribute to the final interface.

Testing in practice

In a real-world MFE e-commerce application, teams begin with unit and component tests to validate individual UI components, business logic, and rendering behavior within each MFE. Integration tests then verify how related components work together within the same MFE, such as form validation combined with data fetching or local state management. A small set of end-to-end tests exercises critical user journeys, including browsing products, adding items to the cart, and completing checkout across multiple MFEs in a production-like environment. Visual regression tests help maintain UI consistency as independently deployed MFEs evolve, while performance tests measure load times and resource usage at both the individual MFE and composed application levels. Finally, security testing is applied through static analysis, vulnerability scanning, and runtime protections to reduce risks introduced by independently developed modules sharing a common runtime.

Principles of effective MFE testing

Regardless of the model followed, a few principles remain consistent across effective MFE testing strategies; isolation is key. Each MFE should be tested as an independent unit with mocked external dependencies. This includes mocking shared APIs, events, and even global styles when needed. Contract testing can also play a vital role, particularly in validating communication between host and remote modules. Tools like Pact or custom schema validation mechanisms can help ensure that changes in one MFE do not break others inadvertently.

Another important aspect is the integration of testing into the CI/CD pipeline. Automated tests should be executed with every build to maintain confidence in the system's integrity. Smoke tests and visual regression tools can be particularly helpful in an MFE environment where visual consistency matters and UI boundaries may span multiple teams. When feasible, running E2E tests on staging environments that mirror the production composition can uncover issues in orchestration, routing, and shared resource management that unit tests might miss.

Continuous evolution of structure and strategy

Rather than thinking of testing and setup as discrete, one-time steps, they should be viewed as evolving practices. As the MFE ecosystem grows and becomes more complex, the project structure and testing approach should be revisited and refined. Teams may choose to gradually migrate from a mono-repo to a poly-repo, or vice versa, depending on their scaling needs. They might also adopt new orchestration tools or introduce advanced testing methodologies like mutation testing or synthetic monitoring.

In summary, project setup and testing in MFE architectures are deeply intertwined and context-sensitive. There is no universal best practice, only strategies that align better with specific team structures, technical goals, and business priorities. Opinionated frameworks offer a smoother start and encourage uniformity, while flexible or agnostic setups offer unparalleled control and adaptability. Testing, similarly, must evolve from simple verification to confidence-building, embracing models that reflect real-world complexity. Ultimately, the success of an MFE project depends not on rigid adherence to patterns, but on how thoughtfully those patterns are chosen, adapted, and evolved over time.

Tailoring CI/CD for MFE architectures

The modular nature of MFE introduces unique challenges for **continuous integration and continuous deployment** (**CI/CD**) pipelines, such as coordinating multiple repositories, managing diverse tech stacks, and ensuring seamless integration. Tailoring CI/CD pipelines for MFEs requires a strategic approach to handle these complexities while maintaining speed, reliability, and scalability. This section explores the key considerations, strategies, and examples for configuring CI/CD pipelines to meet the demands of MFE architectures.

Figure 4.8 depicts a typical pipeline in which the code can be built and deployed all the way to the production environment:

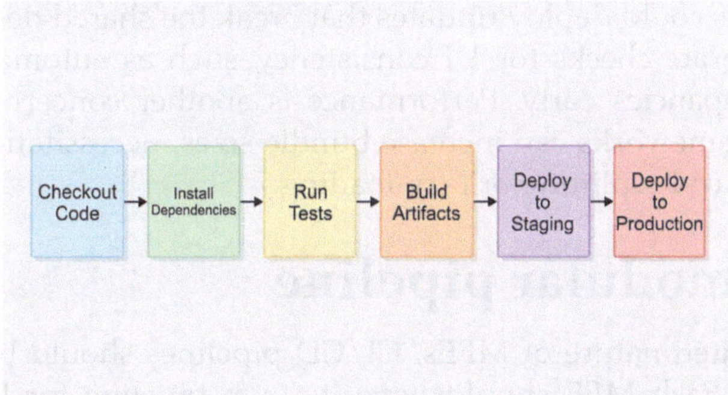

Figure 4.8: *A simple pipeline from code checkout to production deploy*

As shown in the diagram above, deploying code to production is a structured, multi-step process that must be executed in sequence. It begins with a code checkout step, where the latest code is fetched or imported onto the deployment server. This is followed by the install and build process, which sets up the application environment. Next, tests are run, including unit tests, visual regression tests, and optionally functional tests, to verify the reliability of the latest changes. Once validated, the pipeline proceeds to build deployable artifacts, which are first released to a staging or QA environment. Here, additional testing, such as E2E or **user acceptance testing** (**UAT**), is performed. If all tests pass, the exact same artifacts are promoted to production, ensuring consistency. In case of issues, rollbacks may occur either at the staging stage or after the production release.

Pipeline challenges

MFEs differ from monolithic frontends in their distributed nature, where each MFE is a standalone module, often owned by a separate team. This independence allows teams to choose their preferred frameworks, such as React for a product listing module or Vue.js for a user profile widget, but it complicates CI/CD processes. Each MFE may have its own repository, build tools, and deployment schedule, leading to potential integration issues. For example, a checkout MFE built with Angular might need to integrate with a React-based cart module, requiring careful coordination to avoid version mismatches or runtime errors. Additionally, MFEs often rely on orchestration tools like Module Federation, a Webpack feature that enables dynamic sharing of dependencies at runtime, which adds complexity to dependency management in CI/CD pipelines. Ensuring consistent testing, artifact management, and deployment across these diverse modules is a core challenge that requires tailored pipeline configurations.

Another challenge is maintaining a cohesive user experience across MFE. While a monolithic frontend can rely on a single build pipeline to enforce consistent styling and behavior, MFEs risk visual or functional discrepancies if teams do not adhere to shared standards. For instance, a media streaming platform might have a React-based video player MFE and a Vue.js-based recommendation engine, each using different CSS frameworks. Without proper CI/CD governance, these MFEs could deploy updates that break the shared design system. Pipelines must therefore incorporate checks for UI consistency, such as automated visual regression testing, to catch discrepancies early. Performance is another concern, as loading multiple MFEs with different frameworks can increase bundle sizes, necessitating optimization steps in the pipeline, such as code splitting or lazy-loading.

Designing a modular pipeline

To address the distributed nature of MFEs, CI/CD pipelines should be modular, mirroring the architecture itself. Each MFE should have its own pipeline for building, testing, and deploying, allowing teams to work independently. For example, consider an e-commerce application with three MFEs, a product listing (React), a cart (Vue.js), and a checkout (Angular). Each MFE resides in its own repository with a dedicated pipeline. The React-based product listing pipeline might use Webpack to bundle the code, Jest for unit testing, and AWS S3 for deployment. Similarly, the Vue.js cart pipeline could leverage Vite for faster builds and deploy to a different S3 bucket. This modularity ensures that a change in one MFE, such as updating the cart's UI, does not disrupt the others, preserving team autonomy.

However, complete isolation can lead to integration issues when MFEs are combined in the browser. To mitigate this, a central shell pipeline can orchestrate the integration of MFEs. The shell, often a lightweight application using a tool like Single-SPA, a framework-agnostic orchestrator for MFEs, aggregates those into a cohesive application. The shell pipeline runs integration tests to verify that all MFEs work together correctly. For instance, in the e-commerce example, the shell pipeline might use Cypress to test E2E interactions, such as adding a product to the cart and proceeding to checkout. This dual approach of individual pipelines for MFEs and a central pipeline for integration balances autonomy with coordination, ensuring both independence and reliability.

Example of a modular CI/CD stage for an MFE

The following pseudo-code illustrates how a CI pipeline can treat each micro frontend as an independent unit while still following a shared structure. Each MFE runs its own build and test steps, allowing teams to deploy independently without affecting others.

```
mfe-build:
  name: Build and Test MFE
  steps:
    - checkout code
    - install dependencies
    - run unit and component tests
    - build mfe artifact
    - publish artifact to registry
```

Standardizing builds across diverse tech stacks

Micro-frontends often use different frameworks and build tools, complicating the standardization of CI/CD processes. A team building a React MFE might use Create React App or Vite, while an Angular MFE relies on Angular CLI. To streamline this, organizations can adopt a standardized build configuration that accommodates diverse tech stacks while enforcing consistency. For example, a company could mandate Webpack as the bundler for all micro-frontends to leverage Module Federation for dependency sharing. In this setup, a React MFEs pipeline might include a Webpack configuration that exposes a *<ProductCard>* component, while a Vue.js MFEs pipeline exposes a *<ReviewWidget>* component. Both pipelines use a shared Webpack plugin to ensure compatible module formats, reducing runtime conflicts. *Figure 4.9* depicts how the shared webpack config can handle bundling different library assets using a common interface:

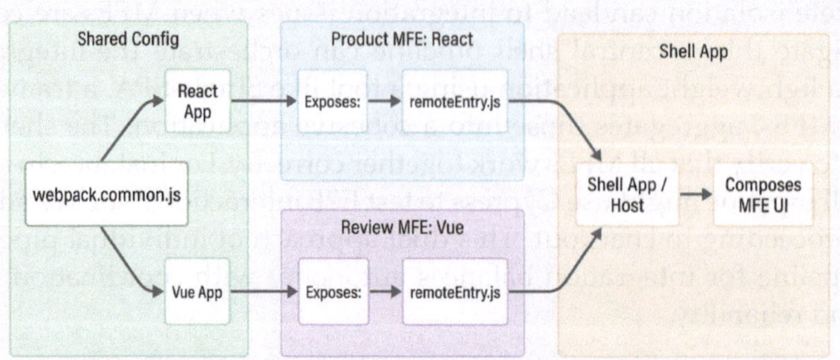

***Figure 4.9:** A shared webpack config used to create independent artifacts*

Standardization also extends to dependency management. MFEs often share dependencies, such as a common UI library like Material-UI for React or Vuetify for Vue.js. Without coordination, teams might use incompatible versions, causing errors when MFEs are loaded together. To prevent this, pipelines can integrate tools like Dependabot to monitor and update dependencies across repositories. For instance, a CI pipeline for a React-based MFE could include a step to check that Material-UI's version matches the one used by other MFEs, ensuring compatibility. Additionally, using a mono-repo tool like Nx or Turborepo can centralize dependency management while allowing separate pipelines for each MFE, simplifying version alignment.

Automating testing for MFE pipelines

Testing is critical in MFE architectures to ensure that independent MFE functions correctly both individually and when integrated. Each MFE's pipeline should include unit tests, integration tests, and visual regression tests tailored to its framework. For example, a Vue.js-based recommendation MFE might use Vitest for unit testing its components, ensuring that a *<RecommendationCard>* renders correctly. Meanwhile, the Angular-based checkout MFE could use Jasmine to test its form validations. These tests run in the MFE's individual pipeline, catching issues early before deployment.

Integration testing is equally important, as MFEs must interact seamlessly in the browser. The shell pipeline can include end-to-end tests using tools like Cypress or Playwright to simulate user interactions across MFEs. For instance, in the e-commerce application, a Cypress test might verify that selecting a product in the React-based listing MFE updates the Vue.js-based cart correctly. Visual regression testing, using tools like BackstopJS, can ensure UI consistency by comparing screenshots of the integrated application against a baseline. For example, if the cart MFE updates its button styling, the pipeline can flag any unintended changes to the shared design system, preventing visual discrepancies.

Performance testing is another key aspect, as MFEs can suffer from increased bundle sizes when multiple frameworks are loaded. Tools like Lighthouse can be integrated into the pipeline to measure performance metrics, such as Time to Interactive, for each MFE. For example, a pipeline might fail a build if a React MFE bundle exceeds a size threshold, prompting the team to optimize with code splitting or lazy-loading. By automating these tests, pipelines ensure that MFEs meet quality and performance standards before deployment.

Deployment strategies for MFEs

In distributed MFE architectures, decoupling deployments is essential to preserve team independence and minimize integration risks. A common strategy is runtime integration, where each MFE is deployed independently and loaded dynamically by the shell application. This avoids build-time dependencies and enables teams to release updates without waiting on others. Organizations often implement multi-environment setups, deploying MFEs to separate paths for development, staging, and production. The shell app adjusts its configuration accordingly, ensuring that each environment loads the correct MFE version. This separation makes it easier to test new features in isolation before exposing them to real users.

To reduce rollout risks further, teams may use feature flags and canary releases. New MFE versions can be deployed behind flags, allowing gradual exposure while monitoring key metrics such as performance and error rates. If issues arise, traffic can be rolled back to a previous version using techniques like blue-green deployments. To manage compatibility, a manifest file maintained by the shell can define which version of each MFE to load. This centralized reference ensures consistency across the system. Combined with immutable deployment URLs that include version identifiers, this approach supports reliable rollbacks, controlled caching, and safer continuous delivery. To ensure reliability, pipelines often use semantic versioning, integration testing, and rollback mechanisms such as blue-green deployments or canary releases. We will explore these strategies in *Chapter 7, Deployment Strategies*.

Governance and monitoring in MFE pipelines

Governance in MFE pipelines ensures that independently developed modules follow shared standards for code quality, design, and accessibility. This is often achieved through automated checks built into each pipeline, such as linters to enforce consistent coding styles or tests to validate adherence to a shared design system. Tools like Storybook can be integrated to verify that visual components render correctly and conform to UI guidelines. A common Tailwind CSS configuration, for example, can be validated in each MFE pipeline to prevent styling conflicts. These governance mechanisms help teams move fast without compromising consistency across the application.

Monitoring complements governance by providing visibility into the runtime behavior of each MFE. Pipelines can include steps to configure observability tools like Datadog, New Relic, or Dynatrace, enabling teams to track performance metrics, error rates, and user behavior. If an issue is detected after deployment, such as high latency in the product listing MFE, the monitoring system can trigger alerts or even roll back to a previous version automatically. By embedding both governance and monitoring into CI/CD pipelines, teams ensure that MFEs not only integrate cleanly during development but also remain reliable and performant in production. We will examine governance and monitoring practices in detail in *Chapter 8, Observability and Monitoring*.

Key takeaways from the above section

Tailoring CI/CD pipelines for MFEs requires addressing the unique challenges of modularity, diverse tech stacks, and integration. By designing modular pipelines for each MFE, standardizing builds with tools like Webpack and Module Federation, and automating comprehensive testing, teams can ensure reliable development and deployment. Deployment strategies like **content delivery network (CDN)** based releases, versioning, and canary deployments enable independent yet coordinated releases, while governance and monitoring maintain consistency and performance. The e-commerce example illustrates how these principles translate into practice, leveraging tools like GitHub Actions, Single-SPA, and Datadog to deliver a scalable MFE architecture. By carefully configuring CI/CD pipelines, organizations can harness the full potential of MFEs, balancing autonomy with cohesion in their frontend ecosystems.

Conclusion

In conclusion, this chapter has provided an overview of the foundational decisions that shape successful MFE architectures, from choosing between framework-specific and framework-agnostic approaches to selecting repository structures that align with team dynamics and project complexity. By examining project setup, testing strategies, and CI and CD practices, readers are equipped with practical guidance for building scalable and maintainable MFE applications. Real-world case studies of mono repo and multi repo implementations further illustrate how these decisions influence autonomy, coordination, and operational tradeoffs in practice.

Together, these discussions highlight several key takeaways. Effective MFE architectures are driven by intentional design choices rather than defaults. Framework selection has a direct impact on developer productivity and long-term adaptability, while repository strategies influence collaboration patterns and delivery independence. Testing practices should prioritize early feedback through unit, component, and integration tests, reserving end-to-end validation for critical user journeys. CI and CD pipelines must balance modularity with standardization to enable independent deployment without compromising quality or governance. Ultimately, the examples in this chapter reinforce that there is no single optimal MFE approach, only context-driven solutions shaped by organizational goals, team maturity, and product needs.

In the next chapter, we will explore the practical aspects of building MFEs using modular and flexible approaches. It will guide readers through effective modularization techniques, explore Web Components and their current landscape, and discuss rendering methods critical for managing state, performance, SEO, and user experience in distributed applications. The chapter will also cover essential component communication patterns, advanced loading strategies like Edge Side Includes and Module Federation, and backend solutions such as **backend for frontend** (**BFF**) patterns, with a brief look at GraphQL. Additionally, it will address integration with native platforms through iframes and highlight common antipatterns and error-handling best practices to ensure resilient MFE applications.

Chapter 5
Implementation Strategies

Introduction

This chapter provides a comprehensive guide for building **micro-frontends** (**MFEs**) through modular and flexible approaches. It begins with modularization techniques, emphasizing the importance of dividing applications into manageable, independently deployable units. Then, we will explore the types of MFEs with respect to the integration techniques. Also, we will talk about techniques to keep in mind while exploring various composition methods, as they play a key role in managing state in a distributed application, and to determine the right approach considering performance, SEO, and user experience needs.

This chapter will slowly get into various implementation patterns that include Web Components, Module Federation, and Siteless UI. Furthermore, we will focus on **backend for frontend** (**BFF**) patterns to tailor services specifically for the frontends and the benefits of doing so. We will touch a bit on GraphQL and how it can favor BFF as a bonus. Also, the section on native apps covers the approach of Iframes for integrating MFE with native platforms, including both desktop and mobile (iOS, Android) apps. Finally, we would see a few common antipatterns that might impact the application performance, along with efficient error handling strategies to mitigate defects in a graceful manner.

Structure

The chapter covers the following topics:

- Modularization
- Integration modes
- Composition strategies
- Implementation patterns
- Component communication
- Antipatterns
- Error handling
- Case study on TuneStream

Objectives

By the end of this chapter, you will understand practical guidelines on implementing MFEs in any organization. It equips you with the knowledge around modules and various types of approaches that an MFE can take. Also, this chapter will discuss different rendering techniques with practical examples. Furthermore, you will understand various communication strategies and a few advanced techniques such as Module Federation, BFF, and Siteless UI. Towards the end, we will look into antipatterns in designing and implementing MFE and strategies that work with native non-browser environments. We will also look into a few error-handling strategies and best practices as well. In the end, we will have a detailed case study with a real-time example application that involves all the above in a practical sense.

Modularization

Researchers say everything on Earth is made up of atoms and molecules. An atom is the smallest unit, and molecules are made up of atoms. There is always a question of why we need molecules when we have atoms. In general, atoms are reusable without context or knowledge of doing anything, whereas molecules, on the other hand, are a wholesome unit that performs a certain task or operation. In the MFE world, we can consider *atoms as components and molecules as modules*. While components are simple reusable units that are not aware of any business context, modules, which are built or composed of more than one component, are context-aware.

Modules

At its core, a module is a self-contained piece of code that encapsulates functionality, exposes only what is necessary, and hides the rest. Think of it as a building block in which small, independent units can be combined to form larger systems.

Modules help developers to organize code into logical chunks, reuse functionality across projects, and avoid naming conflicts by defining the scope for variables and functions. Also, it improves the maintainability by reducing tight coupling between parts of the system.

In frontend development, modularity was not always the norm. Early JavaScript files often contained everything in a single script, polluting the global namespace and making large applications unwieldy. Over time, the JavaScript ecosystem introduced formal module systems to bring order to this chaos.

Evolution of modules

The history of JavaScript modules reflects the broader story of how the web itself evolved from simple scripts to application-scale complexity. Initially, developers relied on global variables and ad-hoc conventions, often wrapping code in **Immediately Invoked Function Expressions**

(**IIFEs**) to simulate private scopes. While this hack worked to some degree, it was not a true solution. The following is an example of how global scope can affect the logic:

```
<!-- index.html -->
<script>
  // script A
  var counter = 0;
  function increment() {
    counter++;
  }
</script>

<script>
  // script B
  var counter = 100; // overwrites script A's counter
  function increment() {
    counter = counter + 10; // different logic, overwrites increment
  }
  increment();
  console.log(counter); // 110, not 1 as script A might expect
</script>
```

In this example, both script A and script B use the same variable and function names because they live in the same global namespace; one silently overwrites the other. This is a problem that only grows worse as more scripts are added.

The following JavaScript had a formal module system, and developers used IIFEs to create a private scope:

```
<!-- index.html -->
<script>
  // script A wrapped in an IIFE
  (function() {
    var counter = 0;
    function increment() {
      counter++;
      console.log("Script A counter:", counter);
    }
    increment(); // Script A counter: 1
  })();
```

```
</script>
<script>
  // script B wrapped in an IIFE
  (function() {
    var counter = 100;
    function increment() {
      counter = counter + 10;
      console.log("Script B counter:", counter);
    }
    increment(); // Script B counter: 110
  })();
</script>
```

In the above code example, both script A and script B are enclosed in an IIFE function, which creates a private scope to avoid conflicting with each other.

The first breakthrough came with CommonJS, a standard introduced in the Node.js ecosystem. CommonJS allowed developers to use require to import functionality and module.exports to define what a module exposes. This seemingly small change had a great impact; it gave developers a predictable, standardized way to organize server-side code. Let us look at a simple CommonJS example in the following:

```
// math.js
module.exports.add = (a, b) => a + b;
// app.js
const math = require('./math');
console.log(math.add(2, 3)); // 5
```

In the example above, we expose the add function from a file math.js via module.exports object. Which can be imported and used anywhere else by using the require function. CommonJS synchronous loading model worked well in Node.js because files were available on disk, but it was not well-suited for browsers, where asynchronous loading is often necessary.

To address the browser use case, the **Asynchronous Module Definition (AMD)** format emerged. AMD allowed developers to declare dependencies that could be loaded asynchronously, ensuring that web applications could fetch and execute modules without blocking the browser. The following shows a simple AMD code in which the math dependency is loaded asynchronously and ready to execute:

```
define(['math'], function(math) {
  console.log(math.add(2, 3));
});
```

The trade-off was verbosity; the syntax was clunky compared to the simplicity of CommonJS. To bridge the gap between server and browser environments, developers introduced **Universal Module Definition** (**UMD**), a flexible format capable of running in either context. UMD became especially popular among library authors, since it allowed them to publish code that would work regardless of the environment in which it was consumed. At this stage, however, all of these approaches were still external conventions layered on top of JavaScript.

The real turning point came with **ECMAScript 2015** (**ES6**), which introduced **ES Modules** (**ESM**) as a language-level feature. With import and export keywords, JavaScript finally gained a native, standardized module system as described in the following code:

```
// math.js
export function add(a, b) {
  return a + b;
}
// app.js
import { add } from './math.js';
console.log(add(2, 3)); // 5
```

ES Modules solved many long-standing problems; they had a static structure that enabled tree-shaking (removing unused code during bundling), they worked natively in browsers without additional tooling, and they provided a clear syntax that felt more intuitive. Over time, ES Modules have become the default choice for modern JavaScript development, even though CommonJS remains entrenched in Node.js for legacy reasons.

Looking back, we can see a progression from global function and IIFEs, to CommonJS for the server, to AMD for the browser, to UMD for portability, and finally to ESM for universal, native modularization. Each stage responded to specific challenges of its time, but together they chart a story of increasing maturity in the JavaScript ecosystem. The following figure illustrates this evolution of the JavaScript module system over time:

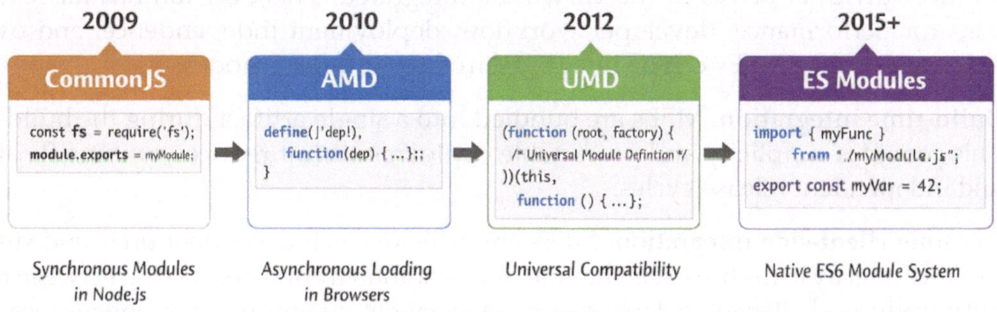

Figure 5.1: Evolution of the JavaScript module system

Module JS

With the arrival of ESM in JavaScript, developers needed a way to distinguish between the old CommonJS format (require, module.exports) and the new import/export syntax. That is where the .mjs file extension comes in.

A file with an extension .mjs explicitly refers to ESM, where a file with a .js extension is ambiguous, which could be either a CommonJS (`.cjs`) or ESM (`.mjs`):

```
// math.mjs
export function add(a, b) {
  return a + b;
}
// app.mjs
import { add } from './math.mjs';
console.log(add(2, 3)); // 5
```

Note the extension `.mjs`, which explicitly tells that it is an ESM. While the .mjs extension is not always mandatory (especially in browser contexts or with bundlers like Webpack, Rollup, or Vite), it serves as a clear signal that a file is using the modern ESM system. In practice, many projects configure their package.json with `"type": "module"`, allowing them to use `.js` for ESM, but when compatibility or clarity is critical, `.mjs` remains a useful option.

Note: In browsers, `.mjs` does not provide any functional advantage over `.js` when using `type='module'`. Its value is mostly in signaling intent, in which it tells both humans and tools that the file is meant to be an ESM.

Integration modes

When organizations adopt MFEs, one of the first architectural choices they face is how and when the individual pieces of the UI will be integrated. This decision has far-reaching implications for performance, developer workflow, deployment independence, and overall user experience. Broadly, MFEs can be integrated in three different modes:

- **Build-time integration**: MFEs are bundled into a single artifact during the build step. This provides simplicity and predictable deployments but reduces runtime flexibility and independent release cycles.
- **Runtime client-side integration**: MFEs are delivered as independent units and stitched together directly in the browser. This maximizes autonomy and decoupling between teams but introduces challenges in dependency management, communication, and performance.
- **Runtime server-side integration**: MFEs are assembled on the server (or edge) before being sent to the client. This enables faster initial load and better caching but requires sophisticated orchestration and infrastructure support.

This section explores each integration mode in detail, from static build-time composition to dynamic runtime approaches, illustrating the trade-offs with examples and code snippets. By the end, you will have a clear understanding of which mode best aligns with your organizational needs and product context.

Build-time integration

In build-time integration, multiple MFEs are packaged together during the build process to produce a single deployable artifact. Each team might develop its own feature or vertical slice of the application, but the final assembly happens before deployment. This approach offers simplicity because the runtime environment does not need to handle dynamic loading or orchestration; everything is already baked into a single bundle. It also allows for consistent dependency management since all MFEs share the same build pipeline and version of libraries.

However, the trade-off is flexibility. If one team needs to make a change, the entire application must be rebuilt and redeployed. This creates tighter coupling between teams and can slow down independent releases. Build-time integration is often a good starting point for organizations experimenting with MFEs, as it minimizes infrastructure complexity while still allowing teams to work in parallel.

Consider a retail application with separate teams responsible for the product list, shopping cart, and user profile. Each team builds its feature as a local package that exposes react components. At build time, a single webpack or vite pipeline bundles these packages into one artifact:

```
// app.js - root application
import ProductList from "product-list";
import Cart from "shopping-cart";
import UserProfile from "user-profile";
function App() {
  return (
    <div>
      <header>Global Retail</header>
      <main>
        <ProductList />
        <Cart />
        <UserProfile />
      </main>
    </div>
  );
}
export default App;
```

Here, the product list, cart, and user profile MFEs are developed independently but consumed as npm packages at build time. Once bundled, they become indistinguishable from a traditional monolithic **Single Page Application** (**SPA**); the entire application must be redeployed if any feature changes. This mode of integration resembles a *modular monolith* and works best when independent deployments are not a top priority, but modular code ownership is. *Figure 5.2* illustrates how the MFEs can be integrated at build time:

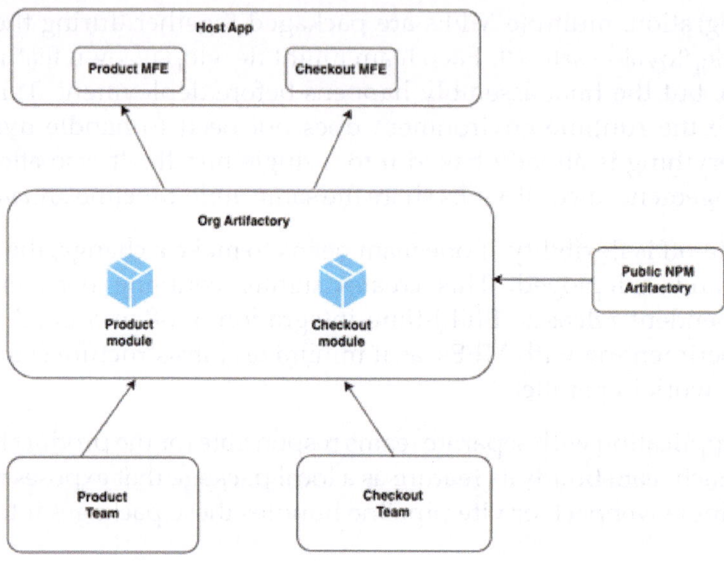

***Figure 5.2**: Build time integration of product and checkout MFE*

Each team develops and publishes its code as a distributed package to an organization-owned artifact registry, which often mirrors the public npm registry for common dependencies. The packages follow **semantic versioning** (**SemVer**) to indicate the impact of changes. It is the host application's responsibility to build and integrate the respective MFE along with its bundle. Note that this is a common strategy followed by many organizations, but exporting as an npm module is not mandatory; other packaging approaches are also possible. The key point is that integration happens at the build step.

Runtime client-side integration

As teams grow and release cycles become more independent, build-time integration starts to show its limits. This is where runtime client-side integration comes into play. The focus here is on *how and when* MFEs are delivered and integrated, instead of being bundled together during build. Each MFE is deployed as its own artifact, and the host application dynamically loads them at runtime.

The simplest version of this approach is to ship MFEs as UMD bundles and embed them via **`<script>`** tags. Imagine the same e-commerce app, but this time the product and checkout MFEs are hosted separately:

```
<!-- host-app/public/index.html -->
<div id="product-list"></div>
<div id="checkout"></div>
<script src="https://cdn.example.com/productMFE.js"></script>
<script src="https://cdn.example.com/checkoutMFE.js"></script>
<script>
  ProductMFE.render(document.getElementById("product-list"));
  CheckoutMFE.render(document.getElementById("checkout"));
</script>
```

This approach is framework-agnostic. One team could write their MFE in React, another in Vue, and as long as each exposes a global render method, they can coexist. However, the burden of managing dependencies, handling version conflicts, and ensuring consistent styling falls on the host.

Figure 5.3 depicts different app teams using separate pipelines to build and deploy their bundle to a static server, such as Amazon S3, and serve the JS bundle via the CDN. Those bundles will be integrated into the host application using the script tag to fetch and execute them at runtime. The advantage clearly is the autonomy of deploying changes without rebuilding or even notifying the host application, and the disadvantage is its lack of versioning the artifact bundles, which is unfortunately not a good candidate to enable browser caching. Also, any unexpected errors from the MFE might bring the entire application down if not handled properly.

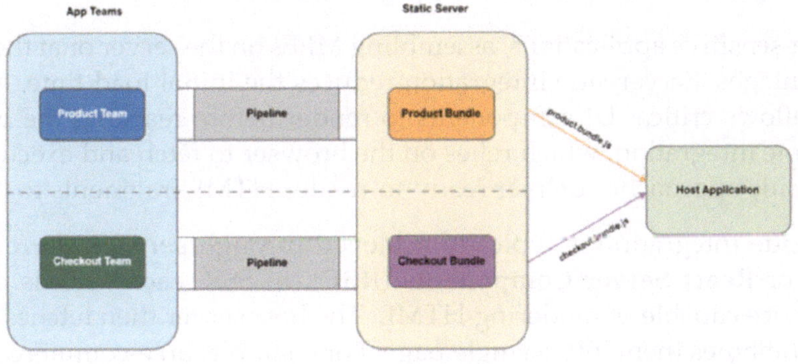

***Figure 5.3**: Runtime client integration example*

A more modern version of runtime integration is *Webpack Module Federation*, introduced in Webpack 5. Instead of hardcoding **`<script>`** tags, the host dynamically loads remote modules at runtime and imports their exposed modules on demand. Conceptually, this works by first loading a remote application's entry file, which registers the remote and makes its modules available to the host. Once registered, these remote modules can be consumed using standard dynamic imports, as shown in the following:

```
// host-app bootstrap
const ProductList = await import("productMFE/ProductList");
const Checkout = await import("checkoutMFE/Checkout");
function App() {
  return (
    <>
      <ProductList.default />
      <Checkout.default />
    </>
  );
}
```

Here, `productMFE` and `checkoutMFE` are independent applications deployed separately, but the host can fetch and execute them as if they were local modules. This allows teams to deploy on their own schedules without forcing host rebuilds. Many large-scale applications, such as Netflix, Spotify, and enterprise **software as a service** (**SaaS**) platforms, use this kind of runtime integration to give teams autonomy while maintaining a unified user interface.

Note: The underlying setup and configuration details for the Module Federation are covered later in the Implementation strategies section.

Runtime server-side integration

For performance-sensitive applications, assembling MFEs on the server or at the edge provides significant advantages. Server-side integration reduces the initial load time, enables caching strategies, and allows critical UI components to render before reaching the browser. Unlike client-side runtime integration, which relies on the browser to fetch and execute independent bundles, server-side approaches deliver ready-to-render HTML fragments to the client.

Modern server-side integration is typically achieved through **server-side rendering** (**SSR**), edge functions, or **React Server Components** (**RSC**). In SSR, each MFE is deployed as an independent service capable of rendering HTML. The host server then fetches these rendered fragments and combines them into a single page. For example, an e-commerce site may serve the Product List and Checkout MFEs from separate services:

```
// server.js
import express from "express";
import fetch from "node-fetch";
```

```
const app = express();
app.get("/", async (req, res) => {
  const productHtml = await fetch("http://localhost:4001/").then(r => r.
text());
  const checkoutHtml = await fetch("http://localhost:4002/").then(r => r.
text());
  res.send(`
    <html>
      <body>
        <h1>My Store</h1>
        <div>${productHtml}</div>
        <div>${checkoutHtml}</div>
      </body>
    </html>
  `);
});
app.listen(3000);
```

Figure 5.4 shows an example of runtime server-side integration where the respective MFEs are fetched and integrated in the server and serve as HTML to the end client:

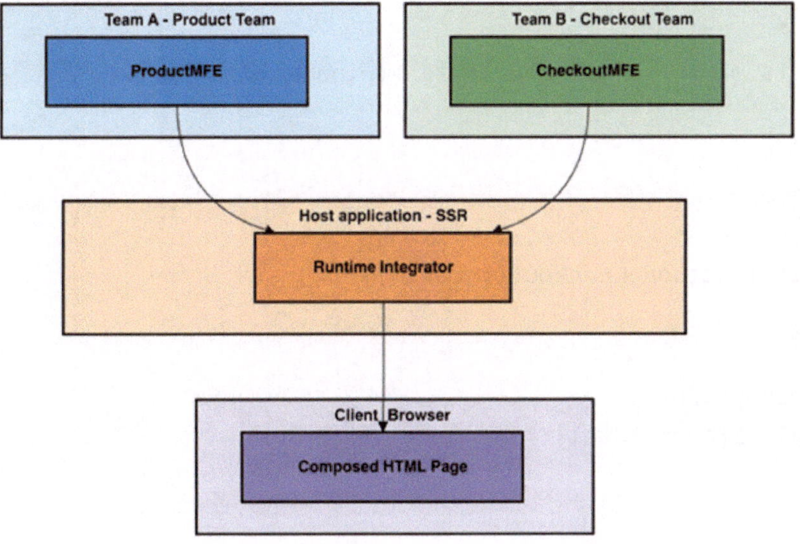

***Figure 5.4**: Runtime server-side integration SSR example*

From the user's perspective, the page loads as if it were a single monolithic app. But under the hood, different services are contributing their slices of HTML.

With **Edge Side Includes** (**ESI**), this assembly can even happen at the CDN level:

```
<html>
  <body>
    <h1>My Store</h1>
    <esi:include src="https://cdn.example.com/productMFE" />
    <esi:include src="https://cdn.example.com/checkoutMFE" />
  </body>
</html>
```

While it is good to know about ESI, it is important to note that it is not being used these days as several other approaches emerge. Edge functions take this concept further by fetching and composing fragments closer to users, reducing latency. Platforms like Vercel Edge Functions or Cloudflare Workers allow MFEs to be assembled dynamically at the network edge without relying on legacy ESI standards.

React Server Components offer a modern twist on server-side integration. With RSC, parts of the UI are rendered on the server and streamed to the client incrementally, minimizing the JavaScript sent to the browser. Each MFE can be implemented as a server component, independently deployed, and imported dynamically by the host:

```
// ProductList.server.js
export default function ProductList({ products }) {
  return (
    <ul>
      {products.map(p => <li key={p.id}>{p.name}</li>)}
    </ul>
  );
}
// Checkout.server.js
export default function Checkout({ cart }) {
  return (
    <div>
      <h2>Checkout</h2>
      <p>Total: ${cart.total}</p>
    </div>
  );
}
// HostApp.server.js
import ProductList from "@server/ProductList.
mfe"; // it can be hosted a npm module or module federation
```

```
import Checkout from "@server/Checkout.
mfe"; // it can be hosted a npm module or module federation
export default async function HostApp() {
  return (
        <main>
          {/* Product MFE rendered on the server */}
          <section>
            <ProductList products={product} />
          </section>
          {/* Checkout MFE rendered on the server */}
          <section>
            <Checkout cart={cart} />
          </section>
        </main>
  );
}
```

This RSC example shows how the host application integrates independently deployed MFEs (**ProductList** and **Checkout**) at runtime using React Server Components:

- The HostApp.server.js fetches the data it needs (products, user cart) from backend APIs.
- It dynamically imports each MFE (**ProductList** from the Product team, **Checkout** from the Checkout team).
- Each MFE is rendered on the server as part of the React tree.
- The server streams the composed UI to the client incrementally, so the browser receives HTML quickly and hydrates only the interactive components.

This approach allows teams to deploy MFEs independently, maintain isolation, and minimize the JavaScript sent to the client.

Choosing the right approach

Selecting the appropriate integration strategy for MFEs is less about technical preference and more about aligning with team structure, release cadence, and user experience requirements. Each of the above-mentioned approaches offers different trade-offs in terms of performance, independence, and operational complexity.

For smaller teams or organizations just starting with MFEs, build-time integration is often the most pragmatic choice. It leverages familiar workflows, like npm packages and monorepos, allowing teams to integrate components during the build process. While this approach reduces runtime complexity and ensures consistent dependencies, it ties deployments together in which the updates to an MFE require a rebuild and redeploy of the host. For applications with coordinated release schedules or limited team size, this trade-off is often acceptable.

As teams grow and release cycles become more frequent, runtime client-side integration offers greater autonomy. Each MFE can be deployed independently, and the host dynamically loads the latest versions at runtime. This flexibility is ideal for organizations with multiple distributed teams or for applications requiring frequent updates to isolated features. However, it introduces complexity in dependency management, error handling, and version coordination, requiring robust CI/CD pipelines and observability.

For performance-critical applications, runtime server-side integration provides significant advantages. By rendering MFEs on the server or edge, teams can deliver HTML fragments pre-assembled for the client, improving load times and enabling effective caching strategies. React Server Components further enhance this model, allowing server-side rendering with minimal client-side JavaScript. This approach is ideal for critical user flows such as checkout, login, or content-heavy pages where speed and reliability outweigh deployment simplicity.

In practice, most organizations adopt a hybrid strategy. For example, a design system may be delivered as a build-time dependency for consistency, core flows may use server-side rendering for performance, and feature teams may leverage client-side runtime integration for maximum independence. Choosing the right mix depends on three guiding questions:

1. How independently should teams release?
2. How important is initial load performance?
3. How much infrastructure complexity can the organization sustain?

Answering these questions provides a framework for selecting the most suitable integration strategies while maintaining flexibility and scalability.

Composition strategies

Once MFEs are delivered, whether through build time, client-side runtime, or server-side runtime, the next challenge is how to assemble them into a seamless user experience. Composition is the process of combining MFEs into a coherent application, determining where each piece is rendered, how it interacts with the rest of the page, and how it maintains consistent behavior and appearance. Poor composition can result in inconsistent layouts, fragile communication, and degraded performance, negating the benefits of MFEs.

There are three main composition strategies:

- **Client-side composition**: The browser is responsible for assembling MFEs at runtime. This allows for high team autonomy and flexible page updates but requires careful orchestration and performance tuning.

- **Server-side composition**: The server assembles MFEs before sending the page to the client. This improves initial load performance and supports caching but increases server-side complexity.
- **Edge or hybrid composition:** Combines server and client-side assembly, e.g., a server-rendered shell with client-loaded MFEs for dynamic features. This balances performance, flexibility, and autonomy.

Each strategy has tradeoffs in responsiveness, complexity, and team autonomy. The right choice depends on the type of application, user expectations, and organizational scale.

Client-side composition

In client-side composition, the host application orchestrates MFEs directly in the browser. The host is responsible for loading, mounting, and rendering each MFE. This approach allows flexibility at runtime and enables MFEs built with different frameworks to coexist.

A classic example is a portal dashboard. Suppose an enterprise wants to show Analytics (React), Notifications (Vue), and User Settings (Angular) within a single page. With client-side composition, the host bootstraps these MFEs in the web page:

```
<!-- index.html -->
<html>
  <body>
    <div id="analytics-root"></div>
    <div id="notifications-root"></div>
    <div id="settings-root"></div>
    <script src="host.js"></script>
  </body>
</html>
```

The above HTML sets the placeholder where each MFE would be rendered. The **`host.js`** is the main script that orchestrates the MFE integration and takes care of routing and so on:

```
// host.js
Promise.all([
  import("analytics/App"),
  import("notifications/App"),
  import("settings/App"),
]).then(([Analytics, Notifications, Settings]) => {
  Analytics.mount(document.getElementById("analytics-root"));
  Notifications.mount(document.getElementById("notifications-root"));
  Settings.mount(document.getElementById("settings-root"));
});
```

In the above code, the MFEs are imported in parallel with a Promise (asynchronous way of fetching dependencies at runtime) and mounted in the respective placeholder (assume a function mount exists in each MFE).

One of the major advantages of client-side composition is the high degree of flexibility it offers. New MFEs can be introduced without requiring a rebuild of the host application, allowing teams to move quickly and deliver features independently. This flexibility extends to technology choices as well, since MFEs built with different frameworks such as React, Vue, Angular, or even plain JavaScript can coexist within the same container, giving teams the freedom to use the tools that best suit their needs. Another important benefit is the autonomy in deployment that allows each team to ship updates to their MFE without coordinating tightly with others, which reduces dependencies across teams and shortens release cycles. This independence not only accelerates development but also empowers organizations to scale their frontend efforts across many teams while still presenting a unified experience to the end user.

Despite its strengths, client-side composition also comes with a set of challenges. One limitation is that MFEs integrated as UMD bundles or Module Federation cannot be easily versioned, which restricts the ability to take advantage of browser-level caching; this can be mitigated by using npm modules, but that comes at the cost of release independence. Even when versioning is possible, teams must carefully manage shared dependencies to avoid conflicts, as different MFEs may expect different versions of the same library. Performance is another important consideration, since multiple bundles may need to be downloaded and initialized in the browser, and the overall time to interact can be slower compared to monolithic builds. This delay can be further compounded if each MFE pulls in its own runtime or redundant dependencies. Finally, because much of the rendering happens on the client, applications that rely heavily on client-side composition may suffer in terms of search engine optimization, as critical content might not be visible to crawlers during the initial load. These trade-offs do not diminish the value of client-side composition, but they highlight the importance of making careful architectural decisions when adopting this approach.

Server-side composition

Server-side composition assembles the application before it reaches the browser, shifting the orchestration away from the client and into the server. Instead of downloading and mounting multiple MFEs in the browser, the server fetches content fragments such as HTML snippets, JSON payloads, or even pre-rendered React components from independent services and stitches them into a single response. This concept is not entirely new. It resembles the older server-side rendering techniques once common with technologies such as JSP, PHP, or ASP, where the server dynamically built pages before sending them to the client. What MFEs add to this pattern is modularity and team autonomy, allowing different groups to own their services while still benefiting from centralized composition.

The primary advantage of server-side composition is the speed of the initial load. This is because the browser receives HTML that is already rendered, the time to first paint(first content on screen), and the time to interactive (when the user can interact) are generally faster compared to applications that render entirely on the client. Yet this benefit depends on several variables. The way the fragments are retrieved from backend services can influence latency. The proximity of the rendering server to the requesting user can reduce or increase response time. The overall load on the aggregation server is another important factor, since a central orchestrator can easily become a bottleneck if it is not scaled appropriately. Server-side composition is therefore not a one-size-fits-all solution but a strategy that requires careful tuning of infrastructure, caching policies, and fallback mechanisms.

In recent years, frameworks have modernized server-side composition with new rendering models. Tools such as Next.js, Nuxt.js, and SvelteKit combine the advantages of server rendering with the flexibility of client interactivity. React Server Components add another dimension by allowing certain parts of the component tree to render on the server while others hydrate on the client, reducing the amount of JavaScript shipped to the browser. Beyond the simple dichotomy of server-side and client-side rendering, we now have more advanced techniques such as static site generation, incremental static regeneration, and streaming server rendering. Each of these methods addresses specific tradeoffs between build time performance, runtime interactivity, and content freshness.

Large-scale consumer sites such as Amazon and Etsy have adopted variations of server-side composition because it improves both performance and search engine visibility. Content-heavy applications like e-commerce platforms, marketplaces, and news portals often benefit from this approach since faster rendering and better indexing can directly translate into improved user engagement and higher conversion rates. At the same time, these platforms usually combine server-side rendering with client-side hydration so that the experience remains interactive after the first load:

```
// app/page.js
import ProductList from "product-mfe/ProductList.server";
import CartSummary from "cart-mfe/CartSummary.server";
// Page component entirely rendered on the server
export default async function Page() {
  // Fetch products on the server
  const products = await fetch("https://api.example.com/products").
then(r => r.json());
  const cartItems = await fetch("https://api.example.com/cart").then(r => r.
json());
  return (
    <main>
        <ProductList products={products} /> {/* Server component */}
        <CartSummary items={cartItems} /> {/* Server component */}
    </main>
  );
}
```

Server-side composition offers several significant advantages. This is because the server delivers fully rendered HTML to the browser, the initial page load is fast, improving perceived performance and time to interactive. This approach also enhances search engine optimization, as crawlers can index content immediately without relying on client-side JavaScript execution. Server components can fetch data securely on the server, keeping API keys and business logic hidden from the client. Furthermore, MFEs remain modular and independently deployable, as each service can provide its content fragment to be stitched into the overall page. Large applications, particularly content-heavy sites or e-commerce platforms, benefit from this model because users receive a complete view of the page quickly, while client-side interactivity can be layered on only where necessary.

Despite these benefits, server-side composition also has some trade-offs. The server can become a bottleneck if it has to fetch and assemble multiple fragments for every request, and latency can increase if backend services or the aggregation server are far from the user. Caching and versioning require careful planning, as content fragments may need to be cached individually or at the edge to maintain performance. Interactivity depends on client hydration, which can complicate the integration of server and client components. Finally, more complex infrastructure and deployment pipelines may be needed to orchestrate independent MFEs on the server while maintaining consistency and reliability across services.

Hybrid composition

Hybrid composition combines the strengths of server-side and client-side approaches to deliver both fast initial rendering and rich interactivity. In this model, critical content such as product listings, headers, or navigation is rendered on the server and delivered as HTML to the browser, ensuring a fast first paint and good search engine visibility. At the same time, interactive MFEs such as carts, forms, or dynamic widgets are hydrated on the client, allowing users to interact with the page without reloading. This separation of responsibilities enables teams to optimize performance while maintaining modularity, as each MFE can decide whether it should render on the server, on the client, or both.

A hybrid approach is particularly useful for large, content-heavy applications. For example, an e-commerce site may render a catalog of products on the server to ensure fast loading and search engine optimization, while client-side MFEs handle shopping cart updates, user preferences, or real-time notifications. Modern frameworks like Next.js make this pattern straightforward by supporting both server and client components on the same page, with the **"use client"** directive marking which parts should hydrate in the browser. Edge functions or serverless platforms can further enhance this model by assembling server-side fragments closer to the user, reducing latency while preserving interactivity on the client:

```
// app/page.js
import ProductList from "product-mfe/ProductList.server";
import CartSummary from "cart-mfe/CartSummary.client";
// Page component that stitches server and client MFEs
```

```
export default async function Page() {
  // Fetch products on the server
  const products = await fetch("https://api.example.com/products").
then(r => r.json());
  return (
    <main>
      <div>
        <ProductList products={products}
/> {/* Server component: rendered on the server */}
      </div>
      <div>
        <CartSummary
/> {/* Client component: hydrated in the browser for interactivity */}
      </div>
    </main>
  );
}
```

The advantages of hybrid composition are clear. It balances performance, interactivity, and modularity, allowing teams to maintain independent deployments while delivering a seamless user experience. By rendering critical content on the server, the application achieves faster first contentful paint and improved SEO, while client-side hydration ensures responsive, interactive features. On the other hand, hybrid composition introduces additional complexity. Teams must carefully manage which MFEs are server-rendered versus client-hydrated, coordinate data fetching across environments, and ensure consistent state management between server and client. Infrastructure and deployment pipelines can also be more complex, as orchestration now involves both server-side rendering and client-side hydration for the same page.

The following table lists the key comparisons:

Aspect	Client-side composition	Server-side composition	Hybrid composition
Rendering location	Entirely in the browser after initial load	Entirely on the server before sending HTML	Critical content on server, interactive components hydrated on client
Time to first paint	Slower for large apps; requires JS download and execution	Fast; HTML is ready on arrival	Fast; server-rendered fragments appear immediately

Aspect	Client-side composition	Server-side composition	Hybrid composition
Interactivity	High; all interactions handled in the browser	Limited; requires full page reloads or server requests	Highly interactive fragments hydrate in the browser
Routing	Managed entirely by client router (React Router, Vue Router)	Managed on server; navigation requires page reload	Mixed; server handles initial routes, client router manages interactive fragments
State isolation	Each MFE manages its own state; careful sharing is required	Server manages state; easier to isolate, but less interactive	Requires coordination; state may span server and client fragments
UX consistency	Can be inconsistent if MFEs load at different times	Consistent; server sends a fully rendered page	Must ensure server and client components render coherently
Caching	Browser caching is possible per bundle	Server or edge caching needed; careful planning	A combination of server-side caching for static fragments and client caching for hydrated components
Edge/layout assembly	Rarely used	Can leverage edge servers to assemble fragments closer to the user	Can combine edge assembly for server fragments with client-side hydration
SEO	Limited; content must be rendered by the client for crawlers	Excellent; fully rendered HTML	Good; server fragments ensure SEO while client interactivity does not block indexing
Complexity	Moderate; mainly frontend build and routing	High; server infrastructure and fragment orchestration	Highest; must coordinate server rendering, client hydration, and state management

***Table 5.1**: List the comparison between different composition techniques*

Choosing the right composition

When choosing a composition strategy, the decision largely depends on the priorities of the application and the organization. Client-side composition is ideal for applications that demand rich interactivity and rapid iterative development, especially when teams want to maintain independent MFE releases. However, it may impact initial load performance and SEO, requiring careful optimization. Server-side composition excels when fast initial rendering, SEO, and controlled data fetching are critical, making it well-suited for content-heavy sites or e-commerce platforms. Its trade-off is limited client-side interactivity and increased server load. Hybrid composition offers a balanced approach by combining server-rendered critical content with client-side interactive MFEs. This provides both performance and interactivity but introduces additional complexity in coordinating state, routing, and a consistent user experience across server and client components. By understanding these distinctions and leveraging the strengths of each model, teams can design MFE architectures that align with both technical requirements and business goals.

Implementation patterns

Implementation patterns define the practical mechanisms through which MFEs are developed, integrated, and delivered across platforms. These patterns not only shape the developer workflow but also influence performance, user experience, and long-term maintainability. There are several patterns in which the component can be built so that it can be distributed across the application. These patterns represent a toolkit that organizations can apply based on their unique constraints and goals. No single pattern fits every scenario, but by understanding their strengths and trade-offs, teams can design implementation strategies that are both resilient and future-proof. We are going to look into a few such patterns in the following sections.

Web Components

Web Components are a framework-agnostic approach to building reusable UI elements that can be used across different front-end frameworks or even plain HTML. At their core, they leverage three browser standards: **Custom Elements**, **Shadow DOM**, and **HTML Templates**. The Shadow DOM encapsulates markup, styles, and behavior, preventing style leakage and conflicts, which is particularly useful when integrating MFEs from multiple teams or frameworks.

A typical use case might be a company like IKEA or Salesforce, which needs to embed reusable UI widgets, such as product cards or dashboards, across multiple applications built with different frameworks. For example, a product-card component can be implemented as follows:

```
// product-card.js
class ProductCard extends HTMLElement {
  constructor() {
    super();
    const shadow = this.attachShadow({ mode: "open" });
    shadow.innerHTML = `
      <style>
        .card { border: 1px solid #ccc; padding: 16px; border-radius: 8px; }
        h3 { margin: 0 0 8px 0; font-size: 16px; }
      </style>
      <div class="card">
```

```
      <h3></h3>
      <p></p>
    </div>
  `;
  }
  connectedCallback() {
    const title = this.getAttribute("title") || "Product";
    const desc = this.getAttribute("desc") || "";
    const shadow = this.shadowRoot;
    shadow.querySelector("h3").textContent = title;
    shadow.querySelector("p").textContent = desc;
  }
}
customElements.define("product-card", ProductCard);
```

Web Components offer several advantages for MFE architectures. They are framework agnostic, meaning the same component can be consumed across different applications regardless of the framework in use. The Shadow DOM ensures encapsulation, keeping styles and behavior isolated and reducing the likelihood of conflicts. Their reusability makes them ideal for large organizations with multiple apps or teams, allowing consistent UI elements to be shared across projects. *Figure 5.5* illustrates the difference between Shadow DOM and the Global DOM in terms of styling and encapsulation:

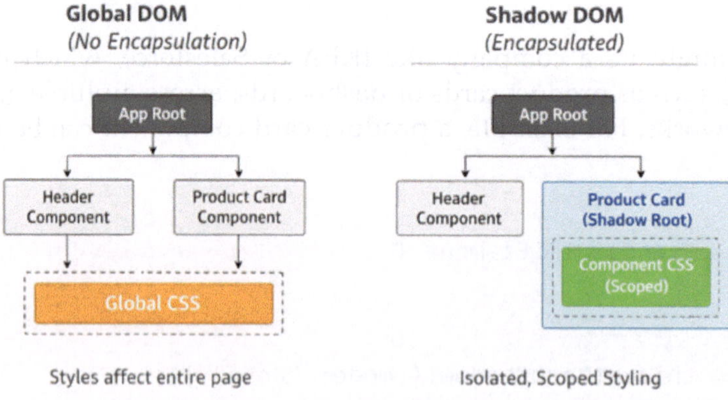

***Figure 5.5:** Comparison of Global DOM vs. Shadow DOM*

Being based on native browser standards, Web Components are stable and likely to be supported for the long term. However, there are trade-offs to consider. The APIs are relatively low-level compared to modern frameworks, so developers may need additional tooling for state management or reactivity. Performance can become an issue if a page contains too many nested shadow roots or heavy DOM manipulation. Integrating Web Components into reactive frameworks sometimes requires wrappers, which can add complexity. Despite these challenges, with libraries such as Lit or SkateJS improving developer ergonomics, Web Components remain a strong option for enterprises seeking framework independence, modularity, and long-term maintainability. Companies like Spotify and IKEA are actively using Web Components to standardize UI across multiple platforms, ensuring consistent experiences without locking into a specific framework.

Module Federation

Module Federation is a feature of Webpack5 that allows JavaScript applications to dynamically share code at runtime, enabling MFEs to consume components or modules from other independently deployed applications. Unlike Web Components, which encapsulate UI elements for reuse, Module Federation allows true code sharing, meaning multiple apps can directly import each other's modules, reduce duplication, and improve maintainability.

Webpack is a popular JavaScript module bundler that takes your application's modules, such as JavaScript, CSS, images, etc., and packages them into optimized bundles for the browser. It allows developers to manage dependencies, perform code splitting, and apply transformations like transpiling or minification.

Producer remote MFE setup

While the host application is responsible for composing the UI, each remote micro-frontend explicitly exposes the modules it wants to share. This is done by configuring the remote application with Module Federation and defining its public interface:

```
// webpack.config.js in product MFE (remote)
const ModuleFederationPlugin = require("webpack/lib/container/
ModuleFederationPlugin");
module.exports = {
  plugins: [
    new ModuleFederationPlugin({
      name: "productMFE",
      filename: "remoteEntry.js",
      exposes: {
        "./ProductList": "./src/ProductList",
      },
      shared: ["react", "react-dom"],
    }),
  ],
};
```

In this setup, the **productMFE** application (Producer) exposes **ProductList** as a federated module. At build time, Webpack generates a **remoteEntry.js** file that acts as the runtime manifest for the remote. The host application loads this file dynamically and resolves exposed modules only when they are requested.

Consumer remote MFE setup

A simple example demonstrates a host app consuming a remote MFE:

```
// webpack.config.js in host app
const ModuleFederationPlugin = require("webpack/lib/container/
ModuleFederationPlugin");
module.exports = {
  plugins: [
    new ModuleFederationPlugin({
      name: "host",
      remotes: {
        productMFE: "productMFE@http://localhost:3001/remoteEntry.js"
      },
      shared: ["react", "react-dom"]
    })
  ]
};
```

The code above shows the Webpack configuration required to consume federated modules, while the following code illustrates how the host can make use of them:

```
// in a host component
import ProductList from "productMFE/ProductList";
export default function HomePage() {
  return (
    <div>
      <h1>Products</h1>
      <ProductList />
    </div>
  );
}
```

Together, the host and remote configurations define a clear contract: the remote controls what it exposes, while the host decides when and how those modules are consumed. *Figure 5.6* illustrates the high-level architecture of Webpack Module Federation, highlighting the roles and interactions between the host application, remote micro-frontends, and shared dependencies:

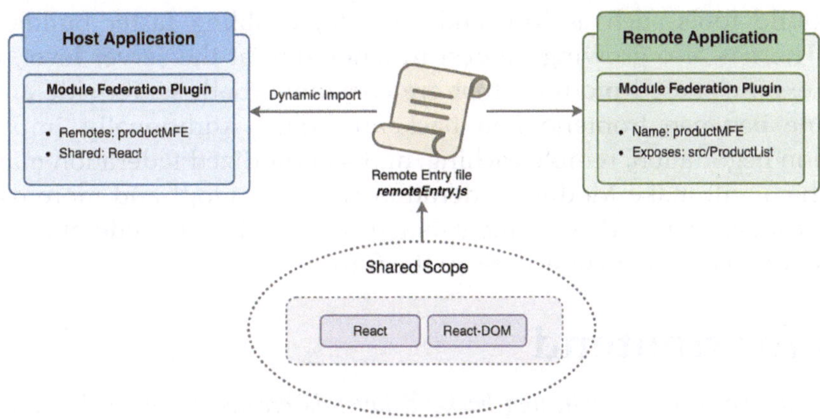

Figure 5.6: Module Federation architecture

In the above diagram, the host acts as the composition layer, initiating runtime loading by fetching the remote application's **remoteEntry.js**, which registers the remote's exposed modules. Once registered, the host can dynamically import these modules as needed. Shared libraries, such as React, are negotiated through a shared scope so that a single instance is reused across the host and all remotes. This approach enables independent deployment, clear ownership boundaries, and runtime composition without requiring host rebuilds, making it well-suited for large-scale micro-frontend architectures.

Module Federation offers several advantages for MFE architectures. It enables true runtime code sharing, allowing MFEs to be independently developed, deployed, and consumed by host applications without requiring a rebuild. Common dependencies, such as React or utility libraries, can be shared across applications, and multiple versions can coexist simultaneously, so one MFE can use React version 17 while another uses React v18 without conflicts. This approach also supports incremental adoption, making it easier for large organizations to gradually migrate parts of a monolithic application to an MFE architecture. Additionally, teams can ship features independently, which accelerates development and reduces coordination overhead.

However, there are trade-offs to consider. Module Federation introduces complexity in configuration and dependency management. Both producers and consumers must have the right tooling and configuration, typically Webpack5 or compatible bundlers like Vite, and understand how to expose or consume federated modules. While multiple versions of shared modules are supported, misconfiguration can still lead to runtime errors or unexpected behavior. Debugging issues across federated modules may be more difficult compared to traditional monolithic or Web Component architectures. Despite these challenges, Module Federation has proven its value in production at large-scale applications and continues to evolve as tooling and ecosystem support improve.

Looking forward, Module Federation is evolving beyond Webpack and gaining compatibility with modern build tools such as Vite and ESBuild, enabling faster builds and simpler configuration. There is also growing interest in federation at the server level, where Node.js services can expose shared modules that are consumed both server-side and client-side, blurring the line between frontend and backend MFEs. Additionally, improvements in automatic version negotiation, remote caching, and standardized federation manifests are on the horizon, which will make Module Federation easier to adopt and more robust in large enterprise applications. These developments suggest that Module Federation will remain a key strategy for scalable MFE architectures in the future.

Backend for frontend

BFF is a design pattern where a dedicated backend layer is created to serve the specific needs of a frontend application or MFE. Instead of exposing a single generic API to all clients, each frontend has a tailored backend that aggregates data, applies business logic, and formats responses optimized for that client. This approach is particularly useful in MFE architectures, where multiple independent teams may have different data requirements or performance constraints.

Imagine an e-commerce site with a Product MFE and a Cart MFE. Instead of having each frontend query multiple services individually, a BFF can aggregate product details, inventory status, and pricing into a single response for the Product MFE, while the Cart MFE receives only the relevant cart data:

```
// bff/productBFF.js (Node.js/Express)
const express = require('express');
const fetch = require('node-fetch');
const app = express();
app.get('/products', async (req, res) => {
  const [productData, inventoryData, pricingData] = await Promise.all([
    fetch('https://api.example.com/products').then(r => r.json()),
    fetch('https://api.example.com/inventory').then(r => r.json()),
    fetch('https://api.example.com/pricing').then(r => r.json())
  ]);
  // Aggregate and format the response for the frontend
  const response = productData.map(p => ({
    id: p.id,
    name: p.name,
    description: p.description,
    price: pricingData[p.id],
    available: inventoryData[p.id] > 0
  }));
```

```
  res.json(response);
});
app.listen(4000, () => console.log('Product BFF running on port 4000'));
```

Frontend MFEs can now call **/products** endpoint and receive aggregated, ready-to-use data, reducing frontend complexity and network calls.

BFF simplifies frontend development by providing tailored APIs, reducing the number of requests and data transformation required on the client. It enhances performance, as each MFE receives only the data it needs, and it allows teams to enforce frontend-specific business rules in a centralized backend. BFFs also improve maintainability in large organizations by decoupling frontend teams from backend services, enabling independent deployments.

BFF with GraphQL

Using GraphQL for a BFF provides distinct advantages over traditional REST APIs; it allows the frontend to request exactly the data it needs, reducing over-fetching and under-fetching, and simplifies aggregation from multiple services into a single query. This makes GraphQL particularly well-suited for MFE architectures, where different MFEs may need varying slices of data from diverse sources, enabling efficient, flexible, and maintainable client-server communication.

GraphQL is a query language for APIs that lets clients request exactly the data they need. It simplifies aggregation from multiple services, reduces over- or under-fetching, and is ideal for modern applications and MFEs.

It is worth noting that while other communication protocols, such as gRPC, are widely used within modern architectures, they are typically employed for backend-to-backend communication rather than directly at the frontend layer. gRPC's binary protocol, strict schema requirements, and transport assumptions make it well-suited for internal service-to-service communication, but less practical for browser-based clients. In MFE architectures, gRPC is often used behind the BFF, while REST or GraphQL remains the primary interface exposed to frontend applications.

On the downside, BFF introduces an additional backend layer to maintain, increasing operational complexity. Teams must ensure consistency between multiple BFFs and underlying services, and excessive aggregation or heavy logic in BFFs can become a performance bottleneck. Moreover, careful versioning is required to prevent breaking changes for dependent MFEs. Successful adoption requires that both frontend and backend teams collaborate on API contracts and tooling.

Companies like Netflix and Spotify leverage BFFs extensively. Netflix uses BFFs to serve different frontend clients, including web, mobile, and smart TV apps, each with optimized payloads and aggregated services. Spotify has implemented BFFs to aggregate data for its web and desktop apps, allowing different teams to independently deploy frontend features without overloading shared backend services.

The BFF pattern is evolving toward serverless and edge-based implementations, where BFF functions can run close to users for lower latency. Integration with MFEs is also improving with frameworks that support server-side composition and incremental rendering, enabling real-time aggregation of data while still leveraging frontend interactivity. There is also a trend toward federated BFFs, where multiple microservices expose their own BFFs that can be composed dynamically for different frontend clients.

Siteless UI

Siteless UI is an emerging concept where the frontend experience is delivered outside the boundaries of a traditional website or application. Instead of users visiting a single *site*, MFEs are embedded directly into third-party platforms, devices, or contexts such as voice assistants, chatbots, smart devices, or even other companies' portals. The UI is essentially decoupled from a dedicated site and consumed where the user already is.

A practical example is a retail company exposing its product catalog as a siteless UI widget that can be embedded in a partner's website. The widget can be served as an MFE using JavaScript and iframes, providing product browsing and purchase functionality without requiring users to leave the host site:

```
<!-- Host website -->
<div id="partner-widget"></div>
<script src="https://cdn.retailer.com/mfe/productWidget.js"></script>
<script>
  // Initialize the MFE
  RetailerProductWidget.init({
    containerId: "partner-widget",
    partnerId: "abc123",
    theme: "light"
  });
</script>
```

Here, the partner site loads the retailer's MFE script and mounts it as part of their own application. Users can browse and buy products seamlessly, and the retailer controls updates centrally without requiring changes in the partner's code. *Figure 5.7* illustrates how this siteless UI MFE is embedded and consumed across different host environments:

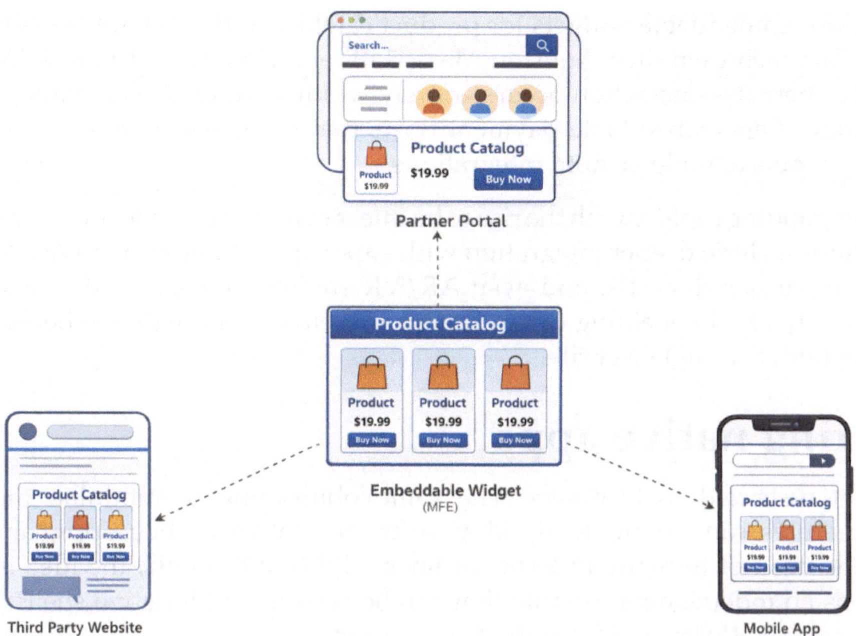

Figure 5.7: *Siteless UI MFE consumed by different host*

The above figure shows a single embeddable MFE, implemented as a product catalog widget, being mounted within multiple external contexts such as a third-party website, a partner portal, and a mobile application. Rather than owning the surrounding page or application, the MFE is delivered as a self-contained unit that is initialized by the host and rendered within its provided container. Each host supplies minimal configuration and integration logic, while the MFE owner retains control over UI behavior, data access, branding, and updates. This model enables organizations to distribute functionality across diverse platforms without duplicating frontend implementations, reinforcing the core idea of siteless UI, delivering experiences wherever users already are, rather than requiring them to visit a dedicated site.

Siteless UI expands reach by bringing functionality directly to users where they already spend their time, whether it is a partner's portal, a social feed, or even a voice assistant. It reduces friction, increases engagement, and allows companies to distribute MFEs across multiple channels without duplicating efforts. It also gives organizations full control over updates and branding, ensuring a consistent experience everywhere the UI is embedded.

On the other hand, this approach introduces challenges around integration and governance. Host environments may restrict styling, JavaScript execution, or network calls, which can limit functionality. Maintaining consistent performance across diverse platforms can be difficult, and dependency on third-party hosts means less control over the end-to-end experience. Security is another consideration, as embedding code in external platforms requires strict sandboxing and data governance to avoid vulnerabilities.

Shopify provides embeddable widgets for product catalogs and checkout flows that partners can integrate into their own sites. Amazon Alexa skills and Google Assistant actions are forms of siteless UI, where the interaction occurs entirely within a voice-driven platform. Similarly, Stripe Checkout offers embeddable payment flows that work across multiple hosts without requiring developers to build custom integrations.

Siteless UI is expanding rapidly with the rise of headless commerce and API-driven experiences. Future directions include deeper integration with super apps, **Progressive Web Apps (PWAs)** distributed via partner channels, and even AR/VR environments. As MFEs evolve, siteless UI will play a key role in enabling organizations to deliver experiences wherever users are, without being tied to a single website.

Supporting native apps

MFEs are not restricted to browsers. The same philosophy of modular, independently deployable features can extend to desktop software, native mobile apps, and smart TV applications. Instead of thinking in terms of JavaScript bundles only, the idea is to package each feature as an independent module that can be consumed by native shells. This creates consistency across platforms while giving teams autonomy.

A practical example is Spotify, which follows an MFE-like model in its desktop and mobile apps. Features like playlists, podcast browsing, and recommendation modules are owned by separate teams and plugged into the client shell. Similarly, Netflix on Smart TVs. composes its app by loading independent feature modules optimized for performance on constrained devices. On mobile, frameworks like React Native, Capacitor, and Flutter make it possible to share MFE logic across iOS and Android while still integrating with native system APIs.

Desktop applications

MFE principles are not limited to browser-based applications; they extend naturally to desktop software, whether built with web technologies or purely native frameworks. The key idea is to treat each feature or module as an independently deployable unit that can be dynamically loaded into a host shell, allowing teams to ship updates without rebuilding the entire app. The following are a few approaches for integrating MFEs into a desktop application:

- **Web-based shells (Electron, Tauri, Neutralino.js)**: Frameworks like Electron enable cross-platform desktop apps using web technologies. Each MFE can be loaded dynamically as a JavaScript module:

```
// Electron shell
const { app, BrowserWindow } = require('electron');
function createWindow() {
  const win = new BrowserWindow({ width: 1200, height: 800 });
  win.loadFile('shell.html');
```

```
}
app.whenReady().then(createWindow);
```

```
<!-- shell.html -->
<div id="chat-container"></div>
<script type="module">
  import('./chatMFE.js').then(module => {
    module.initChat('#chat-container');
  });
</script>
```

Here, **chatMFE.js** is a separate MFE module for chat, independently deployable and dynamically loaded into the desktop shell.

- **Native webview approaches (C++, Java, .NET)**: Traditional native apps can embed web content via **webviews**, enabling MFEs to run inside otherwise native applications:
    - **C++/Qt WebEngine:** Use a Chromium-based WebEngine to host HTML/JS MFEs inside Qt or Win32 apps.
    - **JavaFX WebView/SWT Browser**: Java apps can embed MFEs as HTML/JS content in WebView components.
    - **.NET WebView2 (Edge Chromium)**: Modern Windows apps can embed MFEs in WinForms or WPF applications.

Example using Qt WebEngine (C++):

```
#include <QApplication>
#include <QWebEngineView>
int main(int argc, char *argv[]) {
    QApplication app(argc, argv);
    QWebEngineView view;
    view.setUrl(QUrl("http://localhost:8080/productMFE"));
    view.show();
    return app.exec();
}
```

This allows the native app to host MFEs like a product catalog or dashboard while keeping the rest of the UI native. Communication between native code and MFEs can be achieved via JavaScript bridges or IPC.

Note: The approach is like an Iframed approach, and the result of MFE would be an HTML.

Extending MFEs to desktop applications ensures consistency across platforms, facilitates independent deployments, and enables the reuse of web-based logic. Webview-based approaches allow native apps to embed rich interactive features without rewriting them, while frameworks like Electron provide a fully web-based shell with cross-platform capabilities.

However, there are trade-offs. Resource management is critical because multiple webviews or Chromium instances can increase memory and CPU usage. Communication between native and web layers adds complexity, and dynamic module updates must be coordinated with native app versions. Additionally, purely native approaches (VC++, Java, Qt) may require careful integration to avoid performance bottlenecks or inconsistent UI behavior.

In the Spotify Desktop, Modular features for playlists, recommendations, and playback are dynamically loaded in an Electron shell. At the same time, Slack uses Electron-based MFEs for chat, calls, and integrations. Other real-time examples include Microsoft Teams, which hosts apps and extensions dynamically inside its desktop shell.

The future of desktop MFEs involves smarter auto-update mechanisms, lightweight native shells, and hybrid integration. Newer frameworks like Tauri reduce memory overhead while supporting dynamic module loading. Additionally, we expect hybrid approaches where desktop shells host both native modules and web MFEs, enabling a seamless, modular, and maintainable experience across platforms.

Mobile applications

MFE principles can be extended to native mobile platforms to enable modular, independently deployable features across iOS and Android apps. The goal is to allow teams to ship individual features without requiring a full app rebuild, while maintaining consistency across platforms. Frameworks like React Native, Flutter, and Capacitor make it possible to reuse logic and UI components across mobile apps, while still integrating with native APIs. The following are a few approaches for integrating MFEs into a mobile application:

- **React native example**: In React Native, an MFE module can be distributed as an `npm` package and dynamically imported into the host app:

```
// HostApp.js
import React, { useState, useEffect } from 'react';
import { View } from 'react-native';
export default function HostApp() {
  const [ProductList, setProductList] = useState(null);
  useEffect(() => {
    import('productMFE').then(module => setProductList(() => module.
default));
```

```
  }, []);
  return <View>{ProductList ? <ProductList /> : null}</View>;
}
```

Here, **productMFE** is an MFE encapsulating the product listing feature, which can be developed and deployed independently.

- **Flutter example**: Flutter allows similar modularity through packages or plugins, each feature can be packaged as a module and imported into multiple apps:

```
import 'package:flutter/material.dart';
import 'package:product_mfe/product_mfe.dart';
class HostApp extends StatelessWidget {
  @override
  Widget build(BuildContext context) {
    return MaterialApp(
      home: Scaffold(
        body: ProductMFE(),
      ),
    );
  }
}
```

- **Capacitor/hybrid approach**: Capacitor or Cordova-based apps can embed MFEs as Web Components within a native shell, allowing teams to reuse existing web MFEs on mobile:

```
<ion-app>
  <div id="checkout-widget"></div>
  <script src="https://cdn.example.com/checkoutMFE.js"></script>
  <script>
    CheckoutMFE.init({ containerId: 'checkout-widget' });
  </script>
</ion-app>
```

This approach is similar to Siteless UI but delivered inside a mobile shell, giving access to native APIs while leveraging web-based MFEs.

Smart TV applications

Smart TV devices can benefit from MFE patterns, allowing teams to build modular features that are independently deployable. Many Smart TV platforms, such as Roku, Tizen, and

WebOS, provide ways to load dynamic modules, either as component libraries or web-based bundles, depending on the platform.

On Roku, MFEs can be implemented using BrightScript and SceneGraph components. For example, a product list MFE could be a reusable SceneGraph component that the main app dynamically loads.

Note: A SceneGraph component can be thought of as similar to a React or Vue component. It is a reusable, self-contained UI unit that can be dynamically added to an application. In an MFE context, it plays the same role as a web micro-frontend, encapsulating both structure and behavior.

The following BrightScript snippet demonstrates how the main scene initializes and loads an MFE component dynamically into the Roku SceneGraph application:

```
' MainScene.brs
sub init()
    m.top.productList = createObject("roSGNode", "ProductListComponent")
    m.top.appendChild(m.top.productList)
    m.top.productList.load("http://cdn.example.com/mfe/productList.json")
end sub
```

The following snippet defines the **ProductListComponent** itself, which lays out the UI structure for displaying the product list:

```
<!-- ProductListComponent.xml -->
<component name="ProductListComponent" extends="Group">
    <children>
        <Label id="titleLabel" text="Product List" />
        <RowList id="productRowList" />
    </children>
</component>
```

Here, **ProductListComponent** is an MFE module loaded dynamically via a URL. This approach allows updates to the product list UI independently of the main app, enabling modular development and deployment. Communication between the shell and MFE is handled via events and component APIs. The above code would generate a UI similar to the one illustrated in *Figure 5.8*:

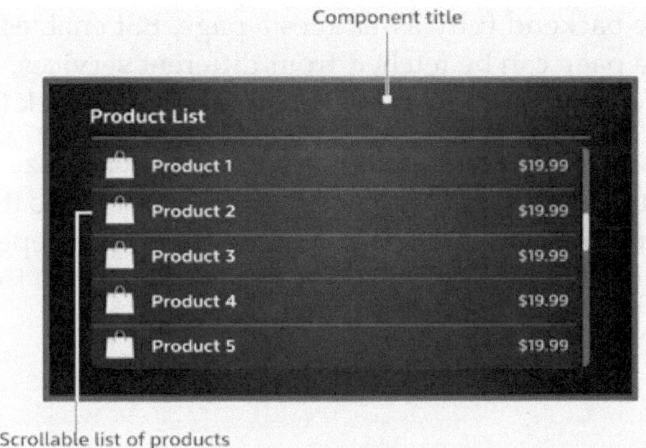

***Figure 5.8:** A screenshot displays how the MFE can be rendered in the Roku app*

Supporting native apps with MFEs provides several advantages. Teams can deploy features independently, reducing the need for full app releases and accelerating time-to-market. Modules can be shared across desktop, mobile, and Smart TV platforms where feasible, enabling cross-platform consistency. Web-based MFEs embedded in native shells allow code reuse, while hybrid approaches integrate seamlessly with native APIs, resulting in modular, maintainable architectures.

However, there are trade-offs. Native shells must handle dynamic loading, communication between web and native layers, and potential version mismatches. Resource management is critical on constrained devices such as Smart TVs Mobile apps still face deployment restrictions from app stores, and hybrid approaches require careful performance optimization to maintain responsive UIs. Despite these challenges, the modularity and independent deployability of MFEs often outweigh the drawbacks, especially in large organizations with multiple development teams.

In the real world, Uber or Airbnb Mobile has feature modules in React Native and Flutter. Netflix and Amazon Smart TVs. have dynamically loaded feature modules optimized for TV displays.

The future of native MFEs involves dynamic over-the-air updates, hybrid shells combining native and web MFEs, and lightweight desktop frameworks like Tauri or Qt WebEngine to reduce memory overhead. Mobile apps will increasingly rely on dynamic module delivery and shared cross-platform modules for consistency. Smart TVs and IoT devices will adopt MFE patterns to deliver modular, independently deployable experiences across constrained hardware.

Edge Side Includes

Edge Side Includes (**ESI**) is a server-driven technique that allows pages to be assembled at the edge or caching layer before being delivered to the browser. Unlike traditional server-side rendering, where the backend fully assembles a page, ESI enables fragmented assembly, where different parts of a page can be fetched from different services, cached independently, and stitched together by a reverse proxy or **content delivery network** (**CDN**).

ESI was popularized by *Akamai*, *Varnish*, and other CDNs to optimize performance for high-traffic websites. For example, a product detail page can be broken into three fragments: header, recommendations, and product details. Each fragment is fetched independently from different services and cached separately at the CDN edge, as illustrated in the following code snippet:

```
<!-- productPage.esi -->
<html>
  <body>
    <esi:include src="/header.esi" />
    <esi:include src="/productDetails.esi?productId=12345" />
    <esi:include src="/recommendations.esi?productId=12345" />
  </body>
</html>
```

Here, **`header.esi`** might be heavily cached across all users, while **`productDetails.esi`** is more dynamic. The CDN assembles the final HTML on the fly before serving it to the client, reducing backend load and improving first byte performance.

ESI is still used in high-traffic e-commerce sites, news portals, and legacy enterprise portals, where caching and modular assembly can significantly reduce server load. Examples include Walmart and BestBuy, which historically leveraged ESI for assembling large catalog pages with dynamic personalization and recommendations.

Limitations and trade-offs

While ESI can improve performance and reduce backend stress, it introduces several limitations:

- **Complexity of caching strategy**: Each fragment may require different caching rules, increasing operational complexity.
- **Limited dynamic capabilities**: Personalization or user-specific content can be harder to implement without bypassing caches.
- **Obsolescence in modern architectures**: With the rise of Next.js, React server components, Module Federation, and edge functions, ESI is less common for new projects. Most modern approaches handle composition at the server or client with finer-grained control and better integration with frameworks.

Although ESI is largely considered a legacy technology, its core concept of fragmented assembly at the edge remains relevant. Modern edge computing platforms like Cloudflare Workers,

AWS Lambda@Edge, and Vercel Edge Functions allow dynamic composition at the edge without relying on ESI syntax. These platforms provide more flexibility, richer programming capabilities, and easier integration with contemporary frameworks, while still delivering the performance benefits of edge assembly.

Component communication

While the following discussion does not replace the detailed treatment of state management and event messaging to be covered in the next chapter, it is important to understand how MFEs communicate with the host container and with each other at a high level. This section focuses on parent-to-child, child-to-parent, and child-to-child communication, providing practical guidance for implementing these patterns in MFE architectures.

Host to MFE

The host application often needs to communicate with its MFEs for several reasons:

- **Initialization with data**: The host provides initial context, such as user identity, authentication tokens, or configuration parameters.
- **Configuration**: The host may define layout options, feature flags, themes, or other settings that the MFE should respect.
- **Re-render or refresh based on external events**: For example, if the user changes the locale or theme, the host may instruct the MFE to update itself.

A common approach is to use a shared context or a singleton object that holds state accessible across MFEs. Examples include Redux, React Context, or a custom global store. While these mechanisms allow the host and MFEs to stay synchronized, they should be used judiciously to avoid tight coupling. The next chapter will cover state propagation and advanced patterns in detail.

Practical example (React props):

```
// HostApp.jsx
<ProductListMFE userId="12345" locale="en-US" />
// ProductListMFE.jsx
export default function ProductListMFE({ userId, locale }) {
  return <div>Loading products for {userId} in {locale} locale</div>;
}
```

Here, the host initializes and configures the MFE, while the **`child(ProductListMFE)`** remains self-contained. This is explained further in detail in *Figure 5.9*:

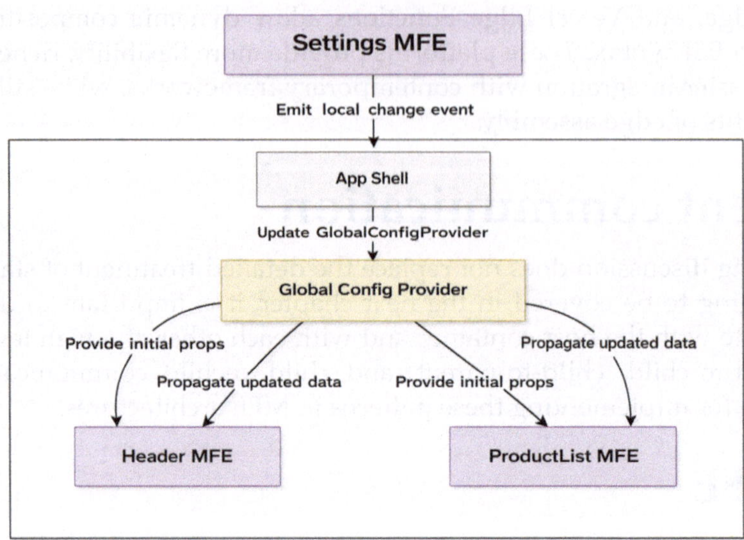

Figure 5.9: Host app to MFE communication

In the above figure, the App Shell acts as the host application and contains the global configuration, such as locale, theme, or feature settings. MFEs like a header or product list, consume this configuration and update themselves automatically whenever it changes. When a user changes a setting like the locale in the settings MFE, it emits an event to the App Shell. The shell then updates its global configuration, which is propagated to all MFEs within the shell, causing them to refresh and reflect the new settings. This approach keeps the Settings MFE decoupled while allowing it to influence the behavior of other MFEs through the centralized configuration managed by the host.

MFE to host

MFEs also need to communicate upwards to the host, for instance:

- **Propagating internal updates**: An MFE may notify the host when an action occurs, such as a form submission or selection.
- **Providing state information**: The host may need to query the state of a particular component within an MFE, such as whether a form input is valid or a feature toggle is active.

  This can be implemented using callbacks, custom events, or exposed APIs.
- **React callback**: The following code snippet shows an example of how a callback function can be used to communicate back to the parent:

```
<ProductListMFE onProductSelect={id => console.
log('Selected product:', id)}
/>
```

In this example, a callback is attached to the **ProductListMFE** as props (**onProductSelect**) from the parent, which will be invoked when triggered from the child. This is a straightforward approach widely used in small-scale applications; however, we would quickly get into the trap of callback hell or prop drilling in React if it has multiple levels of components. In those cases, React context or Redux could help avoid this.

- **Vanilla JS custom event:** The following code uses the native **CustomEvent** to communicate back to the host:

```
// productMFE.js
this.dispatchEvent(new CustomEvent('productSelected',
{ detail: { id: 987 }, bubbles: true }));
```

In the above example, the host can listen and react to these events without tightly coupling to the MFE internals. This works on a fire-and-forget strategy, which could work for some use cases, but not for all use cases, especially when we seek acknowledgement to sequentially operate on other tasks.

- **React hook (useImperativeHandle)**: Another React way of handling the child-to-parent communication is through a React hook called **useImperativeHandle**. Though it has been used very rarely in applications, it is very powerful, especially for component libraries to expose an internal state or the purity of the specific component to its consumer. Though this is a React-only hook, it can be easily replicated as a custom API for a non-react application. Let us look at a code example to understand this better:

```
// child.js
import React, { forwardRef, useImperativeHandle } from "react";
const Child = forwardRef((props, ref) => {
  useImperativeHandle(ref, () => ({
    sayHello: () => alert("Hello from Child!")
  }));
  return <div>Child Component</div>;
});
export default Child;

// parent.js
import React, { useRef } from "react";
import Child from "./Child";
```

```
export default function App() {
  const childRef = useRef();
  return (
    <div>
      <Child ref={childRef} />
      <button onClick={() => childRef.current.sayHello()}>
        Call Child Method
      </button>
    </div>
  );
}
```

In the above code sample, the child component exposes a single method, **sayHello**, using **useImperativeHandle**. The parent obtains a reference to the child and calls this method when the button is clicked. This minimal example illustrates the core concept of child-to-parent communication using a method, showing how a child can expose controlled functionality that the parent can invoke directly.

Figure 5.10 depicts all three approaches while passing the data from the child to its host:

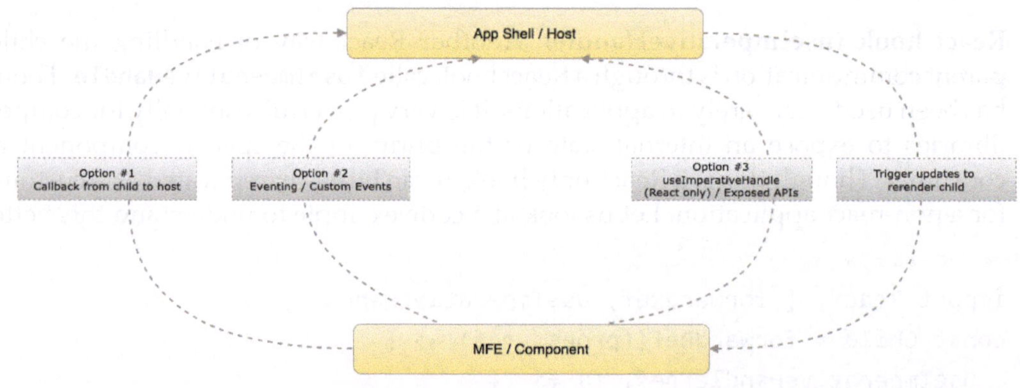

***Figure 5.10**: Different options to pass data from child MFE to host*

MFE to MFE

Direct communication between MFEs is generally discouraged, as it can lead to tight coupling and reduce the independence of deployments. However, in some cases, MFE may need to respond to changes in other MFEs. This is typically done via event messaging or a shared global store.

For example, similar to what we discussed in the previous section, we can leverage event bus or DOM events:

```
// MFE A dispatches
window.dispatchEvent(new CustomEvent('cartUpdated',
{ detail: { items: 3 } }));
// MFE B listens
window.addEventListener('cartUpdated', event => {
  console.log('Cart items changed:', event.detail.items);
});
```

In this code example, the MFE A dispatched the event **cardUpdated**, which will be captured by another MFE B using the native event listener. Remember, in this method, there is no assurance of the delivery of the message. *Figure 5.11* shows how the events can be sent via a centralized event bus or shared store:

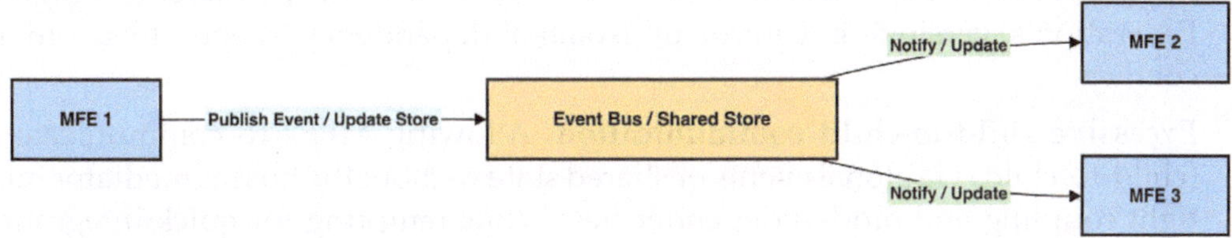

***Figure 5.11**: An example of MFE to MFE communication via event bus*

Although feasible, this approach should be used sparingly. A better alternative is to communicate through the host container, keeping MFEs loosely coupled.

Antipatterns

MFEs offer modularity, independent deployability, and cross-team flexibility, but these benefits can easily be undermined by poor architectural choices. Antipatterns are recurring mistakes that teams often fall into when adopting MFEs, usually because of overengineering, misuse of frameworks, or lack of communication between teams. Recognizing these early is critical to maintain the long-term health and scalability of your application.

At a high level, antipatterns often emerge in communication, dependency management, composition, and deployment strategies. Ignoring them can lead to brittle applications, slower releases, runtime errors, and maintenance nightmares. The following are a few antipatterns that we should avoid in MFEs:

- **Tight coupling between MFEs**: A common pitfall is direct dependency between MFEs, such as one MFE importing internal modules from another. While technically possible, this reduces deployability, increases coordination overhead, and negates the independence benefits. Communication between MFEs should instead flow through the host container or standardized event channels, preserving loose coupling.

- **Overloading the host**: Treating the host as a feature orchestrator with too much business logic creates a bottleneck. The host should manage composition, routing, and shared state sparingly. Overloading it with MFE-specific logic violates separation of concerns and makes upgrades or changes more difficult.
- **Ignoring performance implications**: Composing multiple MFEs without careful attention to bundle sizes, lazy loading, or caching can slow down time-to-interactive, harm SEO, or overload the browser. Relying on UMD-style MFEs without versioning, or embedding too many large modules at once, is a classic antipattern. Modern strategies like Module Federation, siteless UI, or edge-side composition can mitigate these risks, but only if used thoughtfully.
- **Shared dependencies mismanagement**: Sharing common libraries (like React or lodash) seems convenient, but version conflicts and unexpected behavior can arise. MFEs should declare dependencies explicitly and, when possible, leverage Module Federation's versioning control or isolated dependency scopes to avoid runtime conflicts.
- **Excessive child-to-child communication**: Allowing MFEs to communicate directly (child-to-child) via global events or shared state without the host as mediator introduces tight coupling and hidden dependencies. While tempting for quick integrations, this makes testing, debugging, and independent deployments challenging.
- **Ignoring observability and error handling**: Skipping proper logging, monitoring, or error boundaries in MFEs can propagate failures across the entire application. Each MFE should handle errors gracefully and emit meaningful events for the host to monitor health.

Antipatterns often arise when teams prioritize speed over architecture, ignore framework-agnostic boundaries, or attempt to force legacy patterns onto modern MFE strategies. By respecting modularity, limiting direct coupling, managing shared dependencies, and designing for observability, teams can avoid these traps while fully leveraging the benefits of MFEs.

Error handling

In an MFE architecture, each module operates independently, but failures in one MFE can propagate and affect the entire user experience if not handled properly. Unlike monolithic applications, MFEs are designed to be independently deployable, which means that errors can occur in isolation or during interaction with the host container. Proper error handling ensures that failures are contained, observable, and recoverable, maintaining the robustness and stability of the application while preventing one MFE from compromising others.

Types of errors

Understanding the types of errors that can occur is the first step toward designing resilient MFEs:

- **Initialization errors**: These happen during the loading or bootstrapping of an MFE. Common causes include network failures when fetching the MFE's bundle, incorrect versioning of shared dependencies, or runtime errors during the component initialization. If unhandled, initialization failures can prevent the entire page from rendering.
- **Runtime errors**: These occur during the execution of the MFE, such as exceptions in component rendering, event handlers, or internal logic. For example, an MFE rendering a product list may fail due to unexpected data from an API.
- **Communication errors**: Failures in interactions between the host and MFEs, or between MFEs themselves, fall under this category. For instance, a callback or event triggered by the child MFE may not be handled correctly by the host, leading to inconsistent UI or broken workflows.
- **Dependency errors**: MFEs often share libraries or modules with the host or other MFEs. Conflicting versions or missing libraries can lead to runtime failures. These are particularly common in UMD-style integrations or when shared dependencies are not properly versioned under Module Federation.

Strategies for error handling

Error handling in MFEs requires a combination of framework-specific mechanisms and framework-agnostic practices to ensure resilience across the platform. The following are a few strategies that can help with handling errors in MFEs:

- **Error boundaries (React-specific)**: React provides a mechanism called error boundaries to catch runtime errors in a component subtree. When a component fails, the error boundary prevents it from crashing the entire application and renders a fallback UI. This keeps the host container and other MFEs unaffected. The following is the code example of how `Error` boundaries are used in a React application:

```
// ErrorBoundary.jsx
import React from 'react';
export default class ErrorBoundary extends React.Component {
  state = { hasError: false };
  static getDerivedStateFromError(error) {
    return { hasError: true };
  }
  componentDidCatch(error, errorInfo) {
    console.error('MFE Error:', error, errorInfo);
  }
  render() {
```

```
    if (this.state.hasError) return <div>Something went wrong!</div>;
    return this.props.children;
  }
}
```

Usage:

```
<ErrorBoundary>
  <ProductListMFE userId="12345" />
</ErrorBoundary>
```

As stated above, **ErrorBoundary** is a standalone component that can be wrapped around any specific module or component. It implicitly acts as a try-catch mechanism, ensuring that errors do not bubble up and break the entire application. This approach allows errors to be handled gracefully rather than causing the whole application to fail.

- **Fallback UI for Vanilla JS/custom elements**: For MFEs built using Vanilla JavaScript, Web Components, or other frameworks, fallback handling can be implemented using try-catch blocks during initialization or onerror handlers. This allows a graceful fallback in case the MFE fails to load or initialize. The following code snippet shows the usage of the classic try-catch mechanism:

```
try {
  const productMFE = document.createElement('product-mfe');
  document.body.appendChild(productMFE);
} catch (err) {
  const fallback = document.createElement('div');
  fallback.textContent = 'Failed to load product module';
  document.body.appendChild(fallback);
  console.error('MFE load error:', err);
}
```

This approach prevents a single failed MFE from crashing the entire page, maintaining partial functionality for the user.

- **Graceful degradation**: One key principle of error handling in MFEs is graceful degradation. Each MFE should be able to fail silently or with minimal impact on the overall page. For example, if a recommendations MFE crashes, the product list or cart MFEs should continue to function normally. This preserves user experience even in the presence of isolated failures.
- **Centralized error reporting**: While handling errors locally is important, it is equally critical to monitor and log errors centrally for analysis and debugging. Each MFE can emit structured error events that the host listens to, allowing monitoring tools

to aggregate and track issues across all modules. While there are in-built solutions offered by the monitoring tools, the simplest way to get the errors from any MFE is via eventing, as described in the following code:

```
window.dispatchEvent(new CustomEvent('MFEError', {
  detail: { mfe: 'ProductList', message: 'Failed to fetch products' }
}));
```

The host can listen to all `MFEError` events and forward them to a logging service like Sentry, Dynatrace, or Datadog, providing visibility into issues without requiring the MFE to manage logging independently.

Handling network and dependency failures

When dealing with network and dependency failures, it is important to adopt strategies that allow the system to remain resilient under stress. MFEs should be lazy-loaded so that modules are fetched only when required, and retry mechanisms should be in place to recover from transient failures. This ensures that the user is not immediately faced with a broken interface when a script fails to load.

Dependency management also plays a crucial role in error prevention. Using versioned Module Federation or carefully isolating dependency scopes helps avoid runtime conflicts that often occur when different MFEs rely on incompatible versions of the same library. Finally, interactions with backend services should always be wrapped in safe constructs such as try–catch blocks or utility methods designed for error resilience. This prevents unhandled exceptions from bubbling up and allows the MFE to fail gracefully without interrupting the host or other modules.

The following are the best practices:

- **Isolate errors per MFE**: Avoid cascading failures by keeping each MFE self-contained.
- **Handle errors gracefully**: Inform the user of errors using fallback UI without breaking the overall page experience.
- **Emit structured events for monitoring**: Ensure the host can collect and analyze error data.
- **Test failure scenarios thoroughly**: Include cases such as offline mode, API failures, or missing module bundles.
- **Integrate with communication patterns**: Ensure that errors in data updates or events are propagated through the established parent-child or event channels rather than creating ad-hoc paths.
- **Document known failure modes**: Provide clear guidance on expected errors and recovery mechanisms for developers working on new MFEs.

By following these strategies, MFE architectures can remain resilient, maintainable, and user-friendly, even as the number of independently deployable modules grows. Effective error handling ensures that partial failures do not compromise the entire application, supporting modularity and independent releases, which are the core advantages of MFEs.

Case study on TuneStream

TuneStream, a rapidly growing music streaming app, began as a tightly coupled monolith. It worked well during its early growth stages, but as billions of users joined across web, mobile, and desktop, the cracks began to show. Teams were blocked on each other, deployments became risky, and feature velocity slowed down. To address this, TuneStream's leadership made a bold move: migrate to an MFE architecture.

Rendering strategies at TuneStream

When TuneStream moved from its monolith to a micro frontend world, rendering became the cornerstone of its strategy. Each touchpoint, such as web, desktop, and mobile, needed a rendering model that balanced speed, personalization, and resilience.

On the web app, teams split responsibilities by user context. For the Home & Discovery pages, they used SSR so a new visitor could immediately see trending playlists or featured artists. For example, the DiscoveryMFE rendered server-side with SSR to ensure fast time-to-interactive and SEO-friendly metadata. On the other hand, modules like the PlayerMFE or PlaylistMFE, which depend heavily on user interactions and state, were rendered on the CSR. This allowed them to hydrate after login, keeping playback smooth without waiting for server responses for every action.

The desktop app (Electron-based) shared much of the rendering stack with the web. Instead of SSR, it relied on pre-hydrated CSR bundles, because SEO was irrelevant in desktop contexts. Here, MFEs like the DownloadsMFE and OfflinePlayerMFE were shipped as local bundles but still updated dynamically at runtime. The rendering strategy emphasized local-first performance while allowing teams to roll out fixes and enhancements independently.

For mobile, SSR and CSR were not direct fits due to app store constraints and offline use. Instead, TuneStream adopted a Siteless UI SDK approach: rendering happened natively, but components mirrored the look and feel of their web counterparts. For example, the PlayerMFE UI existed as a native module in iOS/Android, but its rendering logic was informed by shared design tokens and data contracts used in the web/desktop MFEs. This way, the rendering experience felt uniform across platforms without duplicating the entire stack.

Crucially, some shared components (like SearchBar, PlaybackControls, and UserAvatar) were abstracted into reusable UI packages. On the web, they were hydrated within CSR or SSR boundaries. On desktop, they were bundled natively. On mobile, they were compiled into native modules. This separation ensured consistency in rendering without forcing a single rendering strategy on all touchpoints. *Figure 5.12* illustrates different rendering strategies on various touchpoints:

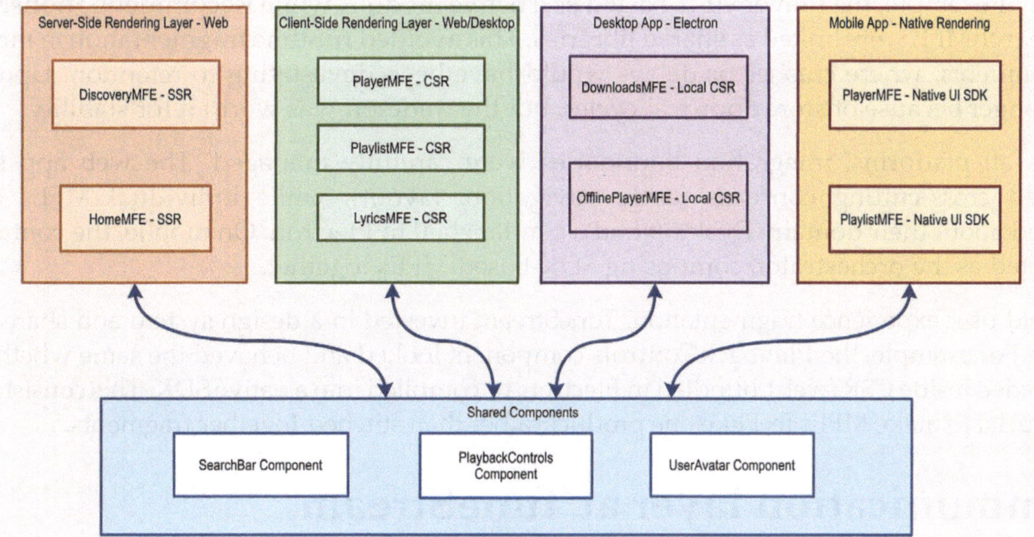

***Figure 5.12**: Rendering patterns used in each layer*

Integration and composition at TuneStream

Once TuneStream settled on rendering strategies, the next big challenge was how to stitch MFEs together into a seamless experience across devices. The engineering teams realized early that composition was not a *one-size-fits-all* problem. i.e., different touchpoints needed different approaches.

On the web app, TuneStream leaned heavily on runtime composition. Using a modern Module Federation approach, each team owned and shipped its own bundle (for example, the PlayerMFE, LyricsMFE, or SocialShareMFE). At runtime, the shell application dynamically pulled the latest version of these MFEs. This gave teams freedom to deploy independently without waiting for monolithic release trains. For instance, when the LyricsMFE shipped a new real-time sync feature, it could go live instantly without redeploying the PlaylistMFE. The trade-off was slightly more runtime complexity, but for a global-scale consumer product, fast iteration mattered more.

On the desktop app (Electron), the story was different. Since users downloaded a local package, stability was prioritized. TuneStream chose build-time composition for core MFEs like DownloadsMFE and OfflinePlayerMFE. These MFEs were composed during packaging, ensuring no surprises at runtime. However, less critical modules (like LyricsMFE) were still pulled dynamically, allowing **over-the-air** (**OTA**) updates. This hybrid strategy kept the experience reliable while still giving room for quick fixes.

On mobile, TuneStream went with release-time composition. Each MFE was distributed as a native UI SDK in which the integration happened at compile or build time before going to the app store. For example, the PlayerMFE existed as a native module, while RecommendationsMFE and SearchMFE were linked as shared libraries. This avoided runtime fragmentation in mobile environments, where crashes or delays would have been devastating to retention. Updates took longer because of store approval cycles, but the trade-off was worth it for stability.

Across all platforms, integration boundaries were carefully managed. The web app shell handled cross-cutting concerns (auth, navigation, layout), while individual MFEs only worried about their domain. Desktop had a similar shell in Electron. On mobile, the container app acted as the orchestrator, composing SDK-based MFEs together.

To avoid user experience fragmentation, TuneStream invested in a design system and shared UI library. For example, the PlaybackControls component looked and behaved the same whether it was loaded inside CSR (web), bundled in Electron, or compiled into a native SDK. This consistency was crucial to make MFEs feel like one product rather than stitched-together fragments.

Communication layer at TuneStream

Once rendering and composition were in place, TuneStream faced a new challenge: how should MFEs communicate without creating tight coupling or cascading failures?

The guiding principle was autonomy with controlled interaction. Each MFE was responsible for its own domain, but some features naturally needed cross-module communication. For instance:

- The `PlayerMFE` broadcasts the currently playing track.
- The `LyricsMFE` subscribes to this event to display synchronized lyrics.
- The `SocialShareMFE` consumes the same event to update *Now Listening* feeds.

Instead of direct imports or a shared global state, TuneStream used a lightweight event bus/pub-sub system. MFEs emitted events and consumed them via a central event broker. This ensured loose coupling: MFEs did not need to know about each other's implementation, only the events they cared about.

For shared data like user preferences, authentication status, or playback state, TuneStream relied on API contracts and a BFF layer. MFEs never called backend services directly; they went through the BFF, which normalized data and handled caching. This avoided duplication and reduced network chatter.

Error handling was built into the communication layer as well. For example, if the LyricsMFE failed to render due to a network issue, it simply gets unsubscribed and displays fallback text. Circuit breakers prevented repeated failed calls from affecting other MFEs. Event bus messages were also versioned, so old MFEs would not break when new events were introduced. *Figure 5.13* depicts how various MFEs can communicate through the shared event bus:

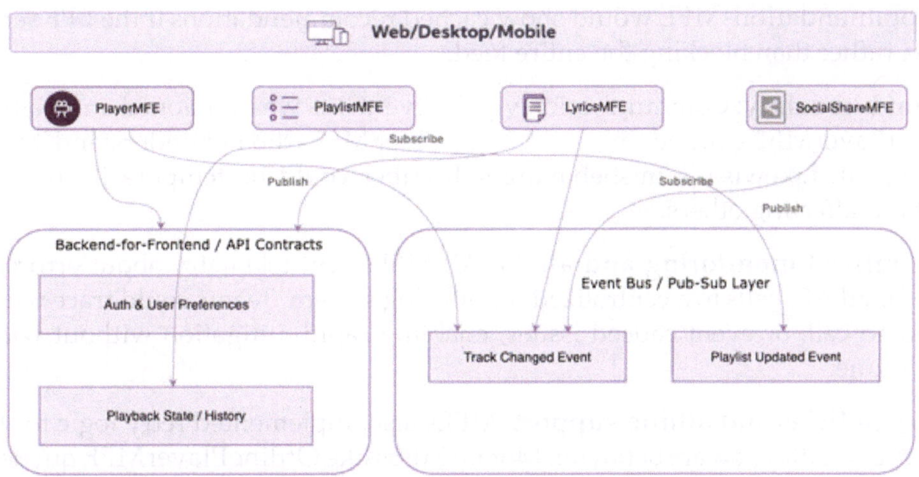

Figure 5.13: *Communication layer at TuneStream*

On mobile, the principle was the same, though implemented natively: MFEs communicated via a publish-subscribe system within the container app, ensuring smooth updates even when MFEs were compiled into the app.

Error handling and cascade failure prevention

With billions of users relying on TuneStream, even a small error could affect millions of streams. In a micro frontend architecture, a single MFE failure had the potential to ripple across other modules, so resilience was a top priority.

The engineering teams applied several strategies:

- **Isolation by design**: Each MFE was isolated in its own runtime environment. On the web, React error boundaries wrapped each MFE so that a crash in the LyricsMFE would not break the PlayerMFE or PlaylistMFE. On desktop, Electron processes were sandboxed per MFE where possible. Mobile MFEs compiled as native SDKs lived in separate containers inside the main app. This ensured a single failing module could fail gracefully without bringing down the entire app.
- **Circuit breakers for backend calls**: MFEs like PlayerMFE or PlaylistMFE relied heavily on BFF APIs. To prevent a slow or failing API from cascading, circuit breakers were implemented. For example, if the PlaybackService became unresponsive, the PlayerMFE would temporarily stop calling it and fall back to cached playback data, while notifying users gracefully with a message Playback temporarily offline.
- **Fallback UIs and graceful degradation**: Whenever MFEs failed, users still had a functional app. If LyricsMFE failed to load, it displayed static lyrics or a Lyrics unavailable message, while PlayerMFE continued playback uninterrupted. Similarly,

RecommendationsMFE would show cached recommendations if the BFF service was slow, rather than blocking the entire feed.

- **Event bus safety**: Communication via the event bus was versioned and namespaced. If the PlayerMFE emitted a new event that older MFEs did not understand, they simply ignored it. Likewise, a misbehaving subscriber could be temporarily unsubscribed without affecting others.
- **Centralized monitoring and alerts**: All MFEs sent telemetry about errors, latency, and failed API calls to a centralized monitoring system. Teams could trace which MFE, backend call, or event caused issues, enabling rapid mitigation without widespread downtime.
- **Retry policies and offline support**: MFEs also implemented retry logic for transient errors and offline-aware behavior. Mobile MFEs like OfflinePlayerMFE queued events locally when connectivity was lost, replaying them once the network returned.

Conclusion

In this chapter, we explored the many ways MFEs can be implemented, from foundational module systems to modern mechanisms like Web Components, Module Federation, siteless UI, and native app integration. Each approach comes with trade-offs in complexity, performance, and developer autonomy, but together they demonstrate the remarkable flexibility of the MFE paradigm. By considering composition strategies, communication patterns, and error handling upfront, teams can design systems that scale both technically and organizationally while avoiding common pitfalls.

The key takeaway of this chapter is an important principle: MFEs succeed not because of any single technology, but because of the architectural discipline behind their use. Decisions around where composition happens, how isolation is enforced, and which capabilities are shared must be made intentionally and revisited as systems evolve. Teams that prioritize clear boundaries, explicit contracts, and runtime flexibility are better equipped to adapt to changing requirements, onboard new platforms, and scale ownership without accumulating hidden coupling. In this sense, MFEs are less about splitting the UI and more about designing systems that enable sustainable, long-term collaboration.

Yet, implementation is only one side of the coin. A collection of independently deployed MFEs must still work together as a seamless product. This is where communication and interoperability become critical. How does state flow across MFEs? How can events trigger coordinate changes without tight coupling? How do shared dependencies and routing strategies maintain consistency without blocking independent evolution? These are the questions the next chapter will explore. By mastering communication, teams move from building isolated fragments to delivering a unified and coherent user experience.

CHAPTER 6
Communication and Interoperability

Introduction

This chapter explores the essential techniques that enable effective communication across MFEs. While they are designed to be autonomous, they must still collaborate to create a seamless and consistent user experience. Achieving this balance requires well-defined patterns for sharing data, broadcasting events, managing dependencies, and coordinating navigation.

We begin with state management, examining how local and shared state can be handled across MFEs. Several popular libraries, including Redux and Recoil, will be discussed to show how they provide robust solutions for synchronizing application state. Next, we will discuss event messaging, which allows MFEs to communicate dynamically through patterns such as publish–subscribe, custom events, and the Broadcast Channel API. Event-driven communication preserves modularity while enabling modules to react to changes in real time.

The chapter also explores shared dependencies, which serve as a communication bridge and provide a common ground for MFEs to interact efficiently. Here, we will see how shared libraries, ranging from contexts for language or currency to business logic utilities, help maintain consistency across otherwise independent modules. Finally, we cover routing strategies, focusing on how navigation can be coordinated across MFEs. Special attention will be given to shared routing configurations and how URL state can be used to synchronize behavior between different parts of the application. Together, these techniques form the backbone of communication and interoperability in an MFE architecture. By understanding their strengths, limitations, and best-use scenarios, teams can design systems that remain loosely coupled at the implementation level while delivering a unified experience for end users.

Structure

The chapter covers the following topics:

- State management
- Event messaging
- Shared dependencies

- Routing
- Case study on SkyTravel

Objectives

The objective of this chapter is to explore how independently developed MFEs can communicate and interoperate to deliver a seamless user experience. While MFEs provide autonomy and flexibility, they must still coordinate to share state, propagate events, align on global settings, and enable consistent navigation. This chapter examines the key patterns that make such collaboration possible, which include state management, event messaging, shared dependencies, and routing, thereby highlighting both their benefits and trade-offs. Through practical examples and a case study, you will gain a clear understanding of how these techniques can be combined to balance independence with cohesion in an MFE ecosystem.

State management

In any application, state represents the data that determines how the UI should look and behave at a given moment. Things like whether a user is logged in, what items are in their shopping cart, or which tab is currently active. Without a state, applications would be static pages with no sense of continuity.

Maintaining state is essential because it ensures consistency, predictability, and personalization across user interactions. Whether a customer resumes browsing after adding products to their cart or a dashboard reflects the latest data without a page reload, state management enables a seamless flow. In modern web applications, especially those with multiple MFEs, handling state effectively becomes the backbone of a smooth and unified user experience.

Unidirectional vs. bidirectional state flow

In any modern application, the way data moves between components determines how predictable and maintainable the UI is. In large applications, especially those built with MFEs, choosing the right data flow pattern is crucial to avoid unintended side effects and hidden dependencies.

Data flow defines not just how state is read or written, but also how changes propagate through the system and how developers reason about those changes. There are mainly two ways data can flow in the modern web application, unidirectional or bidirectional; both have their own pros and cons, which we discuss in the following sections.

Unidirectional flow

Unidirectional flow refers to a design where data moves in a single direction, typically from a parent or host component down to its children, and any updates are sent back through clearly defined events or actions. This approach ensures that the source of truth is centralized, making it easier to trace how state changes affect the UI. By enforcing a single direction of data movement, unidirectional flow reduces the risk of unexpected side effects that can occur when multiple components independently mutate shared state. It also simplifies testing and debugging, since developers can follow a clear path of how data travels through the system, from the origin to the affected components. In distributed architectures like MFEs, this predictability becomes even more important because each module is developed, deployed, and potentially updated independently. Maintaining a consistent flow of data across these boundaries prevents tightly coupled modules and reduces the chances of one MFE inadvertently breaking another.

Another advantage of unidirectional flow is that it encourages explicit contracts between components. Each child component only receives what it needs through either **properties** (**props**) or input parameters and communicates changes via defined callbacks or events.

Note: **React coined the term "props" to emphasize read-only inputs, reinforcing unidirectional flow and functional purity.**

This makes each component's behavior transparent and reduces hidden dependencies, which is particularly important in large applications with multiple teams working on separate MFEs. Moreover, unidirectional flow aligns well with concepts like time-travel debugging and state snapshots in libraries such as Redux, where the entire application state can be captured, inspected, and replayed to understand exactly how the system arrived at its current state. This is depicted in *Figure 6.1*:

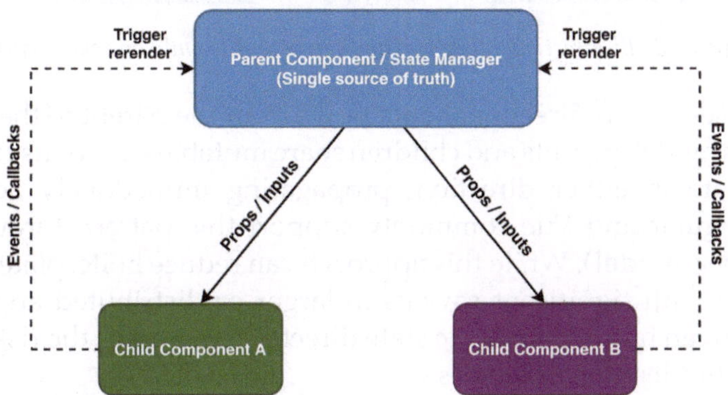

***Figure 6.1:** Unidirectional flow where the data flows from parent to child*

In *Figure 6.1*, we can see how unidirectional data flows from the parent to the child components. In this model, the Parent Component or State Manager acts as the single source of truth. Data flows downward into child components via props or input parameters. When children need to communicate changes, they send events or callbacks upward. The parent then processes these updates, modifies its state, and may trigger a re-render so that the new data flows back down to the children. This cycle keeps the data flow predictable and traceable. The pattern applies equally well in React, Angular, Vue, or any component-based framework.

Bidirectional flow

Bidirectional flow is a design pattern in which components can both consume and directly modify shared state. Unlike unidirectional flow, where data moves predictably from a single source of truth, bidirectional flow allows the state to be updated from multiple points in the component hierarchy. This can simplify certain interactions because components do not need to explicitly emit events or callbacks to a parent, in which the updates propagate automatically to all consumers of the shared state.

For example, consider a settings panel in an application with multiple UI components that depend on the same user preferences. When a user toggles a dark mode option, bidirectional flow allows the settings component to update the shared state directly, causing all other components reading that state to reflect the change immediately. A practical showcase of bi-directional flow is explained in *Figure 6.2*:

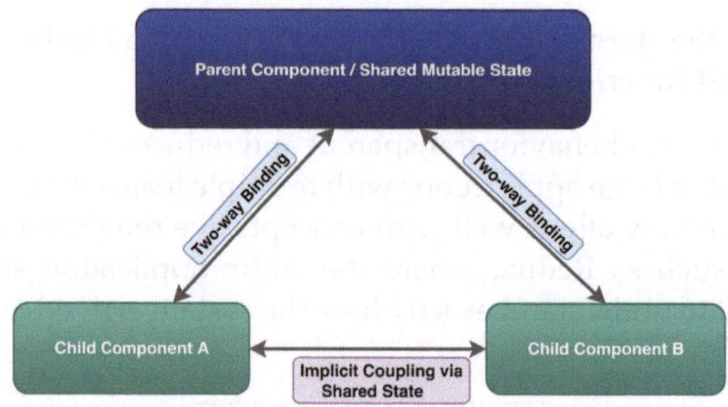

Figure 6.2: Bi-directional flow of data from parent to child and vice versa

In *Figure 6.2*, we can see how bidirectional data flows from the parent to the child components and vice versa. In this model, parents and children share mutable state or use two-way bindings. Changes can originate in either direction, propagating immediately across components. Frameworks like Angular and Vue commonly support this pattern through two-way data binding (ngModel or v-model). While this approach can reduce boilerplate and simplify local UI updates, it comes with significant caveats in larger or distributed applications. Because multiple components can modify the same state directly, it increases the risk of tight coupling, race conditions, and hidden dependencies.

In component-based architectures, bidirectional flow is often best reserved for local or internal state within a single module. When multiple modules or teams are involved, such as in an MFE setup, unidirectional flow is generally preferred to maintain clarity and predictability. If bidirectional updates are necessary across modules, careful design with immutable updates, centralized stores, or event-driven architectures can help mitigate risks.

Managing state across SPA, MPA, and ISG models

State management strategies vary significantly depending on the rendering model of the application. In a **single page application** (**SPA**), the entire UI runs in a single JavaScript runtime, allowing state to be shared easily across components. Centralized stores such as Redux, Zustand, or MobX are commonly used to maintain a single source of truth. This makes unidirectional data flow simple to enforce and predictable. However, SPAs also introduce challenges such as managing long-lived client-side state, persisting data across route changes, and avoiding tightly coupled modules, especially in large applications or MFE architectures.

In contrast, **multi-page applications** (**MPAs**) reload the page for each route, meaning that state typically exists only per page unless explicitly persisted. While local component state is sufficient for short-lived interactions, maintaining continuity across pages requires server-side sessions, query parameters, or client-side storage mechanisms like cookies or local storage. This is because the client-side runtime is reset on each page load, unidirectional state patterns are harder to maintain globally, and careful design is required to avoid inconsistencies when data must be shared across pages.

Incremental Static Generation (**ISG**), or static rendering strategies, deliver pre-rendered HTML that may be generated at build time or on demand. Client-side state only becomes relevant after hydration, when the static content is *activated* with JavaScript. Post-hydration, local component state or lightweight client-side stores can manage interactions, while server-driven state can be embedded in initial props. To address data freshness, ISG is often paired with **Incremental Static Regeneration** (**ISR**), which allows statically generated pages to be revalidated and regenerated in the background. This enables applications to serve fast, cached content while gradually reflecting updated server state without requiring a full rebuild. The main challenge in ISG is synchronizing dynamic client-side interactions with the statically generated content, ensuring that updates are predictable and consistent. *Figure 6.3* shows each of these state flow techniques:

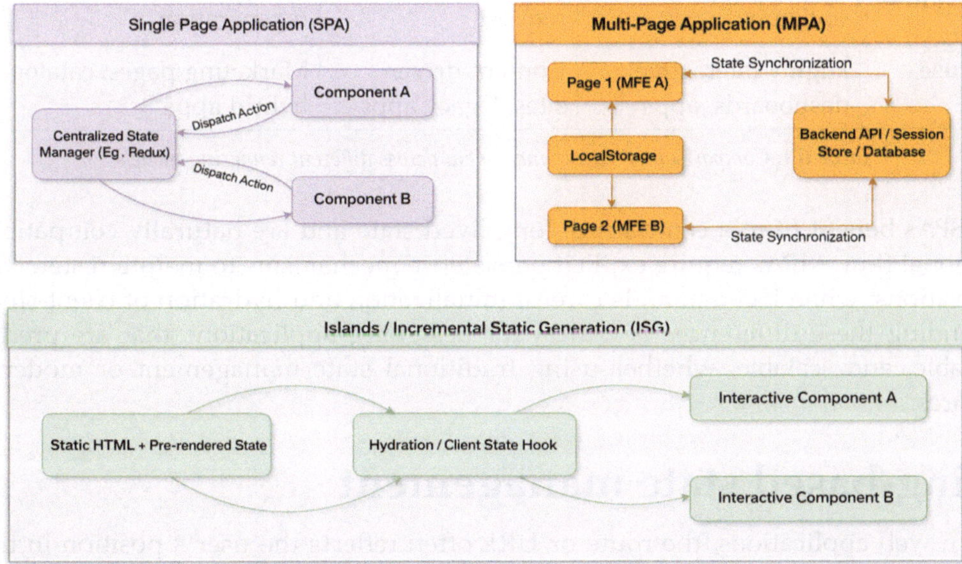

***Figure 6.3:** State flow in SPA vs. MPA vs. ISG*

Figure 6.3 illustrates how data or state is managed in SPA, MPA, and ISG. In SPA, A centralized state manager coordinates all components, making the state predictable across the single-page runtime. Whereas in MPA, each page (or MFE) reloads independently, so shared state is managed via the backend rather than in-browser. At last, in ISG, pages start with a static, pre-rendered state. Interactivity is added later as components *hydrate* and attach their own client-side state.

The following table lists the comparison of state management across rendering models:

Aspect	SPA	MPA	ISG/ISR
Rendering model	Client-side rendering after initial load	Server-rendered HTML per page	Pre-rendered static HTML (build time or on demand)
Page navigation	Client-side routing, no full reload	Full page reload on navigation	Static page load, then hydration
State lifetime	Long-lived in browser memory	Short-lived, reset on navigation	Snapshot at generation time, client state after hydration
State store	Client(stores, component state)	Server or browser storage	Server snapshot + client post-hydration state
Hydration Required	Yes (initial load)	No	Yes
Sharing state across pages	Easy via global stores	Requires backend or storage	Via URL, embedded props, or APIs
Data freshness	Real-time via client updates	Always fresh per request	Managed via ISR or regeneration
Typical use cases	Highly interactive dashboards, apps	Content-driven sites, legacy apps	Marketing pages, catalogs, hybrid apps

***Table 6.1**: Comparison of state management across different rendering models*

Overall, SPAs benefit from a centralized, long-lived state and are naturally compatible with unidirectional flow. MPAs require explicit persistence mechanisms to maintain state between page transitions, while ISG demands careful initialization and hydration of client-side state. Understanding these differences is critical for designing applications that are predictable, maintainable, and scalable, whether using traditional state management or modern MFE architectures.

Routing-based state management

In modern web applications, the route or URL often reflects the user's position in the app, selected filters, or current context. Treating routes as part of the application state ensures that the UI is consistent with navigation, and that state can be restored simply by revisiting a URL.

For example, in a product catalog, the current category, search query, and page number can all be encoded in the URL. This approach enables features like deep linking, browser back or forward support, and bookmarking.

Routing-based state management is particularly useful in SPAs, where the URL does not automatically cause a page to reload. By keeping the route synchronized with the application state, developers can implement unidirectional flow: changes to the route trigger updates to the state, which then update the relevant components. Conversely, changes in the state that should reflect navigation (like selecting a new filter) can update the URL programmatically, keeping the two in sync. Libraries like React Router, Vue Router, or Angular Router facilitate this pattern, allowing developers to push state into query parameters, path segments, or even the hash fragment.

In MPAs, routing is naturally coupled with page loads, so the route inherently determines the page state. However, additional client-side routing state may still be needed for dynamic elements within a page. In ISG or static-generated apps, routing-based state management is crucial after hydration: the initial static page must be augmented with dynamic state, often derived from query parameters or path variables, to enable interactivity without reloading the page.

Routing-based state management can also be combined with centralized or unidirectional state stores, especially in complex SPAs or MFE architectures. The route acts as a single source of truth for navigation-related state, and all components can derive their state from it. This helps avoid inconsistencies where some components reflect outdated filters or contexts while others have updated data. The following is a code sample showing the state management via routes:

```
// Centralized state
let state = { category: 'all' };
// Function to update state and route
function setCategory(newCategory) {
  state.category = newCategory;                    // update application state
  updateURL(newCategory);                          // reflect state in the URL
  render();                                        // update UI
}
// Function to render UI based on state
function render() {
  console.log(`Showing products for category: ${state.category}`);
}
// Simulated user action
setCategory('books'); // user selects a new category
// Browser navigation restores state from URL
```

```
onBrowserNavigation(() => {
  state.category = getCategoryFromURL();
  render();
});
```

In the above code example, the state object holds the current category and serves as the single source of truth. Whenever the state changes, the URL is updated to reflect it, enabling features like deep linking and bookmarking. Components consume this state to render their output but do not modify it directly, preserving a unidirectional data flow. When the user navigates with the browser's back or forward buttons, the application restores state from the URL, ensuring the UI remains consistent with navigation history.

Finite state machine

Modern applications often have complex state requirements. Users may interact with multiple components, perform asynchronous operations, or navigate across different views. Managing such a state with ad-hoc logic or conditional statements can quickly become fragile and unpredictable. A **Finite State Machine** (**FSM**) is a formal model that brings structure and predictability to these scenarios. At its core, an FSM models a system as a set of finite, discrete states, where the system can only occupy one state at a time. Transitions between states are triggered by events or inputs, and each transition follows explicit rules. This guarantees that at any given moment, the application behaves predictably, making debugging, testing, and reasoning about the system significantly easier.

Consider a typical scenario where a product checkout flow is in an e-commerce application. The FSM may define states such as idle, cart, processing, success, and error. When a user adds a product to the cart, the system transitions from idle to cart and triggers UI updates, such as highlighting the cart icon. Initiating checkout moves the system into a processing state. Depending on the outcome of the payment, the FSM transitions to either success or error, with corresponding actions like displaying a confirmation page or an error message. Each state defines the allowed events and permissible transitions, which eliminates ambiguity and prevents invalid operations, unlike traditional conditional logic that can become tangled in nested if statements. FSMs provide a clear and testable blueprint of application behavior.

FSMs are widely adopted in modern web development. Libraries such as XState and Robot3 allow developers to define FSMs declaratively, visualize states and transitions, and simulate workflows before implementation. In MFE architectures, FSMs are particularly valuable. Individual modules can maintain their own state machines while communicating key transitions, such as `checkoutComplete` or userLoggedIn, to the host application. This allows each MFE to remain independent while adhering to predictable state flows. FSMs can also integrate seamlessly with routing-based state management in which a state transition can trigger a route change, and conversely, route changes can trigger state transitions. This approach ensures synchronization between the UI, URL, and underlying logic, while maintaining predictable behavior.

FSMs are also ideal for managing complex UI components beyond checkout flows. For example, consider a media player where states might include stopped, playing, paused, buffering, and error. User actions like play, pause, or stop trigger transitions, while network events like **`bufferingComplete`** or **`playbackError`** also dictate state changes. Another example is a filter workflow in a product catalog, where multiple filters, sorts, and pagination controls interact. Using an FSM ensures that each filter change produces a valid, predictable state and that the UI renders consistently without conflicting or invalid combinations. The following is a code sample of FSM using a traffic light:

```
// A simple finite state machine for a traffic light
class TrafficLightFSM {
  constructor() {
    this.state = "RED"; // initial state
  }
  transition() {
    switch (this.state) {
      case "RED":
        this.state = "GREEN";
        break;
      case "GREEN":
        this.state = "YELLOW";
        break;
      case "YELLOW":
        this.state = "RED";
        break;
    }
    console.log(`Light is now: ${this.state}`);
  }
}
// Example usage
const light = new TrafficLightFSM();
light.transition(); // Light is now: GREEN
light.transition(); // Light is now: YELLOW
light.transition(); // Light is now: RED
```

This example models a traffic light as a finite state machine. The light can only be in one of three states: RED, GREEN, or YELLOW. The transition method defines the allowed paths: red | green | yellow | red. At any moment, the FSM has a well-defined state, and invalid transitions (like jumping directly from red to yellow) are not possible.

Let us also look at how we can write the same code using XState, a popular FSM library:

```
import { createMachine, interpret } from 'xstate';
// Define the machine
const trafficLightMachine = createMachine({
  id: 'trafficLight',
  initial: 'red',
  states: {
    red: { on: { NEXT: 'green' } },
    green: { on: { NEXT: 'yellow' } },
    yellow: { on: { NEXT: 'red' } }
  }
});
// Create a service to run the machine
const service = interpret(trafficLightMachine)
  .onTransition((state) => console.log(`Light is now: ${state.value}`))
  .start();
// Example usage
service.send('NEXT'); // Light is now: green
service.send('NEXT'); // Light is now: yellow
service.send('NEXT'); // Light is now: red
```

The above code sample illustrates how XState enforces explicit, predictable state transitions. It constructs the machine using the createMachine function, where the steps or actions are clearly defined. The interpret function runs the machine, and we can observe state changes with the onTransition listener. By sending events **(`service.send('NEXT')`)**, we step through the traffic light cycle. This approach ensures we have a predictable state, which makes it particularly useful in complex UIs such as multi-step forms, wizards, or workflows in MFEs where state consistency is critical.

The benefits of FSMs extend beyond clarity and predictability. They simplify testing, as each state and transition can be verified independently. They prevent invalid operations by constraining the system to allowed states, reducing bugs and unexpected behaviors. FSMs also serve as formal documentation in which the set of states, events, and transitions provides a blueprint of system behavior, improving maintainability and onboarding for new developers. Furthermore, FSMs naturally encourage unidirectional state flow where the events are emitted, the FSM transitions, and components react. Side effects such as API calls, animations, or route updates can be executed as actions during transitions, preserving a clean separation between state logic and UI rendering.

Even in simpler SPAs or static-hydrated pages, FSMs improve reliability. Components like multi-step forms, interactive dashboards, or chatbots benefit from FSMs by ensuring that every interaction follows a controlled path. In MFEs, where modules are independently deployed, FSMs provide a consistent and predictable framework for inter-module communication. By modeling state transitions explicitly, developers can reason about complex workflows, enforce valid behavior, and maintain a maintainable, scalable architecture.

MFE state management techniques

Each MFE encapsulates a feature or domain, allowing teams to work autonomously. While this approach offers scalability and flexibility, it introduces unique challenges in state management, as MFEs must maintain local state while sometimes synchronizing shared state across the application. Effective state management techniques are essential for predictable behavior, consistent UI, and smooth user experience. Here are a few techniques that can be useful:

- **Local state within MFEs**: The simplest form of state management in an MFE is through local state, where each module manages its own data independently. This works well for features that do not need to communicate with other modules, such as a product recommendation MFE maintaining its own carousel position or selected filters.

  Local state can be handled with plain JavaScript objects or classes, or by using framework-specific mechanisms like React's useState and useReducer, Vue's component data, or Angular's services. Lightweight state libraries such as Zustand or MobX are also sometimes used when components grow in complexity.

  The advantage of this approach is its strong encapsulation, where MFEs remain independent, easy to test, and low risk to the rest of the system. The downside, however, is that local state cannot naturally be shared across MFEs, and duplicate logic may emerge if several modules need to track similar information.

- **Shared state across MFEs**: When multiple MFEs need access to the same information, local state quickly becomes insufficient. In such cases, applications often adopt a shared state model, where data is lifted into a common store or context that serves as a single source of truth. This could be a Redux or Recoil store exposed as a singleton, a Vuex module, or even a dependency injected via Module Federation or **Universal Module Definition** (**UMD**) so that all MFEs reference the same instance. Shared state is particularly useful for scenarios like authentication, shopping carts, or language preferences, where consistency across MFEs is essential to the user experience.

  For instance, if a shopping cart MFE needs to update a cart icon displayed by a header MFE when an item is added to the cart. It can simply update the global cart state, which would in turn update the icon automatically without knowing which MFE triggers them.

  While this approach improves coordination and predictability by enabling unidirectional data flow, it introduces tighter coupling and requires careful governance to prevent multiple store instances or version mismatches. If overused, the shared state can make the system feel monolithic again, reducing one of the core benefits of the MFE approach.

- **Event-driven architecture:** Event-driven architectures are a common pattern in MFEs to allow decoupled communication. MFEs emit events when state changes occur, and other MFEs subscribe to these events to update themselves accordingly. For instance, when the product listing MFE emits an event after an item is added to the cart, the cart summary MFE can update its badge, and the analytics MFE can record the action. This approach preserves modularity, since MFEs do not need direct references to one another, and it works across frameworks and runtimes. The trade-off is that overusing events can lead to complexity, sometimes called *event soup*, where it becomes difficult to trace the source of changes or debug an inconsistent state. Clear event contracts and logging are therefore essential. We will revisit event messaging in a later section, where we explore its role as a broader communication pattern.

- **Routing-based state**: Using the route or URL as a source of truth is an elegant way to manage state that requires visibility across MFEs, especially in SPAs. In this model, state is encoded directly in the URL, whether as path segments (e.g., `/products/electronics`), query parameters (e.g., `/products?category=books&page=2`), or hash fragments for lighter, internal state. Each MFE can read from the URL and render itself accordingly, ensuring that all modules share a consistent context without directly depending on each other. Updates to filters, selections, or sorting can be reflected in the URL, enabling deep linking, bookmarking, and natural browser navigation to maintain the same state across MFEs. This makes the approach transparent and user-friendly. However, not all states belong in the URL. Sensitive information such as tokens must be excluded, and encoding large, complex states into query parameters can quickly become unwieldy. Routing-based state works best when applied to lightweight, serializable data that benefits from being shareable. We will revisit this in a later *Routing* section, where we explore its role as a broader communication pattern.

- **Server synchronized state (BFF/API-driven)**: For MFEs that depend on persistent or authoritative data, server-synchronized state becomes essential. In this pattern, the **backend for frontend** (**BFF**) or API acts as the source of truth, while each MFE maintains only a local cache or reactive state synchronized with the server. For example, an MFE might fetch its initial state via a REST or GraphQL call during initialization, or it might subscribe to real-time updates over WebSockets.

  Some MFEs implement optimistic updates by rendering changes immediately in the UI while awaiting server confirmation in order to keep the user experience responsive. This approach ensures consistency across distributed MFEs, supports offline caching strategies, and avoids conflicts in multi-user scenarios by centralizing updates. On the other hand, it introduces latency, increases reliance on network connectivity, and demands robust error handling and rollback mechanisms. Despite these challenges, server-synchronized state is often the most reliable option for multi-device and multi-session consistency.

Let us discuss the key takeaways. In practice, no single state management technique is sufficient for every scenario in an MFE architecture. Local state works best for isolated UI concerns, while shared state provides consistency for global contexts such as authentication or language. Event messaging enables lightweight decoupling, and routing-based state is ideal for user-facing data that should be bookmarkable or shareable. For scenarios requiring persistence or multi-device synchronization, server-synchronized state through a BFF or API is often the most reliable approach.

As a best practice, teams should begin with the simplest possible option, such as local or routing-based state for lightweight needs, and only introduce shared stores or backend synchronization when clear requirements demand them. For highly structured workflows, FSMs covered earlier in this chapter offer an additional layer of predictability. The key is to balance autonomy and cohesion, choosing the right tool for the scope of the state being managed rather than applying a one-size-fits-all solution.

Challenges of distributed state in MFEs

Managing state across multiple micro-frontends presents unique complexities that differ significantly from traditional monolithic applications. One of the primary challenges is state duplication. In a distributed system, each MFE may maintain its own local state for performance or isolation reasons, which can lead to multiple sources of truth. Duplication increases memory usage and can result in inconsistencies when different MFEs attempt to modify the same underlying data independently. For example, in a retail application, two MFEs, one displaying a product catalog and another handling a shopping cart, may each cache product availability, and if one updates its view, the other may not immediately reflect the change, causing stale or conflicting information.

Synchronization between MFEs is another critical concern. This is because each MFE can be developed and deployed independently, and ensuring that state updates propagate correctly across the system is non-trivial. Event-driven mechanisms, shared global stores, or APIs can be used to broadcast changes, but these introduce latency and complexity. Developers must carefully design how and when state updates are propagated to avoid performance bottlenecks or race conditions. Moreover, the frequency and granularity of synchronization must be balanced, where too frequent updates can overwhelm the system, while infrequent updates can result in inconsistent user experiences.

Closely tied to synchronization is the problem of stale state. Users may interact with an MFE that is temporarily out of sync with the global state or other MFEs. This can lead to actions being performed on outdated information, such as submitting a form based on old data or displaying incorrect inventory levels. Handling stale state often requires optimistic updates, version checks, or reconciliation strategies, each introducing additional development and testing overhead.

Versioning and backward compatibility present another layer of complexity. This is because MFEs are independently deployable, and state schemas and APIs may evolve at different rates.

One MFE may expect a newer data structure while another still produces an older version. Without proper versioning and compatibility checks, these mismatches can lead to runtime errors, subtle bugs, or even user-facing data corruption. Maintaining consistent contracts between MFEs, along with robust migration strategies, is essential to prevent cascading failures.

Finally, distributed state in MFEs impacts debugging and observability. Tracing the source of state-related bugs becomes more challenging when the state is fragmented across multiple independently running modules. Tools for centralized logging, monitoring, and state inspection become vital, but they can also introduce performance overhead or require additional infrastructure.

In conclusion, while MFEs offer modularity and independent deployment, distributed state management introduces significant challenges, including duplication, synchronization difficulties, stale state, versioning conflicts, and debugging complexity. Addressing these issues requires careful architectural design, clear contracts between MFEs, and thoughtful use of shared state mechanisms or event-driven communication patterns to maintain a consistent, reliable user experience.

Exploring state management libraries

While the principles of state management are framework-agnostic, in practice, developers often rely on well-established libraries to handle complexity, enforce patterns, and improve maintainability. These libraries provide ready-made solutions for problems like unidirectional data flow, distributed state synchronization, and reactive updates, saving teams from reinventing the wheel. For MFEs, choosing the right library is especially important, as it affects not only local component logic but also how multiple MFEs interoperate when sharing or synchronizing state.

In this section, we will look at a few widely used state management libraries, such as Redux, MobX, Recoil, RxJS, and Zustand, and discuss how each approaches distributed state, what trade-offs they bring, and how they can be integrated into MFE architectures. While none of these tools is universally superior, understanding their philosophies and patterns helps teams select the one that best aligns with their application's scale, complexity, and communication needs.

Redux toolkit

Redux is a predictable state container that works well for both SPA and MFE architectures. Because it uses a single global store, it can act as a central source of truth shared across MFEs. This helps mitigate duplication and stale state issues, and its explicit action-based updates make versioning and backward compatibility more manageable. However, synchronizing updates across multiple independently deployed MFEs requires careful orchestration, often via middleware or custom event bridges. The following is a code sample of how Redux is used in practice:

```
// store.js
import { configureStore, createSlice } from '@reduxjs/toolkit';
const cartSlice = createSlice({
  name: 'cart',
  initialState: { items: [] },
  reducers: {
    addItem: (state, action) => { state.items.push(action.payload); },
  },
});
export const { addItem } = cartSlice.actions;
export const store = configureStore({ reducer: { cart: cartSlice.reducer } });
```

In the above code sample, the createSlice function bundles together state, actions, and reducers for a particular feature, in this case, the cart. The reducers section defines how state changes. Here, addItem pushes a new item into the items array. While this looks like a mutation, Redux Toolkit uses Immer internally to keep state immutable.

The **`cartSlice.reducer`** is then registered with the store using **`configureStore`**. This sets up the Redux store and makes the cart slice part of the global state tree, so the resulting state shape looks like:

```
{
  cart: {
    items: []
  }
}
```

With this setup, you can dispatch actions like **`store.dispatch(addItem({ id: 1, name: 'Shoes' }))`**, and the reducer will update the state accordingly. In an MFE setup, slices like this can be registered per MFE and then combined into a shared store (via Module Federation or as a singleton dependency). This makes Redux a practical option for distributed state management across multiple teams.

Zustand

Zustand is a lightweight, hook-based state library. It is a shared in-memory state that allows multiple MFEs to synchronize without heavy boilerplate. Zustand is well-suited for distributed state scenarios where MFEs need to quickly read and update common state, though it lacks built-in tools for versioning or handling schema changes. Developers often pair it with events or custom subscriptions to ensure consistency across MFEs. Let us see a sample code:

```
import create from 'zustand';
export const useCartStore = create(set => ({
  items: [],
  addItem: (item) => set(state => ({ items: [...state.items, item] }))
}));
```

In this example, **useCartStore** is a hook that components can call directly to access or update state. For instance:

```
// CartBadge.js
import { useCartStore } from './store';
function CartBadge() {
  const { items, addItem } = useCartStore((state) => state);
  return (
    <div>
      <span>Cart: {items.length}</span>
      <button onClick={() => addItem({ id: 1, name: 'Shoes' })}>
        Add Item
      </button>
    </div>
  );
}
export default CartBadge;
```

This hook-based approach makes Zustand particularly natural in React MFEs, as state can be consumed with minimal wiring and without the need for explicit providers or reducers. Unlike Redux, Zustand does not require wrapping components in a provider. This reduces integration friction when embedding MFEs inside an app shell. Also, Components can subscribe only to slices of the state, minimizing unnecessary re-renders and improving performance in complex UIs. Zustand can also interop with Redux using its middleware, making it flexible for hybrid setups in MFEs.

Note: Zustand works perfectly fine outside React; you can use it in Vanilla JS or even in Angular/Vue MFEs if you wire it up manually.

Recoil

Recoil provides an atom-based state, enabling MFEs to subscribe only to the pieces of state they care about. This granularity reduces unnecessary re-renders and helps prevent stale state in distributed scenarios. For multiple MFEs, shared atoms can act as a lightweight distributed store, but careful design is needed to avoid versioning mismatches when state structures evolve. A sample code is as follows:

```
import { atom, useRecoilState } from 'recoil';
const cartState = atom({ key: 'cartState', default: [] });
function Cart() {
  const [cart, setCart] = useRecoilState(cartState);
  return <button onClick={() => setCart([...cart, 'item1'])}>Add Item</
button>;
}
```

Here, cartState is an atom that represents the list of cart items. The useRecoilState hook works much like React's useState, giving both the current value and a setter. When the setter is called, all components subscribed to cartState re-render with the updated value.

In Recoil, components re-render only when the specific atoms or selectors they depend on change, improving performance in large UIs, thus offering granular subscriptions. Selectors can be used to compute any complex state logic, and that derived state can be shared with other MFEs. Despite the advantages, Recoil is supported only for React-based applications.

RxJS or observables

Reactive Extensions for JavaScript (**RxJS**) is a library for working with asynchronous data streams, most commonly used in Angular but equally applicable in other frameworks. While it is often associated with event handling, RxJS can also serve as a lightweight state management layer.

A common approach is to use a **`BehaviorSubject`** to hold the current state and expose it as an observable. Components can subscribe to the observable to react to updates and use **`next()`** to push new values. The following is a sample code of RxJS:

```
import { BehaviorSubject } from 'rxjs';
const cartState = new BehaviorSubject([]);
export const cart$ = cartState.asObservable();
export function addItem(item) {
  const current = cartState.getValue();
  cartState.next([...current, item]);
}
// CartBadge.js (pseudo-code)
cart$.subscribe(items => {
  console.log('Cart items:', items.length);
});
```

This pattern works especially well in MFEs because observables are framework-agnostic. A React MFE, Angular MFE, and even vanilla JavaScript code can subscribe to the same stream and stay synchronized.

The main benefit of RxJS is its powerful operators, which allow state to be transformed, filtered, or combined with other streams in expressive ways. The trade-off, however, is complexity; RxJS comes with a steep learning curve, and teams must be disciplined about unsubscribing to prevent memory leaks. We will discuss this in detail under Event messaging.

MobX

MobX takes a different approach to state management than Redux or Recoil. Instead of enforcing immutability and strict reducers, MobX relies on observable state and reactions. In MobX, you create state objects that are made observable, and any component that consumes those observables will automatically re-render when the state changes. This makes state management feel almost effortless, in which the changes flow naturally from state to UI without explicit wiring. The following is an example of using MobX code:

```
// cartStore.js
import { makeAutoObservable } from 'mobx';
class CartStore {
  items = [];
  constructor() {
    makeAutoObservable(this);
  }
  addItem(item) {
    this.items.push(item);
  }
}
export const cartStore = new CartStore();
```

Here, cartStore is observable thanks to **makeAutoObservable**. When addItem mutates the items array, MobX automatically notifies any observer components, which re-render without needing manual subscription logic as depicted in the following code:

```
// CartBadge.js (React)
import { observer } from 'mobx-react-lite';
import { cartStore } from './cartStore';
const CartBadge = observer(() => (
  <div>
    <span>Cart: {cartStore.items.length}</span>
    <button onClick={() => cartStore.addItem({ id: 1, name: 'Shoes' })}>
      Add Item
    </button>
  </div>
));
```

MobX can be attractive because of its minimal boilerplate, where there are no reducers, no action creators, just stateful objects and methods. Also, the automatic reactivity ensures that the components stay in sync with state changes without manual subscriptions. As it allows direct mutation of state, debugging flows in large, distributed teams can be harder compared to strict unidirectional stores like Redux. In MFE systems where multiple teams collaborate, careful conventions are needed to prevent unexpected side effects.

Event messaging

While state management provides a structured way to share data and maintain consistency across MFEs, there are scenarios where a more dynamic, lightweight communication channel is necessary. This is where event messaging plays a crucial role. Event messaging is a design pattern where different parts of an application communicate by sending and listening for events. Instead of invoking each other directly, components broadcast a message (*an event*) and let others decide whether to react. This principle is not unique to MFEs. It is widely used in operating systems, desktop applications, and even hardware systems. For example, when you press a key on your keyboard, the operating system broadcasts a *keypress* event, and whichever program is active can respond.

Event-driven communication enables components or modules to signal changes, notify other modules, or trigger workflows without requiring direct dependencies or centralized state. By adopting messaging patterns, developers can enhance modularity and preserve the independence of modules while still allowing them to respond to user interactions and system-level events. In this section, we will explore practical event messaging techniques such as the **Publish-Subscribe** (**Pub-Sub**) pattern, custom DOM events, the Broadcast Channel API, and other mechanisms that allow MFEs to interact fluidly within the browser environment. Each of these approaches comes with trade-offs in terms of performance, scalability, and ease of debugging, which we will evaluate in detail.

Pub-Sub pattern

One of the most widely used event messaging strategies is the Pub-Sub pattern. In this model, a component publishes an event to a central event bus, and any number of subscribers can listen to that event and react accordingly. In a chat application, when a new message arrives, the message service publishes an event. The UI component subscribes to render the message, while the notification component subscribes to show an alert; neither knows about the other.

The Pub-Sub pattern is widely used in MFEs, where one MFE can publish the event for others to listen to and react. For instance, as described in *Figure 6.4*, the CartMFE publishes a CART_UPDATED event. Both HeaderMFE (to update the cart badge) and RecommendationMFE (to suggest products) subscribe:

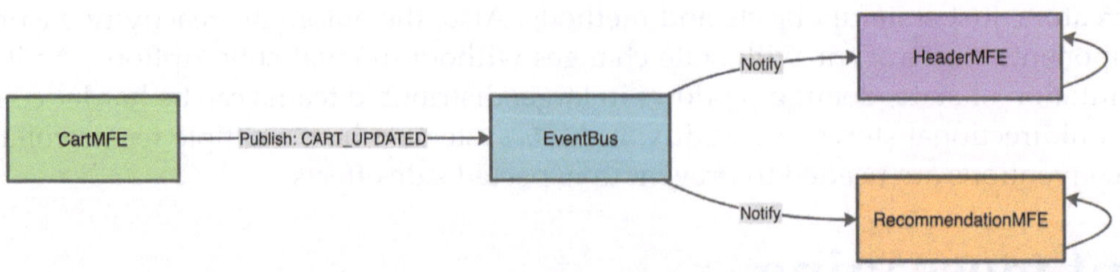

Figure 6.4: Example of Pub-Sub pattern

The key advantage of Pub-Sub is that publishers and subscribers are completely decoupled. The component emitting the event does not need to know who is listening. This reduces dependencies and fosters modularity. However, Pub-Sub systems require a shared event bus, which itself becomes a dependency that needs to be carefully versioned and distributed across MFEs. Additionally, if events are not documented or standardized, it can become difficult to trace which module is listening to what, potentially leading to debugging complexity in larger applications.

Custom DOM Events

Browsers natively support Custom Events via the CustomEvent API. Developers can dispatch and listen for events directly on the DOM, making this a simple and lightweight approach. A simple example is when a video player dispatches a *video:paused* event whenever playback stops. Any component in the page, like analytics or UI overlays, can listen and react.

The DOM has long supported event-driven programming, and MFEs can leverage this feature without introducing additional libraries. An MFE can dispatch a custom event using the CustomEvent constructor, attaching any necessary payload, and other MFEs can simply listen for that event on the window or a shared DOM element.

For instance, the LoginMFE might dispatch a user:loggedin event as shown in the following:

```
const event = new CustomEvent("user:loggedin", { detail: { userId: 123 } });
window.dispatchEvent(event);
```

A ProfileMFE listening for that event could respond like this:

```
window.addEventListener("user:loggedin", (e) => {
  console.log("User logged in:", e.detail.userId);
});
```

The advantage of this approach is that it is simple, lightweight, and built into the platform. Developers do not need external dependencies, and the pattern fits naturally with the web's existing event system. On the other hand, broadcasting everything via the DOM can become messy in very large applications. Event names must be carefully managed to avoid collisions, and the global scope can lead to unintended side effects if multiple MFEs emit events with similar names.

Broadcast Channel API

The Broadcast Channel API is designed for cross-context communication in browsers. It allows different tabs, windows, iframes, or workers to exchange messages through a shared channel. Imagine you open a news site in two tabs. If you log out in one tab, the logout event is broadcast through the channel, so the other tab also logs you out automatically, as explained in the following code:

```
// Tab 1 (Publisher)
const channel = new BroadcastChannel("news");
channel.postMessage({ type: "logout" });

// Tab 2 (Listener)
const channel = new BroadcastChannel("news");
channel.onmessage = (event) => {
  if (event.data.type === "logout") {
    console.log("User logged out in another tab, clearing session here too.");
  }
};
```

This would be ideal in an MFE context, especially when MFEs are running in different execution contexts, such as across iframes, web workers, or different browser tabs. Broadcast channels allow different browsing contexts to exchange messages in real time, enabling MFEs that are sandboxed from each other to still share events. Imagine a scenario where a ChatMFE runs in one iframe and a NotificationMFE runs in another. Using a broadcast channel, when a new message arrives, the ChatMFE can notify the NotificationMFE instantly without requiring server polling. Similarly, a ThemeSwitcher MFE can broadcast a change event, ensuring that multiple MFEs running in separate frames or tabs update their styling consistently.

The Broadcast Channel API is extremely useful for cross-context communication, but it is limited to contexts running within the same origin. It also introduces potential performance issues if not throttled properly, as too many broadcast events may flood communication channels.

Note: Though the Broadcast Channel API looks fascinating, this is not a go-to solution for many common use cases and should be used only if the use case strictly needs cross-context communication.

Eventing in frameworks

Beyond these approaches, developers often combine event emitters or message buses with framework-level solutions. For example, in React, a lightweight event emitter library can be paired with context providers, giving MFEs an isolated yet flexible messaging channel. In Angular, RxJS subjects are commonly used to implement event streams, where observables serve as channels that multiple MFEs can subscribe to. These patterns make use of ecosystem-specific tools but still follow the same principle:

- Emit an event
- Allow interested parties to react
- Avoid hard dependencies

This flexibility makes event messaging particularly appealing in polyglot MFE architectures, where different MFEs may be written in different frameworks but can still exchange events using platform-native APIs or lightweight adapters.

Event messaging in Angular with a shared service

Angular applications naturally lend themselves to event-driven communication because the framework is tightly integrated with RxJS, a powerful library for managing asynchronous streams of data. Instead of building a custom event emitter from scratch, Angular developers typically use services with RxJS Subjects to act as lightweight event buses. This approach makes it easy for one component to emit events and for other components to subscribe, without creating direct dependencies between them.

In the following example, we create a very simple event bus service using Subject. A publisher component (**CartButton**) emits an event whenever the user adds an item to the cart. A subscriber component (**CartBadge**) listens for this event and updates its own display accordingly. This demonstrates how event messaging keeps components decoupled: the button does not need to know about the badge, and the badge does not need to know about the button. Both communicate indirectly through the shared service, making the system more modular and maintainable. The following is a simple event bus service for communication across components:

```
// event-bus.service.ts
import { Injectable } from '@angular/core';
import { Subject } from 'rxjs';
@Injectable()
export class EventBusService {
  private eventSubject = new Subject<any>();
  events$ = this.eventSubject.asObservable();
  emit(event: any) {
```

```
    this.eventSubject.next(event);
  }
}
```

It acts as the central event bus, like a **mailbox** where messages (events) can be sent and received. We use RxJS Subject, which is both an observable (others can listen) and an observer (we can push values into it). **emit(event)** pushes a new event into the subject, whereas **events$** is the observable stream that other parts of the app can subscribe to. Let us explore the cart button component, which acts as a publisher in this case:

```
// cart-button.component.ts
import { Component } from '@angular/core';
import { EventBusService } from './event-bus.service';
@Component({
  selector: 'app-cart-button',
  template: `<button (click)="addToCart()">Add to Cart</button>`
})
export class CartButtonComponent {
  constructor(private bus: EventBusService) {}
  addToCart() {
    this.bus.emit({ name: 'cart:add', item: { id: 1, qty: 2 } });
  }
}
```

It publishes the message whenever the user clicks **Add to Cart**. The **addToCart()** method calls bus.emit and sends an event object with name **cart:add** and payload. Notice that the button does not know who will use this event; it just broadcasts it. The following code is the subscriber counterpart that received the published message:

```
// cart-badge.component.ts
import { Component } from '@angular/core';
import { EventBusService } from './event-bus.service';
@Component({
  selector: 'app-cart-badge',
  template: `{{ count }}`
})
export class CartBadgeComponent {
  count = 0;
  constructor(bus: EventBusService) {
    bus.events$.subscribe(event => {
      if (event.name === 'cart:add') {
```

```
          this.count++;
        }
      });
    }
  }
```

The above code shows a typical subscriber. It listens to all events coming through the event bus. Inside the constructor, it subscribes to **bus.events$**. Whenever an event with the name cart:add arrives, it increases the local counter. The counter is then displayed in the template ({{ count }}).

Event messaging in React with a custom event emitter

React developers often use libraries like mitt, eventemitter3, or even RxJS to build event-driven architectures. These libraries provide lightweight and reliable event emitter utilities that can be easily integrated across components or even across MFEs. However, to truly understand how event emitters work, it is useful to build one from scratch. The following example demonstrates a simple custom event emitter, wrapped in React Context so it can be shared across multiple components or MFEs. This approach keeps publishers and subscribers decoupled while showing how React's hooks and context system naturally support event-driven communication.

The following is the custom event emitter:

```
// eventBus.js
export function createEventBus() {
  const listeners = {};
  return {
    on(event, callback) {
      if (!listeners[event]) listeners[event] = [];
      listeners[event].push(callback);
    },
    off(event, callback) {
      if (!listeners[event]) return;
      listeners[event] = listeners[event].filter(cb => cb !== callback);
    },
    emit(event, data) {
      if (!listeners[event]) return;
      listeners[event].forEach(cb => cb(data));
    }
  };
}
```

This file defines the core of our event bus. The **createEventBus** function returns an object with three methods: **on**, **off**, and **emit**. The on method registers a new callback for a given event name, ensuring that multiple subscribers can listen to the same event. The off method removes a previously registered callback, which is important for cleanup and avoiding memory leaks. The emit method takes an event name and optional data, then notifies all registered listeners for that event. Internally, the bus maintains a listeners object, where each event name maps to an array of subscribed callbacks. This is a minimal but complete event emitter implementation, and it forms the foundation for communication across React components:

```
// EventBusContext.js
import React, { createContext, useContext, useMemo } from "react";
import { createEventBus } from "./eventBus";
const EventBusContext = createContext(null);
export const EventBusProvider = ({ children }) => {
  const bus = useMemo(() => createEventBus(), []);
  return (
    <EventBusContext.Provider value={bus}>
      {children}
    </EventBusContext.Provider>
  );
};
export const useEventBus = () => {
  const bus = useContext(EventBusContext);
  if (!bus) throw new Error("useEventBus must be used inside EventBusProvider");
  return bus;
};
```

Here, the event bus is wrapped in React Context so it can be accessed anywhere in the component tree. The **EventBusProvider** creates a single instance of the event bus using useMemo, ensuring that all child components share the same emitter. This instance is passed down through context, and any component inside the provider can retrieve it. The **useEventBus** hook provides a convenient way for components to access the event bus. If a component tries to use it outside of the provider, an error is thrown, making the usage explicit and safe. This pattern is idiomatic React: it uses **Context** for dependency injection and hooks for ease of access:

```
// CartButton.js
import { useEventBus } from "./EventBusContext";
export default function CartButton() {
  const bus = useEventBus();
  const addToCart = () => {
```

```
    bus.emit("cart:add", { id: 1, qty: 2 });
  };
  return <button onClick={addToCart}>Add to Cart</button>;
}
```

The code above illustrates a simple **event publisher** implemented as a button component. When the user clicks **Add to Cart**, the component emits a **`cart:add`** event through a shared event bus, passing the item details as the event payload. The component itself does not manage cart state or know which part of the application will handle the event; it simply publishes an intent.

This is because the interaction is expressed as an event rather than a direct function call. This component can be reused anywhere in the application where an *Add to Cart* action is required, as shown in the above code example. Any MFE or component interested in cart updates can subscribe to the **`cart:add`** event and react accordingly. This approach promotes loose coupling and makes the component portable across different parts of the application. Let us now see how another component can consume this event:

```
// CartBadge.js
import { useEffect, useState } from "react";
import { useEventBus } from "./EventBusContext";
export default function CartBadge() {
  const [count, setCount] = useState(0);
  const bus = useEventBus();
  useEffect(() => {
    const handler = () => setCount(c => c + 1);
    bus.on("cart:add", handler);
    return () => bus.off("cart:add", handler);
  }, [bus]);
  return <span>Cart {count}</span>;
}
```

Beyond browser scope

Event messaging is not confined to the browser. In distributed systems, it often extends to the backend, where the server acts as a message broker. In this model, MFEs emit events that are sent to a backend via APIs or WebSockets. The backend then redistributes those events to other MFEs, services, or even external systems. This is especially useful when MFEs are deployed across different domains or platforms, where direct client-to-client communication is not possible due to security restrictions.

A common example is real-time analytics, as shown in *Figure 6.5*. An analytics MFE might capture every user action, such as page views, clicks, form submissions, and forward these events to the server immediately. The backend aggregates this data, processes it, and forwards relevant updates to other MFEs, such as a dashboard that displays live statistics or a notification panel that alerts users to important changes.

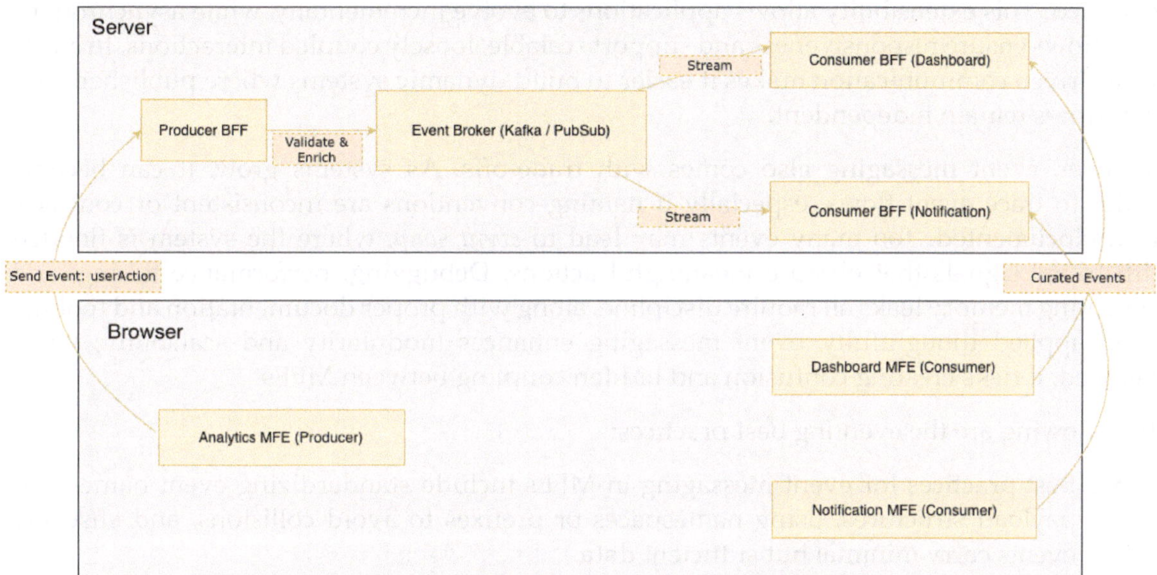

***Figure 6.5**: Real-time analytics example using event emitters*

To implement this at scale, organizations often use event streaming platforms such as Apache Kafka, RabbitMQ, or NATS. These tools allow the backend to function as a highly reliable and distributed message broker. For instance, an MFE can publish a user:purchaseCompleted event to the backend, which pushes it into a Kafka topic. From there, multiple subscribers, such as a recommendation MFE, an order history MFE, and even external billing systems, can consume the event asynchronously. This decouples the event producer (the frontend) from all consumers, enabling systems to scale independently. In an ideal scenario, there can be a BFF layer (Refer to section *Implementation patterns* in *Chapter 5, Implementation Strategies*) in the middle, which can facade the logic of the streaming system used behind, and MFEs do not need to know about Kafka topics, message schemas, or service-level routing. They simply talk to a familiar API.

Server-assisted coordination is also increasingly popular in microfrontend and microservices ecosystems. The backend does not just serve as a message broker but also as a contract enforcer, ensuring that only valid events are accepted and that consumers receive events in the correct format. Cloud providers offer managed services like AWS Kinesis, Google Pub-Sub, or Azure Event Grid, which can simplify event distribution at a global scale, though they lock teams into vendor ecosystems.

Benefits and tradeoffs

The biggest strength of event messaging lies in decoupling. MFEs can communicate without knowing each other's internal details, preserving modularity and independence. Events also bring flexibility, since they can be selectively consumed, ignored, or extended as new MFEs are added. This extensibility allows applications to evolve incrementally, while asynchronous event flows ensure responsiveness and support scalable, loosely coupled interactions. In short, event-driven communication makes it easier to build dynamic systems where publishers and subscribers remain independent.

However, event messaging also comes with trade-offs. As systems grow, it can become harder to trace event flows, especially if naming conventions are inconsistent or contracts are undocumented. Too many events may lead to *event soup*, where the system is flooded with trivial signals that obscure meaningful actions. Debugging, performance tuning, and preventing memory leaks all require discipline, along with proper documentation and tooling. When applied thoughtfully, event messaging enhances modularity and scalability; when overused, it risks creating confusion and hidden coupling between MFEs.

The following are the eventing best practices:

- Best practices for event messaging in MFEs include standardizing event names and payload structures, using namespaces or prefixes to avoid collisions, and ensuring events carry minimal but sufficient data.
- Events should represent meaningful actions (user:loggedIn, cart:itemAdded) rather than low-level state changes, making them easier to understand and reuse.
- Developers should also prefer unidirectional flows wherever possible, with clear event producers and consumers, instead of circular dependencies where modules trigger each other in loops.
- Finally, events should complement state management and should not replace it. For data that must be consistently shared, a global store may still be preferable; events should focus on notifications, triggers, and side effects.

Shared dependencies

Shared dependencies are not only about reducing bundle size by avoiding multiple copies of the same library; they also serve as a communication bridge between MFEs. When multiple MFEs coexist on the same page, it is common for them to rely on some shared concepts, such as language, theme, user identity, or feature flags that need to remain consistent across the entire application. A change initiated in one MFE often needs to propagate seamlessly to others. Shared dependencies provide a way to establish this common ground, ensuring all MFEs can interact efficiently and cohesively.

Consider a practical scenario where several MFEs are displayed on the same page, and the user changes the language preference in one of them. If MFE A updates its language selector, this change must immediately affect the UI of MFE B, MFE C, and so on. One way to achieve this is through eventing (as described in the previous section), where the app shell listens for the change in MFE A and triggers a global state update that impacts the other MFEs. While this is valid, it can become harder to trace as the system grows. A more direct approach is to use a shared dependency. For example, a React Context or a small library that holds the language state as a singleton. If this shared context is injected into the app shell (perhaps as a UMD module or a federated singleton), then updating the context in one MFE automatically reflects across all other MFEs that consume it.

Note: A shared context remains a true singleton only when it is provided by the App Shell. For example, injected as a UMD script or configured as a shared dependency through Module Federation. If the same context is distributed as an npm package and imported separately by each MFE, each one will end up with its own copy, breaking the singleton behavior.

The following code is an example of how language change can be propagated to other MFEs:

```
// LanguageContext.js
import React, { createContext, useContext, useState } from "react";
// Create context
const LanguageContext = createContext();
// Provider that holds global language state
export function LanguageProvider({ children }) {
  const [language, setLanguage] = useState("en");
  return (
    <LanguageContext.Provider value={{ language, setLanguage }}>
      {children}
    </LanguageContext.Provider>
  );
}
// Hook for consumers
export function useLanguage() {
  return useContext(LanguageContext);
}
```

This file defines a shared **`LanguageContext`**. It exposes a provider, which maintains the current language, and a hook, which any MFE can use to access or update the language. The key idea is that this file is distributed as a shared library (UMD bundle, or via Module Federation as a singleton). All MFEs import it from the same source, ensuring there is only one context instance in the page:

```
// MFE A - Language Selector
import { useLanguage } from "languageContext";
export default function LanguageSelector() {
  const { language, setLanguage } = useLanguage();
  return (
    <select value={language} onChange={e => setLanguage(e.target.value)}>
      <option value="en">English</option>
      <option value="fr">French</option>
      <option value="de">German</option>
    </select>
  );
}
```

Here, an MFE provides the user with a dropdown to change the application language. When the user selects a new language, it updates the shared context:

```
//MFE B - Greeting Component
import { useLanguage } from "languageContext";
export default function Greeting() {
  const { language } = useLanguage();
  const messages = {
    en: "Hello",
    fr: "Bonjour",
    de: "Hallo"
  };
  return <h1>{messages[language]}</h1>;
}
```

In MFE B, the greeting automatically updates whenever the shared language context changes. No events or external wiring are required; both MFEs simply consume the same shared dependency:

```
// App Shell
import { LanguageProvider } from "languageContext";
import LanguageSelector from "MFE_A/LanguageSelector";
import Greeting from "MFE_B/Greeting";
export default function App() {
  return (
    <LanguageProvider>
      <LanguageSelector />
```

```
      <Greeting />
    </LanguageProvider>
  );
}
```

Finally, the App Shell hosts the MFEs and wraps them with the shared **LanguageProvider**. This ensures all MFEs read and write to the same language state.

The shared context pattern works well because it provides a single source of truth for cross-cutting concerns like language, theme, or authentication. It is not limited to React. Angular can achieve the same with a shared service, and Vue with a global store. The core idea is that the shared dependency acts as a neutral, framework-agnostic bridge. However, this approach comes with trade-offs: it introduces tighter coupling between MFEs, because they now depend on the shared library's version and contract. Careful governance, semantic versioning, and documentation are required to ensure stability when multiple teams contribute to or consume the same dependency.

In practice, many organizations adopt a hybrid model: lightweight, decoupled communication for feature-specific interactions via events, and shared dependencies for global concerns that must remain consistent across the entire application. By drawing this line carefully, teams can achieve both independence and cohesion, allowing MFEs to evolve autonomously while still presenting a unified user experience. While shared dependencies provide a powerful way to coordinate MFEs, they must be managed carefully. Version mismatches can lead to duplicate runtimes and subtle bugs, making alignment critical and often requiring tools like Module Federation to enforce singletons.

It is also important to remember that shared dependencies go beyond UI libraries; they often include domain logic, API clients, and even type definitions to ensure consistency across the system. This is because these libraries are widely used; they demand clear ownership and governance so that updates are well-coordinated and breaking changes are avoided. Finally, since a single vulnerability can affect all MFEs consuming a shared dependency, regular audits and timely patching are essential. When governed properly, shared dependencies become more than just a convenience; they form the backbone of cohesion in a micro-frontend ecosystem.

Routing

Routing determines how users navigate through an application, shaping both the user experience and the developer experience. In a monolithic SPA, a single router typically controls all navigation, mapping URLs to components or views. This works well when the entire application is developed as one unit. In an MFE architecture, the situation becomes more complex. This is because the application is composed of multiple independently developed and deployed modules; routing must not only ensure seamless navigation for users but also respect the autonomy of each MFE.

The challenge lies in balancing independence and coordination. On one hand, each MFE may want to define its own routes internally, allowing its developers to work without worrying about the structure of other parts of the application. On the other hand, the application as a whole must present a unified navigation system to the user. For example, navigating to `/checkout` should always render the checkout MFE, regardless of which page the user was previously on, while a nested route like `/checkout/shipping` should be controlled by the checkout MFE itself. This means routing in MFEs often involves layering: some routes are controlled globally by an app shell, while others are handled internally by individual MFEs.

App shell routing

One common approach is App shell routing, where the shell owns the global router and decides which MFE to mount for a given route. For example, the shell might map /products to the product MFE, `/cart` to the cart MFE, and `/checkout` to the checkout MFE. Once the shell mounts an MFE, that MFE can manage its own internal navigation. This model gives the shell full control over the high-level structure of the application while allowing MFEs to remain responsible for their own sub-routes. App shell routing is often paired with technologies like Webpack Module Federation or iframe-based integration, where the shell determines which code to load based on the route. The benefit of this model is consistency: the shell ensures that global navigation behaves predictably. The drawback is that MFEs are somewhat constrained; they must register their routes with the shell, which introduces a level of coordination.

Figure 6.6 illustrates how respective MFEs can be mounted on a SPA based on a specific route:

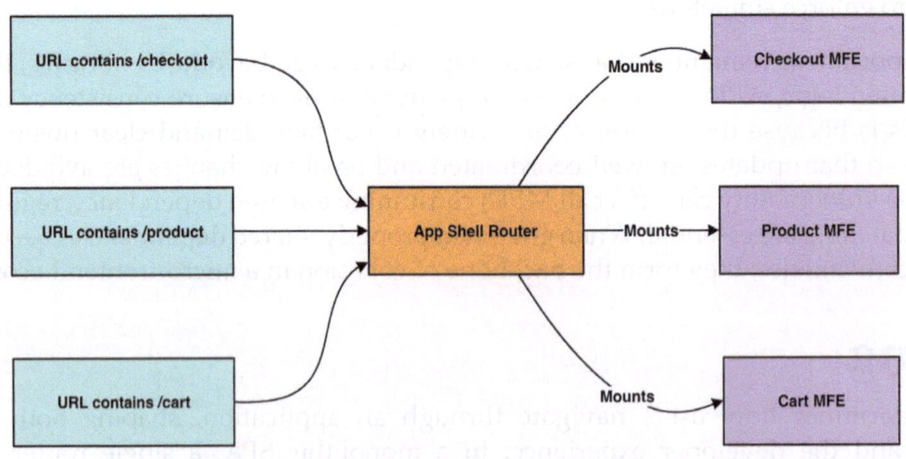

Figure 6.6*: Routing different routes to its MFEs via App Shell Router*

In an app shell routing model, the shell owns the global router and decides which MFE to mount based on the current URL. For example, if the user navigates to `/product`, the shell's router identifies that this route belongs to the product domain and mounts the Product MFE into a placeholder within the page. The same logic applies to other routes, such as **/cart** mounts the Cart MFE, **/checkout** mounts the Checkout MFE, and so on. This ensures that navigation across top-level features is consistent and centralized, while the MFEs themselves can still manage their own local state and UI once they are mounted.

There are multiple ways to implement app shell routing, depending on the framework or library being used. In a React-based shell, a popular choice is React Router, which is an external library that maps routes to components or placeholders. Frameworks like Next.js bring their own file-based routing mechanisms, while Angular includes a powerful built-in router that can also be leveraged for MFE integration. The key idea is that the shell remains the single authority for high-level navigation, and each route corresponds to the mounting of a specific MFE. This model is especially effective for keeping user experience seamless, since the shell enforces consistency across global navigation paths, while still allowing teams to own their MFEs independently.

Independent routing

At the other end of the spectrum is independent routing, where each MFE is fully responsible for handling its own navigation without relying on the app shell. In this model, the shell plays little or no role in routing. It may simply act as a container for mounting MFEs, or in some cases, it is bypassed entirely. Each MFE declares its own routes, manages its own router, and controls how users move within its boundaries.

A common example of this model is found in MPAs, where each page is owned by a different MFE. Navigating from **/products** to **/checkout** triggers a full page reload, unloading the previous MFE and loading the new one. Because each MFE has complete control of its routing, development teams enjoy maximum autonomy: they can use their preferred routing libraries, set their own conventions, and evolve independently of other teams. This is particularly attractive in polyglot environments where MFEs are built with different frameworks, such as React for one and Angular or Vue for another.

The downside, however, is that this independence can create a fragmented user experience. Without coordination, MFEs may implement navigation differently, leading to inconsistencies in behavior or appearance. Features such as global authentication guards, persistent layouts, or shared dependencies (discussed in the previous section) are more difficult to achieve. Furthermore, because each MFE reloads independently, there may be performance costs compared to a single-page experience. Independent routing, therefore, works best for applications where MFEs are more loosely coupled, such as a suite of tools or dashboards, rather than for tightly integrated user journeys like e-commerce checkouts.

Even though independent routing does not allow MFEs to communicate directly in the browser, interoperability is still achieved through contracts defined at the routing layer. Each MFE must agree on consistent paths, query parameters, and payload formats so that navigation itself becomes a form of communication. *Figure 6.7* illustrates the behavior in which the contract is shared via the URL as a query param:

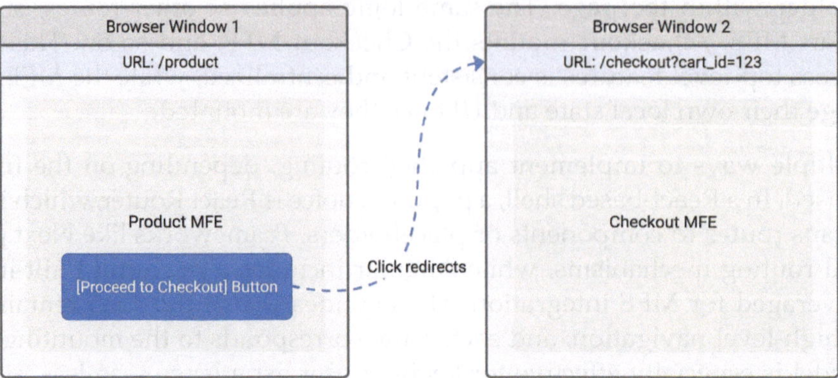

Figure 6.7: *Example of Independent routing with a contract passed in URL*

In *Figure 6.7*, the first browser window shows the Product MFE at `/product`. When the user clicks the **Proceed to Checkout** button, the application redirects to `/checkout?cart_id=123`. The second browser window illustrates what the user sees after the redirect: the Checkout MFE mounted at the new URL. The query parameter `cart_id=123` acts as the contract between the two MFEs, ensuring that the checkout module knows which cart to load. It ensures continuity of user experience, even though each page load replaces one MFE with another. In practice, these contracts are documented and enforced much like API contracts, giving independent MFEs a common language for navigation and data exchange through the URL and backend services.

Note: This example is for illustration purposes only. In a real-world scenario, passing context between MFEs through the URL would typically be combined with backend APIs to retrieve the relevant state. This often involves additional concerns such as authentication, validation, and data consistency, making the actual implementation more complex than what is depicted here.

Hybrid approach

The hybrid routing model combines the strengths of both app shell routing and independent routing. In this approach, the app shell owns the top-level navigation, ensuring that global routes such as `/products`, `/cart`, or `/checkout` consistently map to the correct MFE. Once an MFE is mounted, however, it takes over responsibility for its nested routes and manages them internally using its own router.

Consider the example of a checkout flow. When the user navigates to `/checkout`, the app shell recognizes this global route and mounts the Checkout MFE into the page. From that point forward, navigation inside the checkout experience, such as `/checkout/shipping`, `/checkout/payment`, or `/checkout/confirmation`, is fully managed by the Checkout MFE's internal router. The shell no longer needs to be aware of these details. This division of responsibility ensures that the user's navigation feels seamless while preserving autonomy for the team owning the checkout domain.

Hybrid routing works well in complex applications where some routes need to be consistent and globally recognized, while others are better left to local ownership. It also mirrors how organizations often structure teams: the shell team defines and enforces global navigation rules, while product teams control their feature-specific flows. This balance provides global cohesion without sacrificing local independence.

As with other routing models, hybrid routing requires clear contracts between the shell and MFEs. The shell must know which top-level routes map to which MFEs, while MFEs must be able to handle their sub routes without interfering with the global router. Frameworks like React Router, Angular Router, and Vue Router can all support this model, often with the shell passing control down to the MFE once it is mounted. Done well, hybrid routing creates a smooth and unified navigation experience while allowing MFEs to evolve independently. As illustrated in *Figure 6.8*, the App Shell Router controls the top-level contract, when the user navigates to **`/checkout`**, the shell mounts the Checkout MFE:

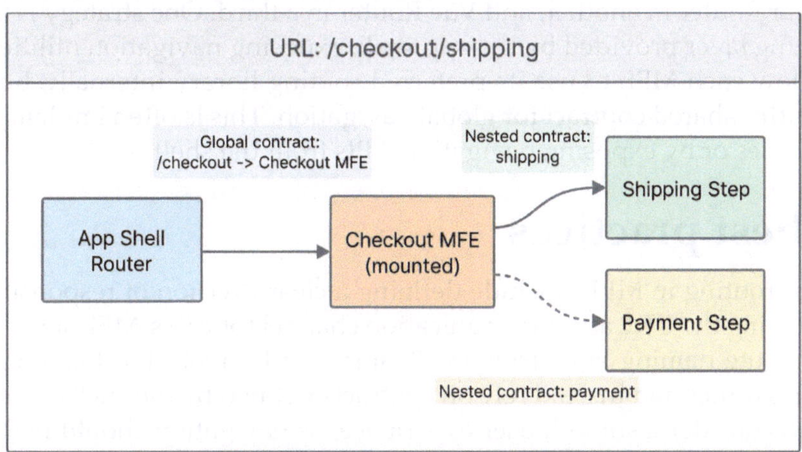

Figure 6.8: *Example of hybrid routing with the main route and the nested route fetched from the URL*

Once mounted, the Checkout MFE's internal router takes over and manages its own nested contracts, such as **`/shipping`** or **`/payment`**. This separation of responsibility makes it clear where global navigation ends and local ownership begins.

Handling state via routing

Routing in MFEs is not only about navigation, but it can also serve as a state-sharing mechanism. The URL itself can act as a source of truth, allowing multiple MFEs to synchronize their behavior without direct dependencies. For instance, a FilterMFE might update the query parameter **`?category=shoes`**, and a ProductListMFE can read that parameter to display the correct products. Similarly, a SearchMFE might update the route to **`/search?q=laptops`**, and a RecommendationsMFE can adapt its results accordingly. Using routing as a communication bridge has the advantage of being transparent, bookmarkable, and shareable. A user can copy and paste a URL, and the state of the entire application can be reconstructed across MFEs.

Of course, this approach comes with trade-offs. Using the URL for state works well for serializable, user-facing data such as filters, queries, or navigation state, but it is less suitable for transient or sensitive data such as session tokens or ephemeral workflow steps. Moreover, relying too heavily on the URL can lead to verbose and unwieldy query strings. Teams must carefully decide what belongs in the URL and what should be managed internally through state or events.

Note: Query parameters are useful for lightweight state sharing, but they have practical limits (often around 1024 characters) in certain browsers or servers. They should carry simple values like filters or IDs, not large data payloads.

Another consideration is the consistency of routing libraries. If MFEs are written in different frameworks, handling routing strategies could be tricky because we might have React Router in one MFE, Angular Router in another, and Vue Router in a third. One strategy is to standardize on a shared routing layer provided by the app shell, exposing navigation utilities to all MFEs. Another is to allow each MFE to use its preferred routing library internally, but require that they integrate with a shared contract for global navigation. This is often implemented through shared dependencies or by exposing navigation APIs from the shell.

Routing best practices

Best practices for routing in MFEs include defining a clear division of responsibility between shell and MFEs, using the URL as a communication channel for cross-MFE state, and enforcing conventions for route naming and structure. Teams should avoid hard-coding assumptions about each other's routes and instead rely on contracts defined by the shell or a shared library. They should also consider a smooth user experience, as navigation should feel seamless and consistent, regardless of how many MFEs are involved behind the scenes.

In summary, routing in MFEs extends beyond simply mapping URLs to views. It is a fundamental mechanism for coordinating independent modules, maintaining global consistency, and even sharing state. Whether implemented through app shell routing, independent routing, or hybrid models, the key challenge is balancing autonomy with cohesion. By treating routing as both a navigation and communication tool, teams can ensure that their MFE applications remain modular yet unified, delivering a smooth user experience across boundaries.

Case study on SkyTravel

To illustrate how communication and interoperability patterns work in practice, let us step into the world of *SkyTravel*, a fictional global travel booking platform. SkyTravel helps millions of travelers search for flights, book hotels, arrange car rentals, and manage loyalty rewards.

Like many large-scale consumer platforms, SkyTravel evolved from a monolithic application into an MFE ecosystem where independent teams build, deploy, and scale their domains separately. While this architecture grants autonomy, it also creates a pressing need for clear communication channels so that the overall user experience remains cohesive.

SkyTravel's front-end is composed of several MFEs, such as:

- **Search MFE**: Provides the search bar and input form for flights, hotels, and rental cars.
- **Results MFE**: Displays available options based on user queries.
- **Booking MFE**: Collects traveler details, seating preferences, and special requests.
- **Payment MFE**: Processes payments securely and handles billing.
- **Loyalty dashboard MFE**: Tracks points, upcoming trips, and past bookings.
- **Analytics MFE**: Observes and logs user activity for personalization and insights.

Each of these MFEs is owned by a different product team. The challenge is ensuring that they communicate effectively while remaining loosely coupled.

State management in SkyTravel

The state is central to SkyTravel's operation. When a user enters a flight search, for example, a trip from San Francisco to New York City on December 15, the Search MFE captures this information. To ensure consistency, it encodes the search criteria into the URL, producing a path such as:

```
/results?from=SFO&to=NYC&date=2025-12-15
```

The Results MFE, mounted by the app shell, simply reads the query parameters and fetches matching flights. In this way, the URL doubles as a state-sharing mechanism, acting as a lightweight contract between the MFEs.

Not all states can be expressed in query parameters. However some data, such as user authentication and session context, must persist across MFEs without being exposed in the URL. SkyTravel solves this by exposing a shared dependency, a session context library injected as a singleton by the app shell. Every MFE imports this shared context, ensuring that they all recognize the same logged-in user, whether displaying loyalty points or pre-filling traveler details at checkout. This combination of URL-based contracts and shared session state keeps the application coherent without tightly coupling MFEs.

Event messaging across MFEs

SkyTravel also relies heavily on event messaging to coordinate actions that cut across domains. For example, as illustrated in *Figure 6.9*, when a user confirms a reservation in the Booking MFE, an event named **`booking:completed`** is emitted. The Loyalty Dashboard MFE, listening for this event, updates the traveler's rewards points in real time. At the same time, the Analytics MFE captures the same event and forwards it to the backend, where it feeds into reporting pipelines and personalization models.

A similar flow occurs during payments. The Payment MFE emits a *payment:success* event once a transaction is cleared. This event not only triggers the display of a booking confirmation page within the Booking MFE but is also consumed by the notification system, which sends an email receipt to the traveler. These events ensure that SkyTravel's MFEs remain loosely coupled; the Booking MFE does not need to know about the Loyalty MFE, nor does payment need to know about notifications. Each module simply reacts to events relevant to its domain.

To prevent *event soup*, SkyTravel enforces a strict event naming convention and requires that all events be documented in a central catalog. This makes debugging easier and ensures that events serve as reliable contracts between teams.

Shared dependencies

Global concerns like currency, language, and user profile are handled using shared dependencies. SkyTravel serves a global audience, so currency selection is critical. If a user chooses *EUR* as their preferred currency in the Search MFE, that choice must be reflected consistently in the Results MFE, the Booking MFE, and especially the Payment MFE. To achieve this, SkyTravel provides a currency context library as a shared singleton dependency. Injected at the app shell, this context ensures that all MFEs read and write to the same source of truth.

The same strategy is used for language preferences, enabling the Header MFE's language selector to instantly update the UI of all other MFEs without requiring direct dependencies between them. These shared contexts act as bridges that unify the platform, while still letting teams own their implementations independently.

Governance is essential here; the platform team at SkyTravel owns and maintains these shared libraries, ensuring version consistency and publishing guidelines for how MFEs should consume them. Without this, there would be a risk of multiple versions being loaded, breaking the promise of a singleton.

Routing for navigation and contract

Routing provides the glue that ties the SkyTravel experience together. The app shell router controls top-level navigation. Routes like **`/results`**, **`/booking`**, and **`/payment`** map directly to their respective MFEs. Once mounted, each MFE manages its own nested flows internally. For instance, the Booking MFE controls routes like **`/booking/passenger`** and **`/booking/seats`**. This hybrid routing model provides global consistency while empowering teams to own their sub-flows.

Routing also acts as a contract. For example, when the Search MFE redirects to **`/results?from=SFO&to=NYC`**, it assumes that the Results MFE will understand the query parameters. Likewise, the Booking MFE knows that **/booking?tripId=456** is the standard way to pass trip context. These agreements on paths and parameters are as critical as API contracts. They allow MFEs to interoperate through URLs, even if they never share runtime state.

To make these communication patterns more concrete, *Figure 6.9* illustrates how SkyTravel's MFEs collaborate during a typical booking journey. Rather than focusing on UI flow, the diagram highlights the primary communication mechanisms such as routing, shared dependencies, and event messaging and shows how they are orchestrated by the app shell to enable loose coupling between independently owned MFEs.

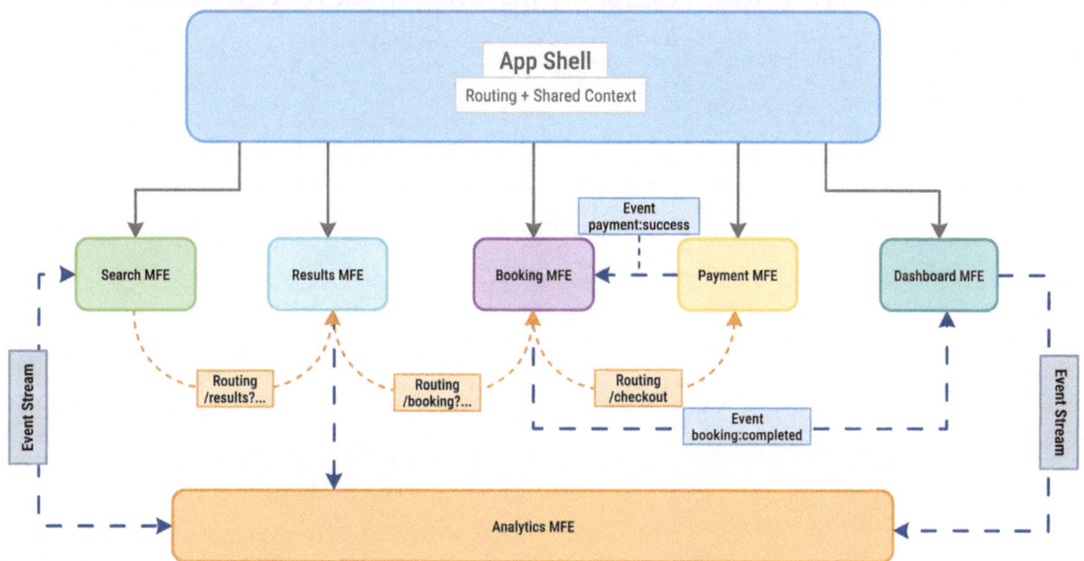

***Figure 6.9**: Communication patterns across SkyTravel MFEs*

Taken together, these strategies enable SkyTravel's teams to work independently while delivering a unified user journey. A traveler searching for flights, booking a trip, and paying for it experiences a seamless flow, even though behind the scenes, the application is composed of multiple independent MFEs. The lesson is clear: in an MFE ecosystem, communication and interoperability are not optional; they are the foundation of a coherent, scalable platform.

Conclusion

Communication and interoperability are at the heart of successful MFE architectures. While MFEs offer autonomy, they must still cooperate to deliver a seamless user experience. In this chapter, we explored the key mechanisms that enable this cooperation via state management, event messaging, shared dependencies, and routing. We saw how local and shared state can be balanced, how events provide loose coupling between modules, how dependencies create common ground, and how routing synchronizes navigation and context. Together, these techniques provide the foundation for MFEs to remain independent yet cohesive, avoiding the pitfalls of tight coupling while ensuring that users experience the application as a unified whole.

With the building blocks of interoperability in place, the next challenge is how to package and deliver MFEs efficiently. In the next chapter, we will move from runtime communication to build-time and delivery concerns, exploring how artifacts are created, bundled, and deployed. We will examine bundlers and transpilers, the role of npm packages, and how formats like UMD and Module Federation shape interoperability at the distribution level. We will also look at CI/CD pipelines and close with a case study that brings these concepts together.

Chapter 7
Deployment Strategies

Introduction

Deploying MFEs goes beyond moving code to production; it is about managing independence at scale. Each MFE must be built, tested, and delivered on its own cadence while ensuring the entire system remains coherent and reliable. This chapter explores how deployment strategies achieve that balance, through well-defined artifacts, optimized builds, versioned packages, and automated pipelines that connect independent releases into a unified experience.

The discussion begins with the concept of artifacts, the deployable outputs that represent tested and versioned units of software, before moving into bundlers and transpilers such as Webpack, Rollup, and Babel that prepare code for production. It then examines npm packages as a foundation for distributing MFEs as reusable modules and revisits key module formats like CommonJS, **Asynchronous Module Definition** (**AMD**), and ES Modules. The chapter also highlights the enduring value of **Universal Module Definition** (**UMD**) for cross-environment compatibility and concludes with Webpack Module Federation, which enables MFEs to share code dynamically at runtime. Together with CI/CD pipelines, these practices form the backbone of scalable, automated, and reliable delivery for modern frontend ecosystems.

Structure

The chapter covers the following topics:

- Introduction to artifacts
- Bundlers and transpilers
- Node packages
- Universal Module Definition
- Runtime integration patterns
- Federated artifacts
- Deployment pipelines

Objectives

By the end of this chapter, readers will have a clear understanding of how modern frontend teams deliver MFEs in a predictable and scalable manner. They will learn why artifacts are central to deployment, how they serve as stable, versioned units of delivery, and how build tools transform raw code into optimized, portable bundles ready for production. Readers will also gain practical insight into distributing MFEs through npm packages, along with the implications of different module formats and compatibility strategies. They will understand how patterns like UMD and more advanced approaches, such as Webpack Module Federation, enable MFEs to be consumed across diverse environments, promote reuse, and support dynamic code sharing at runtime. In addition, they will learn how CI and CD pipelines automate validation, packaging, and rollout, ensuring that independent teams can ship reliably without sacrificing cohesion. The chapter also equips readers with the ability to evaluate governance practices, versioning discipline, and rollback strategies that are essential for maintaining stability in a distributed delivery model. Collectively, these objectives help readers develop a strong mental model of how MFEs move from development to production, how independence is balanced with coordination, and how automation and consistent standards enable teams to operate at scale with confidence.

Introduction to artifacts

The word artifact (pronounced ar·te·fact) originates from the Latin phrase arte factum, meaning *something made with skill* (Source: **dictionary.com**). Historically, it described any human-made object that carried traces of craftsmanship. In the world of software engineering, the term retained this essence. It came to represent the tangible by-product of a creative process that can be deployed, distributed, or reused. An artifact is more than just a file; it is the result of effort, design, and verification, something made with intention and skill.

In earlier stages of software evolution, artifacts were often monolithic, either a single binary or an archive deployed in one piece. Over time, as systems became modular, the concept expanded to include smaller, self-contained units: **Java Archives (JARs)** in Java ecosystems, Docker images in cloud-native systems, or npm packages in the JavaScript world. In modern web development, particularly in MFE architecture, artifacts represent the deployment-ready identities of independently owned application fragments.

Artifacts in the modern frontend landscape

In the frontend ecosystem, an artifact refers to the final, versioned unit of code generated after a successful build. It encapsulates everything needed for execution from compiled JavaScript, minified styles, configuration metadata, and sometimes even pre-rendered templates. Depending on the approach, these artifacts might exist as a compressed ZIP or TAR file in a CI/CD pipeline, a published npm package ready for consumption by other teams, or a bundle hosted on a **content delivery network (CDN)** that the host shell dynamically loads at runtime.

For example, in the *TuneStream* platform from *Chapter 6, Communication and Interoperability*, the **`Playlist`** MFE may produce an artifact named playlist-ui.1.2.0.js, containing optimized and versioned code for playlists, while the **`Recommendations`** MFE might publish its own independent build **`recommendations-ui.3.1.1.js`**. Each artifact carries its own lifecycle. It is built, tested, and promoted through environments without interfering with the others. This separation not only enables parallel delivery but also guarantees that each component can evolve at its own pace.

Artifacts also serve as **contracts**. Once created, they capture a moment in time: a specific codebase, dependency state, and configuration. When deployed, they can be traced back to the source commit or build number. This traceability ensures accountability and reproducibility which is a cornerstone of reliable deployment practices. In other words, artifacts are not simply technical outputs; they are representations of ownership, accountability, and versioned truth in a distributed system.

Semantic Versioning

Semantic Versioning (**SemVer**) provides a standardized way to communicate changes in software through version numbers. Each release is expressed as MAJOR.MINOR.PATCH (for example, **`2.4.1`**), where the patch number increases for bug fixes and non-breaking updates, the **minor** number increments when new features are added while maintaining backward compatibility, and the major number changes when breaking changes are introduced. The illustration of how this works is mentioned in the following figure:

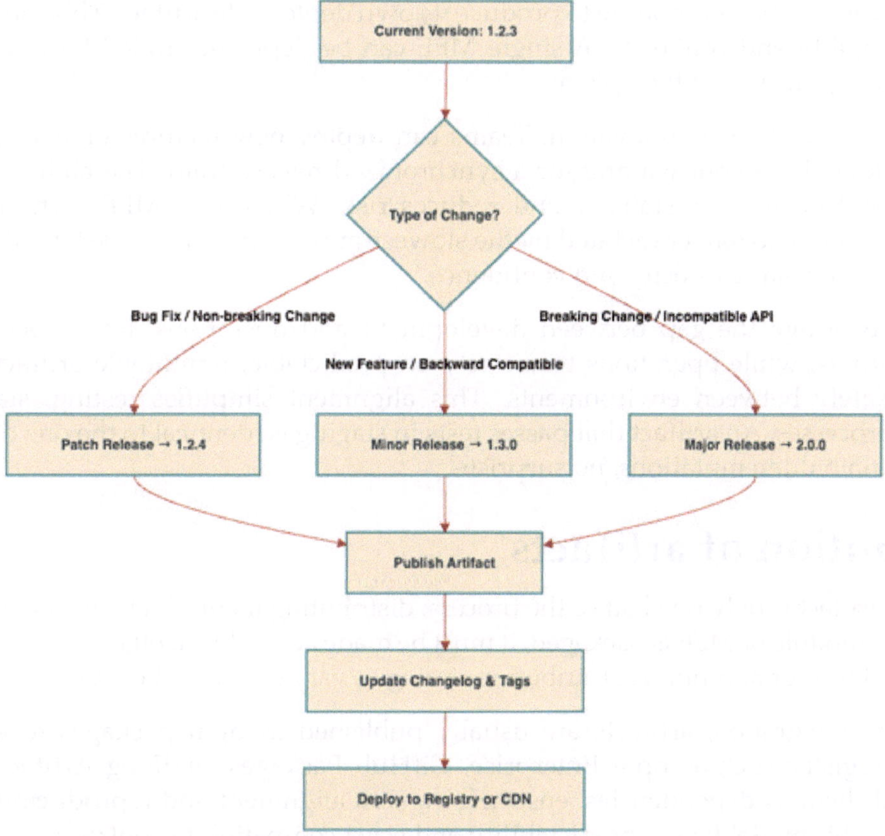

Figure 7.1: Semantic version in action

Figure 7.1 explains how the current version of 1.2.3 will be updated in a semantic version workflow. The next version will be decided in the pipeline based on the commit message example, feat: for new feature, fix: for bugfix, and BREAKING CHANGE: for breaking change in the package that needs a major version upgrade. Following SemVer allows both human readers and automated systems to understand how safe it is to upgrade a dependency. Many teams enforce version governance through automation using tools like semantic-release or Changesets often executed as release bots within CI pipelines. These tools analyze commit messages (provided the commit messages follow the conventional commit standard), determine the type of change, and update versions, changelogs, and tags automatically. This consistency ensures that every published artifact clearly reflects its impact and compatibility across the ecosystem. In a MFE architecture, this discipline is especially important, as unmanaged version drift between independently deployed MFEs can lead to subtle runtime incompatibilities, broken shared contracts, or unexpected behavior in the host application.

Importance of artifacts in MFE

In a monolithic application, a single artifact defines the entire release. One deployment contains all features, and any change requires a complete rebuild. MFEs transform this model by allowing each feature or module to produce its own deployable artifact. This independence brings both agility and resilience. A single MFE can be deployed, rolled back, or replaced without affecting the rest of the system.

This autonomy accelerates innovation. Teams can deploy new features or fixes as soon as they are validated, without waiting for a synchronized release train. The ability to rollback individual MFEs improves stability and reduces risk. When each MFE owns its artifact, release frequency is no longer dictated by the slowest-moving part of the system. It becomes a reflection of each team's velocity and confidence.

Artifacts also bridge the gap between development and operations. Developers focus on building features, while operations teams rely on predictable, immutable artifacts that can be moved safely between environments. This alignment simplifies testing, staging, and promotion processes. An artifact that passes tests in staging is identical to the one deployed in production: no hidden mutations, no surprises.

Distribution of artifacts

Building an artifact is only one half of the process; distributing it effectively is what gives it real value. Once a module or MFE is packaged, it must be made accessible to other parts of the system either at build time or at runtime. Distribution strategies vary based on the integration model.

In build-time integration, artifacts are usually published as npm packages to an internal or external registry such as npm Enterprise, GitHub Packages, or JFrog Artifactory. Other teams install them as dependencies, ensuring version alignment and reproducibility during compilation. This model favors predictability and strict compatibility contracts.

For runtime integration, the artifact is hosted as a static bundle on a CDN or edge node. The host application references it dynamically, often through a manifest file or a remote entry defined in Webpack's Module Federation configuration. This approach enables independent deployment and instant availability so that a new version can be released to production without rebuilding the host.

Distribution also involves metadata, small files like **`manifest.json`** or **`remoteEntry.js`** that describe module entry points, version numbers, and dependency relationships. These allow the host to discover, cache, and load the correct version at runtime. In this sense, artifact distribution is not just about delivering code; it is about enabling orchestration and discovery in a federated ecosystem.

Best practices

Successful organizations treat artifact management as a discipline, not an afterthought. It requires structure, consistency, and governance. A few guiding principles are universal.

- Artifacts must remain immutable; once published, they are never modified. Any change should result in a new version, maintaining a clear history of evolution. Versioning, when done consistently using SemVer, communicates the intent behind a release, whether it is a patch, a new feature, or a breaking change.
- Equally important is traceability. Each artifact should carry metadata that links it back to the source commit, build ID, and environment. This transparency allows teams to diagnose production issues, verify integrity, and perform safe rollbacks. Organizations also benefit from a centralized repository in which a single, trusted system stores artifacts, manages access, and provides audit trails.
- Automation further enhances artifact reliability. Instead of manually copying files or uploading builds, artifacts should flow through continuous integration and deployment pipelines, ensuring consistent validation, promotion, and verification at each stage. Finally, in multi-MFE systems, it is crucial to scope or namespace assets to prevent **Cascading Style Sheets** (**CSS**), font, or resource collisions across independently deployed modules.
- Beyond versioning and publishing, artifacts must also be verified for runtime compatibility before promotion. Artifacts should be tested in both Node and browser environments before being published. A common practice is to release prerelease versions such as **`testpackage@1.0.1-beta.1`** or **`testpackage@1.0.1-rc.1`**, allowing teams to validate the output of transpilation and bundling before promoting it to a stable release. As part of the CI pipeline, these prerelease artifacts are automatically installed, executed, and tested to confirm that the transpiled modules function correctly across environments.

Together, these practices elevate artifacts from simple outputs to governed entities, which is the foundation upon which reliable MFE deployments are built.

Bundlers and transpilers

Once the source code has been developed, the next step in the deployment lifecycle is transforming it into a production-ready artifact. This transformation is handled through two essential instruments of the modern frontend ecosystem: bundlers and transpilers. These tools collectively convert developer-friendly code into optimized assets ready for browsers, encapsulating logic, dependencies, and performance optimizations into deployable units. Optimization is vital, not only to minimize the amount of code sent over the network, conserving bandwidth and improving load times, but also to protect the integrity of the code exposed in the browser. Techniques such as minification and obfuscation compress and disguise the source code, making it unreadable to casual inspection and reducing the risk of misuse while maintaining the same functionality.

Early days of the frontend build system

Before the rise of sophisticated bundlers, frontend development was largely manual. Developers included multiple script tags in HTML, loaded files in strict sequence, and managed dependencies by hand. This approach worked when applications were small, but as web interfaces grew in complexity, so did the need for automation and consistency. The first generation of build tools: Grunt and Gulp, emerged to automate repetitive tasks. Grunt, introduced in 2012, was a task runner that allowed developers to define a series of build tasks, which include minifying JavaScript, compressing images or running tests and executing them through a unified command-line interface. It marked the beginning of build automation in the JavaScript ecosystem. Gulp soon followed, bringing a more elegant, stream-based approach that processed files through pipelines rather than temporary directories. Both tools transformed frontend development into a programmable workflow, setting the stage for reproducible and automated builds. The following code explains how the Gulp workflow was used to automate the build:

```
// gulpfile.js
const { src, dest, series } = require('gulp');
const concat = require('gulp-concat');
const uglify = require('gulp-uglify');
const babel = require('gulp-babel');
const cleanCSS = require('gulp-clean-css');
// Transpile and minify JavaScript
function scripts() {
  return src('src/js/**/*.js')
    .pipe(babel({ presets: ['@babel/preset-env'] }))
    .pipe(concat('bundle.min.js'))
    .pipe(uglify())
```

```
    .pipe(dest('dist/js'));
}
// Minify CSS
function styles() {
  return src('src/css/**/*.css')
    .pipe(concat('styles.min.css'))
    .pipe(cleanCSS())
    .pipe(dest('dist/css'));
}
exports.build = series(scripts, styles);
```

This simple Gulp setup automates the build process by transpiling ES6 code with Babel, concatenating multiple files, and minifying both JavaScript and CSS into a **`dist`** folder. Before modern bundlers like Webpack or Rollup became standard, tools such as Grunt and Gulp performed these discrete tasks using plugin-based workflows.

However, these task runners did not inherently manage module dependencies. Developers still had to manually link scripts or use patterns like **Immediately Invoked Function Expressions** (**IIFEs**) to avoid global namespace collisions. The web needed a structured approach to handle modularity, and that is where Browserify stepped in.

Browserify pioneered the concept of bundling JavaScript modules for the browser. It allowed developers to use the Node.js-style **`require()`** syntax to import dependencies, which it then compiled into a single file that browsers could execute. This innovation made it possible to write frontend code as small, reusable modules rather than monolithic scripts, marking the birth of client-side modular development. Browserify laid the conceptual groundwork for everything that followed from Webpack's dependency graph to Rollup's tree-shaking.

Rise of modern bundlers

As web applications became richer and more dynamic, bundlers evolved from convenience tools into critical infrastructure. Webpack emerged as the dominant solution, building on Browserify's idea of dependency graphs but expanding it into a complete ecosystem. Every asset, such as JavaScript, CSS, fonts, or images, was treated as a module that could be imported, processed, and optimized. Webpack introduced the concept of loaders and plugins, allowing developers to extend the build process and control how different file types are handled.

The flexibility of Webpack came at the cost of complexity, prompting the creation of alternative tools. Rollup emphasized simplicity and output quality, focusing on libraries and reusable components. It was the first bundler to natively support ES modules, producing cleaner, smaller bundles ideal for MFEs, distributed via npm packages. Parcel introduced zero-configuration builds, automatically inferring settings from project structure. More recently, Vite took advantage of native ES module imports and the speed of modern JavaScript runtimes, delivering near-instant development builds and lightning-fast hot module replacement. Its ecosystem has also begun exploring federation-style plugins that enable dynamic module loading without the traditional weight of Webpack. The difference between each bundler is explained in the following figure:

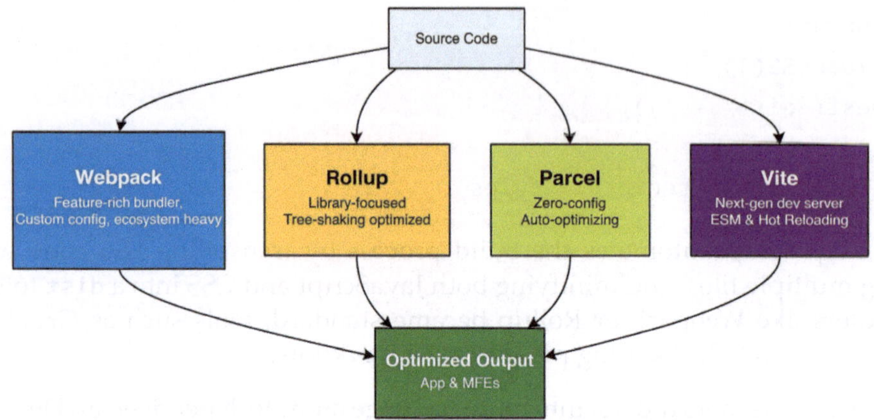

Figure 7.2: *Comparison of modern bundlers, different paths to producing optimized build outputs*

Together, these tools represent an evolutionary continuum, from manual scripts to intelligent build orchestration. Each generation improved abstraction and performance, allowing developers to focus on feature development rather than file management.

Transpilers in modern JavaScript

While bundlers solve the problem of packaging, transpilers solve the problem of compatibility. As the JavaScript language evolves rapidly, not all browsers support the latest syntax or features. Transpilers translate modern code into a form that remains backward compatible, ensuring consistency across environments.

The most prominent of these is Babel, which gained popularity by allowing developers to write ES6+ syntax years before browsers could natively interpret it. Babel's transformation pipeline turned next-generation features such as arrow functions, classes, and Async-Await into ES5 syntax, bridging innovation with reliability. Around the same time, TypeScript introduced static typing to JavaScript, and its compiler (tsc) not only performed type checks but also acted as a transpiler, outputting pure JavaScript for browsers to consume.

This separation of authoring and execution environments freed developers from compatibility constraints. They could adopt modern programming patterns while still targeting older browsers or constrained devices, which is a crucial capability in global-scale web applications.

Packaging across MFEs

In MFE architecture, bundlers and transpilers acquire new significance. Each MFE is an independent build unit, often owned by a different team and potentially using different frameworks or versions of dependencies. The bundler defines how each MFE is packaged, scoped, and exposed to others; the transpiler ensures that all modules, despite their internal differences, remain compatible in the shared runtime environment.

Webpack's Module Federation, discussed in the previous chapter, changed how bundlers operate by enabling multiple builds to coexist dynamically at runtime. Instead of producing one static application bundle, each MFE exposes its compiled output as a remote entry point. The host application, acting as a composition layer, can then dynamically load these remote bundles on demand. This capability turned the bundler from a static packaging tool into a runtime integration engine, capable of stitching together independently deployed artifacts.

Other bundlers followed suit. Rollup and Vite can generate ES module outputs that are directly imported by host shells or edge functions. These formats are increasingly favored in modern deployments, where speed, composability, and portability matter as much as compatibility.

Optimization and governance

Bundlers and transpilers are not just technical utilities; they embody organizational discipline. Without consistency, distributed teams can easily produce incompatible bundles, some using ES modules, others CommonJS, some minified, others not. Establishing shared conventions such as uniform Babel configurations, standardized Webpack presets, and consistent target environments prevents integration issues downstream.

Beyond consistency, optimization remains a key goal. Tree-shaking removes unused exports, minification compresses code, and code-splitting enables lazy loading of only the necessary chunks. These optimizations directly influence performance, bandwidth, and user experience. In a large organization, where multiple MFEs may load simultaneously, consistent optimization practices ensure predictable performance across the application.

Governance completes the picture. By maintaining a set of organization-wide build templates, teams can ensure that every MFE, regardless of ownership, produces output aligned with the platform's technical expectations. In essence, bundlers and transpilers become instruments of both technology and culture, translating architectural intent into operational consistency.

Node packages

In the evolution of modern frontend development, **Node Package Manager** (**npm**) became the backbone of software distribution, the registry that connects developers, teams, and applications through reusable, versioned modules. Introduced in 2010 as part of the Node. js ecosystem, it quickly grew beyond its original purpose, transforming into the universal repository for JavaScript dependencies across both backend and frontend systems.

For MFEs, npm offers more than just dependency management; it provides a standardized way to distribute and consume independently built application fragments. Each MFE can be packaged, versioned, and installed just like any other dependency, turning the act of deployment into a predictable, governed process.

Packaging MFEs as deployable modules

Packaging an MFE begins once the bundler produces its build output. The compiled code, along with any styles, assets, and metadata, is arranged into a structured folder, defined by a **package.json** manifest that describes its entry points and compatibility targets. From that point forward, the MFE ceases to be just a project; it becomes a product: a deployable, versioned artifact that can be installed anywhere within the organization.

This packaging model introduces predictability. Once an MFE is published, it can be consumed by other teams at specific versions, ensuring stable builds and traceable dependencies. Versioning, usually managed through SemVer, communicates the intent behind every release: patch updates for fixes, minor increments for features, and major versions for breaking changes. By enforcing these conventions, organizations prevent integration drift and maintain coherent dependency graphs across distributed teams.

Private npm registries, such as GitHub Packages, JFrog Artifactory, or Verdaccio, are frequently used to host internal MFEs. They act as curated ecosystems where only approved artifacts are accessible, ensuring quality control, compliance, and security. Within such registries, each MFE is treated as a standalone unit, fully testable and independently deployable.

Module formats and compatibility

In *Chapter 5, Implementation Strategies*, we explored the evolution of modular JavaScript from CommonJS and AMD to **ECMAScript** (**ES**) modules, and how those systems shaped modern application design. In the deployment context, these same module formats determine how packaged MFEs can be consumed across diverse environments. When publishing an MFE as an npm package, the module format defines compatibility boundaries. A backend or Node.js process may rely on CommonJS exports, while frontend applications increasingly depend on ES modules for their static import/export semantics and tree-shaking capabilities. Many modern build pipelines therefore produce dual-format outputs, exposing both `main` (for CommonJS consumers) and `module` (for ES module consumers) fields in `package.json`. as described in the following:

```
{
  "name": "@test/package",
  "version": "5.0.0",
  "main": "dist/index.cjs.js",      // CommonJS build
  "module": "dist/index.esm.js",  // ES Module build
```

```
  "types": "dist/index.d.ts",      // Optional: TypeScript declarations
  "files": [
    "dist"
  ],
  "scripts": {
    "build": "rollup -c"
  }
}
```

Modern bundlers resolve these fields differently based on their execution model. For example, Webpack and Vite will prefer the **`module`** field when building for modern browsers, enabling tree-shaking and smaller bundles, while Node.js or older tooling may fall back to **`main`** for CommonJS compatibility:

```
// ESM consumption (Vite, Rollup, modern Webpack)
import Playlist from "@tunestream/playlist-ui";

// CommonJS consumption (Node.js, legacy tooling)
const Playlist = require("@tunestream/playlist-ui");
```

This duality ensures flexibility. A host application built on legacy tooling can consume the same artifact that a modern, **ECMAScript Module** (**ESM**)-compatible bundler would. The bundler or runtime selects the appropriate entry point automatically, maintaining interoperability without additional configuration. For MFEs, this pattern is invaluable as it allows independently developed packages to integrate smoothly, even when built with different frameworks or tooling generations.

Mixed dependency graphs and edge cases

While dual-format publishing improves compatibility, it can introduce complexity when applications consume a mix of CommonJS and ES modules. In large MFE ecosystems, this often results in mixed dependency graphs, where some MFEs import ESM builds while others rely on CommonJS variants of the same dependency. These situations can lead to subtle issues such as duplicated dependencies, broken tree-shaking, or inconsistent singleton behavior for shared libraries like React.

Bundlers typically resolve these conflicts heuristically, but teams must remain disciplined. Clear ownership of shared dependencies, consistent publishing strategies, and runtime enforcement mechanisms such as singleton configuration in Module Federation are essential to prevent version drift and unexpected behavior. As ecosystems continue to move toward ES modules as the default, these edge cases are becoming less common, but they remain an important consideration in transitional architectures.

Build-time integration

Publishing MFEs as npm packages aligns naturally with build-time integration, one of the key deployment models discussed in *Chapter 5, Implementation Strategies*. In this approach, the host or shell application installs MFEs during its own build process, compiles them into a single deployable bundle, and releases the composed application as a unified artifact.

This model prioritizes stability and reproducibility. This is because the dependency graph is resolved at build time, every component version is locked, tested, and verified before deployment. Rollbacks are straightforward; simply revert to a previous version of a dependency, and integration errors are caught before runtime. However, this predictability comes at a trade-off: updating an MFE requires rebuilding and redeploying the host.

Organizations that emphasize predictable delivery pipelines often favor this approach. The ability to trace every dependency, reproduce builds exactly, and promote versioned artifacts through environments development, staging, and production, which offers operational confidence that dynamic runtime loading sometimes sacrifices.

For more flexible environments, hybrid systems often emerge, with core MFEs distributed as npm packages, while fast-moving or user-facing ones are deployed via runtime federation or CDN hosting. Together, these models allow for both reliability and agility within a shared ecosystem.

Governance, versioning, and organizational discipline

In large-scale ecosystems, packaging discipline is crucial. Without it, version conflicts, redundant dependencies, or uncontrolled updates can erode the benefits of modularization. The `package.json` file, therefore, becomes more than a configuration; it is the contract between producers and consumers. It defines not only entry points and versioning but also visibility (public vs. private) and dependency boundaries.

Immutability is a fundamental principle: once a version is published, it should never be overwritten. Each new change must increment the version, maintaining a permanent audit trail of releases. Continuous integration systems can automate this through pipelines that lint manifests, tag releases, generate changelogs, and publish artifacts automatically after successful builds.

Scoped naming conventions (such as `@tunestream/playlist-ui`) help prevent namespace conflicts and create clarity across hundreds of internal packages. Dependency updates can be governed centrally using automated tools or bots, which ensure that host applications always reference the latest compatible versions. When applied consistently, these practices elevate npm from a simple registry to a governance framework, enabling teams to move independently while remaining synchronized through controlled versioning.

Universal Module Definition

As JavaScript evolved into a shared language across environments, developers faced a dilemma: write one module for Node, another for the browser, and maintain both. In response, the community sought a way to unify these ecosystems. The result was the UMD, a pattern designed to make modules compatible everywhere.

UMD was not an official specification but a pragmatic convention. It emerged organically around 2013, combining the portability of AMD with the simplicity of CommonJS. The goal was elegant in its simplicity: a single module definition that works in any environment: Node, browser, or both.

A typical UMD wrapper looks like this:

```
(function (root, factory) {
  if (typeof define === 'function' && define.amd) {
    // AMD
    define([], factory);
  } else if (typeof module === 'object' && module.exports) {
    // CommonJS
    module.exports = factory();
  } else {
    // Browser global
    root.MyLibrary = factory();
  }
}(this, function () {
  return {
    greet: function() {
      return "Hello from UMD!";
    }
  };
}));
```

This small yet ingenious pattern detects the environment dynamically, registering the module appropriately. It made JavaScript libraries *universal* long before the ES module standard existed. This is further explained in the following figure:

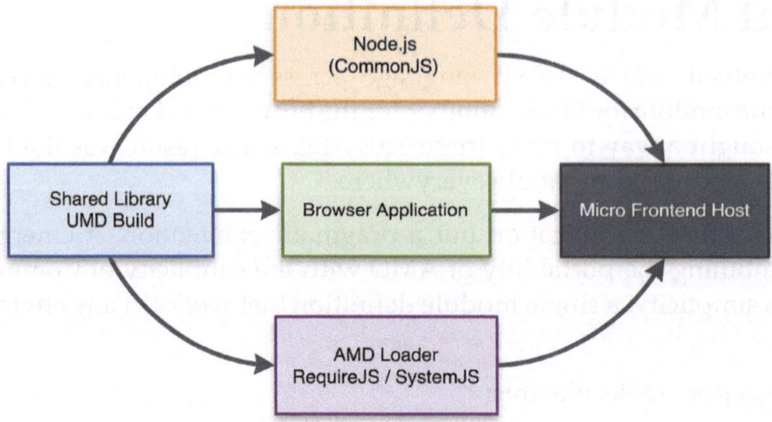

***Figure 7.3:** UMD as a shared bridge*

Figure 7.3 illustrates how the UMD bundle can act as a shared bridge in which a single library distributed once can be used by disparate systems operating under different environments.

Reusable frontend with UMD

During the 2010s, as the frontend ecosystem grew more modular, UMD became the default output format for distribution. Whether it was jQuery plugins, visualization libraries like D3.js, or utility frameworks like Lodash, UMD ensured that a single build could run in a browser script tag, a Node environment, or through a bundler like Browserify. For early adopters of component-based design, UMD was the bridge that made reusable frontends practical. It enabled developers to distribute their code as self-contained, framework-agnostic units, which aligns perfectly with the modern idea of MFEs.

Federated modules with UMD

When tools like Webpack and Rollup arrived, they embraced UMD as one of their standard output targets. Developers could build their applications or libraries once and expose them universally. This flexibility paved the way for modular ecosystems to flourish, long before the official ESM standard became widely supported in browsers.

Although UMD originated in the pre-ESM era, its influence extends directly into the runtime federation model used in MFE architectures today. Both concepts share a common vision: self-contained modules discoverable and loadable at runtime. When Webpack introduced Module Federation, the **`remoteEntry.js`** file that exposes shared components to the host application echoed UMD's spirit, which defines a consistent interface that can be dynamically imported regardless of its source. In essence, Module Federation is UMD reimagined for the modern web, which is still universal, but with asynchronous loading, dependency negotiation, and version sharing built in.

UMD's design patterns also inspired early plugin-based architectures in enterprise applications. A host could expose a global **`window.AppPlugins`** array, and individual UMD bundles would register themselves upon load. While primitive by today's standards, this mechanism demonstrated the earliest form of runtime composition in the browser.

UMD in action today

Even though ES-Modules have largely replaced UMD for modern builds, UMD remains deeply embedded in the JavaScript ecosystem. Many widely used libraries, such as Moment.js, Chart.js, and Lodash, still distribute UMD builds for backward compatibility. In large enterprises, UMD continues to play a role in systems where legacy and modern stacks must coexist. For example, a legacy AngularJS dashboard can dynamically load a new React MFE via a UMD wrapper, avoiding a complete rebuild. The wrapper acts as a compatibility layer, exposing the React component tree as a global variable accessible to older codebases.

In the previous TuneStream example, UMD proved useful during its transition phase. Before adopting Module Federation, the **`@tunestream/analytics`** MFE was exported as a UMD bundle and embedded into multiple host applications via script tags. This allowed the analytics module to evolve independently, while still integrating seamlessly with legacy frontends, which is a testament to UMD's continuing relevance as a transitional bridge.

Transition from UMD to federated modules

UMD represents a pivotal stage in the evolution of JavaScript deployment. It unified a fragmented ecosystem, introduced the notion of universal packaging, and laid the conceptual groundwork for the distributed module systems of today. Its legacy endures not because it is perfect, but because it solved an existential problem: how to make code reusable across incompatible environments.

In MFE architecture, UMD occupies a unique historical niche that offers the missing link between traditional libraries and dynamic federation. For teams modernizing legacy systems, it remains a practical stepping stone that is easy to adopt, universally compatible, and supported by every major bundler. However, the future belongs to federated artifacts and native ESM, where universality is achieved not by wrapping environments, but by letting them communicate directly through runtime resolution and composition mechanisms. In that sense, UMD is not an endpoint, but a bridge, the one that carried web development from isolated scripts to the federated, modular world we now inhabit.

Runtime integration patterns

Before moving to federated modules, it is important to understand runtime integration patterns that decouple deployment from build-time assumptions. These patterns shift integration decisions to runtime, allowing MFEs to be resolved, composed, and updated without rebuilding the host application. By introducing mechanisms such as import maps and edge-based integration, teams gain finer control over versioning, rollout, and rollback across environments. This runtime-first approach lays the foundation for more advanced composition models, including federated artifacts.

Import maps

Import maps introduce a standards-based way to control how JavaScript modules are resolved at runtime. Instead of relying on bundlers to hardcode dependency paths during build time, import maps allow applications to define mappings from module specifiers to concrete URLs that the browser or runtime uses when loading modules. This shifts dependency resolution from the build phase to deployment, giving teams greater flexibility in managing versions across environments.

In an MFE architecture, import maps act as a lightweight coordination mechanism between independently deployed MFEs and the host application. Each MFE can be built and published in isolation, while the host controls which versions are active by updating the import map. This enables safer rollouts and rollbacks, as changing a version no longer requires rebuilding or redeploying the host. Instead, the runtime simply resolves imports based on the current map:

```
{
  "imports": {
    "@tunestream/playlist-ui": "https://cdn.tunestream.com/playlist/2.5.3/
index.js",
    "@tunestream/recommendations-ui": "https://cdn.tunestream.com/
recommendations/3.1.1/index.js",
    "react": "https://cdn.tunestream.com/shared/react/18.2.0/react.esm.js"
  }
}
```

While import maps do not provide built-in dependency sharing guarantees or singleton enforcement, they integrate seamlessly with native ES modules and modern tooling. As browser support and edge runtimes continue to mature, import maps are increasingly used as a foundational building block for runtime integration, complementing more advanced composition techniques such as federated artifacts.

Edge-based integration

Edge-based integration extends runtime composition by moving routing, orchestration, and delivery decisions closer to the user. Instead of resolving all integration logic within the browser or host application, edge platforms such as CDNs or edge runtimes participate in determining which MFEs are served, from where, and under what conditions. This approach decouples delivery concerns from application code, enabling faster responses, localized behavior, and finer-grained control over rollouts.

In an MFE architecture, the edge can act as an intelligent control plane. It can dynamically route requests to different versions of MFEs, rewrite URLs to point to specific artifacts, or select variants based on geography, device type, or experimentation flags. These decisions are made without rebuilding or redeploying the host application, making edge integration particularly effective for progressive delivery strategies such as canary releases, AB testing, and phased rollouts.

By externalizing integration logic to the edge, teams reduce coupling between MFEs and the host while improving resilience and performance. Edge-based integration complements import maps and federated artifacts by focusing on *where* and *when* components are delivered, rather than *how* they are built. As frontend systems continue to scale globally, the edge is increasingly becoming a first-class participant in MFE deployment strategies.

Federated artifacts

As applications grew larger and teams became more independent, the traditional bundling and packaging approaches began to show strain. Build-time integration using npm packages offered predictability but limited agility: each time an MFE changed, the host application had to rebuild and redeploy. On the other hand, legacy approaches like UMD provided runtime flexibility but lacked fine-grained dependency management and version safety.

In this gap emerged Webpack Module Federation, which is a groundbreaking feature introduced in Webpack 5 that fundamentally redefined how frontends could share and consume code at runtime. Instead of packaging and redeploying entire bundles, MFEs could now expose their build artifacts dynamically, allowing other applications to import them when needed. This idea transformed front-end integration from a static pipeline into a federated runtime network.

With Module Federation, Webpack became more than a bundler; it evolved into an application composition engine. It allowed teams to treat their builds as *federated artifacts,* which can be independently versioned, discoverable, and loadable modules across deployments, without prior coupling at build time.

Understanding the concept of Module Federation

At its core, Module Federation enables multiple Webpack builds to share modules with each other at runtime. Each build, typically representing an MFE, can act as both a host (consumer) and a remote (provider). The federation system orchestrates these relationships through configuration objects that declare which modules are exposed and which remote modules can be consumed.

A minimal setup might look like this:

```
// webpack.config.js for Product MFE
module.exports = {
```

```
  name: "productMFE",
  filename: "remoteEntry.js",
  exposes: {
    "./ProductList": "./src/ProductList",
  },
  shared: ["react", "react-dom"],
};
```

Here, the producer of the ProductMFE has to set up the webpack config, which can create the ProductMFE artifact and expose it via the **remoteEntry.js** file. Along with that bundle, it can also expose any specific asset directly via the exposes object (ProductList in this case). Finally, it provides an option to share any common dependencies (ex: **react** and **react-dom**) which are required to run the ProductMFE. Let us see how this can be integrated on the consumer side:

```
// webpack.config.js for Shell App (host)
module.exports = {
  name: "shellApp",
  remotes: {
    productMFE: "productMFE@https://cdn.example.com/product/remoteEntry.js",
  },
  shared: ["react", "react-dom"],
};
```

At runtime, when the Shell App needs to render the ProductList component, it dynamically fetches it from the remote entry URL. The code executes seamlessly, as though it were locally bundled, except it was not part of the host's original build.

This ability to compose applications at runtime marked a turning point in MFE architecture. It allowed teams to achieve true deployment independence, where one MFE could update and deploy without rebuilding others.

Internals of federated artifacts

When Webpack builds a federated module, it generates a **remoteEntry.js** manifest, an artifact that describes what the remote exposes and how its dependencies are structured. The host application references this manifest at runtime, enabling it to import exposed components dynamically using asynchronous module loading.

For example, a shell application can import a remote component like this:

```
const ProductList = React.lazy(() => import("productMFE/ProductList"));
```

When the shell runs, Webpack automatically resolves this import from the remote entry, fetching the corresponding bundle from the CDN or deployment location. Because the manifest defines dependency versions, Webpack can share common libraries such as React or Lodash, ensuring they are loaded only once and reused across all MFEs.

This design results in two key advantages:

- **Reduced duplication**: Shared dependencies are cached and reused across MFEs, cutting load times and bundle sizes.
- **True independence**: MFEs can be built and deployed independently yet still integrate seamlessly at runtime.

Together, these features make Module Federation ideal for large-scale, distributed applications maintained by multiple teams, which is the very challenge MFEs were designed to solve.

Runtime loading and negotiation flow

While federated artifacts are produced at build time, their true power emerges at runtime. Unlike traditional bundling, where integration is resolved before deployment, Module Federation defers composition until the browser executes the application. This allows MFEs to remain independently deployable while still forming a cohesive user experience.

At runtime, the shell application does not directly import code that was bundled ahead of time. Instead, it participates in a structured loading and negotiation process orchestrated by the federation runtime. This process determines *where code is loaded from, which dependencies are shared*, and *how compatibility is enforced*, all while the application is already running. This is illustrated in the following figure:

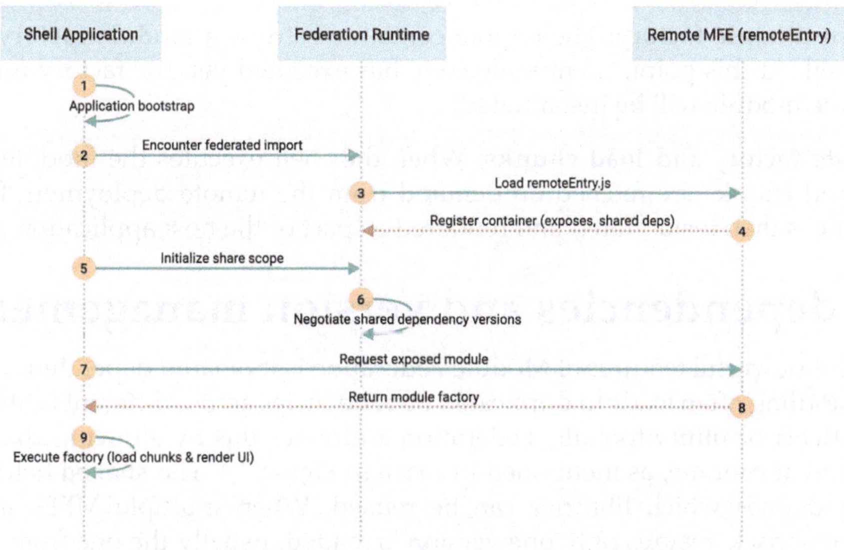

Figure 7.4: *Runtime loading and negotiation flow of federated artifacts*

The runtime flow shown in *Figure 7.4* can be understood as a deterministic sequence of steps:

1. **Application bootstrap**: The shell application loads its own bundle and initializes the Webpack runtime. At this stage, no remote code is involved.
2. **Encounter federated import**: When execution reaches a federated import, resolution is deferred. The shell signals that the module must be resolved dynamically at runtime rather than from its local bundle.
3. **Load remoteEntry file**: The federation runtime injects the remote's **`remoteEntry.js`** as a script tag. This file serves as a manifest and entry point, describing exposed modules and shared dependency requirements.
4. **Register remote container**: Once loaded, the remote entry registers a container in the global runtime scope. The container exposes module factories and metadata but does not execute application logic.
5. **Initialize share scope**: The shell initializes the remote container with its shared dependency scope, declaring which libraries it can provide and which versions it expects to consume.
6. **Negotiate shared dependency versions**: The federation runtime resolves compatible versions of shared dependencies across host and remote builds. Depending on the configuration, it may select a singleton instance, isolate incompatible versions, or fail fast if constraints cannot be satisfied.
7. **Request exposed module**: After dependency negotiation succeeds, the shell requests a specific exposed module from the remote container.
8. **Return module factory**: The remote container returns a **module factory function** to the shell. At this point, no module code has executed yet; the factory merely defines how the module will be instantiated.
9. **Execute factory and load chunks**: When the shell executes the module factory, any required chunks are fetched on demand from the remote deployment location. The module is then instantiated and rendered as part of the host application.

Shared dependencies and version management

One of the most powerful features of Module Federation is its shared dependency mechanism. Traditional bundling often leads to duplicated dependencies across different builds, especially libraries like React or utility toolkits. Federation addresses this by allowing shared modules to be negotiated at runtime, as mentioned in *step 6* in *Figure 7.4*. The **`shared`** field in Webpack configuration defines which libraries can be reused. When multiple MFEs use the same dependency, Webpack ensures only one version is loaded, usually the one from the host or a designated provider. In practice, this often means designating certain libraries as singletons, ensuring that only one instance is loaded across the entire application. Frameworks such as

React are commonly configured this way to preserve hook semantics, context propagation, and state continuity.

Version requirements further constrain this process, allowing teams to specify compatible ranges while preventing silent incompatibilities. In the ideal case, both the shell and the remote agree on a compatible version range and explicitly enforce a singleton. This ensures that only one instance of the library is loaded and reused across all MFEs. The following code explains how the config is setup in the host and the remote:

```
// webpack.config.js – Shell Application
shared: {
  react: {
    singleton: true,
    requiredVersion: "^18.2.0"
  },
  "react-dom": {
    singleton: true,
    requiredVersion: "^18.2.0"
  }
}


// webpack.config.js – Product MFE (Remote)
shared: {
  react: {
    singleton: true,
    requiredVersion: "^18.2.0"
  },
  "react-dom": {
    singleton: true,
    requiredVersion: "^18.2.0"
  }
}
```

This is because both applications declare compatible requirements, the federation runtime selects a single React instance, typically provided by the shell. The library is loaded once, cached, and shared across MFEs. Hooks, context, and state flow correctly across application boundaries, and no duplicate framework code is downloaded.

When versions align, the result is both performance and correctness: a single shared library instance is downloaded once, cached, and reused by all MFEs. When versions drift, however, the system must make trade-offs. Consider a remote MFE that upgrades React independently.

```
// webpack.config.js – Shell Application
shared: {
  react: {
    singleton: true,
    strictVersion: true,
    requiredVersion: "^18.2.0"
  }
}

// webpack.config.js – Remote MFE
shared: {
  react: {
    singleton: true,
    strictVersion: true,
    requiredVersion: "^18.3.0"
  }
}
```

As you can see in the above Remote MFE code, the React version is **`18.3.0`**, and it mismatches with the host React version. At runtime, the federation layer must resolve this mismatch. Depending on the **`strictVersion`** configuration, one of two outcomes occurs:

- If teams enable strict version checks, the federation runtime rejects the incompatible remote at startup, surfacing the mismatch as a clear runtime error. While disruptive, this behavior prevents silent correctness bugs and forces teams to resolve version alignment before deployment.
- If strict version enforcement is not enabled, Webpack may load a second copy of React for the remote MFE. While the application continues to function, subtle failures can emerge: hooks may break, context may not propagate across MFEs, and state shared through React internals becomes inconsistent. These issues are often difficult to diagnose because the system does not fail immediately.

This behavior underscores an important reality of federated artifacts: runtime flexibility does not eliminate the need for coordination; it merely moves it from build time to governance and contract management. When two MFEs depend on incompatible library versions, the federation layer may isolate them, negating sharing benefits. Many organizations mitigate this by maintaining approved dependency baselines or version contracts, ensuring compatible versions across teams.

Advantages of federated artifacts

Federated artifacts revolutionized how teams build and release frontends by shifting integration from build time to runtime. The benefits are profound:

- **Dynamic code sharing**: MFEs can load modules from one another without recompiling, reducing redundancy and enabling live updates.
- **Independent deployment**: Teams can release features autonomously, supporting continuous delivery at scale.
- **Optimized performance**: Shared libraries load once and persist in cache, cutting down bundle size and improving load times.
- **Progressive modernization**: Legacy applications can incrementally adopt MFEs without full rewrites by simply consuming federated bundles.
- **Flexible composition**: Hosts can decide which remote MFEs to include, allowing runtime configuration and feature toggling.

These capabilities make Module Federation a key enabler of scalable front-end ecosystems, aligning technical architecture with organizational autonomy.

Challenges and considerations

Despite its strengths, Module Federation introduces a new layer of operational complexity. Teams must carefully coordinate version compatibility and deployment sequencing. Unlike static builds, runtime integration means that an incompatible update can break the host unexpectedly. Strong contract testing and integration validation are therefore crucial. Caching and CDN invalidation are also challenging. Because federated bundles load from remote URLs, aggressive caching may cause hosts to pull outdated versions, similar to the issue with UMD. Proper cache-busting strategies such as versioned filenames, query hashes, or manifest updates are essential.

Security is another dimension. Loading remote code dynamically can expose applications to injection risks if not properly controlled. Enterprise-grade implementations typically include allowlists of trusted origins or signed manifests to mitigate such threats. Finally, tooling and developer experience remain evolving areas. Debugging distributed runtime code, tracing performance bottlenecks across MFEs, or ensuring source map alignment can be complex. Advanced monitoring and observability tools are required to maintain confidence in production systems.

Best practices for federated MFE deployments

To succeed with federated artifacts, teams adopt structured governance and technical consistency:

- Align on shared dependency versions and regularly audit them.
- Host all remote entries behind versioned CDN URLs with proper cache-control.
- Implement integration testing pipelines that validate host-remote compatibility before promotion.
- Use semantic versioning and manifest-based discovery to manage updates safely.

Apply observability and error isolation at runtime, ensuring one faulty MFE does not impact the entire application. These practices transform runtime composition from an experimental feature into a reliable enterprise discipline.

Deployment pipelines

Every change in an MFE's codebase begins a journey, from a developer's local machine to a live, running application. The system that automates this journey is the deployment pipeline. It takes raw code, tests it, builds it into a deployable artifact, and promotes it through environments until it reaches production. In earlier web projects, these steps were mostly manual and slow, often depending on scripts or human coordination. Today, automation handles almost everything. This approach is known as **continuous integration** (**CI**) and **continuous deployment** (**CD**).

CI is the practice of merging code changes frequently into a shared mainline so that every developer always works with the most recent version of the application. Each integration triggers an automated process that builds, tests, and validates the combined codebase. This approach helps teams detect integration issues early and ensures that all contributors stay aligned with the latest source, preventing long-lived branches and painful merge conflicts.

CD extends this principle by automatically promoting the successfully integrated code through testing and staging environments into production. Together, CI and CD form an automated delivery pipeline that keeps software always in a releasable state, reducing manual steps and making releases routine rather than risky. This is explained in the following figure:

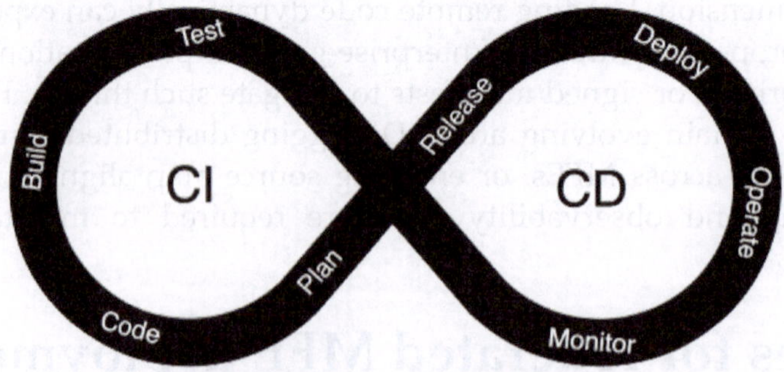

Figure 7.5: CI/CD process in action

Figure 7.5 illustrates the CI and CD cycle, represented in an infinity-shaped loop to emphasize its ongoing nature. The left side of the loop, labeled CI, captures the activities that transform source code into a validated, ready-to-deploy artifact. These steps include *Code, Build, Test,* and *Plan,* forming a closed system of continuous improvement within development. The right side of the loop, labeled CD, represents the delivery and operational phases, which include *Deploy, Operate, Monitor,* and *Release*. These stages ensure that validated artifacts are released to production, observed for performance and reliability, and continuously refined based on insights and feedback.

Together, both loops create a seamless lifecycle that connects development and operations. The intersection between Plan and Release signifies collaboration between teams and the iterative handoff that keeps software delivery in motion. This model reinforces the DevOps philosophy, a continuous, repeatable process that enables rapid, reliable, and resilient delivery from code commit to customer feedback.

CI/CD in the context of MFE

MFEs mirror the evolution of microservices: small, focused units developed and deployed by independent teams. Each MFE can move at its own pace, but the user experiences them as a unified product. In a typical setup, every MFE runs its own CI pipeline, triggered by commits or pull requests. The pipeline lint's code, runs tests, performs type checks, and builds the deployable artifact (an npm package, federated bundle, or static asset set). Once validated, the artifact is pushed to a versioned repository such as a private npm registry or a CDN, becoming a candidate for deployment.

The CI phase is typically illustrated in the following code:

```
name: Frontend CI/CD

on:
  push:
    branches: [main]
  pull_request:

jobs:
  pipeline:
    runs-on: ubuntu-latest
    steps:
      - name: Checkout source code
        uses: actions/checkout@v4

      - name: Install dependencies
```

```
        run: npm ci

      - name: Build application
        run: npm run build

      - name: Run tests
        run: npm test

      - name: Deploy
        run: npm run deploy
```

At its simplest, a frontend CI/CD pipeline follows a predictable sequence: install dependencies, build the application, validate it through tests, and deploy the resulting artifacts. The exact tooling may vary, but this structure is consistent across most modern delivery systems.

The CD phase builds on this foundation. Depending on the integration model, the artifact may be:

- Published as a versioned npm package and consumed by host applications during their next build,
- Uploaded as a remoteEntry.js bundle to a CDN, and dynamically discovered by hosts at runtime, or
- Promoted through multiple environments (development | staging | production) using a manifest-based orchestration layer.

Each MFE pipeline operates independently, but together they form a federated delivery ecosystem. The success of CI/CD in this environment depends not only on automation tools but also on cultural alignment in which the teams must trust their pipelines enough to release frequently, and coordinate through contracts rather than shared codebases.

From centralized to distributed delivery

In traditional frontend deployments, a single DevOps or release engineering team owned the deployment pipeline. All commits are merged into a central branch, and one build represents the product. This created bottlenecks: one team's delay could halt an entire release cycle. With MFEs, that model no longer fits. Each team is responsible for the full lifecycle of its feature from commit to deployment, but within a shared ecosystem of standards and guardrails.

The introduction of federated CI/CD, where each MFE has its own independent pipeline governed by common conventions, brings both power and complexity. Builds happen in parallel. Releases are asynchronous. Updates flow continuously without coordination meetings or *release trains*. Yet, because each pipeline outputs versioned artifacts, the system remains traceable and recoverable. If something fails, rollback is a matter of redeploying a known artifact, not undoing a massive monolithic change.

This decentralized model introduces a new dimension of organizational scalability. Teams can innovate at their own pace, experiment safely, and deliver value faster, all while the larger application remains stable. In effect, CI/CD becomes not just a technical automation, but an operational philosophy, the one that enables continuous delivery at scale through structure, governance, and trust in automation.

Frontend pipelines vs. backend pipelines

While CI/CD principles are universal, frontend pipelines differ subtly from backend ones. Backend services often deploy to long-running environments in containers, functions, or servers. Frontend MFEs, however, deploy immutable artifacts: static files that must be versioned, cached, and served globally through CDNs or edge networks.

This distinction introduces unique considerations:

- **Build reproducibility**: The same artifact must behave identically across environments.
- **Caching and invalidation**: Frontend deployments require explicit strategies to handle browser and CDN caching.
- **Static vs. dynamic delivery**: MFEs may be static bundles (npm artifacts) or dynamic remotes (Webpack Federation), demanding different CD workflows.
- **Observability and rollback**: Once deployed to a CDN, rollback involves version switching, not redeploying code.

Thus, while backend CI/CD focuses on container orchestration, frontend CI/CD emphasizes artifact governance, dependency consistency, and delivery integrity. This is illustrated in the following figure:

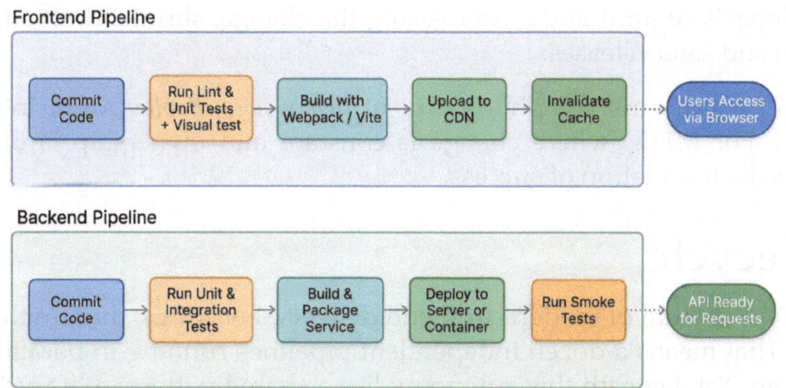

Figure 7.6: *Typical frontend and backend pipeline showing code commit to deployment*

Figure 7.6 depicts a typical frontend and backend pipeline steps that are needed to deploy the changes for consumption. A frontend pipeline is designed to build, test, and deliver static assets that run directly in the user's browser. The process begins when developers commit code, triggering automated checks such as linting and unit tests to maintain code quality. The code is then bundled and optimized using tools like Webpack or Vite, producing lightweight assets that improve performance. These optimized files are uploaded to a CDN, ensuring global availability and faster load times. Once uploaded, caches are invalidated so that users immediately receive the latest version of the application. The final stage of the pipeline results in an updated **Single Page Application** (**SPA**) that users can access seamlessly from their browsers.

In contrast, the backend pipeline focuses on preparing and deploying the logic that powers APIs, authentication, and data services. Similar to the frontend process, it begins with a code commit, followed by automated unit and integration tests that verify business logic and service interactions. The backend code is then packaged, often as a Docker image, and deployed to containerized or server environments such as Kubernetes or **Elastic Container Service** (**ECS**) containers. After deployment, smoke tests validate the health and readiness of the service before it starts handling live traffic. While the frontend pipeline ends with assets on a CDN, the backend pipeline culminates in a running API service, ensuring that both layers of the system are independently built, tested, and deployed in harmony.

Need for CI/CD in MFEs

For a distributed frontend ecosystem, CI/CD is not optional. It is the glue that keeps independent pipelines coherent. Without automated build, test, and deployment flows, teams quickly lose synchronization. Version drift, inconsistent dependencies, and untested integrations can cascade into instability.

Automation brings discipline. Every change passes through a consistent pipeline of validation and release. Testing becomes enforceable rather than aspirational. Artifacts become traceable, auditable, and reproducible. Most importantly, deployment velocity, which is the time between a developer's commit and a user seeing the change, shrinks dramatically, enabling faster innovation and safer releases.

Therefore, CI/CD transforms the philosophy of *deploy less, deploy safely* into *deploy often, deploy confidently*. For MFEs, where change is constant and ownership is distributed, this transformation is the foundation of success.

CI/CD lifecycle

CI and CD form the rhythm of modern frontend delivery. For MFEs, that rhythm is not linear but distributed. That means a dozen independent pipelines running in parallel, each owned by a separate team. Yet, beneath this autonomy lies a shared pattern: a lifecycle that ensures every change is tested, versioned, and deployed with precision. This section breaks down that lifecycle from the moment code is committed to the moment it reaches users, highlighting how automation, validation, and governance align to make continuous delivery possible across a federated ecosystem.

From commit to build

Every lifecycle begins with a commit. A developer merges code into the MFE's repository, triggering the CI pipeline. The first stage focuses on verification, which ensures fast, deterministic checks that catch issues early.

Common CI tasks include:

- Static analysis through linting and type checks.
- Unit and snapshot tests to validate functionality.
- Security scanning for dependency vulnerabilities.
- Code style and coverage thresholds enforced automatically.

This is the guardrail stage, which ensures that only code that meets baseline standards progresses downstream. Pipelines are triggered automatically (via Git hooks or CI services like GitHub Actions, GitLab CI, or Jenkins) and execute in isolated environments to maintain reproducibility.

Once validation succeeds, the pipeline moves into the build stage, in which the raw code will be transformed into deployable output. Depending on the architecture, this could be a compiled JavaScript bundle, a Webpack federated module, or a versioned `npm` package. The bundler and transpiler (Webpack, Rollup, or Vite) handle minification, tree-shaking, and source map generation.

By the end of this stage, the MFE produces a candidate artifact that is the digital equivalent of a manufactured component ready for quality inspection.

Artifact creation and versioning

After building, the artifact is prepared for deployment. This involves versioning, packaging, and publishing to a central repository.

Artifacts might take different forms:

- A package published to an npm registry for build-time integration.
- A remoteEntry.js file deployed to a CDN for runtime federation.
- A zip or tar bundle stored in artifact repositories like Artifactory or Nexus.

Versioning follows SemVer as discussed in the previous section. Each versioned artifact is immutable, ensuring traceability. If `@tunestream/playlist-ui@1.2.3` is promoted to staging, the same binary artifact moves to production. This immutability makes debugging, rollback, and audit logging reliable. A pipeline step typically signs and tags the artifact, producing metadata such as commit hash, build timestamp, and dependency versions. These details are stored alongside the artifact to enable precise tracking later in the delivery chain.

Publish and store artifacts

Once validated and versioned, the artifact is published to its destination repository, which would be a single source of truth for deployment.

For MFEs, this could be:

- npm or JFrog or GitHub Packages (for private package distribution).
- S3 buckets, CloudFront, or Fastly CDNs (for runtime bundles).
- Internal artifact stores (for hybrid deployments or offline environments).

Publishing automatically updates manifests that record the artifact's location and version. Host applications or orchestration layers can use these manifests to discover the latest compatible versions dynamically. In federated setups, the output might include a **`remoteEntry.json`** or manifest file describing the MFE's exposed modules and shared dependencies. This metadata allows runtime loaders to fetch and mount the MFE on demand, which is a core aspect of runtime composition as discussed earlier in *Chapter 3, Designing Micro-frontends.*

Staging and integration testing

Once the artifact is published, the CD pipeline begins promoting it through environments. The first stop is usually staging, where integration and end-to-end tests validate that the artifact behaves correctly within its host ecosystem.

Here, automated test suites verify:

- Host and remote compatibility (API contracts, event schemas).
- UI consistency through visual regression tools (e.g., Storybook, Chromatic).
- Functional correctness using E2E tests (e.g., Cypress, Playwright).
- Performance benchmarks and accessibility checks.

For federated MFEs, the staging environment also confirms that remote entry URLs resolve correctly, and shared dependencies load as expected. In large organizations, staging environments may be ephemeral, in which the environment will be automatically created for each pull request and destroyed afterward to save cost and ensure isolation. Only after passing these integration gates does an artifact qualify for promotion.

Promotion to production

The promotion phase represents the final stage of the CI/CD lifecycle. Instead of rebuilding, the same artifact from staging is simply promoted to production. Promotion can be triggered automatically after successful tests or manually for added control in sensitive systems.

For npm-based MFEs, this means publishing to a production registry namespace (e.g., moving from **@internal/dev** to **@internal/prod** or **@test/pkg-1.0.0-beta** to **@test/pkg-1.0.0**). For runtime-federated bundles, it means replicating assets to production CDNs and updating manifest endpoints.

Production deployments are often versioned using immutable URLs or hashed filenames to ensure cache safety. For example:

```
// versioned url
https://cdn.tunestream.com/playlist/1.3.2/remoteEntry.js

// hashed url
https://cdn.tunestream.com/playlist/remoteEntry.9f2b7c1a4d.js

// version + hashed url
https://cdn.tunestream.com/playlist/1.3.2/remoteEntry.9f2b7c1a4d.js
```

This guarantees users always load a predictable, tested version of the artifact. In some cases, pipelines implement canary or phased rollouts, that is, gradually routing a percentage of users to the new version and monitoring performance metrics before full rollout. If regressions occur, rollback is instantaneous: revert the manifest pointer to the previous version, no rebuild required.

Observability and feedback loop

Once in production, the lifecycle does not end; it loops instead. Observability systems monitor performance, error rates, and deployment success. Dashboards track metrics like load time, render success, and API error frequency. We will look into various observability and monitoring approaches in the next chapter.

If anomalies arise, the CI/CD pipeline provides instant rollback or triggers automated alerts. Logs, metrics, and user feedback all feed back into development, closing the loop and enabling continuous improvement.

This observability-driven feedback ensures MFEs remain healthy and responsive long after deployment, thus reinforcing confidence in automation.

End-to-end flow

The following figure illustrates this continuous loop of integration, delivery, and feedback:

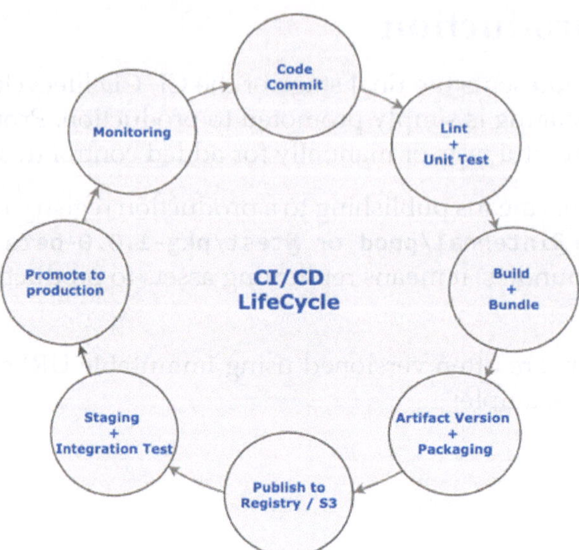

Figure 7.7: CI/CD lifecycle

Figure 7.7 illustrates the complete lifecycle of a frontend CI/CD pipeline, showing how every stage from code commit to production deployment forms a continuous loop of improvement. The circular representation emphasizes that delivery does not end with deployment but instead cycles back through monitoring, feedback, and iteration. This loop reflects the principles of Agile and the broader **software development life cycle (SDLC)**, where teams continuously build, test, release, and refine their applications. Each transition between stages represents a key automation point that ensures consistency, reduces human error, and promotes faster and more reliable software delivery.

Each MFE follows this loop independently but within a shared framework of standards, ensuring consistent quality, traceability, and control across teams. CI/CD pipelines orchestrate this process with precision, transforming human-driven releases into automated, verifiable flows. From code commit to monitoring, each stage reinforces trust: code is tested, artifacts are immutable, environments are consistent, and feedback is immediate. When multiplied across dozens of teams, this structure transforms complexity into order, thus allowing organizations to scale their frontends without losing control.

Pipeline architecture and tooling

The power of continuous delivery lies not just in automation, but in how automation is architected. In an MFE ecosystem, every pipeline is both autonomous and interconnected. Each MFE builds, tests, and deploys independently, yet collectively forms the experience users see. To keep this distributed system reliable, the underlying CI/CD architecture must balance flexibility with control, thus allowing teams to innovate freely while adhering to common operational standards.

Architecting pipelines for MFEs

While tool selection matters, the architecture of pipelines is what determines scalability and stability in a multi-MFE ecosystem where each MFE is built and deployed in an independent fashion, and must communicate seamlessly without friction. A mature organization structures its pipelines around three design principles:

- **Autonomy per MFE**: Each MFE owns its full lifecycle, from build scripts to deployment triggers. Pipelines are defined within the same repository as the code to minimize dependencies. This isolation allows teams to deploy at their own pace, a critical factor for organizational scalability. This step has prerequisites, though, as each team should be aware of its dependencies and have them sorted out upfront. Though it has the freedom to create bundles, it should follow a common standard or tools to avoid friction at a later stage while integrating with the host.
- **Shared templates and governance**: Despite autonomy, consistency matters. Most enterprises maintain a shared pipeline template repository containing standardized configurations, such as build stages, testing thresholds, and artifact publishing steps. Teams import these templates into their pipelines, ensuring alignment without restricting freedom. For instance, a common YAML snippet might define artifact signing, test coverage enforcement, or publishing conventions.
- **Federated orchestration**: While each MFE deploys independently, a higher-level orchestrator (or registry service) tracks artifact states and compatibility. Hosts and shells consume manifests to discover the latest remote entries or `npm` package versions. This orchestration model provides visibility and control, which forms the foundation for a federated CI/CD architecture.

Connecting pipelines across teams

In distributed MFE ecosystems, though pipelines seem to exist in isolation, it has to communicate. When one MFE is updated, downstream consumers may need to rebuild or verify compatibility. To manage this dependency network, organizations adopt a manifest-driven model.

Each MFE publishes metadata after a successful build:

```
{
  "name": "playlistMFE",
  "version": "1.3.2",
  "remoteEntry": "https://cdn.tunestream.com/playlist/1.3.2/remoteEntry.js",
  "shared": ["react", "react-dom"]
}
```

The host application or shell fetches this manifest dynamically during its own pipeline, as referenced in the following conceptual code section, ensuring it always references the latest tested version:

```
// Host application resolving which federated artifact to load
async function loadManifest() {
  const response = await fetch("/mfe-manifest.json");
  return response.json();
}
const manifest = await loadManifest();
const playlistRemote = manifest.playlistMFE.remoteEntry;
```

At runtime or during deployment, the host resolves federated dependencies through the manifest rather than hard-coded URLs. This indirection allows the host to consume the latest validated version of an MFE without rebuilding or redeploying downstream applications. This design eliminates manual dependency updates and allows asynchronous deployment. One team can release without requiring others to rebuild, in which the host simply pulls the latest manifest on the next deployment.

Note: In this model, the manifest is a coordination mechanism, not a loading mechanism. It allows hosts and pipelines to agree on which federated artifact is active, while Module Federation remains responsible for how that artifact is loaded, shared, and executed at runtime. By separating version selection from module loading, teams avoid entangling deployment decisions with application code.

More mature platforms extend this idea by promoting a centralized, versioned manifest that governs all MFEs collectively, as described later in the *Manifest-driven discovery* section.

Strategies for coordinated delivery

Over time, organizations have evolved several models for managing distributed pipelines. The right model depends on scale, organizational culture, and technical maturity. The following are a few types of pipelines that can be used:

- **Fully independent pipelines**: Each MFE maintains its own end-to-end pipeline from code commit to production without centralized orchestration. Artifacts are published to a shared registry or storage, such as an npm repository or an S3 bucket, and are consumed by the host application. When the host dynamically loads these artifacts at runtime through a manifest or remote entry, using techniques like Webpack Module Federation or a versioned manifest file, each MFE can deploy independently without requiring the host to rebuild. This enables true asynchronous delivery, allowing updates to appear immediately after validation.

If the host instead imports MFEs during its own build process, for example, by consuming npm packages or static dependencies, then it must be rebuilt to incorporate the latest versions. In this case, integration is semi-independent rather than fully decoupled. Regardless of approach, this model relies heavily on strict versioning discipline and clearly defined interface contracts between teams. Consumer applications must handle backward compatibility through semantic versioning and runtime configuration to maintain stability across independent releases.

For example, TuneStream's `@tunestream/recommendations-ui` pipeline operates completely independently of `@tunestream/playlist-ui`. The host shell fetches each remote's manifest dynamically, ensuring that even if one MFE deploys ahead of another, the overall application remains functional without requiring a rebuild.

- **Semi-coordinated releases**: Here, pipelines remain independent but share integration checkpoints. Before deploying to production, MFEs are automatically validated in a shared staging environment. Contract tests verify that APIs, events, and visual layouts remain compatible. This approach provides a safety net without introducing rigid coupling. Changes can still be released individually, but every new build passes through a cross-MFE integration suite that mirrors real-world composition.

  For example, a CI job in the shell application triggers after any MFE publishes a new version. It loads all remotes from the registry, performs smoke tests, and reports integration results. If any incompatibility arises, the release is paused until it is resolved.

- **Orchestrated rollouts**: In tightly coupled ecosystems, such as shared navigation layers or global state providers, MFEs may need orchestrated deployment cycles. An orchestration pipeline coordinates version compatibility across teams, ensuring that shared dependencies (like React or design systems) remain aligned. This model often uses manifest orchestration in which a centralized service would track the latest validated versions of each MFE and define which combinations are approved for deployment. Hosts then load MFEs based on this manifest rather than live registry data. More details on manifest-based discovery are mentioned in the next section.

  For example, TuneStream's global shell references a manifest JSON that looks like:

```
{
  "playlistMFE": "1.3.2",
  "recommendationsMFE": "2.1.0",
  "analyticsMFE": "1.8.5"
}
```

When staging tests validate a new combination, the manifest updates automatically. Production hosts fetch this manifest to ensure only approved builds are deployed. This guarantees coherence across independently deployed modules.

Manifest-driven discovery

While earlier examples show manifest usage at an individual or host level, large-scale systems typically converge on a single, production-grade manifest that serves as the authoritative source of truth across all MFEs. Rather than hardcoding URLs or versions, the host application reads from a manifest file that maps each MFE to its latest deployed artifact. This allows deployments to remain flexible and decoupled while still maintaining consistency across environments.

During an orchestrated rollout, each MFE's pipeline updates its own entry in the manifest after a successful deployment. The orchestrator then validates and promotes the manifest as a single versioned asset, ensuring that all participating MFEs are released in sync. This is because the manifest can be promoted independently of the host build, and new versions of MFEs can be activated instantly or rolled back simply by reverting to a previous manifest version. Here is a production-grade manifest example:

```
{
  "version": "2025.10.16",
  "environment": "production",
  "lastUpdated": "2025-10-16T08:24:12Z",
  "apps": {
    "playlist-ui": {
      "url": "https://cdn.tunestream.com/playlist/2.5.3/remoteEntry.9a7f2b1c.
js",
      "integrity": "sha384-H2S7h3l0...XaA==",
      "module": "PlaylistApp",
      "team": "playlist",
      "version": "2.5.3"
    },
    "recommendations-ui": {
      "url": "https://cdn.tunestream.com/recommendations/3.1.1/remoteEntry.
f2b9d31a.js",
      "integrity": "sha384-pJ3l92p...tZQ==",
      "module": "RecommendationsApp",
      "team": "recommendations",
      "version": "3.1.1"
    },
    "analytics-ui": {
      "url": "https://cdn.tunestream.com/analytics/1.9.0/remoteEntry.c89d23af.
js",
      "integrity": "sha384-Xa23F9k...gTQ==",
```

```
      "module": "AnalyticsApp",
      "team": "analytics",
      "version": "1.9.0"
    }
  }
}
```

In a real-time environment, the host application typically downloads the manifest file at startup or at regular intervals. Each manifest entry points to a specific, immutable version of a remote module, ensuring that the application always loads the exact version intended for that release. When a team deploys a new version of its MFE, the corresponding entry in the manifest is automatically updated by the CI/CD pipeline to reflect the latest artifact and its metadata. If a rollback is required, the system can simply revert to an earlier version of the manifest, such as **`manifest-2025.10.15.json`**, allowing the entire frontend ecosystem to return instantly to a previously verified state without rebuilding or redeploying the host.

Cross-pipeline dependencies

Even when pipelines are autonomous, they often share common dependencies such as UI libraries, frameworks, or analytics SDKs. Coordinating these shared dependencies requires dependency awareness across pipelines.

Common techniques include:

- **Shared dependency contracts**: Defining a central baseline (e.g., React 18.2.0, TypeScript 5.x) that all MFEs must align with.
- **Peer dependencies**: Declaring shared libraries as peers in each MFE's **`package.json`**, ensuring the host provides the runtime instance.
- **Automated compatibility checks**: CI bots that scan dependency manifests across all repositories and flag inconsistencies before integration.

This alignment minimizes bundle duplication and runtime version conflicts, which are common pitfalls in federated applications.

Best practices for CI/CD in MFE ecosystems

As MFE ecosystems mature, the complexity of managing multiple pipelines, environments, and deployment targets increases exponentially. Best practices become the foundation that keeps the system coherent. They transform automation from a collection of scripts into a predictable, governed workflow that supports independence without chaos. While tools and frameworks vary, successful teams share a common set of principles that guide how they build, test, and release.

A strong starting point is standardization. Each MFE may have its own repository and pipeline, but the structure of those pipelines should remain consistent. Shared templates ensure that every build follows the same sequence, such as lint, test, build, package, publish, and promote using common conventions for naming, artifact storage, and environment variables. These templates reduce cognitive load, accelerate onboarding, and allow governance to evolve centrally without disrupting individual teams. Mature organizations treat their pipeline definitions as versioned assets, distributed and updated like any other piece of code.

Another essential practice is isolation of configuration. Each artifact must define its own build logic and environment settings, independent of others. This prevents accidental coupling and allows a single pipeline failure to be contained within its domain. Teams that adopt infrastructure-as-code approaches, using tools like Terraform or CloudFormation, extend this principle to deployment environments, ensuring that infrastructure is reproducible and portable across regions or stages.

Security and integrity checks are woven throughout modern pipelines. Before any artifact is promoted, dependency scanning tools verify that open-source libraries meet policy requirements and do not expose vulnerabilities. Secrets management systems inject credentials securely at runtime instead of embedding them in configuration files. Every publish event is signed and auditable, providing a clear chain of custody from source to deployment. These controls turn CI/CD from a convenience into a trust framework.

When MFEs load code dynamically at runtime, CI/CD pipelines become part of the application's trust boundary. Hosts should restrict remote loading to explicitly allowed origins, preventing untrusted sources from injecting code. Artifact integrity can be strengthened through checksums or signature validation, ensuring that only outputs produced by approved pipelines are eligible for consumption. By enforcing provenance and integrity checks during build and promotion, teams preserve the flexibility of runtime composition without compromising security.

Automated testing at multiple levels remains the most effective guardrail. Unit tests verify logic, integration tests confirm cross-MFE compatibility, and end-to-end tests validate the user experience across hosts and remotes. When combined with visual regression testing and performance benchmarking, these automated checks transform quality from a manual review process into a measurable outcome enforced by the pipeline itself.

Observability and feedback complete the loop. Pipelines should not end at deployment but feed runtime metrics back into planning. Build durations, test success rates, rollback frequency, and release cadence all provide insights into system health. Teams that review these metrics regularly can identify friction, remove bottlenecks, and continuously refine their delivery process.

Finally, successful MFE organizations cultivate a culture of continuous improvement. Pipelines are not static; they evolve as technologies and practices mature. Teams experiment with new testing strategies, containerization techniques, or build optimizations and share their learnings across the organization. Over time, these shared insights turn best practices into institutional habits, making quality, security, and automation part of the everyday rhythm of development.

Well-designed CI/CD systems are not defined by their tools but by their discipline. Consistency, isolation, security, and feedback are the traits that allow a distributed architecture to move as one. When these principles are embedded in every pipeline, the complexity of MFEs becomes manageable, predictable, and, most importantly, continuously deliverable.

Operational complexities

Implementing CI/CD for MFEs introduces a level of complexity that few teams anticipate at the start. Each pipeline may run smoothly on its own, yet coordinating hundreds of them across different repositories, frameworks, and release cadences exposes new organizational and technical challenges. Over time, these challenges become valuable lessons that shape how teams evolve their delivery practices.

Challenges

The first and most common challenge is fragmentation. When every MFE maintains its own build configuration, testing setup, and deployment script, inconsistencies inevitably emerge. Small differences in naming conventions, dependency versions, or release triggers can lead to drift and make system-wide governance difficult. The lesson here is standardization. Shared templates and centralized CI/CD libraries ensure every team operates under the same structure while retaining autonomy over their feature code.

Another recurring challenge lies in dependency synchronization. MFEs often rely on shared libraries, frameworks, or APIs. When one MFE upgrades a dependency without coordination, others may break silently. Over time, organizations learn to establish dependency contracts, shared version baselines, and automated compatibility checks that run as part of every pipeline. These controls keep distributed systems cohesive even as teams move at different speeds.

Operational visibility also becomes harder as pipelines multiply. Failures, slow builds, or security issues can hide among the noise of continuous activity. Centralized dashboards and observability tools become essential, not optional. They provide a unified view of build health, deployment status, and artifact freshness across all MFEs, allowing teams to act before small issues escalate into widespread outages.

Learnings

Resource management poses another lesson. Large numbers of concurrent builds can overwhelm shared infrastructure, consuming compute time, caching space, and network bandwidth. Teams learn to optimize build caching, parallelization, and pipeline concurrency limits to keep CI systems performant. Over time, mature organizations treat building infrastructure as a first-class product that will be monitored, optimized, and evolved like any other service.

Perhaps the most important lesson is cultural. CI/CD for MFEs is not just a DevOps task but a collective discipline. It succeeds only when teams trust automation, respect versioning principles, and see testing and deployment as shared responsibilities rather than peripheral steps. Collaboration replaces coordination meetings, and governance shifts from control to enablement.

In practice, most teams discover that success comes from iteration. The first version of a pipeline may work, but it rarely scales. Each improvement, such as better caching, clearer manifests, and stricter tests, adds resilience. Over months and years, these refinements accumulate into a delivery fabric strong enough to support an entire ecosystem of independent applications.

The journey toward mature CI/CD for MFE teaches that automation alone is not enough. What matters most is consistency, visibility, and culture. When these elements align, distributed pipelines become more than build systems. They become the nervous system of the product, continuously integrating, validating, and delivering value without friction.

Conclusion

Deployment strategies form the backbone of a successful MFE ecosystem. This chapter explored how artifacts, packaging formats, and build pipelines come together to enable consistent and scalable delivery. From understanding the role of bundlers and transpilers to exploring module systems such as CommonJS, ESM, and UMD, we examined how modern build processes ensure portability and compatibility across environments. We also discussed federated artifacts using Webpack Module Federation and the ways in which CI/CD pipelines automate delivery through independent or orchestrated rollouts, balancing team autonomy with system coherence.

Ultimately, effective deployment is not just about shipping code; it is about delivering stable, observable, and verifiable experiences. Once an MFE reaches production, its lifecycle continues through observation, measurement, and iteration. The next chapter, *Observability and Monitoring*, builds on this foundation by examining how teams track performance, detect errors, and understand user behavior across distributed frontends. It introduces the principles and tools of modern observability, covering performance metrics, logging, error tracking, and distributed tracing to ensure that every deployed MFE remains reliable, performant, and aligned with user expectations.

Chapter 8
Observability and Monitoring

Introduction

This chapter emphasizes the importance of tracking performance, errors, and user behavior in modern web applications, particularly within an MFE architecture. As frontend systems have grown more dynamic and distributed, observability has become essential to understand how users experience the application, how independently deployed modules behave at runtime, and where failures originate. Modern MFEs operate in an environment where asynchronous boundaries, shared infrastructure, and independent release cycles make visibility critical to ensuring reliability. The chapter begins by outlining the core pillars of observability: logs, metrics, and traces. Also, we would see how they apply to frontend applications. It introduces several observability tools commonly used to monitor and debug MFEs, including **application performance monitoring** (**APM**) systems, log aggregation platforms, RUM analytics providers, and error-tracking solutions. These tools collectively help uncover bottlenecks, script failures, slow interactions, and degraded user experiences.

The challenges in the MFE section explore the unique issues that arise in MFE monitoring, such as tracing errors across independently deployed modules, tracking runtime failures in remote components, and managing decentralized telemetry data across teams. To address these challenges, the chapter explores logging and distributed tracing, detailing how shared correlation IDs, context propagation, and standardized logging schemas enable teams to form a unified view of user flows across MFEs. In addition, the chapter highlights the complexity of gathering consistent Analytics data in an MFE environment, where product metrics can easily fragment across separate modules. It presents strategies to centralize instrumentation, enforce governance, and create a uniform analytics layer that ensures accuracy, consistency, and meaningful insights.

Structure

The chapter covers the following topics:

- Necessity of monitoring in modern web
- Observability tools in modern web and MFE

- Observability challenges in MFEs
- Observability testing in MFEs
- Logging and distributed tracing in MFEs
- MFE analytics

Objectives

The objective of this chapter is to explain how performance, errors, and user behavior can be effectively monitored in an MFE-based application, where independent modules introduce complexity and fragmented visibility. This chapter outlines why modern web applications require consistent and proactive monitoring, introduces the tools and techniques used to gather meaningful performance and error data, and explains how observability restores clarity in a distributed environment. You will learn how to address the unique challenges that arise when MFEs generate decentralized logs, inconsistent metrics, and disconnected analytics signals. The chapter concludes by demonstrating how unified logging, distributed tracing, and shared analytics practices create an integrated view of user journeys and system health across all MFEs.

Necessity of monitoring in modern web

Modern web applications have evolved into highly interactive, stateful, and performance-sensitive systems that run substantial logic directly inside the browser. What was once a document rendering layer has expanded into a sophisticated application runtime responsible for orchestrating UI state, routing, data access, component rendering, caching, and meeting high performance expectations. With this shift, the browser has become a critical execution environment, and understanding its behavior is essential for building reliable and user-centric products. Monitoring, historically associated with backend systems, is now an indispensable requirement on the frontend. Many failures that directly impact users originate not from backend APIs but from issues within the browser environment itself. JavaScript errors, script initialization failures, layout instability, long task blocking, memory leaks, slow component updates, and unreliable third-party integrations all affect the user experience before a backend service is ever involved. Traditional server-side monitoring cannot capture these issues because the backend only sees requests; it does not see how long it took a component to render, whether the UI froze, or whether a script failed to load entirely. The diversity of end-user environments amplifies this need. Frontend performance and stability can vary dramatically across devices, browsers, network conditions, CPU capability, OS versions, and geographic regions. A feature that performs flawlessly on a high-end desktop may behave unpredictably on a mid-range mobile device with constrained resources. Without monitoring based on real-user conditions, these problems remain invisible, often emerging only through user complaints or support tickets. To illustrate the point, *Figure 8.1* highlights the layers of a modern web application where failures occur and why backend-only monitoring provides an incomplete picture:

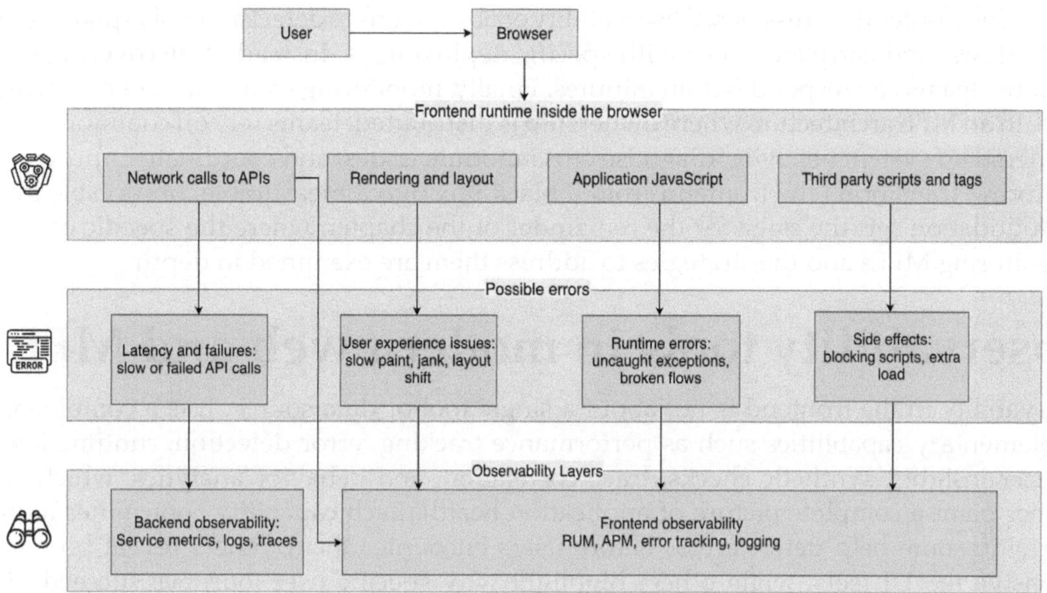

Figure 8.1: *Various frontend-specific errors that might arise and are captured at their respective observability layers*

This figure shows the various operations that happen in the browser engine and how many failures and performance issues occur, which span across rendering, JavaScript, network calls, and third-party scripts. Backend monitoring sees only a narrow part of this path, while frontend observability is required to capture the full user experience.

Monitoring MFEs

The transition toward MFEs intensifies the necessity of monitoring even further. MFEs allow independent teams to build, deploy, and evolve their own slices of the UI. While this decentralization increases velocity and flexibility, it also introduces new observability challenges. Failures can originate in one MFE but manifest in another. Performance degradations might only appear when multiple MFEs load simultaneously on the same page. Error signatures may differ across modules, and analytics funnels can become fragmented. Without a strong monitoring baseline, it becomes difficult or sometimes impossible to determine which MFE caused a regression, when it happened, and why. Additionally, modern businesses rely heavily on digital performance metrics. Even subtle degradations, such as an extra half-second in page load, a delayed interaction, a layout shift, or a broken scroll behavior, can reduce engagement and conversion. Through Core Web Vitals, Google established a widely adopted benchmark for modern web performance, making user experience measurable and comparable across products. Robust monitoring provides the data needed to detect regressions early, validate improvements, and ensure competitive performance.

Monitoring also supports operational excellence and rapid iteration. Continuous delivery pipelines, feature flags, canary releases, and real-time experimentation increase the risk of unintended frontend regressions. Observability enables teams to detect anomaly spikes, identify broken flows, and correlate issues with specific deployments. Instead of discovering failures days later, teams can respond within minutes. Finally, monitoring creates a shared truth across teams. In an MFE architecture where ownership is distributed, teams rely on common visibility to understand system behavior, diagnose cross-module issues, and coordinate improvements. Monitoring transforms the frontend from a black box into a measurable, observable system. This foundation sets the stage for the remainder of the chapter, where the specific challenges of monitoring MFEs and the strategies to address them are examined in depth.

Observability tools in modern web and MFE

Observability in the frontend is not about a single tool or data source. It is a combination of complementary capabilities such as performance tracking, error detection, runtime logging, real user insights, synthetic checks, trace correlation, and behavior analytics, which would together paint a complete picture of application health. Each capability contributes a unique viewpoint: some help detect errors before users encounter them, others reveal how fast or responsive the UI feels, while others highlight why specific user journeys succeed or fail. Viewed in isolation, these signals provide partial visibility. Viewed together, they form a cohesive, actionable understanding of the system.

In the context of modern web applications and especially from an MFE perspective, these capabilities serve distinct roles that map to different layers of the runtime experience. Some focus on measuring how the application performs in real-world environments, others on capturing the operational footprint of distributed UI modules, while others help validate stability through controlled testing or correlate a user session across independently deployed MFEs. Understanding what each category of observability does is essential to designing a balanced, scalable monitoring strategy.

The following subsections break down these categories, not by specific products, but by the function they serve in a modern frontend architecture. Each subsection explains the purpose of a particular observability capability, the type of insight it contributes, and how it fits into an MFE environment. Together, they form the foundational layers that we build upon in later sections when discussing the challenges and implementation patterns unique to MFEs.

Overview of the observability landscape

At the highest level, the landscape can be viewed through the lens of *what questions each capability answers*. Performance monitoring helps to determine how quickly the application loads and how responsive it feels. Error monitoring reveals which failures users encounter and how frequently they occur. Logging captures detailed diagnostic information that is invaluable during investigation. Real user monitoring provides insights into actual user behavior under real conditions, while synthetic monitoring verifies stability through controlled, repeatable checks. Distributed tracing enables teams to follow a user's journey across multiple MFEs and backend services, preserving continuity that is otherwise lost in distributed UI architectures. Finally, behavior and product analytics expose how users navigate the system, highlighting friction points and validating whether application flows behave as intended.

Together, these categories define the core of frontend observability. Each one focuses on a different layer of the runtime experience, but they collectively form a cohesive model of system health. In the subsections that follow, we explore each category in more detail, thus clarifying what it measures, what value it provides, and how it contributes to a complete observability strategy for MFEs.

Real user monitoring

Real user monitoring (**RUM**) focuses on capturing performance and behavioral data directly from actual users as they interact with the application. Unlike synthetic tests or controlled lab measurements, RUM reflects real-world conditions using different devices, network speeds, CPU capabilities, browsers, geographic regions, and usage patterns. It provides the most authentic representation of how users truly experience the application in production.

At its core, RUM answers questions such as:

1. How fast does the application load for real users?
2. Which devices or networks experience slower performance?
3. Are certain user segments more affected by layout shifts or interaction delays?
4. How do performance metrics vary across browsers, geographies, or connection types?
5. Which MFE contributes to specific performance degradation?

RUM typically captures standardized web performance metrics, including Core Web Vitals such as **Largest Contentful Paint** (**LCP**) or **Interaction to Next Paint** (**INP**), navigation timings, resource loading patterns, long tasks, and interaction latency. It also collects device and environment characteristics that help contextualize performance issues, such as screen size, CPU type, memory availability, and connectivity. This enables teams to understand not just how the system performs on average, but how it behaves across the vast diversity of user environments.

In an MFE architecture, RUM becomes particularly important. This is because MFEs are loaded and executed independently; they may not uniformly affect all users. For example, one MFE may slow down the first interaction on lower-end mobile devices, while another may introduce layout instability only in specific viewport sizes. RUM reveals these nuances by correlating performance regressions with specific modules, versions, user segments, or usage contexts. Without this visibility, teams may incorrectly attribute performance issues to backend latency or global application logic when the root cause sits within a specific MFE.

Many RUM platforms, such as those included in Datadog RUM, New Relic Browser, and performance-focused solutions like SpeedCurve, provide dashboards for visualizing how metrics trend over time and across different user categories. While these tools vary in implementation, they share the common goal of surfacing real-world user impact early and providing data-driven insights that guide performance improvements.

RUM also often acts as the earliest signal for detecting regressions. Because it observes every user session, shifts in LCP, increased layout instability, or spikes in long tasks appear quickly as part of the system's continuous performance baseline. These signals can reveal whether a newly deployed MFE affected responsiveness, whether a bundle size increase impacted low-power devices, or whether a network resource became unreliable in certain geographic regions. By grounding performance insights in real user data, RUM forms the foundation of frontend observability. It helps teams understand the true quality of the user experience and provides the necessary context for deeper analysis through application performance monitoring, tracing, and logging. The next subsection extends this visibility by shifting from real-world signals to system-level browser instrumentation through APM.

Application performance monitoring

While real user monitoring focuses on the experience observed by actual users, **application performance monitoring** (**APM**) provides a deeper, system-oriented view of how the frontend behaves within the browser. APM tools instrument the application at runtime to capture detailed performance signals such as resource waterfalls, JavaScript execution timelines, long tasks, memory patterns, and correlations between frontend activity and backend dependencies. This creates a complementary perspective to RUM: RUM shows *what* users experience, while APM reveals *why* those experiences occur.

APM helps answer questions such as:

1. Which scripts, bundles, or MFEs consume the most execution time?
2. How much work is the main thread performing, and where does it get blocked?
3. Are network requests, caching patterns, or backend latency contributing to slow interactions?
4. How does the browser's event loop behave under load?
5. Are certain MFEs introducing long tasks or heavy rendering operations?

These insights are derived from browser-level instrumentation: PerformanceObserver APIs, resource timing entries, long-task detection, script evaluation timings, and interaction event processing. Unlike RUM, which focuses on high-level experience signals, APM explores the mechanics of how the browser processes work, making it especially valuable for diagnosing issues that are not immediately visible to users but accumulate into noticeable latency.

In MFE architectures, APM provides the granularity needed to understand the performance cost of each independently deployed module. MFEs often load their own JavaScript bundles, initiate their own network requests, and render components independently of the host application. While each MFE may be optimized in isolation, their combined runtime footprint can exceed the performance budget of the page. APM surfaces these interactions, showing whether a particular MFE introduces long tasks, blocks the main thread, increases memory usage, or creates unexpected re-renders when integrated with others.

High-percentile performance metrics such as p95 and p99 execution time, high-percentile interaction latency, and tail-end long tasks are especially important here. These values help teams assess how MFEs behave in the most constrained environments and detect regressions that might be invisible in averages or medians. In practice, small increases in script size or execution time introduced by one MFE may disproportionately affect users on slower devices, and APM gives visibility into these effects.

APM solutions such as Datadog Browser APM, New Relic Browser, and Dynatrace frequently integrate both frontend and backend views, linking browser interactions to the services they ultimately invoke. While the chapter is not focused on specific tooling, it is worth noting that this end-to-end correlation is particularly valuable in MFE systems, where a single user interaction may trigger multiple backend calls initiated by different MFEs. APM helps teams trace how frontend performance characteristics relate to backend behaviors, enabling holistic optimization.

Finally, strong APM instrumentation significantly reduces **mean time to detect** (**MTTD**) and **mean time to resolve** (**MTTR**). Performance regressions introduced by an MFE release become visible within minutes, and teams can quickly isolate which module, bundle, or network call caused the slowdown. In distributed frontend architectures where independent deployments happen frequently, this level of insight is essential for maintaining reliability and ensuring that teams can respond quickly when degradations occur.

The next subsection builds on this concept by shifting from performance-oriented visibility to error monitoring, which focuses on the failures, exceptions, and faults that occur across both host and MFE boundaries.

Error monitoring

While performance monitoring reveals how the application behaves under normal conditions, error monitoring exposes what happens when things go wrong. Modern frontend applications run substantial logic in the browser, creating many opportunities for failures that never reach backend logs. JavaScript exceptions, failed resource loads, unhandled promise rejections, aborted API requests, cross-origin script errors, and component-level rendering failures all directly impact the user experience but remain invisible without dedicated error tracking.

Error monitoring focuses on capturing, categorizing, and analyzing these failures, answering questions such as:

1. What errors are users encountering, and how often do they occur?
2. Do failures correlate with specific browsers, devices, or regional conditions?

3. Which component, script, or MFE introduced the error?
4. Did a recent deployment cause a spike in client-side exceptions?
5. How severe is the impact? Is it isolated, intermittent, or widespread?

To support this, error monitoring systems capture stack traces, device information, browser versions, contextual events, user actions leading up to a failure, and the environmental conditions under which the issue occurred. They often include features such as grouping similar errors, mapping stack traces using source maps, and surfacing regressions introduced by new releases. While examples include platforms like *Sentry, Rollbar, Bugsnag,* or *Raygun,* the specific tools matter far less than the capability they provide, i.e, visibility into client-side failures at scale.

Error monitoring becomes significantly more complex and more essential in MFE architectures. Because MFEs are independently built and deployed, each one introduces its own potential failure surface. A seemingly harmless update to one MFE can break a shared dependency, introduce unexpected global state changes, or create cascading effects that appear within another module. Without unified error tracking, teams may chase symptoms rather than causes, and root-cause analysis becomes slow, fragmented, and error-prone.

Another challenge is attribution. In a page composed of multiple MFEs, determining *which module* generated an error is not always straightforward. Without consistent metadata such as module name, version, build hash, and deployment timestamp, the error events lack the context needed for rapid diagnosis. A shared client-side error instrumentation library, commonly maintained by a platform or infra team, helps ensure that all MFEs emit errors using the same schema and attribution model.

Framework-level mechanisms also play a role. React error boundaries, Angular error handlers, and global window error listeners provide structured ways to catch exceptions before they crash the application. When used consistently across MFEs, these tools prevent individual module failures from propagating and improve the completeness of captured error data. Finally, error monitoring directly influences operational performance. Clear visibility into client-side failures reduces MTTD and MTTR by enabling teams to detect spikes early, isolate them to specific MFEs, and deploy targeted fixes. In distributed architectures with frequent deployments, this capability is essential for maintaining user trust and minimizing the blast radius of faulty releases. From here, we turn to another important aspect of observability: synthetic monitoring, which provides controlled, predictable tests that complement real-world data and ensure that critical flows remain stable across independently deployed MFEs.

Synthetic monitoring

Synthetic monitoring provides a controlled, predictable way to evaluate application performance and stability by executing scripted tests against the system at regular intervals. Unlike RUM, which reflects the unpredictable conditions of actual users, synthetic monitoring operates in a consistent environment that has fixed device characteristics, known network profiles, and repeatable interactions. This makes it ideal for detecting regressions early, validating critical user journeys, and ensuring that the system remains reliable across independently deployed MFEs.

Synthetic monitoring helps answer questions such as:

1. Do key user flows (login, search, checkout, onboarding) still work after recent deployments?
2. Has page load time or Core Web Vitals degraded for the baseline test profile?
3. Are critical APIs, assets, or remote bundles consistently accessible?
4. Are MFEs loading, initializing, and rendering within expected thresholds?
5. Has an MFE deployment introduced intermittent failures that do not immediately surface in RUM?

Because synthetic tests run on a fixed schedule: every 5 minutes, every 15 minutes, hourly, or as part of CI/CD, they act as an early-warning system. They detect issues even when user traffic is low, and they catch failures that might only appear under first-load conditions or specific execution sequences. This predictability is particularly useful for identifying regressions caused by new MFE releases or remote module failures triggered by **content delivery network (CDN)** propagation, version mismatches, or caching inconsistencies.

In MFE architectures, synthetic monitoring plays a uniquely important role. MFEs may be loaded lazily, conditionally, or based on runtime composition rules. A synthetic test can validate these integration points before real users encounter them. For example, a test might catch a scenario where a remote MFE bundle has been deployed, but its manifest is not yet available on edge caches, resulting in *module not found* errors. While such issues might only affect a subset of users temporarily, synthetic testing surfaces them immediately and consistently.

Synthetic testing also helps ensure functional stability across independently evolving MFEs. Even if each module works correctly in isolation, their interactions, which include shared state, routing transitions, global event listeners, or styling dependencies, may break when combined on a page. A test suite executed against the host application can verify that critical flows continue to work as expected despite independent deployments happening throughout the day. Examples of synthetic monitoring capabilities can be found in solutions like SpeedCurve Synthetic, Catchpoint, Pingdom, Lighthouse CI, and Playwright or Cypress scripted synthetic checks. These tools vary in sophistication, from basic uptime checks to fully scripted, multi-step flows that mimic user journeys. Regardless of the platform, the objective remains consistent: to provide a stable baseline against which changes in performance, availability, or reliability can be measured.

Synthetic tests also serve as a governance mechanism. They reinforce performance budgets, prevent regressions from slipping into production, and ensure key user flows remain operational even as MFEs evolve independently. When integrated into CI/CD pipelines, synthetic tests can block risky deployments, reducing the operational burden on frontend teams and decreasing overall MTTD for critical failures. By complementing real-world signals from RUM and granular insights from APM and error monitoring, synthetic monitoring provides the controlled perspective necessary to validate that the application remains stable, performant, and predictable regardless of how many moving parts exist in the underlying MFE system. The next subsection expands this visibility further by exploring logging and aggregation, the backbone of diagnostic investigation and root-cause analysis.

Logging platforms and aggregation

Logging provides the detailed, diagnostic signals required to understand why failures, performance issues, or unexpected behaviors occur within a web application. While RUM, APM, and synthetic monitoring reveal symptoms, logs often reveal the underlying cause. In modern frontend applications, where significant logic runs in the browser, client-side logging has become just as important as server-side instrumentation. Logs capture fine-grained information about user actions, application state transitions, business events, rendering behavior, and the internal conditions leading up to errors or regressions.

Logging helps answer questions such as:

1. What was the application state immediately before a failure occurred?
2. Which MFE, version, or component triggered a specific behavior?
3. What sequence of actions led a user into a broken or unexpected UI state?
4. Did a specific API response, network timeout, or configuration mismatch cause the issue?
5. Are certain logs or warnings increasing after a recent deployment?

While traditional backend logs often reside in platforms like **Elastic Stack** (**ELK**), Splunk, Grafana Loki, or cloud provider logging services, frontend applications typically forward logs to the same aggregation pipelines or to specialized browser-log ingestion endpoints. The value lies not in the specific tool but in the ability to centralize signals from all MFEs into a unified destination where they can be searched, correlated, and analyzed.

In an MFE architecture, logging becomes more challenging and more critical. Each MFE may be built by a different team, follow a different release cadence, or use a different technology stack. Without standardization, logs quickly become fragmented with varying structure, naming conventions, severity levels, context, and schema. Fragmented logs lead to duplicate effort, incomplete investigations, and difficulty correlating problems across independently deployed modules. A unified logging strategy is therefore essential. We will discuss this in detail in the following sections.

A consistent logging approach typically involves:

- A shared logging schema (defining fields like module name, version, environment, trace ID, and severity).
- A single, platform-provided logging client used across all MFEs.
- Correlation or trace IDs that tie logs to user sessions, request flows, or distributed traces.
- Log sampling rules to balance visibility and cost.
- Version metadata so teams can correlate spikes to releases.

These conventions ensure that logs emitted from MFEs blend into a coherent system of record rather than a collection of isolated messages. When issues arise, teams can trace the chain of events across MFEs, link logs with RUM signals and APM timelines, and isolate the precise module or version responsible for a regression. Client-side logs also play a critical role in investigating intermittent or hard-to-reproduce issues such as race conditions, rendering timing problems, inconsistent API behavior, or MFE lifecycle conflicts. Many of these problems do not result in explicit errors, and without structured logs, they remain invisible. Detailed browser logs make it possible to reconstruct the exact conditions under which these issues appear.

In addition, logging is fundamental to maintaining low MTTD and MTTR. When a regression occurs, such as a sudden increase in failed network requests or a spike in console warnings, logs often provide the first clue. With unified aggregation, teams can instantly see whether a single MFE caused the spike, whether the issue is global or isolated, and whether a rollback or hotfix is needed. With logging forming the diagnostic backbone of frontend observability, the next subsection builds on this foundation by exploring distributed tracing, which connects the dots across MFEs and backend services to create an end-to-end view of user journeys and system dependencies.

Diagnostic trails with logs and traces

Logs and traces form the diagnostic trails that help teams understand what happened inside an application at runtime. While other observability signals such as RUM, APM, or synthetic checks could highlight symptoms, logs and traces provide the detailed evidence needed to investigate root causes. They act as breadcrumbs, revealing the paths taken through the system and the state of key components at the moment an issue occurred. In modern frontend architectures, especially MFEs, these diagnostic trails are indispensable for reconstructing the story behind failures, regressions, and unexpected behaviors.

Logs capture fine-grained, event-level details from within the browser: state transitions, user actions, warnings, configuration mismatches, network responses, and application-specific events. They help answer questions such as:

1. What happened immediately before this error occurred?
2. Which component, script, or MFE triggered the behavior?
3. What user actions or environmental conditions preceded the failure?
4. Is a particular MFE emitting new warnings or errors after a deployment?

In MFEs, logs must be consistent across independently deployed modules. Without a shared logging schema, capturing fields like module name, version, trace ID, and severity, the logs become fragmented and difficult to correlate. A unified logging strategy enables teams to trace issues across MFE boundaries, quickly identify which module is responsible, and reduce both MTTD and MTTR when investigating regressions.

While logs provide information on a particular event, tracing extends this idea beyond individual events by constructing an end-to-end narrative of a user's journey. A trace links together operations originating in the browser, such as rendering events, network requests, or MFE lifecycle hooks, with the backend services that fulfill them. While backend tracing has existed for years, frontend tracing is increasingly important in applications where multiple MFEs contribute to a single user interaction. Without tracing, it is difficult to determine whether a slowdown originates from the host, a remote MFE, a downstream API, or a combination of all three.

High-level tracing platforms supported through standards like **OpenTelemetry** (**OTel**) and solutions such as Jaeger, Zipkin, or Datadog Traces offer the ability to visualize latency across multiple hops. When applied to MFEs, tracing shows:

1. Which MFE initiated a request?
2. How long each MFE's initialization or rendering took?
3. Whether backend latency or frontend execution contributed to the overall delay
4. How a user interaction propagated across services?

Together, logs and traces provide the complete diagnostic trail: logs offer detail, context, and specificity; traces provide structure, continuity, and narrative. In MFE ecosystems, where responsibility is decentralized, releases occur frequently, and failure boundaries are blurred, these trails are essential for making sense of the system. They help engineers reason across independently deployed modules, correlate frontend events with backend operations, and understand how a user's experience unfolds across distributed components.

Later in the chapter, we will explore logging and distributed tracing in greater depth, focusing on the patterns, standards, and propagation techniques required to implement them effectively in an MFE architecture. With the major observability capabilities now introduced, the next sections explore the deeper challenges of applying these practices in a distributed MFE architecture.

Observability challenges in MFEs

While modern observability tools offer deep insight into how web applications perform, behave, and fail, applying these capabilities to an MFE architecture introduces a distinct set of challenges. MFEs distribute responsibility across multiple independently deployed modules, each with its own codebase, lifecycle, and operational surface area. This decentralization complicates everything from logging and trace continuity to performance attribution and analytics consistency. Issues that are straightforward to observe in a monolithic frontend become significantly harder to detect, correlate, and diagnose when the application is composed of many moving parts assembled at runtime. The following sections highlight the most impactful challenges that make observability uniquely complex in MFE environments and set the foundation for the deeper strategies and solutions explored later in this chapter.

Fragmented telemetry causing inconsistency

One of the most pervasive challenges in MFE architectures is the fragmentation of telemetry across independently developed modules. Each MFE often arrives with its own opinionated approach to logging, error reporting, analytics naming conventions, and performance instrumentation. These inconsistencies create a scattered landscape of signals that do not align, cannot be correlated, and frequently contradict one another. A single user action might generate three or four different logs from different MFEs, each using different schemas, severity levels, and metadata fields, thus making it nearly impossible to assemble a coherent narrative of what occurred. As teams evolve, onboard new engineers, or adopt new tools, this inconsistency widens, creating telemetry drift that grows more pronounced with every release cycle.

The result is an observability ecosystem that produces a large volume of data but surprisingly little insight. Debugging becomes slow because engineers must sift through incompatible logs, missing fields, or mismatched event names. Analytics dashboards become misleading because similar behaviors are logged differently by different MFEs, breaking funnels and skewing metrics. Even error monitoring becomes unreliable when one MFE captures detailed errors while another reports only generic exceptions. Fragmented telemetry is the root cause behind many downstream observability problems in MFEs, and addressing it requires unified instrumentation practices such as common schemas, shared **Software Development Kit** (**SDKs**), standardized metadata, and coordinated governance, which we will explore in later sections.

Lack of cross-MFE traces

Another major challenge in an MFE architecture is the loss of trace continuity as user interactions traverse multiple independently loaded modules. In a monolithic frontend, a single application is responsible for generating and maintaining the context required to trace user actions from the UI to backend services. In an MFE setup, however, each module executes within its own boundary, loads independently, and often initializes its own instrumentation. As a result, the trace context created by the host or shell application rarely propagates automatically into child MFEs, and even less so into nested or lazy-loaded modules. This breaks the chain of events needed to understand the full path of a user interaction, which can convey what triggered a request, which MFE handled, and how backend services responded.

Without shared trace continuity, observability tools present only a fragmented view of the user journey. A trace might show a backend request taking too long, but fail to indicate which MFE initiated it. A performance spike in the host application may appear disconnected from an expensive rendering operation triggered by a child MFE. Investigations become time-consuming because engineers must manually correlate logs, APM data, and error events across modules and services. Cross-MFE workflows such as onboarding flows, dashboards with composed widgets, or checkout sequences are especially affected, as the user experience spans multiple MFEs with no consistent mechanism to link the pieces together. Establishing trace continuity across MFEs is one of the core problems addressed later in the chapter through shared context propagation, instrumentation standards, and platform-level tracing strategies.

MFE runtime failures

MFEs introduce a new class of runtime failures that do not typically exist in traditional monolithic frontend architectures. This is because MFEs are composed at runtime, often loaded from independent origins, deployed asynchronously, or resolved through a remote module manifest; they can fail before any of the application code begins to execute. Remote script loading errors, version mismatches between host and child MFEs, stale manifests cached at the CDN edge, or cross-origin resource restrictions can cause an MFE to fail silently or throw errors long before the user interacts with the UI. These failures are difficult to detect without client-side observability, because the backend has no visibility into whether a module loaded successfully, initialized correctly, or rendered at all. Even simple issues like an MFE's bundle being unavailable after a deployment or a temporary CDN outage can break critical parts of the UI without generating any server-side signals.

In addition to loading issues, MFEs experience failure modes triggered by lifecycle and integration mismatches. The host application and its child MFEs may initialize in different orders, rely on different versions of shared libraries, or assume inconsistent global states. A child MFE might try to access shared context before the host provides it, or the host might unmount an MFE unexpectedly, creating race conditions that surface only under specific timing or device conditions. These failures tend to be intermittent, environment-specific, and difficult to reproduce locally, making them especially challenging to diagnose. Without strong client-side logging, runtime error tracking, and clear traceability of module boundaries, teams often misattribute these failures to backend latency, caching issues, or user-specific anomalies. Understanding these unique failure modes is essential before exploring the solutions presented later in this chapter, where we examine how consistent instrumentation and distributed tracing mitigate these integration risks.

Performance attribution across MFEs

Determining which MFE is responsible for a performance regression is one of the most difficult aspects of operating a distributed frontend. In a monolithic architecture, performance metrics map directly to a single bundle, runtime, and rendering pipeline. In an MFE environment, however, multiple modules contribute independently to load times, rendering phases, network requests, and main-thread work. An increase in LCP might originate from a slow asset belonging to one MFE, while a spike in interaction latency could be caused by long tasks introduced by another. This is because MFEs may load conditionally, lazily, or based on user-specific contexts; performance regressions do not always affect every user uniformly, making root-cause analysis even more challenging. Without proper instrumentation, teams are often left guessing which part of the UI initiated the slowdown.

This problem becomes more visible in real-user performance metrics, where high-percentile measurements (p95, p99) reveal the impact of MFEs on constrained devices and low-bandwidth networks. A single MFE that increases CPU usage, performs heavy rendering work, or introduces layout shifts can disproportionately affect users at the edges of the performance distribution, even if the average metrics remain stable. The inability to attribute performance issues to specific MFEs leads to misaligned optimizations, finger-pointing between teams, and costly investigations. To resolve this, teams need consistent metadata on performance events such as module name, version, and lifecycle timings paired with unified RUM and APM instrumentation. These strategies will be explored later when we examine how MFEs can participate in shared performance budgets and contribute meaningful telemetry to a unified observability layer.

Fragmented user journeys

User journeys in modern applications rarely exist within a single interface surface; they span multiple screens, components, and, in MFE architectures, multiple independently deployed modules. This distribution complicates analytics and behavior tracking because each MFE may implement its own event definitions, naming conventions, and data-capture logic. A checkout flow, for example, might begin in the host application, transition through a product details MFE, and complete in a payments MFE, yet each module may emit different event names or omit key metadata. As a result, analytics funnels become fragmented, with missing steps or inconsistent event properties making them appear incomplete or erratic. This leads product teams to draw incorrect conclusions about user drop-off points or engagement issues simply because the instrumentation is not aligned across MFEs.

The fragmentation becomes even more problematic when MFEs operate with different levels of observability maturity. One module may thoroughly instrument its interactions, while another emits only high-level events, and a third logs nothing at all. This inconsistency makes it difficult to measure the true impact of design changes, feature rollouts, or new MFE deployments. Without unified analytics schemas and common event contracts, organizations struggle to build holistic dashboards, evaluate user behavior across MFEs, or understand the cause behind behavior shifts. Later in the chapter, we explore how shared analytics libraries, governance models, and event dictionaries help restore continuity across MFEs, enabling end-to-end insight into user journeys that traverse distributed UI boundaries.

Observability testing in MFEs

Observability in MFEs does not begin in production; it begins much earlier, during testing. Because MFEs are independently developed, independently deployed, and often independently instrumented, testing plays a critical role in preventing issues that would otherwise surface as noisy signals in logs, traces, RUM metrics, and user analytics. The goal of observability testing in MFEs is not to replace monitoring, but to strengthen it by catching integration failures, performance regressions, and compatibility issues before they reach real users. The following approaches represent the most impactful testing strategies that directly support a clean, reliable observability pipeline in distributed frontend architectures.

Testing layers that help MFE

Testing provides an essential preventative layer in distributed UI systems, where independent deployments can introduce regressions that observability tools later detect. This is because MFEs can fail to load, miscommunicate with the host, or introduce side effects without affecting backend systems; many problems must be caught before runtime. Automated tests reduce the amount of noise that reaches logging and monitoring platforms by preventing predictable issues from entering production, which in turn improves MTTD, MTTR, and the overall signal quality of observability data. Testing becomes the first filter that ensures observability systems spend their resources highlighting the unexpected, not the avoidable.

Contract testing between the host and MFEs

Contract testing is one of the most effective MFE-specific testing techniques because it ensures compatibility across independently deployed modules. These tests validate shared boundaries such as API schemas, event names, props, routing conventions, analytics contracts, and shared library versions so that changes in one MFE do not break another. By enforcing interface stability, contract tests prevent a large class of runtime errors: module-not-found issues, version mismatches, incorrect payload shapes, or broken event listeners. Strong contract testing reduces the frequency of client-side errors and broken interactions, allowing downstream observability tools to surface true anomalies rather than predictable integration mismatches.

E2E integration testing for composed pages

While individual MFEs can be thoroughly tested in isolation, most real user journeys span multiple modules assembled at runtime. **End-to-end (E2E)** integration tests validate that the composed experience continues to function as expected by ensuring the routing between MFEs, shared state transitions, UI composition, and cross-module flows like onboarding, dashboards, and checkout. These tests act as safety nets against regressions introduced by independent MFE deployments and help ensure that critical user journeys remain intact. By catching UI integration failures early, E2E tests prevent a flood of runtime errors, broken analytics funnels, and confusing RUM patterns that would otherwise pollute observability pipelines.

Performance regression testing

Because each MFE contributes its own bundle, rendering logic, and resource footprint, even small changes can have meaningful performance implications. Performance regression tests allow teams to guard against increases in bundle size, new layout shifts, long tasks, or CPU-heavy operations introduced by a single MFE release. These tests are often run in CI/CD, comparing the new version of an MFE against previous baselines. When performance budgets are exceeded or execution characteristics degrade, changes can be blocked before deployment. This prevents high-percentile regressions from reaching production, where they would distort RUM metrics, complicate APM investigations, and make performance attribution harder in distributed UI environments.

Visual, accessibility, and UI stability testing across MFEs

A major source of observability noise in MFEs stems from subtle UI regressions that occur when independently built modules share global layout space. Visual regression tests help detect unintended changes in layout, spacing, typography, or component positioning, especially when MFEs rely on shared design tokens or global styling rules. Accessibility testing ensures consistent standards across modules, preventing fragmented experiences that may degrade user interaction metrics. UI stability tests verify that MFEs mount and unmount cleanly without producing rendering errors or layout shifts that skew performance metrics. Together, these testing layers reduce the number of visual and structural issues that escape into production and distort behavior analytics or RUM data.

Logging and distributed tracing in MFEs

Logging and distributed tracing are foundational pillars of observability, but their implementation becomes significantly more complex in MFE architectures. In a traditional monolithic frontend, all events, logs, errors, network calls, and user actions originate from a unified runtime. A single bundle initializes instrumentation, manages state, and consistently enriches telemetry with metadata. In MFEs, however, each independently deployed module brings its own runtime behavior, lifecycle, and integration boundaries. MFEs load at different times, execute in different contexts, and interact with shared resources in unpredictable ways. This fragmentation creates observational blind spots where trace continuity breaks, logs lack necessary metadata, and performance events cannot be attributed to the correct module.

Moreover, the distributed nature of MFEs introduces new failure surfaces and timing sensitivities. A remote MFE may fail to load due to a network issue, conflict with a shared dependency, or initialize before the host has provided the required context. These issues occur entirely in the browser and often leave no backend footprint, making them invisible to traditional observability systems unless logging and tracing are implemented with careful coordination. Tracking how user interactions flow across MFEs, how each module contributes to performance, and how each component participates in UI-level failures requires a level of consistency and interoperability that cannot be achieved through ad-hoc instrumentation.

This section explores the essential strategies needed to build unified logging and distributed tracing across independently deployed MFEs. We examine how shared logging standards, common metadata, trace context propagation, and cross-MFE span linkage create continuous diagnostic trails, allowing teams to analyze complex runtime behaviors with confidence. By the end of this section, you will see how consistent instrumentation transforms a fragmented collection of MFEs into a coherent, observable system where debugging is faster, regressions are easier to isolate, and user journeys remain traceable end-to-end.

Unified client-side logging strategy

A unified client-side logging strategy is the foundation of observability in an MFE architecture. Without a consistent approach to logging, the signals produced by each MFE become fragmented, incomplete, and difficult to interpret. Each MFE is often built and deployed independently, which means teams naturally introduce their own logging styles, event structures, and metadata conventions. Over time, this leads to telemetry drift, where logs from different MFEs cannot be correlated or compared. A shared logging SDK solves this problem by providing a single, authoritative way of emitting logs across all MFEs. The SDK defines how events are created, how severity is categorized, and how essential metadata is attached. This creates a uniform observability surface that allows every MFE to participate in the same diagnostic and monitoring ecosystem, regardless of the team or technology involved. The following figure shows an example of using the shared logging SDK to create centralized and generic metrics across MFEs:

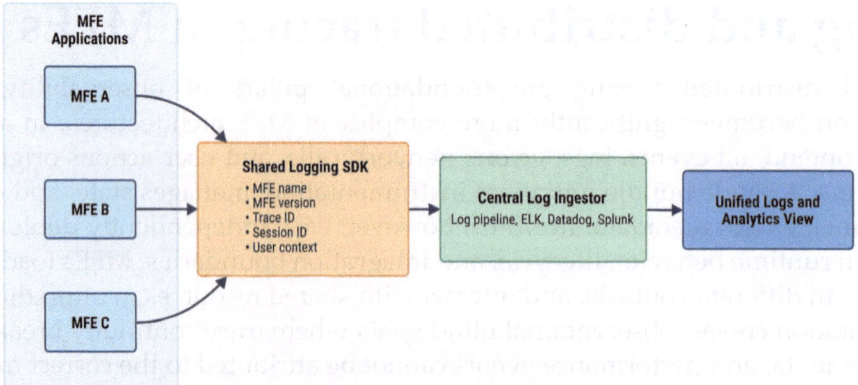

Figure 8.2: Example of using the shared logging SDK to create a unified logging experience

Figure 8.2 illustrates how multiple MFEs send structured events through a shared logging SDK, which standardizes fields such as MFE name, version, trace ID, and session ID before forwarding them to a central log ingestion system, enabling a unified analytics and diagnostics view across the entire application.

A unified SDK also reduces noise by enforcing structure and quality at the source. Without guardrails, MFEs may produce redundant messages, verbose debug logs, or overly generic errors that dilute the signal-to-noise ratio. The shared SDK can automatically normalize error objects, prevent duplicate entries, enforce sampling rules, and ensure that sensitive user information is never logged. It can also wrap global browser listeners, such as console error and unhandled promise rejection, to guarantee complete coverage for unexpected failures. By centralizing these behaviors, the platform reduces the operational burden on individual teams and establishes a stable foundation for deeper analysis using distributed tracing and correlation techniques. The next two subsections describe the essential elements that make this unified approach successful: shared metadata fields and consistent trace context propagation.

Metadata standards across MFEs

Consistent metadata is essential for correlating logs and events across independently deployed MFEs. Without shared fields, observability systems cannot reconstruct user journeys, compare versions, or identify which MFE introduced a regression. Every MFE must attach a standard set of metadata fields to every log, error, performance event, and network call. These fields usually include the MFE name, MFE version, environment, session identifier, trace identifier, and page or view identifier. When structured consistently, these fields allow observability tools to group, filter, and analyze events in a way that reveals patterns across the entire application rather than isolated signals from individual MFEs.

A unified metadata contract becomes easier to understand when expressed through a concrete example. The following sample illustrates a recommended baseline that every MFE should attach to its observability signals. While the exact fields may vary by organization, this structure captures the minimum information required to correlate events across MFEs and reconstruct complete user journeys:

```
{
  "mfeName": "profilePage",
  "mfeVersion": "3.14.0",
  "environment": "production",
  "sessionId": "7f0a23d9",
  "traceId": "4c9cda52b8f149c3",
  "spanId": "e19c2f4b82",
  "userId": "optional",
  "pageId": "profile_overview",
  “timestamp”: “2025-11-17T21:45:10.123Z”,
```

```
  "device": {
    "type": "mobile",
    "os": "iOS",
    "browser": "Safari"
  },
  "network": {
    "connectionType": "4g",
    "downlink": 5.5
  }
}
```

Each field plays a specific role. The MFE name and version identify the exact module and deployment responsible for the event. The session identifier ties together events across MFEs, while the trace and span identifiers ensure that distributed tracing remains continuous. The page identifier clarifies which screen or views the user interacted with, and the timestamp ensures correct ordering when MFEs load at different times. Optional device and network data help diagnose performance issues, especially for users in constrained environments. With a structured and shared metadata contract like this, engineering teams gain the ability to search, aggregate, and correlate observability data with confidence, turning a distributed MFE environment into a coherent diagnostic system.

Trace context propagation across MFEs

Trace context propagation ensures that the diagnostic trail remains continuous as user actions flow across MFEs and into backend services. In a single application, the trace identifier created at startup naturally persists through all operations. In an MFE architecture, however, each module loads independently, initializes at different times, and may not automatically inherit the trace context created by the host. Without a shared mechanism for passing this context into every MFE, the observability system receives disconnected spans and incomplete traces. A single user action may generate logs and network calls from several MFEs, but without a common trace identifier, none of these events appear linked. This breaks the diagnostic story and makes the investigation significantly harder.

The following figure illustrates how a host application can generate an initial trace identifier and pass it to multiple MFEs as they mount. Each MFE then creates a child span connected to the root trace, and any API requests made by those MFEs carry the same trace identifier into backend services. This enables observability tools to reconstruct the full end-to-end path of the user action, including contributions from each MFE and each backend service involved.

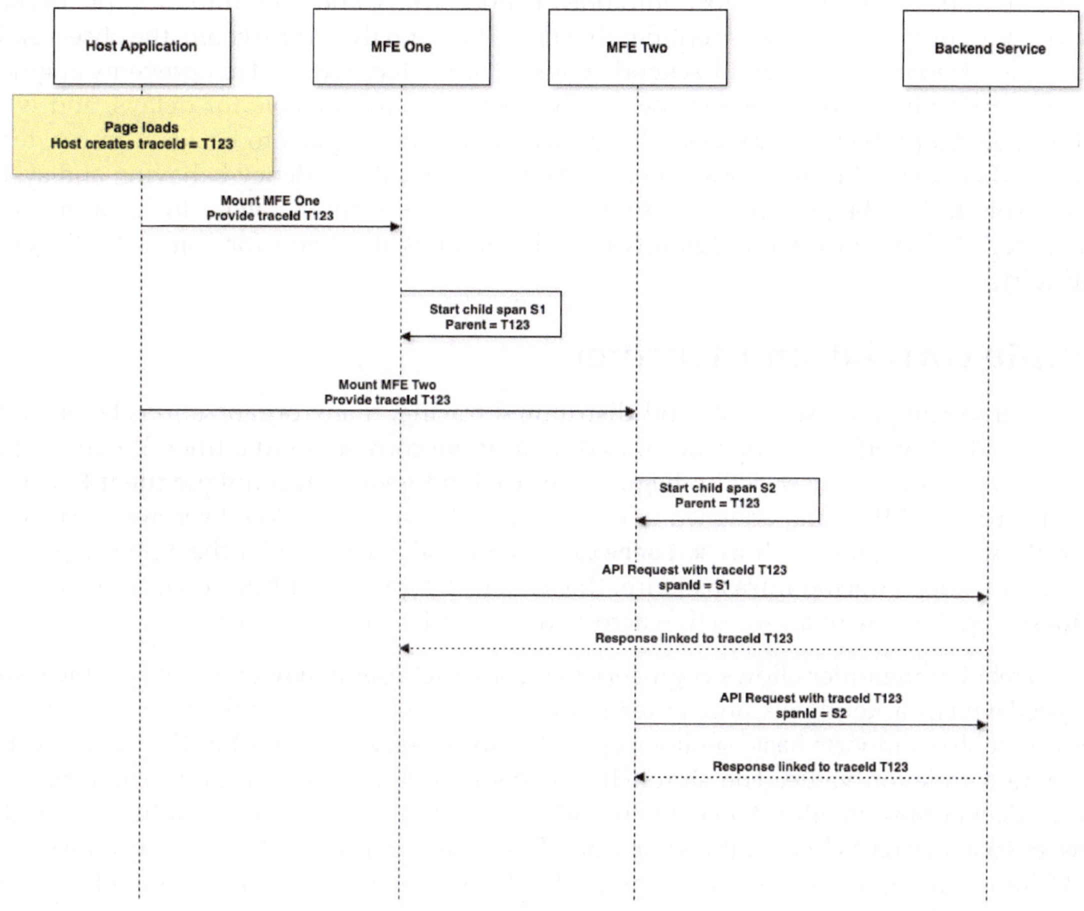

Figure 8.3: *Example of a trace context*

Maintaining this continuity requires all MFEs to participate in a shared contract. The host must generate the initial trace identifier and supply it to each MFE when it mounts. MFEs must accept and use this identifier when creating their own spans and when making network requests. They must also propagate updated context when nested MFEs or lazy-loaded modules appear later in the session. When done correctly, the result is a seamless diagnostic trail that spans the entire system. Observability tools can display how a user action moves from the host to each MFE and into backend services, revealing timing, dependencies, and failures at every step. Trace context propagation transforms a distributed MFE landscape into a coherent and analyzable application.

Linking browser spans to backend traces

Linking browser spans to backend traces is the step that transforms observability from a collection of isolated signals into a complete end-to-end narrative. In an MFE architecture, user actions often pass through the host, into one or more MFEs, and then into multiple backend services. Without a shared trace identifier that flows through this entire chain, the observability system sees frontend spans and backend spans as unrelated events. This prevents engineers from understanding where time is spent, what service is responsible for delays, and which MFE initiated a problematic request. By connecting frontend spans to backend traces, teams gain a unified view of user interactions, API performance, dependency behavior, and system health. This section begins with the simplest and most effective strategy for creating cross-system correlation and then builds toward full span-based tracing for complete diagnostic continuity.

Simple correlation identifier

Before introducing browser spans and distributed tracing, many organizations begin with a simple and highly effective approach based on a single correlation identifier. When the page loads or when a major user action begins, the frontend generates a unique identifier that is shared across all MFEs and attached to every network request. Backend services receive this value through a header such as **`x-correlation-id`** and include it in their own logs. Even without advanced tracing infrastructure, this creates a lightweight but powerful mechanism for following the flow of a user action across MFEs and backend systems.

This correlation identifier allows engineers to reconstruct user behavior, identify which MFEs triggered which backend calls, and understand cross-system interactions by filtering logs across services. It also supports basic session replay because every event within the session carries the same correlation value. The simplicity of this approach makes it an excellent first step toward deeper observability. Once this foundation is in place, teams can gradually introduce browser spans, parent-child relationships, and full trace continuity without disrupting existing workflows. The following code is an example of how a simple correlation identifier can be reused across the application,

```
// Simple platform utility for creating or retrieving a correlation identifier
export function getCorrelationId() {
  let id = sessionStorage.getItem("correlationId");
  if (!id) {
    id = crypto.randomUUID();
    sessionStorage.setItem("correlationId", id);
  }
  return id;
}
export function fetchWithCorrelation(url, options = {}) {
  const id = getCorrelationId();
  const headers = {
    ...options.headers,
```

```
    "x-correlation-id": id
  };
  return fetch(url, { ...options, headers });
}
```

This simple pattern ensures that all MFEs participate in a shared diagnostic identity and provides immediate value with almost no overhead. The next subsections build on this foundation by introducing spans, context propagation, and end to end trace construction.

Creating browser spans within an MFE

Creating browser spans is the next step in establishing rich end to end observability. A span represents a specific unit of work inside an MFE, such as loading data, rendering a component, or handling a user action. Each span is linked to the active trace context, allowing the observability system to understand how the operation relates to the rest of the user journey. In an MFE architecture, spans are especially important because MFEs may load at different times, run separate execution paths, and interact with different backend services. By creating spans at meaningful boundaries, each MFE provides structured timing information that becomes the foundation for linking frontend activity with backend operations.

In an ideal scenario, the entire span process should be created by the platform team and distribute it as an SDK for application teams to consume. The **`createSpan`** method in the platform SDK reads the current trace context, generates a new span identifier, links it to the parent span, and marks the start time. While the span is active, nested work such as network calls inherits its context. When the operation is complete, calling **`span.end()`** records the end time and sends the span to the tracing system.

The following example shows how an MFE would create a span when loading profile data. This pattern ensures that meaningful work is captured with consistent context and precise timing.

```
// Provided by the platform tracing SDK
import { createSpan, fetchWithTrace } from "@example/platformTracing";
export function loadUserProfile() {
  const span = createSpan("loadUserProfile", {
    mfeName: "profilePage"
  });
  fetchWithTrace("/api/user/profile")
    .then(response => response.json())
    .then(data => {
      // update UI
    })
```

```
    .catch(error => {
      // handle error
    })
    .finally(() => {
      span.end();
    });
}
```

This pattern clearly marks when an operation begins and ends. The span inherits the trace context, ensuring continuity, and records accurate timing that helps identify performance or dependency issues. With each MFE following this approach, browser spans become reliable anchors for backend trace continuation.

Injecting trace identifiers into network requests

Once spans are created, the next requirement is to ensure that every network request carries the correct trace information. Without injecting trace identifiers into outgoing API calls, backend services cannot link their spans to the frontend spans that initiated them. A shared fetch wrapper in the platform SDK ensures consistent propagation across all MFEs as described in the following code sample:

```
// Provided by the platform tracing SDK
import { getTraceContext } from ""@example/platformTracing";
export async function fetchWithTrace(url, options = {}) {
  const { traceId, spanId } = getTraceContext();
  const headers = {
    ...options.headers,
    "trace-id": traceId,
    "span-id": spanId
  };
  return fetch(url, { ...options, headers });
}
```

This simple wrapper retrieves the active trace context, attaches it to the request, and sends it to the backend. Backend services then read these headers to create their own spans, forming the next link in the trace.

Backend services for continuity

When backend services receive the trace identifier, they create spans that link directly to the frontend work. This allows observability platforms to construct a complete chain of spans that includes both frontend and backend operations.

A simplified example using OpenTelemetry in Node:

```
const { trace } = require("@opentelemetry/api");
app.get("/api/user/profile", (req, res) => {
  const incomingTraceId = req.header("trace-id");
  const incomingSpanId = req.header("span-id");
  const span = trace.getTracer("userService").startSpan("getUserProfile", {
    links: [
      { context: { traceId: incomingTraceId, spanId: incomingSpanId } }
    ]
  });
  // service logic here
  span.end();
});
```

This backend span becomes part of the same trace as the originating MFE span, enabling full visibility into the sequence of operations.

Alternative approaches to cross MFE observability

Full distributed tracing is powerful, but not every organization has the platform maturity or team alignment needed to implement it across all MFEs. Many teams instead rely on real user monitoring tools as their primary source of cross-system visibility. RUM platforms automatically collect performance metrics, resource timing, JavaScript errors, network failures, and session-level behavior without requiring deep instrumentation in each MFE. When combined with shared metadata such as MFE name, version, and correlation identifier, RUM tools provide a useful way to understand how individual MFEs behave in real sessions and how they contribute to overall user experience. This makes RUM a practical and low-effort alternative to full tracing, especially in environments where MFEs are owned by different teams with varying levels of observability readiness.

In addition to RUM, teams often adopt lightweight strategies such as shared correlation identifiers, structured logging with a common event vocabulary, and simple operation-level metrics emitted by each MFE. These approaches offer enough signal to follow user flows, diagnose common issues, and identify performance bottlenecks without the complexity of span-based tracing. Some organizations also rely on edge or gateway-level request tracing or session replay tools to capture the most important context around user behavior. These techniques do not replace distributed tracing, but they provide meaningful visibility at a lower cost and serve as practical steps toward a more complete observability model that can be expanded as the platform evolves.

Challenges and mitigations

Implementing deep observability across MFEs brings several practical challenges that require coordination, shared standards, and careful design. These issues often arise because MFEs are built and deployed independently, each with its own lifecycle, resources, and ownership. When observability tools operate without a unified contract, the result is fragmented context, partial traces, or inconsistent data that complicates debugging and reduces the value of the system. Addressing these challenges requires combining platform-level solutions with clear engineering practices that ensure all MFEs participate in the same diagnostic framework.

Complex trace context propagation

Distributed tracing depends on the ability to carry a trace identifier from one operation to the next, but this becomes complicated when MFEs mount and unmount dynamically. Each MFE runs in its own scope and does not automatically inherit context from the host. Without a shared mechanism for passing context into each MFE, traces become fragmented and lose their diagnostic value. Propagation also becomes harder when MFEs load from different origins or when asynchronous imports break continuity.

The simplest mitigation is to let the host application create the initial trace context and supply it to each MFE at mount time. MFEs must then use a shared SDK that stores, reads, and updates this context consistently. Clear conventions for when and how to read context, combined with automatic injection of trace identifiers into network calls, greatly reduce the likelihood of broken or missing traces.

Tight coupling with the host

All MFEs rely on the host to supply the shared instrumentation tools, metadata, and trace context needed for observability. If the host is outdated, misconfigured, or incorrectly initializes the tracing environment, every MFE inherits that problem. This creates a fragile dependency where a single failure in the host can cause missing traces, incorrect identifiers, or gaps in logs across the entire application.The best mitigation is to treat the host as a platform component with strict versioning, automated tests, and clear upgrade policies. The host should expose observability tools through stable interfaces, and MFEs should avoid relying on host internals. When the host behaves as a reliable provider of trace context and logging capabilities, MFEs can remain decoupled in implementation while still participating in a shared observability model.

Ordering and timing issues

One of the core challenges in an MFE architecture is the difficulty of maintaining a clear and reliable order of events. MFEs load independently, sometimes in parallel, and often at different times depending on network conditions, device performance, or caching. As a result, trace events may appear out of order, making it difficult to reconstruct what happened or understand the true sequence of operations. Timing accuracy becomes even harder when MFEs perform work before they fully mount or when background tasks continue running after an interaction appears complete.

To mitigate this, teams can use a shared platform clock, ensure every span or event includes precise timestamps, and create clear lifecycle boundaries inside each MFE. It also helps to centralize the recording of key transitions, such as page load or route changes, so that observability tools always have stable anchor points for ordering and visualization.

Backend dependency

Distributed tracing only works when backend services accept, propagate, and emit trace identifiers. If even one service in a request chain ignores the incoming trace information, the trace becomes incomplete. This creates broken segments where the frontend appears disconnected from the backend, even though the operations are related. Missing backend spans also make it difficult to attribute performance issues to the correct service.The mitigation is straightforward but requires organization-wide alignment: all backend frameworks and services must support trace propagation. This includes reading trace identifiers from headers, passing them to downstream services, and emitting spans consistently. Platform teams can provide middleware or service templates that handle tracing automatically so that individual developers do not need to manage context manually.

MFE analytics

Analytics form the backbone of how modern organizations understand user behavior, product usage, and application performance. In a monolithic frontend, data flows through a single codebase and uses a uniform set of tools. Micro-frontends change this dynamic. Each independently built module introduces its own patterns, lifecycle, and sometimes its own analytics library. Without deliberate coordination, data becomes fragmented and unreliable. This chapter explores why analytics drift in an MFE environment and how teams can restore accuracy through consistent tools, shared taxonomies, and lightweight governance.

Types of MFE analytics

Micro-frontends rely on three primary categories of analytics, each essential in understanding the user experience across independently deployed UI fragments.

Product analytics track how users adopt features and move through funnels. Tools like Amplitude, Mixpanel, Adobe Analytics, and Google Analytics help teams understand drop-offs, usage frequency, and how users transition across MFEs. These insights are crucial for ensuring that independently deployed parts of the UI still form a coherent experience.

Interaction analytics capture user behaviors within the interface, click paths, scroll depth, heatmaps, and rage clicks. Solutions such as Hotjar, FullStory, LogRocket, and Microsoft

Clarity provide session replay and visual insights that highlight where friction occurs. Since each MFE can contribute uniquely to the overall interaction flow, these tools help uncover issues that might be hidden in isolated development environments.

Performance analytics focus on how quickly the application loads, how responsive it feels, and how much each MFE contributes to or detracts from overall performance. Tools like New Relic Browser, Datadog RUM, SpeedCurve, and Sentry Performance provide metrics such as Web Vitals, CPU usage, and network timings. Because MFEs load independently, performance monitoring must identify which module is responsible for slowdowns.

Creating a unified analytics layer

To prevent fragmentation, organizations must adopt a unified analytics strategy that applies equally to every MFE. This does not require custom implementation; it starts with shared concepts. The first concept is a centralized analytics strategy that defines the tools, rules, and expectations for event tracking. Whether the chosen platform is Mixpanel, Adobe Analytics, or Datadog RUM, every MFE should rely on the same core stack.

Next is the idea of an analytics router, a conceptual layer either built in-house or using tag managers that standardizes event payloads and forwards them to the correct providers. Rather than each MFE embedding its own SDK, they rely on this shared mechanism to ensure consistency. A common dictionary of events defines naming conventions, event categories, and required metadata. This shared taxonomy prevents the same action from being tracked differently across MFEs. Lightweight governance through documentation, reviews, or automated checks helps avoid naming collisions and ensures that teams follow consistent patterns.

Fragmented analytics in MFEs

Analytics fragmentation is one of the most common issues teams face when adopting micro-frontends. While MFEs bring autonomy and faster delivery, they also distribute responsibility for tracking user behavior across multiple codebases. Without shared practices, analytics quickly become inconsistent or incomplete. Instead of producing a unified picture of the product experience, each MFE generates its own view, making it difficult to understand how users move across the entire application. This section focuses on two practical areas where fragmentation becomes most visible: maintaining cross-MFE funnels and avoiding common data-quality issues.

Ensuring cross-MFE funnels remain intact

One of the first symptoms of fragmentation is the breakdown of multi-step funnels that span several MFEs. A typical product journey, such as onboarding, checkout, or upgrading, often crosses boundaries between independently deployed modules. If each MFE uses different event names, tracking timing, or session identifiers, analytics tools cannot link the steps into a single continuous flow. The result is a funnel that appears to *reset* or lose users between MFEs, even though the user is still progressing normally.

Maintaining funnel continuity requires consistent event definitions and shared session context across all MFEs. Even when teams use different frameworks or deployment cycles, they must agree on simple practices such as standard event names, required attributes, and when events should fire. Many organizations rely on tag managers or host-controlled instrumentation to anchor the beginning and end of important flows. When these shared practices are applied, funnels remain intact, and insights remain accurate, even when the underlying architecture is distributed.

Avoiding data problems

Fragmentation also appears in the form of data-quality issues that arise from how MFEs load, mount, and rehydrate on the client. Because independent modules can re-render or reinitialize as users navigate, events may fire more than once or before the necessary context is available. This leads to inflated counts, missing metadata, or inconsistent attribution. These issues often surface subtly in dashboards: unexpected event spikes, mismatched totals, or inconsistent numbers between MFEs.

Avoiding these problems requires lightweight alignment rather than heavy technical solutions. Simple guardrails, such as ensuring analytics initialization happens only once, avoiding multiple SDK loads, and validating session context before sending events, must solve most issues. Organizations also benefit from shared guidelines on when an event should be triggered and how to handle remount scenarios. These small governance practices significantly reduce duplication and misattribution, keeping analytics trustworthy even when MFEs operate independently.

Analytics fragmentation is less a technical problem and more a coordination challenge. Cross-MFE funnels and data quality suffer when each module defines its own tracking patterns. By aligning around consistent event definitions, shared session context, and simple data-quality guardrails, teams can preserve the accuracy of analytics without sacrificing the independence that micro-frontends offer. These practices ensure that product insights remain reliable and that the entire user journey can be understood as a cohesive experience.

Conclusion

This chapter explored how observability brings clarity to an MFE environment where independent deployments, isolated runtimes, and distributed ownership can easily create blind spots. We examined how unified logging, shared metadata, trace context propagation, browser spans, backend linkage, and RUM platforms help rebuild a complete picture of user interactions across MFEs. We also looked at how analytics can fragment when each MFE logs events differently, and how a unified analytics layer ensures consistent measurement, healthy funnels, and reliable product insight. Throughout the chapter, we saw that observability is not a collection of tools but a coordinated discipline that allows MFEs to function as a coherent system rather than disconnected parts.

In the next chapter, we shift from understanding what is happening inside the system to improving how the system behaves. We will explore performance and security, beginning with practical ways to set and enforce performance budgets, measure MFE performance using browser timing signals, and interpret real-world performance data. We will then move into security concerns such as isolation boundaries, dependency governance, and safe integration between MFEs. Together, these topics build directly on the foundation of observability and prepare us to operate MFEs with greater speed, safety, and confidence.

Chapter 9
Performance and Security

Introduction

Performance and security define the reliability and trustworthiness of any large-scale frontend system. However, in an MFE architecture, they become significantly more complex. Traditional single-page applications operate within a single runtime, a single dependency graph, and a single security boundary. MFEs break that model apart. They load independently, ship their own code, manage their own resources, and communicate with each other across loosely coupled boundaries. This flexibility unlocks autonomy and scale, but it also creates new challenges: performance budgets can drift across teams, payload sizes begin to accumulate, shared dependencies multiply, and distributed execution increases the surface area for security vulnerabilities.

While performance and security are often discussed as separate concerns, in an MFE architecture they are closely connected. Decisions about how MFEs load, share dependencies, and execute at runtime affect not only speed and responsiveness, but also isolation boundaries, trust assumptions, and exposure to risk. Throughout this chapter, we will see how many of the same guardrails, measurement techniques, and governance models help address both performance and security challenges, reinforcing the need to approach them together rather than in isolation.

This chapter presents a practical, engineering-focused guide to handling these challenges systematically. It begins with performance budgeting, a discipline that helps teams set measurable constraints on load time, bundle size, and runtime behavior. These budgets act as a guardrail for every MFE team, ensuring the overall user experience remains predictable and performant as the system grows. We will also investigate options to measure performance in MFEs, introducing key metrics, monitoring tools, and the effective use of browser APIs like the Performance Timing API. These tools help developers capture data directly from the user's environment, identify bottlenecks introduced by individual MFEs, and maintain visibility across independently shipped fragments.

Finally, the chapter explores the security considerations unique to distributed frontends. MFEs introduce additional cross-origin interactions, independent module boundaries, and shared runtime surfaces, all of which expand the attack vector landscape. We will learn how to secure inter-module communication, enforce strict governance, apply the right HTTP security headers, manage cross-origin isolation, and mitigate threats such as **cross-site scripting**

(**XSS**) and **cross-site request forgery** (**CSRF**) in a modular environment. The chapter closes by offering governance recommendations to maintain consistency across teams without compromising their autonomy.

Structure

The chapter covers the following topics:

- Performance budgeting
- Measuring performance in MFEs
- Measuring tools
- Security in MFEs
- Governance and team practices

Objectives

The objective of this chapter is to equip readers with a clear understanding of how to maintain both high performance and strong security within a distributed MFE architecture. By exploring performance budgeting, we will learn how to establish measurable limits for load times, bundle sizes, and runtime behavior that scale across multiple independent teams. The chapter also aims to help readers develop the skills to accurately measure, monitor, and diagnose performance issues using browser-based timing APIs, real-user monitoring, and distributed telemetry. On the security side, readers will gain insight into protecting inter-module communication, enforcing strict access boundaries, applying essential security headers, and mitigating risks that become more complex in MFEs. Ultimately, this chapter provides the knowledge and practical tools needed to build MFE systems that remain fast, predictable, and secure as they grow in size and complexity.

Performance budgeting

A performance budget is a practical way to keep an application fast as it grows. It works like a spending limit, but instead of money, it controls the size and cost of the resources that make up a web experience. A team first measures how the application performs today and uses that information to set limits on things such as how much JavaScript can load during startup, how long the page can take to become interactive, or how many requests can run before the first screen appears. These limits guide design choices, development work, and release decisions. When used well, a performance budget creates a shared understanding of what good performance looks like and gives every team a clear boundary to stay within. It also helps prevent slow regression over time, which often happens as new features and dependencies are added. In short, a performance budget protects the user experience by keeping the application focused and efficient.

Setting the baseline

Ever wondered how we can define the baseline of the application performance, where to start, and what to focus on? *Harry Roberts* explains this clearly in his own terms. He says,

Performance budgets should not be things to work toward; they should be things that stop us slipping past a certain point. They should not be aspirational; they should be preventative.

(**Source: https://csswizardry.com/2020/01/performance-budgets-pragmatically/**)

This idea sets the right mindset for creating a baseline. A baseline is not a dream target or an ideal scenario. It is an honest snapshot of how the application performs today. It shows the current weight of scripts and styles, how long the first content appears, how quickly the browser settles, and how users experience the very first moments of interaction. Without this starting point, any limits we set would be based on hope rather than reality.

With this view, defining a baseline becomes a process of careful observation. Teams gather measurements from synthetic tools, from real user sessions, from different devices, and from both strong and weak networks. They measure how long the page takes to load, how much script is parsed and executed, and which resources slow the page during startup. This initial picture reveals where most of the time is being spent and which areas already push the limits of a good user experience. Once this information is known, teams can set budgets that make sense for their environment. These budgets are not goals to grow into but guardrails that protect the experience as new features and MFEs are added. The baseline provides the ground truth that keeps the entire system steady and predictable over time.

Understanding performance budget

A performance budget is made of a small set of limits that control the parts of a page that most affect the user experience. These limits help teams stay focused on the resources that matter the most, such as script weight, style size, image cost, and how much work the browser must perform before the page feels ready. When teams define these limits, they are not trying to chase a perfect score or an ideal benchmark. Instead, they are placing boundaries around the areas that most often cause slowdowns. This keeps the application predictable and prevents silent growth over time. Each part of the budget acts like a checkpoint that asks a simple question: Is this change safe for the user experience?

A well-defined performance budget usually includes the size of the JavaScript bundles, the cost of images and fonts, the number of requests made in the first few seconds, the time it takes for visible content to appear, and the time the browser spends running and processing code. It also includes key user experience signals such as how stable the layout is and how quickly the page responds to the first user action. These pieces work together to form a picture of what a healthy experience should look like. They remind teams that performance is not only about loading less code but also about reducing work, avoiding delays, and creating a smooth path for the user from the moment the page begins to load. By understanding what the budget contains, teams can make more informed decisions and build features without losing sight of the experience they are trying to protect.

To understand how a performance budget works in practice, imagine a team building an application that loads a home page with a product list. After measuring the baseline, the team learns that the page currently loads around three hundred kilobytes of JavaScript, makes nine requests during startup, and shows the first meaningful content in about two and a half seconds on an average device. Using this information, the team creates a budget that sets a limit of two hundred and fifty kilobytes of JavaScript for the next release, no more than six startup requests, and a target for the first content to appear within two seconds. These numbers are not guesses. They are based on what the application already does and what the team believes is both safe and achievable.

Now imagine the team adds a new image gallery. Without a budget, this feature could easily add large images, a new script library, and extra style sheets. With a budget in place, the team checks their changes before release and sees that the new images push the page over the allowed size. They decide to use more efficient formats and remove an unnecessary library. As a result, the new feature ships without hurting the user experience. This simple example shows how a performance budget guides decision-making, keeps teams honest about the cost of their changes, and prevents slow regression over time. It also shows that a budget is not a barrier to new features but a way to build them without sacrificing speed and quality.

Performance budgets in MFEs

Performance budgets become even more valuable when an application is built with MFEs. In this type of architecture, different parts of the page are created and shipped by different teams, often with their own tools, timelines, and priorities. Each MFE brings its own scripts, styles, images, and startup work. Even when every team is careful, the combined effect can slowly increase the overall cost of the page. A small rise in bundle size here, a new library there, and an extra request from another team can add up quickly. Without a clear budget that everyone follows, the final experience can become slow and uneven, even though no single team intended to cause any harm.

A shared performance budget creates a common foundation for every team working in the system. It sets clear limits for the container and for each individual MFE. It ensures that no single part grows without control and that every team understands the impact of its changes on the entire page. When new features are added, the budget acts as a gentle guardrail that keeps the experience safe. When regressions appear, the budget helps teams identify where the increase came from. This structure encourages thoughtful design, reduces accidental duplication of shared libraries, and protects the overall flow of the page. With a budget in place, an MFE system remains fast, predictable, and stable even as many teams ship updates in parallel. The budget calculation of a page with MFEs is depicted in the following figure:

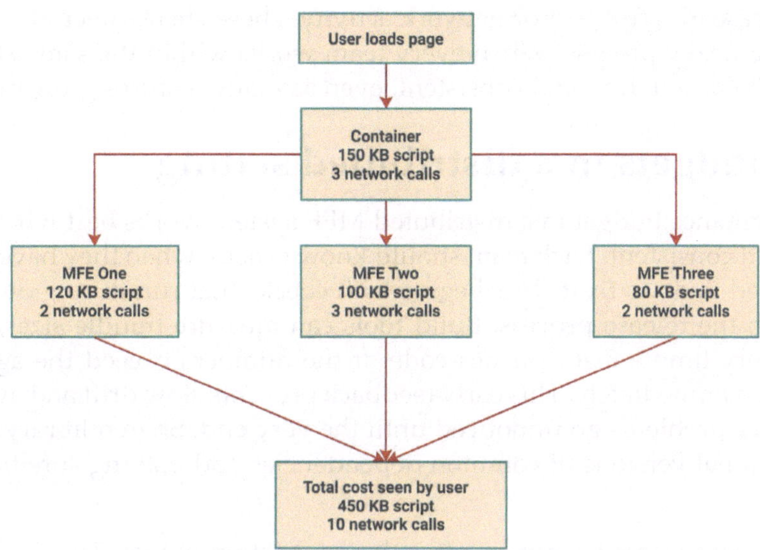

***Figure 9.1**: Cumulative impact of independent MFEs*

Figure 9.1 shows how the cost of a page grows as each MFE adds its own scripts and network calls. The container loads first and brings its own weight, but every MFE that follows contributes more work for the browser. Each contribution may represent a small regression introduced during an independent release and may seem harmless when viewed in isolation, yet all of them combine into the total cost the user must pay before the page is ready. This is the core challenge with MFEs. Even careful teams can unintentionally add more script, more processing, and more requests over time. Without shared limits, the final experience becomes slower with each new feature.

Applying budgets across MFE

Applying a performance budget in an MFE system begins with the idea that every team shares responsibility for the overall experience. The container owns the basic structure of the page and often includes routing, shared libraries, and core assets. Each MFE then receives a portion of the total budget that matches its role and importance. A feature that appears on the first screen may receive a larger allowance than a feature that loads later or only appears in a settings page. This shared view prevents one part of the system from growing without limits and ensures that every team understands the cost of its changes. It also encourages teams to remove unused code, avoid repeated libraries, and ship only what is essential.

Once the budget is divided, the next step is to make sure it is followed in a simple and predictable way. Build steps can alert a team when its MFE grows beyond its allowance. Shared library rules can prevent teams from shipping multiple versions of the same dependency. During integration, the container can check that the total size of all MFEs still fits within the overall limit. **Real user monitoring** (**RUM**) can show which part of the page is responsible for a sudden increase in script cost or network activity. These checks keep the system healthy without creating a heavy process. When every team works within the same shared plan, the entire page stays balanced, fast, and consistent, even as many features grow independently.

Enforcing budgets in a distributed setting

Enforcing a performance budget in a distributed MFE system works best when the process is simple, visible, and consistent. Each team should know exactly when they have crossed a limit and what they need to do to fix it. This begins with checks that run during development and continues through the release process. Build tools can measure bundle sizes, script weight, and asset cost every time a team pushes code. If the numbers exceed the agreed limit, the developer is alerted immediately. This early feedback prevents slow drift and avoids situations where performance problems go unnoticed until the very end. Shared library rules also help by blocking additional versions of common dependencies and making sure the system stays clean and lean.

The other part of enforcement happens after the application is live. This is where real user monitoring becomes important. When the page loads in the browser, the system can record how each MFE performs and how much work it adds to the page. If a sudden slowdown appears, teams can trace it back to the exact feature or update that caused the issue. This type of monitoring makes performance a shared responsibility rather than an afterthought. Instead of relying on guesswork or manual checks, the system itself reveals where a regression came from. With clear limits, simple build checks, and real-world data, teams can keep an MFE system steady, predictable, and easy to scale, even as many groups ship changes at the same time. The following figure shows an approach of enforcing budget at the time of integration:

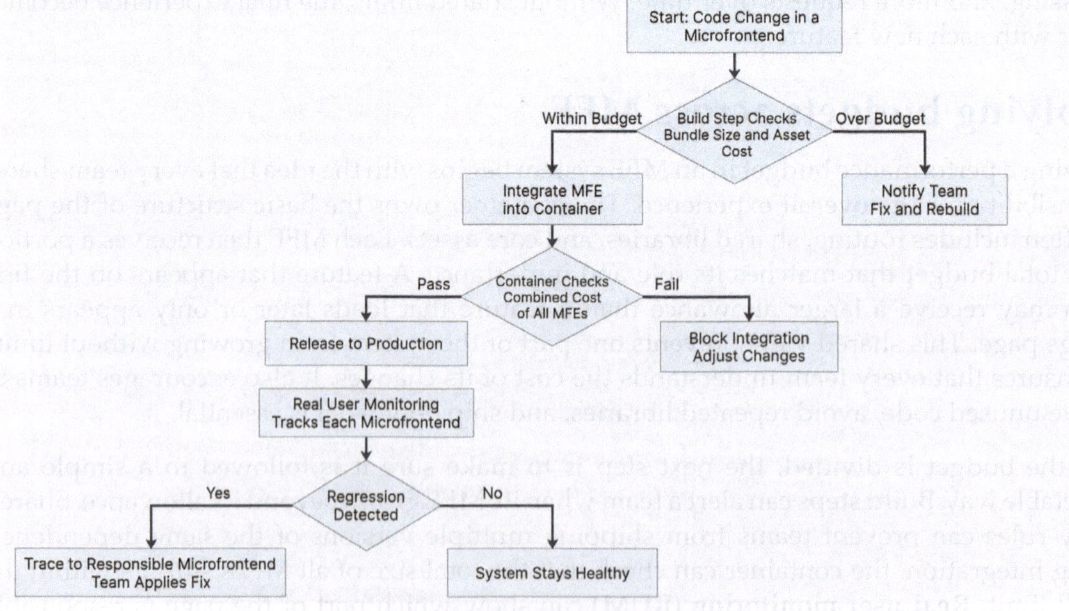

Figure 9.2: A typical MFE performance budget governance workflow

Figure 9.2 shows how performance budgets are enforced as MFEs move from development to production. Each change begins with a local build check that tests bundle size and asset cost. If the change fits within the limit, it is integrated into the container. The container then performs its own check to ensure that the combined cost of all MFEs remains safe. Only when both checks pass does the update go live. Once the application is running in the browser, real user monitoring watches how each MFE performs. If a regression appears, the system can trace it back to the exact MFE that caused the issue, allowing the team to apply a quick fix. This simple flow keeps the entire application steady, predictable, and fast, even as many teams ship updates at the same time.

Note: The above illustration is only an example of how a performance budget can be enforced in a distributed environment. The exact steps may differ from one application to another based on tools, release practices, and organizational guidelines. Some systems might allow changes to reach production even when a budget is crossed, and then notify the MFE team to apply a fix. In other cases, the host may choose to block integration until the issue is resolved. The way these checks influence the flow depends entirely on how the host manages its MFEs and how strict the performance rules need to be.

Measuring performance in MFEs

Measuring performance in an MFE system is more than checking how fast a page loads. It is about understanding which part of the page creates delays, how much work each MFE adds, and how the system behaves in real user sessions. In a traditional application, it is easy to look at one bundle and one runtime, but MFE system is different. Multiple teams own different parts of the experience, and each part loads at its own pace. It is because the measuring performance must be done with careful attention to detail so teams can see both the overall picture and the individual contribution of each MFE.

A good measurement strategy lets teams trace where time is being spent. It shows when a container script slows down the start-up, when a feature is making too many network calls, or when an MFE blocks the main thread. Without this visibility, performance regressions appear slowly and silently over time. With clear measurement in place, teams catch issues early and maintain a smooth and predictable experience even as the system grows.

Key metrics

Performance on the web is shaped by how quickly the page becomes useful, how steady it feels during loading, and how responsive it is when the user interacts. To understand these qualities, teams rely on a set of general performance metrics that describe the experience in simple and practical terms. Core Web Vitals are the industry standards to measure performance. They focus on moments that matter most to users, such as the time it takes for important content to appear, how stable the screen looks as it loads, and how smooth the page feels when the user begins to interact. These values give teams a clear way to judge the experience without getting lost in the details of implementation.

Alongside these user-focused signals, there are several technical measurements that help explain why a page feels fast or slow. These include how much script is downloaded, how many requests are made during startup, and how much work the browser must do on the main thread before it can respond. Browser features such as the Resource Timing API and the Navigation Timing API show how long it takes to fetch and prepare different assets. Resource hints like **`preload`** and **`preconnect`** allow the browser to prioritize important work early in the loading process. When used together, these general metrics create a complete picture of the behavior of the page across different devices and network conditions.

MFE-specific metrics

Once the general performance signals are understood, the next step is to look at how these measurements apply in an MFE environment. An MFE system is made of separate parts that load at different times and are owned by different teams. Because of this, the total performance of the page is not the only thing that matters. Teams need to understand the cost of each MFE on its own. This allows them to see which part adds the most weight, which part introduces delays, and which part affects the early moments of the experience.

One of the most important MFE-specific metrics is the time it takes for each MFE to become ready. This includes the time needed to download its script, the time the browser spends executing that script, and the time needed to fetch any required data. Even a small delay inside one MFE can affect the overall experience when several MFEs appear on the same screen. By measuring readiness per MFE, teams can see which features load quickly and which ones slow down the startup.

Another useful metric is the processing cost of each MFE. In a shared environment, multiple MFEs compete for the same main thread. If one MFE performs heavy work during startup, it can slow down all the others. Measuring how much main thread time each MFE uses helps teams understand where the browser is spending its effort. It also shows which parts might need offloading to a worker or restructuring to reduce heavy computations.

Network behavior is another key area. Each MFE may make its own requests, and without careful attention, these requests can stack up and create long wait times. Measuring request count and request timing per MFE helps teams to avoid unnecessary waterfalls and large bursts of network work. It also encourages MFE to share data when possible, rather than fetching the same information multiple times.

By tracking these MFE-specific metrics, teams gain a clearer view of how each part of the system behaves on its own. This level of detail makes it easier to trace regressions, target improvements, and maintain a consistent experience even as many MFEs evolve independently. It turns performance measurement from a broad view of the page into a more focused and actionable insight that supports both autonomy and quality.

Measuring tools

Measuring performance in an MFE environment requires a clear view of both the overall page and the individual parts that make up the experience. A single application can be measured as one unit, but an MFE system contains many bundles, many loading paths, and many ownership groups. It is because of this, teams need tools that can show how the page behaves from start to finish while also revealing the cost of each MFE on its own. Modern browsers and lightweight instrumentation already provide everything needed to build this understanding. When used together, these tools give teams a complete and trustworthy picture of performance across all devices and networks.

Browser Timing APIs

Browser Timing APIs are the foundation for most performance measurement work. They offer precise information about how long different parts of the page take to load, how resources travel over the network, and how the browser prepares the document for display. These tools require no additional setup, add no weight to the application, and work in every modern environment. Because they come directly from the browser, they provide accurate data that can be trusted when diagnosing performance problems.

Resource Timing API

The Resource Timing API gives a detailed view of how long each file takes to load. It records when a request starts, when the response arrives, and how much time the browser spends fetching and processing different resources. This information helps teams understand which scripts, styles, or images slow down the page. It is especially useful in an MFE system where each MFE ships its own script bundle or assets. By reading resource timing entries, teams can see which MFE has the heaviest file, which one has slow network retrieval, and which one introduces extra requests. With this insight, teams can control asset growth and avoid duplication across multiple MFEs.

Resource Timing data also helps teams understand how changes in the container or shared libraries affect the loading path. A new dependency added by one MFE might show up as a larger file in the timing data, and a slow edge location in a content delivery network might show up as longer fetch times. By capturing these values early, teams can detect patterns and correct issues before they reach users. The API provides the level of detail needed to keep a distributed system predictable, even when many MFEs load on the same page.

The following is a code example of capturing all the resources and their load time cost using the native performance API:

```
// Get all resource timing entries and filter for scripts
const resources = performance.getEntriesByType("resource");
const scripts = resources.filter(entry => entry.initiatorType === "script");
```

```
scripts.forEach(entry => {
  console.log("Script name:", entry.name);
  console.log("Transfer size (bytes):", entry.transferSize);
  console.log("Fetch time (ms):", entry.responseEnd - entry.startTime);
});
```

This helps you quickly see which scripts are slow or heavy. We can extend this a bit to track all the MFEs (the UMD/Module Federation style) load time, provided the MFEs are named with a common convention. In this way, we can identify performance bottlenecks arising from the MFE and inform or fix those before they reach production. The following code sample shows a method to extend the above to the MFE use case, assuming each MFE bundle uses a simple naming pattern such as:

- **`mfe-cart.bundle.js`**
- **`mfe-profile.bundle.js`**

```
function collectMfeResourceTimings() {
  const resources = performance.getEntriesByType("resource");
  const mfeResources = resources.filter(entry =>
    entry.initiatorType === "script" &&
    entry.name.includes("mfe-")
  );
  return mfeResources.map(entry => ({
    name: entry.name,
    transferSize: entry.transferSize,
    fetchTime: entry.responseEnd - entry.startTime,
    startTime: entry.startTime,
  }));
}
window.addEventListener("load", () => {
  const mfeData = collectMfeResourceTimings();
  // Example: send to your monitoring endpoint
  navigator.sendBeacon("/rum", JSON.stringify({
    type: "mfe-resources",
    resources: mfeData,
  }));
});
```

By leveraging the performance API, the utility function would filter resources starting with a specific name to avoid the noise from unrelated scripts, and once it collects all the required data, it can be sent to the tracking or monitoring system using the **sendBeacon** method. This approach of sending performance data looks naive, but very handy and effective. If we closely observe, this only solves one side of the puzzle. Yes, now we can track the load time of MFE at the initial render of the application, but not all MFEs are rendered at the application load time; MFEs tend to load asynchronously in applications such as **Single Page Application** (**SPA**) or Hybrid. The naive approach does not help. We need something better, enter the world of streaming using **PerformanceObserver**. The following is a sample code of how the asynchronous MFE performance can be tracked:

```
if ("PerformanceObserver" in window) {
  const observer = new PerformanceObserver(list => {
    const entries = list.getEntries();
    entries
      .filter(entry => entry.initiatorType === "script")
      .forEach(entry => {
        console.log("Script loaded:", entry.name);
        console.log("Fetch time (ms):", entry.responseEnd - entry.startTime);
      });
  });
  observer.observe({ type: "resource", buffered: true });
}
```

This is helpful when an MFE loads on demand, not only at page start, and it shows the cost of each script at the moment it loads, which is useful for MFEs loaded later in the session.

Navigation Timing API

The Navigation Timing API gives a complete picture of how the browser loads a page from the moment navigation starts until the page is fully ready. It captures key moments in the life cycle of the load process, such as when the request begins, when the first response arrives, and when the document becomes stable enough for interaction. This information helps teams understand where time is being spent and whether delays come from the network, the server, or the browser preparation work. In an MFE environment, navigation timing provides the outer frame for all other timing work because it sets the baseline for when the container becomes ready and when MFEs can begin their own loading process.

To make use of this information, one simple approach is to send the navigation timing values to a monitoring service. This allows teams to observe how real users experience the page across many devices and network conditions. By capturing the key milestones reported by the browser, teams learn whether the container loads slowly, whether the document takes too long to prepare, or whether changes in infrastructure or content delivery affect the first stage of the experience. The following is a code sample of how we can send page navigation data to the RUM service:

```
window.addEventListener("load", () => {
  const [navEntry] = performance.getEntriesByType("navigation");
  if (!navEntry) return;
  const payload = {
    type: "navigation",
    timeToFirstByte: navEntry.responseStart,
    domContentLoaded: navEntry.domContentLoadedEventEnd,
    domComplete: navEntry.domComplete,
    loadEventEnd: navEntry.loadEventEnd,
  };
  navigator.sendBeacon("/rum", JSON.stringify(payload));
});
```

Navigation timing also becomes more powerful when it is combined with simple signals from each MFE. By marking the moment, the container becomes ready, and then listening for events from MFEs when they complete their startup work, teams can see exactly how long each MFE takes to become usable. This creates a clear and traceable view of the MFE startup sequence and helps identify which features introduce delays after the container has already finished its work. This is illustrated in the following code example:

```
// In the container
window.addEventListener("load", () => {
  const [navEntry] = performance.getEntriesByType("navigation");
  if (!navEntry) return;
  const containerReady = navEntry.domContentLoadedEventEnd;
  window.addEventListener("mfe-ready", event => {
    const { name, readyTime } = event.detail;
    console.log(`Microfrontend ${name} ready at (ms):`, readyTime);
    console.log(
      `Time from container ready to ${name} ready (ms):`,
      readyTime - containerReady
    );
  });
});
// In each microfrontend
function markMfeReady(name) {
  const now = performance.now();
  const event = new CustomEvent("mfe-ready", {
    detail: { name, readyTime: now },
```

```
  });
  window.dispatchEvent(event);
}
```

This pattern helps separate container performance from MFE performance, making it easier for teams to see who contributes what to the overall experience. Although this approach works well for tracing when each MFE becomes ready, it does have a few limitations. The container must listen for readiness events, which means any new MFE added to the system often requires an update in the container code. This creates a small but ongoing dependency between the container and individual MFEs. It also requires every MFE team to follow the same pattern and remember to send the correct signal at the right moment. If an MFE forgets to report its readiness or reports it too early, the measurement becomes inaccurate. This method is still a helpful starting point, but it should be treated as a simple technique rather than a complete solution for large and fully distributed systems.

Custom marks and measures

Browser timing APIs provide a good foundation, but they offer only a general view of how the page loads. To understand how each MFE behaves on its own, teams often add custom marks and measures inside their code. These marks allow an MFE to report the exact moment it starts loading, when it mounts in the interface, and when the user can first interact with it. This level of detail becomes helpful because it shows what happens inside each MFE rather than only what the browser sees at the page level. It gives teams a clear sense of which features start quickly, which ones take more time, and where any delays begin.

Custom marks are simple signals created using the browser performance API. They do not add weight to the application, and they work in every modern browser. A team might place a mark at the start of an MFE and another when the MFE becomes ready. With two marks in place, a measure can be created to calculate the time between them. This pattern helps teams understand the internal cost of each MFE, including initialization time, rendering time, and any additional work performed during startup. When used consistently across teams, these marks form a shared language for understanding performance inside an MFE environment.

To illustrate this, consider an MFE that wants to track how long it takes to move from its entry point to its mounted state. A simple approach is to place a mark at the very beginning and another when the component is fully rendered. From these marks, a measure can be created that shows the total time spent in that step:

```
// Inside a microfrontend
performance.mark("mfe-profile-start");
// ... perform setup, fetch data, render components ...
performance.mark("mfe-profile-ready");
// Create a measure for the time between start and ready
performance.measure(
```

```
  "mfe-profile-boot-time",
  "mfe-profile-start",
  "mfe-profile-ready"
);
// Read the measure
const [entry] = performance.getEntriesByName("mfe-profile-boot-time");
console.log("Profile MFE boot time (ms):", entry.duration);
```

This simple structure gives the team a clear and repeatable way to track MFE readiness. It also allows the container or monitoring system to collect these values from different MFEs and compare them over time. As features evolve, the boot time will reveal whether new code introduces unexpected delays, making it easier to catch regressions early.

Custom marks can also be used for business-specific journeys rather than only measuring load. For example, an MFE could track how long it takes to complete a checkout step, open a menu, or render a list of items. These measurements help teams understand not just how fast the MFE loads, but also how fast it feels during real user interaction. This gives a more complete picture of the experience and highlights the areas where improvements matter most.

Custom marks and measures are powerful because they reveal the internal cost of each MFE while still being easy to use and maintain. They fit naturally into a distributed system and give teams a simple way to take responsibility for their own performance work without adding heavy tools or complex processes.

Common pitfalls

While browser timing APIs are powerful, teams can run into a few common pitfalls when applying them across MFEs. One frequent issue is inconsistent resource naming. If each MFE uses a different naming convention for its bundles, it becomes difficult to reliably group and analyze resource timing data. Another challenge is timing skew across MFEs. Because MFEs load at different moments and may execute asynchronously, comparing raw timing values without proper context can lead to misleading conclusions. For example, a later-loading MFE may appear slow simply because it starts after the container has already completed its work. Finally, incomplete instrumentation can reduce accuracy. If some MFEs emit timing signals while others do not, the resulting picture is fragmented and harder to trust. Establishing shared conventions and measuring relative timing rather than absolute values helps avoid these early mistakes and keeps browser-level measurements consistent and actionable.

Real user monitoring

Real user monitoring was covered in detail in *Chapter 8, Observability and Monitoring,* under the *Observability tools* section, where we explored how real-world conditions, device differences, and usage patterns shape the overall experience. For the purpose of this chapter, the role of RUM is more focused. In an MFE environment, RUM acts as the link between browser timing data and how each MFE behaves in production. While browser APIs help measure performance during controlled conditions, RUM shows how those measurements hold up when real users load and interact with the application. This becomes especially valuable when multiple MFEs appear on the same route, and each one behaves differently across devices, networks, or regions.

In this context, RUM serves two main goals. The first is to help teams observe how each MFE performs in real sessions without adding heavy instrumentation. The second is to reveal when a performance shift correlates with a specific MFE rather than the container or backend. A lightweight pattern for this is for each MFE to send a small signal when it becomes ready or completes a key part of its work. These signals are then collected to show trends over time, making it easier to see which MFE caused a slowdown after a new release.

A simple example looks like this:

```
function reportMfeTiming(name, duration) {
  const payload = {
    type: "mfe-timing",
    mfe: name,
    duration
  };
  navigator.sendBeacon("/rum", JSON.stringify(payload));
}
```

Each MFE can call this function after it mounts or completes an important sequence. When viewed in a central dashboard, these small pieces of data help track which MFEs load consistently and which ones introduce sudden slowdowns. This focused use of RUM supports the deeper timing information gathered through browser APIs by placing it in a real-world context. It forms a bridge between internal measurements and how the distributed system behaves for actual users.

Unified observability view

Each tool we have discussed offers a different perspective on performance, but none of them alone can show the full story of how the MFE system behaves. Navigation timing describes the outer frame of the page load. Resource timing reveals the cost of individual assets. Custom marks highlight what happens inside each MFE. Real user monitoring shows how all of this plays out in real sessions. When combined, these tools create a complete and reliable picture of performance across both the container and the individual MFEs.

At the container level, teams can use navigation and resource timing to understand how the shared framework, routing, and common libraries influence the earliest moments of the experience. This helps identify issues that affect every route, such as a heavy shared dependency or slow document preparation. Meanwhile, MFE level marks and telemetry reveal how each feature behaves on its own. They show how long MFEs take to initialize, which ones consume the most main thread time, and where delays appear once the container has finished its work.

A shared dashboard brings these layers together. It may show container load time, ready times for each MFE, network cost per bundle, and trends gathered from real user monitoring. When all these signals are viewed side by side, patterns become easier to spot. Teams can quickly see whether a slowdown comes from the container, from a specific MFE, or from a change in network conditions. This alignment allows different teams to make informed decisions without guesswork, while keeping the entire system predictable and stable as it grows. By combining timing APIs, custom marks, and real user data, teams gain the clarity needed to maintain a fast experience in a distributed environment. This flow has been illustrated in the following figure:

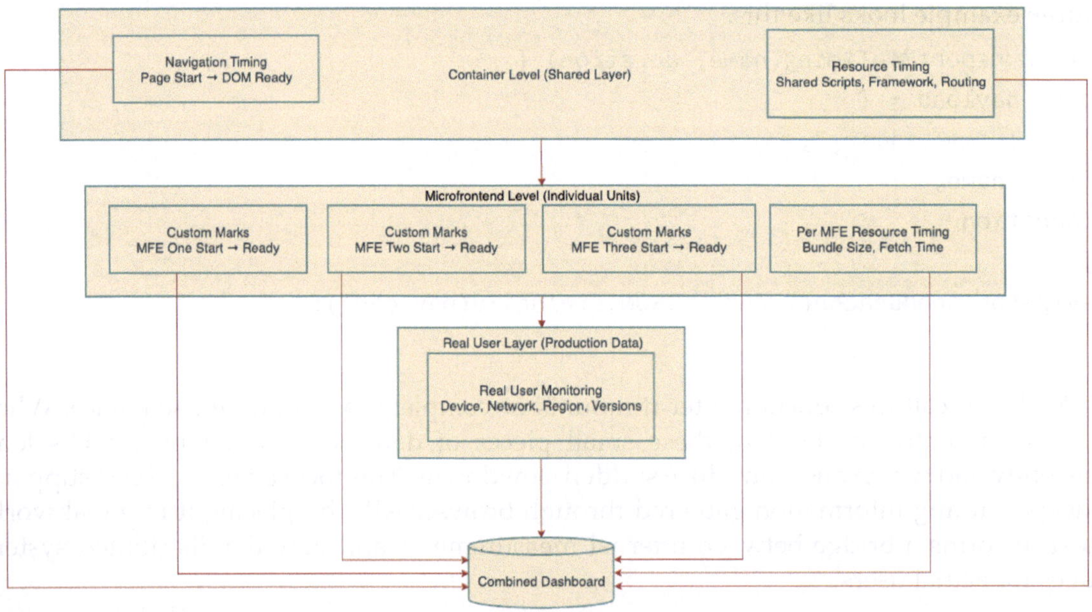

Figure 9.3: *The complete picture of performance monitoring*

The above *Figure 9.3* brings together the full picture of performance measurement in an MFE system by isolating the role of each layer. The container layer records the foundational timing information through navigation and resource timing. These values show how long it takes for the page to begin loading, prepare the document, and download any shared dependencies. The MFE layer then adds its own view through custom marks, measures, and per MFE resource timing. This provides visibility into how each separate feature initializes and how much weight or processing cost it adds.

The outer layer shows real user monitoring, which captures how these timings behave in real environments across varied devices, locations, and network conditions. All these signals feed into a shared dashboard that blends container timings, MFE measurements, and real-world observations into one reliable view. This allows teams to instantly see whether a slowdown comes from the container, a specific MFE, the user environment, or a combination of factors. By isolating each level, the system becomes easier to understand, easier to improve, and far more predictable as it scales.

Security in MFEs

Security becomes more complex in an MFE environment because the system is no longer a single application with one clear boundary. Instead, it is made of many independent parts, each owned by different teams and often shipped on their own schedule. This distributed structure increases the number of places where something can go wrong and creates more opportunities for inconsistent rules, unsafe communication, or accidental exposure of sensitive data. As a result, security must be approached with shared guidelines and consistent practices rather than handled separately by each MFE team. A secure MFE system is one where every part follows the same standards, every boundary is clearly defined, and every team understands how their choices affect the larger application.

Unique challenges in MFE security

MFEs introduce a set of challenges that do not appear in traditional applications. Because each MFE loads its own scripts, styles, and logic, the attack surface increases. A mistake or oversight in one MFE can affect the entire page. When MFEs communicate through shared events, messages, or global objects, there is a risk of unsafe access or unintended information flow. If one MFE assumes a certain level of trust and another does not, it creates gaps that attackers can exploit.

Another challenge is the variety of environments in which MFEs run. They may be served from different origins, use different versions of shared libraries, or interact with different API endpoints. Without a consistent approach to headers, policies, and permissions, the system can become unpredictable and difficult to secure. This is why security in an MFE architecture must rely on shared agreements and a common foundation rather than isolated solutions. Each MFE must follow the same rules when it comes to encoding, sanitizing, requesting data, and handling user input. This protects the entire system from inconsistent behavior and ensures that security does not break down as the application grows.

Securing inter-module communication

Communication between MFE is one of the areas where security risks can appear quickly if it is not handled with care. MFEs often exchange data through shared events, message channels, or global objects. While this flexibility makes the architecture easier to scale, it also creates openings where sensitive information can leak or where one MFE can accidentally gain access to data it should not see. A safe communication pattern begins by keeping the messages simple, limiting what is shared, and ensuring that no MFE can interpret or manipulate data outside of its intended purpose.

A secure approach focuses on two ideas. The first is to avoid passing raw objects or untrusted input between MFEs. Instead, messages should be well defined, small, and free of unnecessary details. This reduces the risk of exposing information that another MFE should not use. The second idea is to keep a clear boundary around the shared communication layer. The container or a dedicated communication module should act as the gatekeeper and validate messages before broadcasting them. This prevents any MFE from sending unexpected data or interfering with events that belong to another feature.

When communication happens across different origins, additional care is needed. Cross-origin messages should always check who the sender is and confirm the target origin before processing any data. This helps prevent spoofed messages or unintended access from untrusted frames or external sources. Even in the same origin setups, it is important to ensure that event names and message channels do not collide. A simple naming convention can prevent one MFE from accidentally listening to another's internal events.

By keeping messages well-scoped, validating communication at the boundary, and avoiding direct data sharing, teams create a safe and predictable environment for MFEs to work together. This approach protects the application from accidental leaks and reduces the risk of one MFE affecting another in ways that were never intended. It allows communication to remain flexible while still providing the structure needed to maintain strong security across a distributed system.

Protecting shared resources

Shared resources are an important part of any MFE architecture, and they can also become a significant security concern if not handled carefully. MFEs often rely on common assets such as design systems, user data, authentication tokens, or shared API layers. When these resources are exposed or accessed without clear rules, one MFE can accidentally access information meant for another. This creates gaps where sensitive data might leak, or where a poorly isolated MFE can interfere with the behavior of the rest of the system. Protecting shared resources starts with clearly defining what each MFE is allowed to access and ensuring that access cannot happen in ways that bypass these rules.

A safe approach to shared resources involves controlling both *what* is shared and *how* it is shared. The container, or a dedicated shared module, should serve as the single source of truth for sensitive information. MFEs should receive only what they need and nothing more. For example, instead of passing full user objects, it is safer to pass only the specific fields required for a given MFE to render its view. API calls should also follow this principle. Each MFE should communicate with backend services through well-defined endpoints, rather than relying on global objects or common request builders that allow unrestricted access to data. This prevents any MFE from making unauthorized calls or reading information meant for a different part of the application. Another approach is to encrypt or sign the data at the server side before passing it to the container or other MFEs, and the consuming MFE can decrypt it.

Shared libraries require similar attention. If MFEs use the same library, the version must be consistent and loaded from a trusted source. Using mismatched versions or unverified copies increases the risk of introducing vulnerabilities. The container can help enforce this by loading critical dependencies itself and making them available in a controlled way. This reduces the chance of accidental duplication and ensures that MFEs cannot bring unsafe or outdated libraries into the page.

By limiting access, validating what is shared, and keeping sensitive resources behind clear boundaries, the system becomes much easier to secure. Each MFE can work independently without the risk of exposing information or affecting the behavior of other MFEs. This protects the entire architecture from mistakes, misuse, or unintended interactions and forms a strong foundation for secure collaboration across teams.

Common web threats in an MFE context

A distributed MFE system inherits all the usual security risks found in web applications, but the impact can be larger because multiple teams contribute code that runs in the same environment. A mistake in one MFE can create a weakness that affects the entire page. This makes it important to understand the common web threats that appear in any frontend architecture and how they become more challenging when MFEs operate together. One of the most familiar threats is XSS, where unsafe input is rendered directly into the page. In an MFE environment, even one unsafe template, unescaped variable, or direct manipulation of rendered content can allow an attacker to run malicious code across the full application. Because MFEs share the same global scope, a vulnerability in one MFE allows attackers to interact with the container, read shared resources, or listen for events from other MFEs. Safe encoding, sanitization, and avoiding direct HTML injection are essential to prevent this kind of exposure.

Another common risk is CSRF, which tricks the browser into executing unintended actions on behalf of the user. MFEs that make API calls must ensure that they follow consistent protection strategies, such as using secure cookies, verifying tokens, or relying on server-side defenses. Inconsistent approaches across MFEs create gaps where these protections can fail. Each MFE must follow the same rules for authentication, token use, and request patterns so that no single part becomes an entry point for unwanted actions. Overly permissive cross-origin settings are another challenge. An MFE might rely on assets or data from a third-party source, but if the container or the MFE uses relaxed content rules, it can expose the system to unsafe origins. This includes loose content security policies, open fetch permissions, or script tags pointing to untrusted locations. This is because MFEs share the same page; unsafe configuration in one MFE affects the entire surface.

Even common mistakes become more serious in an MFE system. Duplicate libraries with known vulnerabilities, outdated dependencies, or unsafe feature flags can extend the attack surface. An MFE may unintentionally make the system heavier, slower to patch, or inconsistent in its security posture. By treating these risks as shared responsibilities and applying consistent rules, teams reduce the chance of introducing vulnerabilities and protect the overall system from threats that are easy to overlook in distributed architectures.

Security headers and policies

Security headers form an important layer of protection in an MFE system because they define what the browser is allowed to load, which origins it can trust, and how sensitive information should be handled. These rules must be applied consistently at the host level so that every MFE operates under the same constraints. Even when MFEs are built and deployed independently, they should still inherit a shared set of headers that keep the system predictable and safe.

One of the most important controls is the content security policy. A CSP limits where scripts, styles, and other resources can come from. For example, a host might allow only its own domain and its trusted CDN, preventing MFEs from introducing unapproved script sources. A simple server setup could look like this:

```
res.setHeader(
  "Content-Security-Policy",
  [
    "default-src 'self'",
    "script-src 'self' https://cdn.example.com",
    "style-src 'self' https://cdn.example.com",
    "img-src 'self' data:",
    "connect-src 'self' https://api.example.com",
    "frame-ancestors 'none'",
  ].join("; ")
);
```

With this policy in place, even if an MFE accidentally inserts unsafe HTML or loads a third-party dependency, the browser will block it before it reaches users. This helps prevent injected scripts from running and keeps the system aligned around trusted sources.

Transport and origin-based protections reinforce this foundation. A strict transport security header ensures that all MFEs load over HTTPS, reducing risks from downgraded or intercepted connections:

```
res.setHeader(
  "Strict-Transport-Security",
  "max-age=63072000; includeSubDomains; preload"
);
```

Similarly, origin-based policies help control how resources are read or embedded across sites. A host may restrict its assets to the same site access using a rule or require trusted conditions when embedding external content, as shown in the following:

```
res.setHeader("Cross-Origin-Resource-Policy", "same-site");
res.setHeader("Cross-Origin-Embedder-Policy", "require-corp");
```

These protections are especially useful when MFEs rely on workers or heavily shared assets, as they prevent untrusted origins from influencing the page.

Additional headers help prevent subtle information leaks. A safe referrer policy, for example, controls how much data is sent during navigation:

```
res.setHeader("Referrer-Policy", "strict-origin-when-cross-origin");
```

This prevents MFEs from passing sensitive path or query details to external sites. Similarly, a permissions policy limits which browser features can be used across the system:

```
res.setHeader(
  "Permissions-Policy",
  "geolocation=(), microphone=(), camera=()"
);
```

This ensures no MFE can access capabilities it does not need.

Finally, cross-origin request rules must be consistent. If an MFE is served from a CDN, the host may expose it only to trusted origins:

```
res.setHeader("Access-Control-Allow-Origin", "https://app.example.com");
```

Loose **cross-origin resource sharing** (**CORS**) settings can expose the entire set of MFE bundles, so the host should define these rules carefully and expect all MFEs to operate within them. When these headers and policies are applied together, they form a strong baseline that protects the application from common threats. They also create a predictable environment where every MFE works under the same constraints. This allows teams to build independently without weakening the overall security of the system.

Governance and team practices

Performance and security in an MFE system depend not only on technical controls but also on the practices that guide how teams work together. Because each MFE is owned and deployed independently, the system needs shared rules that keep the experience predictable without limiting the freedom that makes MFEs valuable. Good governance sets clear expectations, defines how decisions are made, and ensures that every MFE follows the same standards. When done well, governance becomes a support structure rather than a restriction. It helps teams work faster while keeping the entire application safe and efficient.

A core part of governance is establishing guardrails that protect the system without taking away autonomy. Performance budgets, shared security headers, and consistent communication patterns all serve as boundaries that every MFE must respect. These guidelines do not dictate how each team builds its features. Instead, they ensure that decisions made by one team do not negatively affect users or weaken the system. The goal is not to centralize control but to give every team a clear understanding of what *good* looks like, so that independent work remains aligned with the overall health of the application.

Versioning and dependency management play an important role in this. When MFEs load their own libraries, the risk of duplication, outdated dependencies, or mismatched versions increases. A shared dependency strategy helps avoid this. The container can declare which libraries are approved, which versions are supported, and where they should be loaded from. This keeps the page lightweight, reduces security risks from unpatched libraries, and prevents unexpected conflicts between MFEs. Teams retain freedom in feature development, but common dependencies are controlled through shared agreements that protect performance and safety.

Review processes reinforce these standards. Before deployment, MFEs may undergo lightweight checks for bundle size, security headers, unsafe patterns, or dependency issues. These reviews should be simple, consistent, and automated wherever possible. A small performance regression or an unsafe API call in one MFE can impact the entire application, so these checks help catch issues early. Over time, this creates a culture where performance and security are treated as shared responsibilities rather than the job of a single team.

Finally, good governance includes a clear approach to incident response and failure handling. When an MFE causes a production issue, whether from a performance regression, a security weakness, or an expired dependency, the system needs a predictable way to respond. This may include quick rollback paths, alerting that identifies the responsible MFE, and shared logs or dashboards that help teams trace the problem. In a distributed environment, issues should not require guesswork. The system should make it easy to see where the problem originated and how to fix it. By planning for failure, teams protect the user experience and reduce the impact of unexpected issues.

As the number of MFEs grows, governance practices naturally evolve. Early on, lightweight guidelines and informal agreements may be enough to keep teams aligned. Over time, as more MFEs are added and ownership becomes more distributed, governance tends to shift toward clearer standards, automation, and shared tooling. Performance budgets move from advisory to enforced checks, security reviews become part of continuous integration rather than manual oversight, and dependency rules are codified instead of documented. This evolution is not about increasing control, but about reducing friction. By gradually moving guardrails closer to the platform and embedding them into pipelines, organizations maintain consistency and safety without slowing teams down as the system scales.

Together, these governance practices allow MFEs to remain fast, secure, and reliable while still giving teams the independence they need. They form a shared foundation that brings structure to a distributed system and ensures that every MFE contributes positively to the overall application.

Conclusion

This chapter examined how performance and security shape the reliability of an MFE system. We looked at how performance budgets keep growth under control, how browser timing APIs and custom marks reveal the behavior of each MFE, and how lightweight telemetry connects these measurements to real-world usage. We also explored how security boundaries protect the system from injection risks, unsafe resource access, and inconsistent policies, and how shared headers, guarded communication patterns, and common dependency rules help maintain a stable and trustworthy environment. Throughout the chapter, we saw that performance and security are not isolated checklists but ongoing disciplines that require shared agreements, consistent practices, and a clear understanding of how every MFE contributes to the overall experience.

In the next chapter, we shift our focus from the technical foundation to the human and organizational side of MFEs. We will explore how MFEs influence team structure, leadership roles, decision-making, and long-term product strategy. The chapter highlights real-world adoption stories, sector-specific patterns, and the cultural changes that occur when organizations embrace independent deployment, distributed ownership, and shared architectural responsibility. By understanding the organizational impact of MFEs, readers will gain a broader perspective on what it takes to adopt this architecture successfully and sustain it with clarity, alignment, and confidence.

Join our Discord space

Join our Discord workspace for latest updates, offers, tech happenings around the world, new releases, and sessions with the authors:

https://discord.bpbonline.com

CHAPTER 10
Organizational Impact

Introduction

Micro-frontends have moved from a niche idea to a practical approach that many organizations use to scale their frontend work. They allow teams to build and ship parts of the product independently, which helps reduce coordination overhead and supports faster delivery. It is because MFEs have become common in companies of many sizes, from large enterprises to small startups. However, this independence comes with a tradeoff. When teams work more autonomously, it becomes harder to keep the overall product consistent. The more freedom teams have, the more important shared standards and coordination become.

This chapter focuses on the organizational side of MFEs. Rather than exploring technical details, it looks at how MFEs influence team structures, workflows, and decision-making. We begin by reviewing how MFEs are applied in real products and how different companies use them to support parallel development. These examples show why MFEs continue to gain traction across many types of products.

We then look at how MFEs appear in different industries. Finance uses them to isolate regulated areas and manage release risk. Media companies rely on them to scale regional experiences and content surfaces. E-commerce platforms use MFEs to let separate teams own merchandising, checkout, discovery, and personalization without slowing each other down. These patterns highlight the broad applicability of MFEs and the flexibility they offer. Along with benefits, MFEs introduce organizational challenges. Teams may adopt different design practices, create inconsistent analytics, or duplicate logic. Release schedules may drift and cause uneven user journeys. This chapter outlines these issues and explains the approaches that successful organizations use to manage them, such as shared design systems, platform ownership, and stronger governance models.

Leadership support is an important part of making MFEs work. Engineers may see the technical advantages, but leaders look for alignment with business goals. This chapter describes how to present MFEs in a way that matches leadership concerns, such as faster delivery, safer releases, and clearer ownership boundaries. We end with a look at the future of MFEs. Trends in AI-assisted development, edge-based delivery, and composable platforms continue to shape how teams will build large applications. Through all these changes, MFEs remain a strong model for scaling both technology and the organizations that maintain it.

Structure

The chapter covers the following topics:

- MFE in action
- Industry adoption
- Challenges and mitigations
- Gaining leadership support
- Future of MFEs

Objectives

The objective of this chapter is to explain how MFEs influence organizations and the people who build large applications. While earlier chapters focused on architecture, performance, observability, and deployment, this chapter shifts attention to how MFEs are used in real products across companies of different sizes and industries. As MFEs move from theory to widespread practice, their impact extends beyond technical design and into how teams are structured, how work is coordinated, and how decisions are made, and how these changes can improve delivery speed and product quality.

The chapter also examines the common challenges that appear when multiple teams work independently on the same product surface, such as design drift, duplicated logic, inconsistent analytics, and uneven release patterns. It then outlines practical strategies that organizations use to manage these issues through shared systems, stronger governance, and clear communication. Finally, the chapter guides engineering leaders on how to secure management support for MFE initiatives by connecting technical benefits to business outcomes. It concludes with a forward-looking view of how MFEs are evolving and how they will shape future product development. As MFEs become more widely adopted in real products, their impact extends beyond architecture and into how organizations structure teams, manage delivery, and maintain consistency.

MFE in action

This section looks at how MFEs operate inside real product organizations. Rather than focusing on frameworks or technical patterns, it highlights what changes when many teams build and ship parts of the same user experience. MFEs influence how teams plan work, structure responsibilities, and coordinate releases. They also reshape the way features move from idea to production, often reducing delays and making development cycles smoother. By examining these practical shifts, we can understand why MFEs have become an attractive choice for companies that want to scale their frontend development without slowing down delivery.

Improved workflows

MFEs alter the daily workflow of frontend teams in noticeable ways. In a single shared application, teams often wait for one another, merge large branches, and coordinate releases through long cycles. With MFEs, each team controls its own slice of the product and manages development on a smaller and more focused codebase. This reduces friction and creates clearer paths for feature work. Local development becomes simpler because teams work only within their own application boundaries. They can run, debug, and iterate without pulling down the entire frontend or understanding every part of the product. Pull requests become smaller and easier to review, since they touch only the owned area. This speeds up code reviews and lowers the risk of conflicts.

Release planning also improved. Instead of one large scheduled deployment, teams can deploy whenever their work is ready. This independence reduces long waits and frees teams from cross-team coordination. When issues occur, the blast radius is smaller, often limited to the team's part of the application. This makes troubleshooting faster and reduces the pressure that comes with large and risky releases. Quality checks also adapt to the MFE model. Teams take responsibility for accessibility, performance, analytics, and reliability for their area. Automated checks and shared tools help maintain consistency, but the day-to-day ownership sits with each team. This gives developers more control and creates a sense of direct responsibility for their work. Overall, workflow improvement is one of the strongest reasons organizations embrace MFEs. They streamline development, reduce dependency cycles, and let teams move at the speed that matches their product demands.

MFE influencing teams

MFEs influence not only how teams work but also how they are organized. When a product grows as one large frontend, teams often share responsibilities, touch the same codebase, and depend on one another for even routine changes. MFEs shift this model by creating clearer boundaries that align with product journeys or business domains. Each team owns a specific area and takes full responsibility for building, maintaining, and improving it. This change introduces a more focused ownership model. Teams operate as small product units rather than contributors to a large, shared codebase. They handle feature development, UI decisions, quality practices, local performance, accessibility, and telemetry for their part of the experience. This clarity removes the confusion that often appears in large frontends where it is difficult to know who is responsible for what.

MFEs also reduce the need for constant coordination. Since teams work in separate codebases and deploy independently, they no longer need to align every decision across many groups. Dependencies are managed through stable contracts and shared standards rather than shared implementation details. This allows teams to iterate faster without creating friction for others.

At the same time, MFEs encourage stronger collaboration patterns where it matters most. Shared design systems, platform tools, documentation, and review rituals help teams stay aligned without slowing them down. This balance between independence and alignment leads to more predictable delivery and a clearer sense of accountability. As organizations adopt MFEs, the role of engineers begins to shift. Teams develop stronger skills in ownership, observability, quality, and architectural thinking. Developers gain more responsibility for the full lifecycle of their features, including how they behave in production. This creates a culture where teams move with autonomy while also taking full responsibility for the user experience they provide.

Predictable delivery

MFEs enable teams to ship features at a pace that matches their own priorities rather than the schedule of a shared release cycle. In a single large frontend, teams often wait for others to complete work, stabilize branches, or approve changes that affect unrelated areas. With MFEs, each team manages its own deploy pipeline and moves updates to production when they are ready. This removes many of the delays that come from cross-team dependencies and allows teams to maintain steady momentum throughout the development cycle.

This independence also improves the safety of deployments. This is because each MFE is isolated, the scope of a release is much smaller, and problems are easier to detect and roll back. Failures rarely affect the entire application. They usually remain within the boundaries of the MFE that introduced the change, which reduces pressure on both developers and release managers. Teams can experiment more freely, introduce features gradually, and use targeted rollouts without worrying about destabilizing unrelated areas of the product.

Over time, independent deploys shape a more confident and predictable delivery culture. Teams begin to design their workflows around rapid iteration, smaller changes, and continuous validation in production. The organization benefits from shorter lead times, fewer release bottlenecks, and a more consistent flow of improvements to users. The combination of autonomy and safety makes MFEs an appealing model for engineering groups that want to increase velocity without sacrificing reliability.

Platform team evolution

As organizations adopt MFEs, the role of a central platform team becomes increasingly important. While product teams focus on their individual surfaces, the platform team provides the shared foundation that keeps the entire ecosystem consistent and maintainable. This includes the development environment, build tooling, shared libraries, design systems, documentation standards, and deployment workflows. By offering these elements as reliable and well-supported services, the platform team removes friction from product teams and allows them to concentrate on delivering features.

The platform team also plays a key role in shaping governance. They define boundaries and guardrails that help product teams maintain quality while still moving quickly. This can include approved dependencies, performance and accessibility checks, telemetry standards, and integration guidelines. These standards ensure that although each MFE is built independently, the overall product maintains a coherent user experience. The platform team does not act as a gatekeeper but rather as an enabler, helping teams align on practices that support long-term health.

Over time, the platform team becomes a central part of the organization's engineering culture. They help maintain a balance between autonomy and consistency across MFEs, and they drive the adoption of tools and practices that improve reliability at scale. Their contribution becomes especially visible during major transitions, such as introducing a new design system, upgrading shared frameworks, or refining deployment pipelines. By providing a strong and evolving foundation, the platform team ensures that MFEs remain efficient, predictable, and sustainable as the product grows.

Cultural shift from autonomy to accountability

MFEs introduce a strong sense of autonomy within product teams. Each team owns a defined area of the application and has the freedom to design, build, and deploy features without waiting on others. This reduces the coordination burden that often slows down large frontend organizations and gives teams the ability to make decisions based on the needs of their users. Autonomy becomes a natural part of the workflow, encouraging developers to think more independently and take initiative when shaping the product.

With greater autonomy comes an equally significant increase in accountability. Teams are responsible not only for building features but also for the quality, performance, accessibility, and stability of their own MFE in production. This leads to clearer ownership of issues and faster response times when problems arise, since teams no longer rely on others to diagnose or fix failures. Observability, user experience consistency, and operational readiness become shared expectations across the organization. Teams begin to measure their success by outcomes rather than output, which often raises the overall standard of product engineering. In practice, this accountability is reinforced through clear production ownership, defined service-level objectives, performance dashboards, incident reviews, and regular design or platform audits. Autonomy is supported by visible metrics and shared standards that ensure independence does not compromise quality.

Over time, this balance of autonomy and accountability strengthens the engineering culture. Teams learn to collaborate more intentionally through shared practices, design systems, and platform tools while still retaining the independence needed to move quickly. The organization shifts from a model of centralized control to one built on trust, responsibility, and continuous improvement. MFEs do not just change how applications are structured; they encourage a healthier way of working where teams feel ownership, align on quality, and contribute to a more resilient product ecosystem.

Industry adoption

MFEs are now present in many parts of the industry, but they do not appear in the same way everywhere. Some organizations use them to slowly modernize a long-lived product, while others adopt them early to keep growth under control. This section looks at how MFEs show up in enterprises and startups, how they are applied in finance, media, and e-commerce, why teams choose them, and where they are still rare.

Enterprises

Enterprises often adopt MFEs as a response to scale. Large applications that have grown for many years accumulate complexity that slows down development. Many teams contribute to the same frontend, which increases merge conflicts, release bottlenecks, and cross-team dependencies. MFEs provide a controlled way to break the product into meaningful parts that mirror existing organizational structures. Teams can own customer onboarding, billing, admin settings, dashboards, or content surfaces without constantly coordinating changes to a shared codebase.

In enterprise settings, MFE adoption typically happens with strong platform support. A central platform team provides the shared design system, routing model, release pipeline, telemetry standards, and documentation practices. This ensures that each MFE team can work independently while still contributing to a consistent product experience. MFEs also help enterprises modernize legacy applications. Instead of rewriting everything at once, teams gradually carve out parts of the old system into MFEs and retire legacy pages step by step. This reduces risk and fits better with enterprise timelines and budgeting cycles.

Example 1: Zalando

Zalando operates one of the largest fashion e-commerce platforms in Europe, with many teams contributing to the same customer-facing application. As the product expanded, the single frontend became difficult to evolve. Release cycles slowed down due to cross-team dependencies, onboarding new teams became cumbersome, and different parts of the UI needed to change at different speeds. Modernizing the entire frontend at once was considered too risky because of the scale and constant business demand.

Zalando adopted a modular architecture often referred to as *Project Mosaic*, where the storefront was split into smaller applications aligned with real product boundaries. Teams became responsible for surfaces such as product discovery, item detail pages, checkout, and recommendations. Each team worked in its own codebase and shipped independently, while a central platform group provided routing, design standards, and shared tooling. This allowed Zalando to modernize the UI gradually, reduce coordination overhead, and improve the pace at which features reached customers.

Example 2: Upwork

Upwork managed a large and long-lived frontend built over many years, with technologies that had become increasingly difficult to maintain. Multiple teams contributed to the same codebase, and changes often affected unrelated parts of the application. Release cycles were slow, experimentation was limited, and the risk of regression increased as the product grew. A full rebuild was not feasible because the platform had to stay live and support millions of users.

Upwork adopted MFEs to modernize the frontend piece by piece. They identified key domains such as profile management, messaging, job search, and onboarding, and migrated each into its own independently deployed application. Teams were given ownership over their surfaces, including design, performance, and deployment. A platform team provided shared standards, composition logic, and design foundations to keep the experience consistent. This approach allowed Upwork to upgrade its technology stack gradually, shorten release cycles, and reduce the risk associated with changes.

Startups

Startups adopt MFEs for reasons very different from enterprises. While large organizations often move to MFEs to escape coordination bottlenecks, startups adopt them to avoid those bottlenecks from forming in the first place. As teams grow and new products surface, MFEs give startups a way to scale development without constantly restructuring the codebase or slowing down the delivery process. The architecture helps maintain speed even when engineering teams expand rapidly.

Many startups begin with a single frontend owned by a small group of engineers. As the product finds traction and the team expands, this shared codebase becomes harder to manage. Multiple product areas evolve at once, new teams join, and the risk of one change affecting another increases. Release cycles start to slow down because teams must coordinate on branches, code reviews, and testing workflows.

Startups often move to MFEs when they sense that:

- Feature teams are starting to overlap in the same code areas
- Development slows down due to merge conflicts and shared releases
- New hires struggle to understand the entire frontend
- The product needs to scale quickly across new journeys or markets
- A major redesign or re-platforming is coming and must be done gradually

MFEs offer a way to keep autonomy and velocity while the company grows. In very early-stage startups, MFEs are rarely necessary. When a small team is focused on validating product-market fit, speed and simplicity matter more than architectural separation. A single, cohesive frontend allows rapid iteration without the overhead of platform investment. MFEs begin to provide real value in later-stage startups, when multiple teams own distinct product areas, hiring accelerates, and parallel development becomes the norm. At that point, the cost of coordination often exceeds the cost of modularization, making MFEs a strategic choice rather than an architectural experiment.

Adoption across key industries

Key industries such as finance, media, and e-commerce adopt MFEs for very different reasons, but they share one common trait: each operates large, complex product surfaces that evolve continuously and require clear ownership across many teams. MFEs help them reduce dependency chains, manage regulated or fast-changing areas, and deliver updates more predictably. By aligning product boundaries with team boundaries, MFEs allow these industries to scale without losing control of quality or consistency.

Finance

Financial applications often have deeply regulated workflows, strict review processes, and surfaces that must evolve at different speeds. Areas like identity verification, account management, statements, or payments operate under tight compliance requirements. Meanwhile, customer-facing experiences such as dashboards or budgeting tools may need rapid iteration. A single shared frontend becomes a bottleneck when some teams need to move quickly, and others must advance cautiously.

MFEs allow financial organizations to isolate sensitive flows into independent applications owned by specialized teams. These teams follow slower, more controlled release practices, while consumer experience teams iterate faster on features that demand agility. MFEs enforce the separation of responsibilities and reduce the risk that a fast-moving feature affects a regulated flow. Shared design systems, routing frameworks, and security guidelines keep the overall product consistent even when different parts move at different speeds.

Media

Media companies manage dynamic, content-heavy experiences that vary by region, category, event, and platform. They often need to update layouts quickly for promotions, global events, and editorial shifts. At the same time, they serve large and diverse audiences, so reliability and consistency are essential. A monolithic frontend becomes difficult to evolve when design teams and editorial teams require rapid change.

MFEs allow individual teams to manage sections such as home pages, content rails, video experiences, article templates, or region-specific modules. Teams can update surfaces on their own schedules, respond quickly to breaking news or seasonal events, and experiment with new layouts in isolation. The shared runtime ensures that all experiences still feel cohesive, even when many teams contribute independently. MFEs also make it easier to target different regions by letting local teams own localized surfaces without modifying the core application.

E-commerce

E-commerce platforms operate some of the most complex and high-traffic frontends in the industry. They support long customer journeys across merchandising, product discovery, cart, checkout, and account management. Demand spikes during seasons or promotions put additional pressure on teams to iterate safely and quickly. A single shared frontend slows down experimentation and increases the chance that one change affects unrelated areas.

MFEs allow teams to own distinct product surfaces and deploy updates independently. Search, product pages, recommendations, checkout, fulfillment, and post-purchase flows can evolve on different timelines. Teams can optimize performance, run experiments, and update content without waiting for central releases. MFEs also support gradual modernization, letting e-commerce companies replace older flows without disrupting the entire shopping experience. The result is a more responsive product that adapts quickly to customer behavior and business needs.

MFE adoption boundaries

MFEs offer clear advantages in large and fast-growing products, but they are not the right solution for every team or every application. Many products remain more efficient, more maintainable, and easier to evolve when kept as a well-structured single frontend. The decision to use MFEs depends on the scale of the product, the number of teams involved, the stability of the domain, and the organization's willingness to invest in the platform and governance. This section outlines where MFEs are less commonly used and why teams may deliberately avoid them.

Small or single-team applications

MFEs are rarely a good fit for small or single-team applications because the architectural overhead outweighs the benefits. The primary strength of MFEs is that they allow many teams to work in parallel without blocking one another, but this advantage is unnecessary when the same group owns the entire frontend. In these environments, developers already share context, communicate frequently, and move through the codebase with ease. Introducing separate runtimes, independent deployments, and cross-application contracts creates complexity that does not solve any real organizational problem. Instead of gaining autonomy, teams end up maintaining composition logic, shared interfaces, and platform tooling that slow them down.

Small applications are easier to maintain as a unified frontend because the domain is narrow, the number of screens is limited, and developers can comfortably understand most of the system. These products are typically found in early-stage startups, internal dashboards, admin portals, and specialized enterprise tools. In these scenarios, a single codebase supports rapid iteration, direct refactoring, and straightforward release pipelines. Scalability at this stage does not require MFEs. The growth challenges are better addressed with good component boundaries, clear modular organization, a consistent design system, and predictable release practices. A well-structured monolithic application can scale very far before a distributed architecture becomes necessary.

Even in companies known for large-scale engineering, small product surfaces often avoid MFEs entirely. Early versions of tools like *Notion*, *GitLab*, and *Figma* grew successfully inside well-organized monolithic frontends. Many enterprise teams at Google, Meta, and Microsoft also maintain internal applications as single frontends because the cost of building a platform to support MFEs does not match the needs of a small team. These examples show that avoiding MFEs is often a strategic choice rather than a limitation.

Note: MFEs should be introduced only when scaling the organization (team count), not scaling the codebase. Codebase complexity is solved with modular design, not distributed applications.

Choosing not to use MFEs in small applications brings several advantages. The architecture remains simple and easy to reason about. Teams can refactor freely without negotiating boundaries or coordinating releases. Debugging and testing are more predictable because there are no cross-application interactions to manage. The design and user experience stay consistent by default, and onboarding new engineers becomes faster because they learn one system rather than many small ones. Most importantly, the team avoids the burden of maintaining a platform, shared contracts, and governance practices that MFEs require. For small or single-team applications, a unified frontend offers the best balance of speed, simplicity, and long-term maintainability.

Stable domains with minimal change

MFEs are also not a natural fit for applications that evolve slowly or follow predictable and infrequent release cycles. These products often consist of stable workflows, mature interfaces, and business rules that do not change rapidly. In such environments, the primary challenges are reliability, accuracy, and long-term maintainability rather than speed of iteration or organizational scaling. Introducing MFEs in these cases adds operational weight through independent deployments, composition layers, and shared contracts, but offers little benefit in return. The architecture becomes more complex without solving a real coordination problem, since teams do not need to ship features in parallel or avoid overlapping work.

Stable domains often appear in internal enterprise tools, administrative consoles, configuration panels, reporting dashboards, compliance portals, and systems that support back-office operations. These applications typically serve a narrow audience and evolve in measured cycles based on internal priorities or regulatory changes. Because the scope is well understood and the surface area is modest, teams can maintain a single frontend with ease. A conventional application structure with modular components, a clear folder organization, shared UI patterns, and established testing practices is usually sufficient to support the product for many years. In these cases, MFEs would only complicate releases and debugging without delivering organizational advantages.

Organizations without platform investment

MFEs rely on a strong foundation of shared infrastructure, design systems, and engineering practices. Without these elements, the architecture becomes difficult to govern and even harder to scale. Organizations that do not invest in platform capabilities often find MFEs more burdensome than beneficial. Each team ends up solving the same problems independently. Common issues such as routing, build processes, accessibility standards, design consistency, performance checks, and observability must be implemented on its own, which leads to fragmentation across the product. Instead of gaining the autonomy MFEs promise, teams face increased maintenance work and inconsistent outcomes, ultimately slowing down development rather than accelerating it.

The attention required from a platform team is not a small commitment. MFEs depend on common tooling to stitch independently deployed applications into a coherent product. They need shared conventions for dependency management, security baselines, error handling, and performance budgets. A design system must exist to maintain a unified visual identity, and teams must adopt common coding standards to avoid divergence. When none of these elements are in place, MFEs introduce significant operational overhead. A distributed architecture amplifies inconsistencies and creates confusion for both users and developers. A monolithic frontend with good internal boundaries is usually more effective in such environments because it reduces the need for cross-functional coordination and limits the risk of drift.

When platform investment is missing, failure patterns quickly emerge. Teams adopt inconsistent routing strategies, duplicate dependencies, and implement analytics or authentication differently across MFEs. Accessibility and performance standards vary, and incident ownership becomes unclear. Users experience fragmented interactions, and developers struggle with unclear debugging paths and uneven tooling. What was intended to provide autonomy instead introduces operational friction. For organizations with limited engineering bandwidth or early-stage platform maturity, MFEs may not be the right choice. Many successful SaaS products initially favored cohesive frontends supported by evolving component libraries and documented practices. This approach allowed teams to prioritize product value over platform complexity until their scale justified distribution.

Challenges and mitigations

As MFEs spread across an organization, new forms of complexity begin to appear. The architecture gives teams autonomy and clearer ownership, but it also pushes responsibility for consistency, integration, and quality to the edges of many independent surfaces. Challenges emerge not because MFEs are flawed, but because distributed development requires stronger alignment across design, engineering, and platform practices. When teams move quickly in isolation, even small differences in decisions can accumulate into visible issues for users and measurable friction for engineering.

This section highlights the common challenges organizations face when scaling MFEs and outlines practical ways to address them. The goal is not to present rigid rules, but to show how teams can reinforce autonomy with shared standards, platform support, and predictable cross-team workflows. Some challenges are technical, others are organizational, but all of them reflect the same core truth: MFEs succeed when independence is balanced with discipline.

One of the earliest and most noticeable issues to appear is in the user interface itself. As different teams build their own surfaces, visual and interaction patterns often begin to drift. This leads to the first and most visible challenge in any MFE environment.

UX and design fragmentation

UX and design fragmentation is one of the most visible challenges that emerges when multiple teams build separate parts of the same product. As MFEs evolve independently, differences in layouts, spacing, typography, animations, and interaction patterns begin to surface. Even small inconsistencies can accumulate over time and make the interface feel disconnected, especially when users transition across surfaces owned by different teams. The product may appear less polished, and customers may feel as though they are using several different tools rather than one coherent experience. These gaps often start subtly but become more pronounced as more MFEs come online.

This fragmentation happens because MFEs distribute ownership across many teams, each with its own roadmap, priorities, and interpretation of design guidance. When deadlines are tight or requirements shift, teams make local decisions that optimize their surface but unintentionally break global consistency. In some cases, teams create custom components to move faster, or they extend patterns that were never designed for shared use. Teams may also adopt different frameworks, styling approaches, or build pipelines, which increases the likelihood of divergence. Without shared constraints, visual drift becomes a natural outcome of distributed development.

Mitigating UX fragmentation requires strong platform support and a commitment to shared design standards. Successful organizations establish a unified design system with clear principles, reusable components, and versioned tokens for colors, spacing, and typography. The system must be actively maintained, not simply published, and should be supported by documentation, examples, and best practices. Many teams adopt a central component library managed by the platform or design system team, which ensures that visual and interaction patterns remain consistent across all MFEs. Regular cross-team design reviews, audits, and collaboration sessions also help maintain alignment. By combining a strong design foundation with predictable communication, organizations preserve a unified user experience while allowing teams to work independently.

Duplication of logic

As MFEs empower teams to operate independently, a new form of duplication often appears behind the scenes. Different teams begin solving similar problems in parallel, creating their own versions of data fetching logic, formatting rules, error handling patterns, API clients, and even domain-level business rules. Over time, this leads to subtle inconsistencies in how features behave across the product. Users may notice that similar actions yield slightly different responses or error states, while engineers struggle with multiple competing implementations that increase maintenance costs. What starts as harmless duplication quickly becomes technical drift, making it harder to ensure reliability and correctness across the full experience.

This challenge arises naturally when autonomy is not balanced with shared practices. Teams build locally optimized solutions because it is faster in the short term, especially when deadlines are pressured or when ownership boundaries are unclear. Some teams introduce custom utilities or adopt different build tools, while others rely on frameworks or state management approaches that fit their local workflow but create friction when integrated into a larger system. Without explicit alignment on technical foundations, each MFE evolves along its own path, and the architecture loses coherence. The result is a fragmented internal landscape that slows long-term evolution and multiplies the cost of change.

Mitigating duplication and divergence requires strong shared foundations and clear guidance on what should be standardized globally and what should remain owned locally. Certain elements benefit from global consistency. Core domain logic, API clients, authentication flows, validation rules, internationalization frameworks, analytics schemas, and design tokens should typically be standardized to ensure correctness, security, and a unified user experience. These shared modules are often maintained by platform or domain teams and versioned in a way that makes adoption predictable and safe. At the same time, not everything should be centralized. Teams should retain ownership of presentation logic, feature-specific state management, localized UI behavior, and product experimentation within their MFE boundaries. Preserving this local autonomy allows teams to move quickly, tailor experiences to their domain, and evolve independently without waiting for global approvals. The goal is not to eliminate variation, but to control it deliberately. Some companies introduce backend-for-frontend layers that centralize business rules while keeping UI implementation flexible. Clear documentation, architectural decision records, and internal guidelines reinforce these boundaries. When teams understand what is shared and what is theirs to own, collaboration becomes more structured, and the overall system retains coherence even as individual MFEs evolve at their own pace.

Inconsistent telemetry and analytics

When MFEs are introduced across a product, each team gains the freedom to implement its own approach to analytics, logging, error reporting, and performance monitoring. While this autonomy accelerates local development, it often creates inconsistencies in how user behavior is tracked and how issues are detected across surfaces. Funnels break when one part of the journey logs an event differently from another. Error reports become fragmented because each MFE uses slightly different metadata or naming conventions. Even core metrics such as page transitions, latency, or user actions can become difficult to interpret when there is no shared definition. As a result, leaders and analysts lose the ability to understand the holistic user journey, and engineering teams struggle to diagnose problems that span multiple MFEs.

This challenge emerges because telemetry is frequently treated as a local implementation detail rather than a first-class cross-team contract. When deadlines are tight, teams may log events that work only for their surface or interpret tracking requirements in subtly different ways. In some organizations, each MFE integrates its own analytics library or error tracking tool, creating multiple sources of truth. Without a unified system, it becomes difficult to correlate events, connect front-end behavior with back-end traces, or analyze performance trends across the full application. MFEs magnify this problem because each independent deployment introduces more variation in how data is captured and interpreted.

Mitigating these inconsistencies requires treating analytics and observability as shared infrastructure rather than isolated code. Successful organizations establish a central analytics SDK with standard event schemas, semantic naming rules, and clear guidelines for when and how measurements should be taken. A shared event dictionary ensures that every team uses consistent parameters for key journeys such as onboarding, checkout, or account management. The platform team often enforces trace context propagation across MFEs so that logs and events can be correlated end-to-end. Dashboards and data pipelines are built around unified conventions that aggregate events across all surfaces. With these shared foundations, each MFE still tracks its own behavior, but the resulting data aligns into one coherent story, making it easier to understand, debug, and optimize the overall product.

Cross-team coordination

Even though MFEs allow teams to operate independently, they still rely on shared interfaces, data contracts, and integration points that must remain stable across the product. When these boundaries are not clearly defined or consistently maintained, coordination becomes one of the most challenging aspects of an MFE ecosystem. A single breaking change to a shared API or component can ripple across multiple MFEs, causing unexpected issues in areas owned by different teams. These problems often surface late in development or even in production, since each team may test only its own surface without validating how its changes affect the broader system. As more MFEs appear, the need for structured collaboration becomes increasingly important.

This challenge arises because independence can unintentionally hide dependencies. Teams optimize for local delivery, unaware that another MFE depends on their component, API contract, or event flow. Informal communication, tribal knowledge, or unclear ownership boundaries create gaps that surface only when multiple MFEs integrate. Version drift makes the problem more difficult: one MFE may be updated with new contract assumptions while another continues using older definitions. Each team operates with good intentions, but without clear agreements and versioning practices, the product becomes fragile. Integration bugs become harder to trace because they emerge at the boundaries where MFEs meet, not within the isolated code of any individual team.

Mitigating coordination challenges requires establishing explicit contracts and predictable processes for evolving shared interfaces. Organizations that succeed with MFEs introduce versioned APIs, deprecation policies, and architectural decision records that document the intent and impact of changes. Contract tests and integration smoke tests validate that MFEs still function correctly when assembled into the full product. Regular cross-team syncs or working groups help maintain alignment without slowing down delivery. A strong platform team often plays a coordinating role, defining guidelines for data flows, event structures, shared components, and backward-compatible releases. These practices ensure that MFEs remain loosely coupled but not loosely managed, preserving both independence and stability.

Gaining leadership support

Gaining leadership support is essential for any meaningful architectural shift, and MFEs are no exception. While engineering teams often focus on autonomy, performance, or code structure, leaders evaluate initiatives through a broader lens. They look for decisions that strengthen delivery predictability, reduce operational risk, enable team scalability, and improve the overall product experience. To secure leadership alignment, MFEs must be framed not as a technical preference but as a strategic investment that supports long-term organizational goals. A successful case for MFEs connects engineering outcomes to business outcomes and shows how the architecture positions teams to move faster and more confidently as the product grows.

Common concerns

Leaders evaluate architectural decisions through the lens of predictability, risk, and alignment with business goals. They care about how reliably teams can deliver features, how quickly the organization can respond to market needs, and how safely the product evolves over time. MFEs gain leadership attention when they clearly address systemic pain points such as slow-release cycles, heavy coordination overhead, and inconsistent ownership. Leaders want to see that the architecture will remove bottlenecks, support clearer accountability, and improve the overall execution rhythm of the organization.

Leaders also focus on cost, both in the short term and the long term. Any architectural change must justify the investment required to build platform tooling, maintain shared systems, and support new workflows. MFEs must therefore demonstrate that the reduction in coordination cost, the increase in delivery speed, and the improvements in reliability outweigh the expense of implementation. Leaders respond strongly when the conversation highlights cost predictability over time. MFEs introduce upfront platform work, but they reduce the hidden costs of large monolithic coordination, simplify onboarding as teams grow, and lower the downstream cost of regression and recovery. When framed as a shift from unpredictable complexity to predictable operating cost, MFEs become easier for leaders to support.

Measurable outcomes

Leadership responds most strongly when architectural choices connect directly to measurable business outcomes. Teams that adopt MFEs often track improvements in deployment frequency, reduced lead time, fewer cross-team merge conflicts, and lower change failure rates. These operational metrics demonstrate that independent deployment translates into real execution gains. When teams can show shorter release cycles, faster recovery from incidents, and clearer ownership of production issues, the benefits of MFEs become tangible rather than theoretical. Leaders want confidence that the architecture will enhance the organization's ability to move quickly without compromising product quality or stability. When MFEs are positioned as a tool for eliminating bottlenecks and enabling teams to deliver independently, they become part of a broader plan for increasing organizational efficiency.

The most persuasive arguments also highlight how MFEs reduce long-term maintenance costs and avoid the *big rewrite trap* that leaders rightfully fear. Instead of replacing an entire frontend at once, MFEs allow teams to modernize gradually, focusing on the areas that most need improvement while avoiding disruption to the product roadmap. Leaders value approaches that reduce uncertainty and protect ongoing commitments. When they see that MFEs help teams adopt new technologies safely, manage complexity more deliberately, and lower the risk of wide-scale regressions, they are more likely to support the transition. Presenting MFEs as a path toward sustainable growth, safer evolution, and lower operational overhead ensures that leadership views the architecture as an investment in resilience rather than an engineering experiment.

Return on investment

Evaluating architectural changes through return on investment is essential for leadership, especially in organizations where engineering choices must align with financial accountability and long-term planning. MFEs introduce upfront costs in platform tooling, shared governance, design systems, and new workflows, but they deliver ongoing value by reducing the inefficiencies that accumulate in large monolithic frontends. Leaders often see the real ROI not in the initial setup but in the cumulative time saved by lowering coordination overhead, accelerating delivery, and reducing the frequency and impact of regressions. MFEs turn slow, intertwined release cycles into predictable, autonomous deployments, allowing teams to ship improvements without waiting for unrelated work. This increased predictability directly affects the organization's ability to respond to customers and market conditions with speed and confidence.

The long-term **return on investment** (**ROI**) becomes even more compelling when viewed through the lens of sustainability. MFEs eliminate the need for risky, expensive, and disruptive frontend rewrites by enabling modernization to happen incrementally. Instead of halting roadmaps for massive migrations, teams can evolve each surface independently while continuing to deliver features. This protects revenue-generating timelines and avoids the opportunity costs associated with stopping product work to fund a rewrite. MFEs also reduce downstream maintenance costs by enforcing clearer ownership boundaries and narrowing the blast radius of changes. Onboarding becomes faster, cross-team dependencies shrink, and operational risk declines. When leaders recognize that MFEs replace unpredictable complexity with a more stable, efficient, and scalable delivery model, the architecture shifts from being a technical preference to a strategic investment with measurable financial and organizational returns.

Future of MFEs

MFEs have already reshaped how organizations structure frontend development, but their influence is still evolving. What began as a practical solution for scaling teams is now part of a broader shift toward distributed ownership, platform thinking, and composable user interfaces. As the industry continues to modernize its approach to building large applications, MFEs will play a meaningful role in how teams balance autonomy and cohesion, particularly in environments where product complexity grows faster than individual teams can manage. Looking forward, the future of MFEs is defined not by frameworks but by the continued push toward cleaner boundaries, smarter tooling, and experiences that adapt to users and markets with greater agility.

AI-driven development

AI is poised to transform how frontends are designed, assembled, and evolved, and MFEs provide a natural foundation for this shift. Instead of treating UI as a static artifact, teams will increasingly rely on AI systems that generate, test, and refine parts of the interface based on real-time signals and product goals. MFEs make it possible for these AI-driven components to evolve independently, without requiring large, coordinated releases or full application rewrites. They give teams isolated spaces where AI can propose optimizations, introduce new flows, or adjust layouts while the platform ensures that everything still fits together coherently.

One major area of evolution is AI-assisted modular generation. As models improve, they will be able to create isolated MFE units that implement targeted features, experiment with alternative interaction patterns, or replace outdated logic with optimized versions. These units can be deployed as self-contained modules that plug into the existing product without requiring manual integration work. In this model, engineers act as reviewers and orchestrators rather than manual implementers. MFEs offer an ideal boundary for AI-generated code: each module is small, self-contained, and replaceable, reducing the risk of unwanted side effects.

Another direction is automated experimentation and UI evolution. Today, experimentation frameworks rely on predefined variants, but AI will increasingly generate new variants in response to user behavior, performance data, or business goals. MFEs enable this by letting the system swap or modify individual surfaces without touching the entire application. Imagine an AI system that notices a drop in conversion and automatically proposes a new layout for the checkout MFE, then deploys it to a small audience, monitors results, and refines it further. This *continuous design evolution* becomes possible only when interfaces are modularized at the MFE level.

A third frontier is AI-powered developer tooling for MFEs. AI agents will support teams by maintaining shared contracts, auto-repairing dependency issues, suggesting performance optimizations, and generating integration tests across distributed surfaces. They may even detect divergence across MFEs, such as inconsistent tokens, outdated APIs, or duplicated logic, and propose unified refactors. Instead of manually policing alignment across many independent modules, teams will rely on AI to enforce consistency. MFEs amplify this because modular boundaries make it easier for AI tools to reason about each surface in isolation and provide targeted guidance.

Finally, AI will enable domain-aware, context-rich orchestration of MFEs, where the runtime chooses which module to load based on the user, device capability, network conditions, or business objectives. Instead of a fixed composition, the application becomes adaptive. MFEs act as swappable building blocks, and AI determines the best combination for each situation. This unlocks a future where the frontend is not just modular but also intelligent by continuously assembling itself to serve users more effectively. While AI-driven development opens new possibilities, it also introduces constraints that organizations must manage carefully. Automatically generated interfaces must still meet security, accessibility, and performance standards. Overreliance on AI-generated modules can lead to inconsistencies if outputs are not governed by shared design systems and architectural boundaries. There are also risks related to explainability, auditability, and operational control, particularly in regulated environments. As with MFEs themselves, AI works best when paired with strong oversight, clear contracts, and well-defined ownership rather than replacing disciplined engineering practices.

Edge composition

As applications move closer to the user through CDNs and serverless runtimes, MFEs are poised to take advantage of edge-based composition, where individual modules are assembled at the network edge rather than in the browser or a central server. This shift reduces latency, improves perceived performance, and enables finer-grained personalization based on geography, device type, user attributes, or real-time conditions. Instead of delivering a single static shell that loads MFEs in the browser, the edge can assemble the right combination of modules before the user even reaches the page. This aligns naturally with MFE architecture because each module is already self-contained, versioned, and independently deployable. The edge becomes a lightweight but powerful orchestrator, determining which modules to include and how to stitch them together for the fastest and most relevant experience.

Edge-based composition also opens the door to new operational patterns that would be challenging in a monolithic environment. Teams can roll out regional features, test edge-side fallbacks, or serve alternative flows for specific markets without touching the global application.

Personalization becomes more efficient because the edge can select variants dynamically while keeping the core product stable. This approach reduces the complexity of client-side routing and minimizes the cost of rendering logic on the browser, especially for low-power or mobile devices. As edge platforms mature, they will support richer orchestration rules, real-time configuration, and improved observability for distributed UI assembly. MFEs provide the modular structure that makes this evolution not only possible but increasingly inevitable as performance expectations rise.

Design systems evolution

As MFEs continue to expand across organizations, design systems will play an increasingly central role in maintaining coherence. In distributed architectures, it is easy for visual patterns to drift as teams make local decisions to meet deadlines or experiment with new interactions. A strong, token-driven design system becomes the anchor that holds the experience together. Instead of thinking about MFEs purely as technical units, organizations will treat design foundations such as colors, typography, spacing, grid rules, motion patterns, and component behaviors as the real source of consistency. MFEs remain free to evolve independently, but they draw from a shared vocabulary that ensures the product feels unified regardless of how many teams contribute to it. As design tokens become more standardized across tools and platforms, the gap between implementation details and user-facing consistency will continue to shrink.

This evolution shifts the role of design systems from a library of components to a cross-MFE contract. Future design tooling will automatically validate whether MFEs comply with tokens, accessibility rules, and interaction standards, highlighting deviations before they reach production. Automated visual regression systems and AI-driven pattern analyzers will help enforce consistency even as implementation details vary. In this world, the design system becomes the true *platform* for frontend cohesion, offering a stable foundation that allows teams to innovate without creating fragmentation. MFEs benefit because the system absorbs much of the alignment burden, enabling distributed teams to move faster without sacrificing quality. As organizations mature, the design system becomes as strategically important as the MFE architecture itself, shaping how teams think about composition, brand consistency, and long-term maintainability.

Finally, the long-term impact of MFEs is organizational. The future of MFEs is less about technical composition and more about how teams structure themselves around product surfaces. As distributed ownership becomes the norm in fast-scaling companies, MFEs provide a framework for aligning team boundaries with real customer experiences. They encourage platform thinking, reinforce clarity of responsibility, and enable safer, continuous delivery at scale. Even as tooling evolves, the underlying organizational benefits remain relevant. MFEs will continue to influence how companies design, build, and operate their frontends because they address the fundamental challenge of scaling teams without sacrificing consistency.

Conclusion

MFEs began as a response to the growing complexity of modern web applications, but their true value lies in how they reshape the way organizations think about ownership, autonomy, and scale. Throughout this chapter, we explored how MFEs influence team structure, collaboration, leadership decision-making, and long-term product evolution. What becomes clear is that MFEs are not merely a technical pattern; they are an organizational strategy. They help teams move faster without losing alignment, reduce risk without slowing progress, and modernize safely without halting roadmaps. By distributing responsibility across well-defined boundaries, MFEs give organizations a framework for scaling both their products and their people.

At the same time, MFEs introduce challenges that require discipline and thoughtful investment. Consistency, performance, analytics, and coordination all become more complex when ownership is distributed. These challenges are real, but they are also solvable when organizations pair autonomy with strong platform practices and shared foundations. The most successful MFE ecosystems strike a balance between independence and alignment, giving teams room to innovate while maintaining a unified product experience. Leadership plays a pivotal role in achieving this balance by championing standards, supporting platform teams, and evaluating architectural decisions through the lens of long-term organizational health.

Looking ahead, MFEs will continue to evolve alongside new technologies, design systems, and AI-driven tooling. However, the principles behind them, including clear ownership, modular thinking, and safe incremental change, remain timeless. Whether assembled in the browser, at the edge, or through intelligent composition, the idea of breaking the frontend into focused, independently evolving units will continue to guide how complex applications are built. MFEs offer a path not just to better software, but to better organizational structure. They help teams grow without growing apart and create products that evolve with confidence rather than hesitation.

MFEs remind us that architecture is ultimately about people: how they collaborate, how they deliver, and how they build systems that can adapt to change. As organizations scale and user expectations rise, the need for structures that support both autonomy and cohesion becomes increasingly essential. MFEs provide that structure. While implemented thoughtfully, they align how the system is built with how the organization works, enabling teams to move fast without breaking the product apart. They offer a practical, forward-looking way to build modern web experiences that can stand the test of time. MFEs succeed not because they divide the frontend, but because they unite teams around clear ownership, shared standards, and resilient delivery.

Index

G

H

I

J

L

N

O